SUPREME AMBITION

*Brett Kavanaugh and the
Conservative Takeover*

RUTH MARCUS

Simon & Schuster

NEW YORK · LONDON · TORONTO
SYDNEY · NEW DELHI

Simon & Schuster
1230 Avenue of the Americas
New York, NY 10020

First Simon & Schuster hardcover edition December 2019

SIMON & SCHUSTER and colophon are registered trademarks
of Simon & Schuster, Inc.

For information about special discounts for bulk purchases, please contact
Simon & Schuster Special Sales at 1-866-506-1949
or business@simonandschuster.com.

The Simon & Schuster Speakers Bureau can bring authors to your
live event. For more information or to book an event, contact the
Simon & Schuster Speakers Bureau at 1-866-248-3049
or visit our website at www.simonspeakers.com.

Interior design by Paul Dippolito

Manufactured in the United States of America

1   3   5   7   9   10   8   6   4   2

Library of Congress Cataloging-in-Publication Data is available.

ISBN 978-1-9821-2386-4
ISBN 978-1-9821-2388-8 (ebook)

For my family: Jon, Emma, and Julia

CONTENTS

SUPREME
AMBITION

The Beneficiary

Supreme Court Justice Anthony Kennedy had a request: would President Trump have a few minutes to speak privately? It was April 10, 2017, a sparkling spring morning in Washington, and Kennedy was at the White House to preside over the ceremonial swearing-in of the newest justice, Neil Gorsuch—the first time in history that a sitting justice had sworn in one of his former law clerks to join him on the bench. Just eighty days into Trump's chaotic presidency, the confirmation of Gorsuch represented a rare and welcome victory for the beleaguered new administration, reeling from court defeats of its travel ban and, despite controlling both houses of Congress, unable to repeal President Obama's signature health care law.

Perhaps most important, as the prominent conservative lawyers, activists, and judges assembled in the Rose Garden that day understood, Gorsuch's addition was just one step, necessary but not sufficient, in a three-decades-long conservative bid to cement control over the high court. This effort had been as frustrating as it was lengthy. Seeming opportunities for dominance repeatedly slipped away, with Republican nominees, including Kennedy himself, turning out to be less reliably conservative than advertised. But Republicans had learned from those costly errors, assembling a farm team of potential nominees whose judicial records could be carefully scrutinized to detect any risks of ideological deviation.

Gorsuch was among those who came bearing the seal of approval of the Federalist Society, the conservative legal group that had made itself the central actor in this court-shaping exercise and was playing an even more outsize role in the new administration.

Trump took pains to single out one man who was not in the Rose Garden that day, Senate majority leader Mitch McConnell, "for all that he did to make this achievement possible."[1] Indeed, everyone present knew that McConnell had been the indispensable man leading to that moment. Had it not been for McConnell, President Barack Obama would have filled the vacancy created by Justice Antonin Scalia's sudden death in February 2016, and Justice Merrick Garland would be sitting on the high court, anchoring a newly fortified liberal majority. McConnell, with his audacious announcement that the opening would not be filled—no matter that Obama had eleven months remaining in his term—had avoided that fateful outcome. His intervention meant that Gorsuch now occupied Scalia's seat—a conservative-for-conservative swap. The next vacancy was almost certain to be the far more critical one, shifting the court's balance instead of affirming it.

On that score, all eyes were on the eighty-year-old Kennedy, then serving his thirtieth year on the high court and, by dint of age, years of service, and political allegiance, the most likely to depart. The swing justice on an already conservative court, Kennedy was pleased about Gorsuch, but he had another former law clerk on his mind as he was ushered into Trump's private dining room for an unusual session with the president and White House counsel Don McGahn. Justices are routinely invited to the White House for social events, state dinners, and holiday parties. But at least until Trump took office, such one-on-one meetings were rare in the modern era, with its finicky notions about preserving the appearance of judicial independence—unlike the relaxed days when justices did double duty as private counselors to presidents such as Franklin Roosevelt and Lyndon Johnson.

In the chronically leaky Trump White House, aides took pains to keep the Trump-Kennedy meeting secret. There were no public reports about the session, and only a few senior officials ever learned what Kennedy said to Trump that day. The justice's message to the president was as consequential as it was straightforward, and it was a remarkable insertion by a sitting justice into the distinctly presidential act of judge picking. As a candidate, Trump had upended tradition by issuing a list of judges—it ultimately grew to twenty-one, including Gorsuch—from which he pledged to pick his Supreme Court nominees. Now Kennedy had a recommendation for Trump's list. You named one of my former clerks, Kennedy told Trump. You should think about another one: Brett Kavanaugh.

When Anthony Kennedy spoke, the Trump White House listened, with good reason. During the campaign, when Trump, against all expectations, emerged as the Republican nominee and ultimate victor over Hillary Clinton, the issue of judicial selection had been a utilitarian means to an electoral end. The socially conservative and evangelical voters Trump needed to win were deeply, understandably suspicious of the thrice-married, once-Democratic New Yorker. They were particularly dubious about how Trump would approach the critical task of shaping the federal judiciary, especially the Supreme Court.

The list of high court candidates that Trump produced with the help of the Federalist Society, upending convention with typical Trumpian bravado, was explicitly aimed at calming their concerns, and it succeeded beyond the wildest expectations of its creators. On Election Day, more than a quarter of Trump voters identified the Supreme Court as the critical factor in determining their vote. White, evangelical, born-again Christians broke 81 percent for Trump to 16 percent for Hillary Clinton, meaning that Trump outperformed previous Republican nominees Mitt Romney, John McCain, and George W. Bush among such voters.[2]

In office, Trump not only keenly understood the politics of judicial selection and its importance to his reelection, he also gained a new appreciation for what the Supreme Court meant to a president's legacy. Thanks to McConnell's ruthlessness, Trump had inherited what no president had before: the gift of an existing vacancy. The canny Kentuckian had insisted that the Scalia seat would remain unfilled until the next president took office, not so much because he thought Trump would win—that prospect seemed remote—but because it would help shield his Senate majority. Conservative voters would turn out if a Supreme Court seat hung in the balance, and that would help McConnell's members.

But the brazen tactic worked better than McConnell could have imagined. Now, having replaced Scalia with Gorsuch to great acclaim, Trump craved the chance to name another justice, and Kennedy was the most promising target. Indeed, Gorsuch had been selected in part to flatter Kennedy's sizable ego and to reassure Kennedy that, if he chose to retire, Trump would not behave irrationally in filling his seat. The president's tweets might be unhinged, but his judicial nominees would be solid, establishment choices. "The deal is Kennedy, when he sees that Trump's not crazy, we definitely have a deal with Kennedy," one adviser recalled. "It's got to be Gorsuch to replace Scalia. It's a signal to Kennedy."

The new administration already had strong reason to believe that Kennedy's departure would come sooner rather than later—at the end of the court's term in June of 2017, just a few months away. Administration officials were giddy at the prospect: Trump, or so they thought, would be able to name two justices to the high court during his first six months in office, as many as Obama had managed during his full eight years. Depending on what happened, perhaps two additional vacancies could be in the offing. Trump, always shooting high, was inclined to be even more optimistic. "I think I'm going to get five," he liked to tell people.[3]

One clue to Kennedy's inclinations came the weekend after the new administration took office, at the annual dinner of the Alfalfa Club, an elite Washington institution whose sole function is to convene the highest ranks of government officials and business leaders over lobster bisque and filet mignon. While the president himself was a no-show for this swampiest of events, his new administration was out in force. Among those gathered at the Capital Hilton that night were first daughter Ivanka Trump and husband, Jared Kushner; Vice President Mike Pence; chief of staff Reince Priebus; and presidential counselor Kellyanne Conway, fresh off her triumph as the first woman to manage a Republican presidential campaign. As the guests mingled and gossiped, a lanky-haired man speaking with Conway offered the most intriguing of the congratulations she collected that night.

"No one," he told Conway, "was happier about the election than my father."[4]

This was no ordinary observation, because the speaker was no ordinary well-wisher. He was Gregory Kennedy, a Stanford Law School graduate and investment banker then taking a brief detour to work for the new administration as a financial adviser at NASA. More to the point, he was Anthony Kennedy's son.

"That's good to know," Conway replied. "That happiness has consequences." She promptly reported the encounter to her White House colleagues, including Trump himself.

That wasn't the only indication. The administration had a secret and valuable back channel to Kennedy courtesy of Leonard Leo, the Federalist Society executive vice president who had been instrumental in assembling Trump's Supreme Court list and bragged privately about his secret meetings with one of Kennedy's sons. As early as the transition, Leo was convinced—and was insisting to Trump's advisers—that, based on these conversations, Kennedy was ready to retire.

The Trump White House would do whatever it took to make that happen. In his remarks at the Gorsuch ceremony, Trump seized the opportunity to woo Kennedy. During the campaign, Trump had excoriated Kennedy's far more conservative colleague, Chief Justice John Roberts. "A disaster in terms of everything we stand for," Trump called Roberts in one primary debate.[5] Now he had no qualms about lavishing praise on Kennedy, who had infuriated conservatives with his votes to protect abortion and expand gay rights. "A great man of outstanding accomplishment" who "has been praised by all for his dedicated and dignified service," Trump said of Kennedy.[6]

And he clearly heeded the justice's advice. In the weeks after the Gorsuch swearing-in, musing about the prospect of another vacancy, Trump began to mention: there are a few of Kennedy's clerks that we ought to take a hard look at. And he would ask friends and advisers what they knew about Brett Kavanaugh and what they thought of him. The president wanted to know: Would he be a good choice? A strong Trump justice?

Any Supreme Court retirement is enormously consequential. A Kennedy departure, if and when it came to pass, would be cataclysmic because of the pivotal role he had played on the closely divided court. No longer would conservatives be subject to the idiosyncratic jurisprudence of a Tony Kennedy, who one day could author the ruling in *Citizens United v. Federal Election Commission*, which ushered in a new era of unbridled campaign spending, and another day could declare that the Constitution's unwritten regard for dignity included the right to same-sex marriage. A predictable, consistent conservative would lock in a reliable five-vote majority. A young enough one, to replace the octogenarian Kennedy, could ensure that the majority would last for years to come.

This was a conservative project decades in the making—a project that stretched back to Kennedy's own selection by Ronald Reagan in 1987. Kennedy had been chosen to replace the retiring Lewis Powell only after the failure of Robert Bork, the conservative legal icon whose Senate defeat had left wounds that remained raw all these years later. Kennedy was an establishment Republican, but it was clear even at the time that he was no Bork. Time and again, over the previous decades, conservatives had watched as the nominees of Republican presidents veered to the left and disappointed them once confirmed. Perhaps most painfully, when the court appeared ready in 1992 to jettison the constitutional right to abortion it had declared in 1973, three Republican-appointed justices betrayed the cause, as conservatives saw it. Instead of overturning *Roe v. Wade*, as had been expected, Kennedy—joined by Reagan's first appointee, Sandra Day O'Connor, and George H. W. Bush nominee David Souter—intervened to save it. Conservatives were determined not to allow another Republican president to make any more such mistakes. Through those bitter lessons, and through the emergence of the Federalist Society and its allied entities, they had built the legal infrastructure to help avoid another catastrophe.

No one better understood the significance of the conservative enterprise to reshape the federal judiciary, and no one had been a more energetic participant in it or as eager a beneficiary of its influence than Kavanaugh, the former clerk whose merits Kennedy praised to Trump that day. Then fifty-two, Kavanaugh, a graduate of Yale College and Yale Law School, had risen meteorically through the conservative legal ranks: a clerkship with Kennedy; a stint as a prosecutor for independent counsel Kenneth Starr as he investigated Bill and Hillary Clinton; five years in the George W. Bush administration; and, for the previous dozen years, a seat on the prestigious federal appeals court in Washington.

Much as the conservative movement had spent decades making certain that it would not again squander the opportunity of a Supreme Court vacancy, Kavanaugh had spent a lifetime preparing for it—angling for it, as some observers saw it. After eight years under a Democratic president, Trump's unexpected ascendance could be Kavanaugh's opportunity at long last. A Kavanaugh candidacy for the high court could help induce Kennedy to retire. Kavanaugh had a lengthy record that could attest to his reliability as a conservative jurist; notwithstanding jitters among some conservatives, there was little risk he would be, as they most feared, another Souter or even another Kennedy. And as the conservative legal project shifted from combustible social issues like abortion and gay rights to what Trump adviser Steve Bannon called the "deconstruction of the administrative state," Kavanaugh's belief that administrative agencies had been given too much leeway to regulate was in sync with this business-oriented conservative agenda. He had amassed squadrons of well-placed allies like Kennedy, who helped him secure the nomination, and George W. Bush, who rallied to his defense when, at the eleventh hour, his once certain confirmation appeared in jeopardy. He was, in short, a man whose résumé was perfectly crafted for this moment.

The story of Kavanaugh, his ultimate selection, and what turned out to be the contentious road to his confirmation is in part a story of paradoxes. A president who came to office promising to drain the swamp, a president who disdained all things Bush, ended up choosing for his nominee a lobbyist's son who had spent nearly his entire career inside the confines of the Beltway—a man who not only worked for years at Bush's elbow but had also married the president's secretary. A nominee who was chosen because of those very establishment credentials, including a glittering résumé that seemed to mark him as the safest choice in a closely divided Senate, turned out to be not so safe after all, his confirmation nearly derailed by last-minute allegations of sexual misconduct. A nominee whose selection was almost torpedoed by social conservatives who feared he would be another unreliable "squish"—and who mounted a desperate effort to block his selection—ended up with those very conservatives coalescing behind Kavanaugh and celebrating him as a martyr to Democratic desperation.

The story of Kavanaugh's confirmation is also the story of history converging and repeating itself. The Kavanaugh nomination battle evoked the high ideological stakes of the Bork fight—this time waged in the unhinged new era of Twitter and 24-7 cable television and accompanied by a multimillion-dollar advertising onslaught financed by secret donors on both sides. The Kavanaugh fight echoed the ugly and contested sexual drama of the Clarence Thomas hearings—this time amid the unforgiving atmosphere of the #MeToo movement.

The fusion of those two previous episodes occurred in the already combustible environment of Donald Trump's Washington, a world in which norms of civility were shredded, partisan battle lines hardened, and a win-at-any-cost mentality prevailed. As the confirmation battle unfolded, each side operated from the conviction that the opposition would stop at nothing. Democrats believed that Republicans would do anything to muscle through their nominee; Republicans were equally convinced that Democrats would do whatever it took to defeat him. And both sides well understood: Kavanaugh's nomination offered conservatives the opportunity they had been seeking for decades—the reliable, entrenched majority that had so long eluded them.

Before all that could happen, there was just one problem, a hurdle that Kennedy referenced in his meeting with Trump that day. The president had promised to pick Supreme Court nominees only from his list. Brett Kavanaugh was not on it, and this was no mere oversight.

The Choice

The Missing Man

In the summer of 2016, Brett Kavanaugh was celebrating his tenth year on the bench, and his growing ranks of law clerks had gathered for a reunion. This one, held in June at the Chevy Chase Club, not far from Kavanaugh's home, came at an odd, even awkward moment, with Donald Trump about to claim the Republican nomination. Some of the clerks were Democrats, and though more were Republicans, few if any were Trump Republicans. All of them, it is safe to say, had been astonished a few weeks earlier when Trump released a list of eleven potential Supreme Court nominees that was notable for the name it did not include: Brett Kavanaugh. By this stage in his career, Kavanaugh was an obvious if not leading choice for any Republican president or presidential contender. He had been on Mitt Romney's short list for the Supreme Court during the 2012 campaign and no doubt would have been at the top of the roster for any of the establishment GOP candidates in 2016, such as Jeb Bush and Marco Rubio, except that they had long before fallen to Trump.

Still, at that point the prospect of the blowhard New York reality television star actually winning the presidency seemed fanciful. So when Travis Lenkner, an early Kavanaugh clerk who was serving as master of ceremonies for the event, referred to Trump's glaring omission, it was more in the nature of gentle joshing than painful jab. Here's to Judge Kavanaugh, he toasted—the twelfth man on Trump's eleven-person list.

·　·　·

Trump had been toying with the notion of that list for months before the plan became public. Before the Iowa caucuses, when New Jersey governor Chris Christie, at the time a Trump rival but also a friend of long standing, asked Trump how he was going to manage the problem of attracting evangelicals, Trump threw out a suggestion: what about getting the Federalist Society to produce a list for him? Good idea, Christie responded; you should talk to Leonard Leo. Trump wasn't going to secure the nomination, he figured, so offering Trump advice was like giving away snow in winter.

Ted Cruz, the conservative senator from Texas, came in first in the Iowa caucuses on February 1, thanks in large part to his support among evangelicals, the very constituency that Christie had identified as a Trump vulnerability. Trump won the New Hampshire primary eight days later. Then came the event that upended the campaign—and, as it played out, helped catapult Trump to victory. Don McGahn, the Trump campaign's general counsel and, in his spare time, guitar player for a rock-and-roll cover band, was on his way to a gig that Saturday afternoon when he received a text from his wife: "Scalia died."[1] McGahn pulled to the side of the road to collect his thoughts. There was a primary in South Carolina that night, and the candidate needed to be prepared for questions on this new front.

Scalia's death generated an instantaneous miniversion of the Trump list—and the first inkling that Kavanaugh might have a problem making it. As Trump did his once-over-lightly form of debate prep later that day—forty-five minutes in a room with key advisers as well as others who called in—McGahn pressed the point: the candidate couldn't simply rely on a generic pledge to name a justice in the Scalia mold. That wouldn't be convincing, not from Trump. Voters listening to the debate wouldn't have any worries about Cruz filling Scalia's seat, McGahn argued. Trump, on the other hand, was an unknown, and untrusted, quantity. He had been, not so long ago, in favor of abortion rights and a ban on assault weapons. He needed to back up his promises with some specifics. So that evening, when moderator John Dickerson of CBS raised Scalia's death as the first question of the debate, Trump not only echoed McConnell in calling for "delay, delay, delay" until a new president could be elected, he also took the unusual step of volunteering names of those he would consider for the vacancy. "We could have a Diane Sykes, or you could have a Bill Pryor, we have some fantastic people," Trump offered. Those names were significant—a calculated signal to the conservative base that Trump would pick judges to their liking.[2]

Sykes, a former justice of the Wisconsin Supreme Court named to the Seventh Circuit by George W. Bush, was a darling of social conservatives for, among other things, striking down the Affordable Care Act's requirement that employers provide no-cost contraceptive coverage, a mandate that Sykes said infringed on the religious freedom of Catholic business owners.[3] She had attracted the attention of McGahn, an election lawyer who detested campaign finance regulation, with a ruling striking down major parts of Wisconsin's campaign finance law on First Amendment grounds.[4] (After the election, Sykes made it to a first-round interview with the president's advisers. But Trump was put off by her marriage to a leading Republican Trump critic, talk radio host Charlie Sykes, although he kept forgetting the key fact: the Sykeses were divorced.)

Pryor, a former attorney general of Alabama tapped for the Eleventh Circuit by Bush, was even more controversial—and therefore an even more potent signal for Trump to send to conservatives. Among other things, Pryor had dismissed the Supreme Court as "nine octogenarian lawyers" and criticized *Roe v. Wade* as "the day seven members of our highest court ripped the constitution and ripped out the life of millions of unborn children."[5]

As McGahn later described Trump's approach to the debate, "I knew then that President Trump was a different kind of guy. For him to go up in a debate and say 'Judge Pryor' showed me he was the real deal when it was going to come to judges. There was no hesitancy. There was none of this, 'Well, you know, who are the moderates?'"[6]

There was one name McGahn floated on the night of Scalia's

death, as his candidate did his debate prep, that Trump waved off. No one from the swamp, Trump instructed. That meant no Kavanaugh.

There was another, related problem as well. "When people think of Brett," one campaign official explained, "they think of Bush." That was not exactly a plus in Trumpworld, and certainly not with the candidate himself. Jeb Bush, the brother of the president for whom Kavanaugh had worked, was still in the race—he dropped out a week later—and even after that the hostility between the Trump and Bush camps festered.

Scalia's death—and McConnell's vow to hold the seat open for the next president—transformed the campaign equation. For voters in the Republican base—far more than for Democrats—courts, and the Supreme Court in particular, are always a motivating force. These voters are tired of what they view as unelected judges writing policy preferences into constitutional law. For decades, these liberal judges prevented ordinary citizens from protecting the lives of the unborn and from allowing their children to pray in school. Now they were trying to tell them not only that gays and lesbians had a constitutional right to marry but also that a baker whose religion held that same-sex marriage was sinful had to bake a cake to celebrate the marriage or else be put out of business. Now Scalia's death brought those concerns to the forefront. Hillary Clinton could not be permitted to replace Scalia with a liberal justice.

The future of the court was comfortable terrain for Cruz, a Harvard-trained lawyer, clerk to Chief Justice William Rehnquist, and former Texas solicitor general. The Texas senator was delighted to exploit the issue not only against Clinton but also, more immediately, against Trump. And he had a handy weapon to wield against his rival: Trump's sister Maryanne Trump Barry. Older than Trump by nine years, Barry was a veteran federal judge, first appointed to a federal trial-court judgeship by Reagan and elevated to the Third Circuit in 1999 by Bill Clinton. Trump

had raised the prospect of tapping his sister for the high court—
"jokingly," he insisted—and managed to dig himself into an even
deeper hole with social conservatives.[7]

"I think she'd be phenomenal. I think she'd be one of the best,"
Trump told *Bloomberg Politics* in August 2015 about the idea of
his sister as a justice. "But frankly, we'd have to rule that out now,
at least temporarily." Again, in October 2015, he told Fox News
about the idea of naming his sister to the high court, "I would love
to, but I think she would be the one to say, 'No way, no way.'"[8]

Trump may have been joking, but conservatives were not
amused. Barry was anathema to conservatives for a 2000 ruling
in which she struck down a New Jersey law banning the procedure known as partial-birth abortion. The Supreme Court had just
overturned Nebraska's nearly identical law, but that didn't matter.[9] Conservative activists—and Trump's Republican rivals—still
railed against Barry.

Trump's "breezy adulations—'phenomenal' and 'one of the
best'—gloss over the reality that Barry is a pro-abortion judicial
activist," warned Carrie Severino of the Judicial Crisis Network,
the Leo-linked group that eventually fell into line and spent millions of dollars promoting Trump's Supreme Court picks after the
election. In a *USA Today* op-ed piece headlined DON'T TRUMP
THE SUPREME COURT, she cautioned that Trump "has yet to
prove that he can be trusted with that most precious of presidential
powers: the power to shape the high court."[10]

Likewise, conservative activist Penny Nance of Concerned
Women for America called Trump's praise for his sister "alarming
and disturbing," adding, "That Mr. Trump can so easily offer effu-
sive praise of a judge who is in favor of giving constitutional protection to partial-birth abortion—simply based on the fact that the
judge is his sibling—calls into question not just his readiness to be
the nominee for the party that fights for the unborn, but his overall
fitness for the most important job in the world."[11]

In the days after Scalia's death, Cruz flayed Trump for the comments about his sister. A "Bill Clinton–appointed federal appellate

judge who is a radical pro-abortion extremist," Cruz said.[12] For
Trump, producing that list, and getting it right, was going to be
more important than ever.

By the end of March, Trump was improbably—alarmingly, to much
of his party—on the verge of clinching the GOP presidential nomination. But he faced the same vexing problem he had discussed
with Christie in Iowa: winning the trust of social conservatives and
persuading them to turn out for him in November. On a triumphal
trip to the capital as the party's all-but-certain nominee on March
21, Trump visited the *Washington Post* for a session with the editorial board, unveiling a list of foreign policy advisers and, ever
the real estate developer, complimenting the newspaper's gleaming
new offices. He toured the new Trump International Hotel under
construction on Pennsylvania Avenue, touting its granite exterior—
"they don't build them like that anymore, that I can tell you"—and
the cavernous lobby, soon to be adorned with "marble, beautiful
marble, from different parts of the world."[13] He pledged fealty to
Israel before the American Israel Public Affairs Committee, assuring the crowd, "My daughter Ivanka is about to have a beautiful,
Jewish baby."[14]

     And he convened a group of conservative lawmakers and
activists—including Alabama Republican Jefferson Sessions, the
first senator to endorse Trump; Heritage Foundation president and
former South Carolina senator Jim DeMint; and former House
leaders Newt Gingrich and Bob Livingston—to help him tackle the
conservative problem.

     "The meeting wasn't philosophical. The meeting was polit-
ical," Gingrich recalled of the session in a conference room at
Jones Day, McGahn's law firm. "The meeting was—there are a
large number of conservatives who are still not convinced you're
a conservative. What can he do to reassure people that he's really
a conservative?"[15]

     Judges were the obvious answer, and Trump now floated his

audacious solution before the group: releasing a list of prospective Supreme Court nominees. Under normal circumstances, with normal presidential candidates, such short lists of potential nominees are closely guarded secrets. Trump turned that convention on its head, much to the discomfort of some of his advisers. It wasn't having the list that mattered, as Trump saw the situation—it was making the names public. "I don't think any experienced politician would have done that," said Trump adviser and former New York mayor Rudy Giuliani. "But he's different. And I think he felt because I'm different I have to do things differently to satisfy people that I know what I'm doing."[16]

Trump, never a man to keep a secret, telegraphed his plans later that day in a news conference held amid the construction of the Trump hotel. "I'm gonna submit a list of justices, potential justices of the United States Supreme Court that I will appoint from the list," he said. "I won't go beyond that list. And I'm gonna let people know. Because some people say, maybe I'll appoint a liberal judge. I'm not appointing a liberal judge."[17]

As the group discussed the judges list, the Heritage Foundation's DeMint volunteered his organization's services in putting together some names. But one man in the room that day had come forewarned by McGahn of Trump's desire to have a list and was forearmed with a roster of names. The Federalist Society's Leo stayed behind after the gathering broke up to speak with Trump and McGahn. He reached into his jacket pocket and pulled out a list of six possibilities.

"I was really hoping for twelve," Trump told him.

"We can try," Leo replied.[18]

Leo's answer was telling. As Trump pressed him to come up with more names, there was one obvious candidate whom Leo nonetheless omitted. Once again, Kavanaugh was the missing man.

Kavanaugh's absence from Leo's list was no accident. Kavanaugh and Leo had known each other for years; they had worked together on judges back when Kavanaugh was at the Bush White House. But privately, Leo harbored concerns about the reliability of Kavanaugh's conservatism—worries prompted by, but not limited to, the fact that Kavanaugh had demurred a few years back, when he had the chance, to vote to overturn Obama's signature health care law.

Leo "didn't trust that Brett wasn't going to pull a Souter because of his background, being a swamp creature, born and raised in the D.C. area, being very much a Bush Republican," said one close observer. "All the credentials . . . pointed to someone who was high risk."

Those worries weren't well known outside conservative circles, but—much as his Bush ties served as a black mark with Trump—they threatened to keep the well-credentialed jurist from the Supreme Court seat that he had long coveted.

Well before the meeting at Jones Day, the Federalist Society had become the conservative movement's established clearinghouse for legal talent. For Trump, the Federalist Society's imprimatur served as a kind of Good Housekeeping seal of approval for judicial nominees. If the Federalist Society blessed Trump's picks, conservatives could relax.

Not in their wildest, most ambitious dreams did the founders of the Federalist Society imagine that their group would eventually wield such influence when they organized their first event, held at Yale on the last weekend of April in 1982. "A Symposium on Federalism: Legal and Political Ramifications," the gathering was called, a reflection of the wonky inclinations of the society's creators, a group of Yale, Chicago, and Harvard Law students.[19] As the proposal for the event explained, "Law schools and the legal profession are currently strongly dominated by a form of orthodox liberal ideology which advocates a centralized and uniform society." It was time to formulate "a comprehensive conservative critique."[20]

Robert Bork, who would be nominated to the Supreme Court five years later, was present at that first event. So were Antonin Scalia, then a University of Chicago law professor, and Ted Olson, then head of the Justice Department's Office of Legal Counsel.

The conference was the first of many networking opportunities—Woodstock for the conservative legal movement, as one attendee put it.[21] As much as the Federalist Society was conceived and continues to operate as an intellectual enterprise, it evolved to serve an even more influential and initially unforeseen purpose: attracting, developing, and credentialing the foot soldiers of the burgeoning conservative legal movement.

With Republicans in control of the White House for the next decade, members of the Federalist Society formed the beginnings of a new legal ruling class. The students who once were outliers in the legal academy, oddballs in liberal-dominated class discussions, found themselves holding a valuable new credential. Federalist Society members—the group soon expanded from law school campuses to outposts among practicing lawyers nationwide—provided the legal infrastructure for the Reagan and Bush administrations. Like a stocked pond from which to fish, the Federalist Society supplied the kind of originalist judges that Reagan attorney general Edwin Meese and his successors had committed to putting on the bench, nominees who pledged to hew to the original meaning of the Constitution and avoid substituting their policy preferences for the intent of the framers.

After eight years of a Democratic White House, and with control of the Supreme Court in the balance, the outcome of the 2016 election was of immense importance to the Federalist Society and Leo, especially after Scalia's death. Conservatives feared that their work of decades would be undone in a matter of months. "When we lost Justice Scalia . . . it seemed the court would once and for all become the instrument of the progressive liberal agenda," Leo recalled.[22] He put the stakes in apocalyptic terms. "Staring at that vacancy," Leo said, "fear permeated every day in that countdown to November 8th."[23]

Leo had once disdained advances from the Trump campaign. In February 2015, four months before Trump's fateful escalator ride into the lobby of Trump Tower, the candidate-in-waiting was already making the rounds with the party faithful, speaking at the annual Conservative Political Action Conference. In the hallways of the Gaylord National Resort in suburban Maryland, amid the conservative radio hosts and the Tea Party activists dressed in colonial garb, Trump's eager young aide Sam Nunberg, who had met Leo when Nunberg was a student at Touro Law Center on Long Island, buttonholed the Federalist Society official.

"I'm working for Mr. Trump: he's speaking here, and he's going to be running," Nunberg recalled telling Leo. "I just want you to understand that he's going to run. The judiciary is a very important issue to him. He gets it, and you're going to get everything you want." Leo, Nunberg said, replied, "Oh, that's great. Follow up with me." Leo, as Nunberg interpreted it, "was being nice. He wasn't being dismissive. But it also wasn't something that was going to be such a top priority to him."[24]

But Trump turned out to be a candidate to be taken seriously— a top priority, in fact. By January 2016, as the Iowa caucuses approached, the tables—and the balance of power—had turned: the Federalist Society was now eager to connect with the surging Trump campaign. Federalist Society vice president Jonathan Bunch tracked down Trump campaign lawyer McGahn, saying the group wanted to discuss judicial selection. "You have nothing to worry about," McGahn recalled telling him. "I've known Leonard for years."[25]

The two men made the oddest of couples—Leo, with his highbrow talk of the "structural Constitution," and Trump, who knew so little of the document that he once referred to its nonexistent Article XII. Leo cared about judges because he cared about reining in what he viewed as the excesses of an out-of-control judiciary. Trump cared about judges because caring about judges might help get him elected. If it was a marriage of convenience, it was an arrangement that worked out well for both parties to the transaction.

By the time of the 2016 campaign, Leo had made himself into a central, perhaps the central, player in conservative legal circles.

During the George W. Bush administration, he was one of a group known as the Four Horsemen: the other three were Meese, George H. W. Bush White House counsel Boyden Gray, and Jay Sekulow of the American Center for Law and Justice, later to become Trump's personal lawyer. The Four Horsemen coordinated closely with the Bush White House, including a young lawyer in the counsel's office named Brett Kavanaugh, to ensure that judicial openings would be filled with reliable conservatives. When a Supreme Court vacancy arose, first with O'Connor's retirement and then with Rehnquist's death, Leo would take a leave from the Federalist Society to help shepherd the nominees—John Roberts and Samuel Alito—through confirmation.

An alumnus of Cornell University and Cornell Law School, where he founded the Federalist Society chapter before graduating in 1989, Leo clerked on the D.C. Circuit court for conservative Raymond Randolph and has worked for the Federalist Society ever since. An owlish-looking man with a penchant for tailored suits, Leo combines devout Catholicism—the father of seven, he has attended daily Mass since the death in 2007 of his oldest daughter, born with spina bifida—with a taste for fine clothes and fine dining.[26] He keeps a wine locker at Morton's, the downtown Washington steak house, and his wine buyer is the chief steward at the Trump International Hotel.[27]

Leo's twin driving forces, mutually reinforcing, are Catholicism and judicial conservatism. In public, he disavows any zeal for overturning the constitutional right to abortion. He has accused the left of "using *Roe v. Wade* as a scare tactic," adding, "This is not about overturning a particular case. It's about getting the Constitution right."[28] That public posture is at odds with his private comments. "For Leonard, it's all about *Roe*," said one friend. As conservative blogger Ed Whelan wrote in December 2016, defending Leo against improbable attacks from the right, "No one has been more dedicated to the enterprise of building a Supreme Court that will overturn *Roe v. Wade* than the Federalist Society's Leonard Leo."[29]

As the years went on, a significant part of Leo's influence stemmed from one essential skill he brought to the conservative legal enterprise: raising the money needed to run it. This was no easy lift. Big donors—the kind of financiers who can afford the enormous sums needed to underwrite a modern nomination fight—prefer to see a more immediate return on their investments than a judicial confirmation, whose impact could take years if not decades to manifest itself. Leo excelled at explaining the stakes and securing the checks.

Federal tax law allowed Leo to keep the identity of his donors secret, and Leo was adept at batting aside questions about the sources of his funding. There was a storied history of anonymous money being used to support worthy causes, he argued: just look at the civil rights movement. And he disavowed deep involvement in financial operations. "I'm not particularly knowledgeable about a lot of it," he told the *Washington Post*. "I don't waste my time on stories that involve money and politics because what I care about is ideas."[30]

This was beyond disingenuous. The greatest source of Leo's power was his singular knack for coaxing huge checks, some as large as eight figures, out of billionaire donors. The *Washington Post* added up the amount that Leo-affiliated nonprofit organizations had raised between 2014 and 2017 alone and produced the staggering sum of more than $250 million.

Doing good for the conservative cause, it turned out, also offered Leo the ability to do well for himself. He made in excess of $400,000 a year at the Federalist Society, but that accounted for only one of his income streams. He has identified himself in campaign finance filings as an employee of the BH Group, an otherwise unknown Virginia company that has in turn received more than $4 million in payments from Leo-affiliated entities for unspecified consulting, research, and public relations services. In August 2018, Leo paid off the mortgage on the northern Virginia home he had purchased in 2010 for $710,000. Two months later, as the Kavanaugh confirmation was coming to a final vote, Leo closed on a

$3.3 million, eleven-bedroom, eight-bathroom waterfront home in Mount Desert Island, Maine. In a statement to the *Washington Post*, he described it as "a retreat for our large family and for extending hospitality to our community of personal and professional friends and co-workers."[31] Real estate records show that the mortgage on the Maine home was paid off in July 2019.[32]

As Leo's influence grew and his profile rose with the new administration, there was, as there is for anyone with such outsize success, a degree of bristling at his new prominence. "It really did become like he had a little bit of a God complex, as if he were doing the court appointments," said one person who watched Leo from up close. "People were going to him to pitch themselves . . . 'If I can get in front of Leonard', 'Can you make an introduction to Leonard?', 'What do you think Leonard would think?', 'How do I get to Leonard?' It's become the Leonard primary—that's what it's become under Trump."

This elevation of Leo's influence was more than a little inflated, but at least initially that puffery served Leo and the White House simultaneously. "His role both in the selection and even through the confirmation process was a lot more limited than people assume, but it was to our benefit," said one White House official. "That guy is the stamp of approval."

Over time, one person who was put out by Leo's new prominence was Trump himself. At one point, after Kennedy retired and Leo was making the rounds of the Sunday talk shows, Trump exploded, not once but repeatedly, about Leo's ubiquity. "Who's this little fucking midget?" he complained, a reference to Leo's short stature. "That fucking Leonard Leo yapping his mouth," Trump told another adviser. "Everybody should just keep quiet. I make the decisions here."

Leo, whose ego had a tendency to get the better of his judgment, would generally remember to acknowledge that the president had the final say. But in an interview after the Kavanaugh confirmation, he offered a revealing comment about the way he perceived his own role in the universe of judicial selection. "I was here long before this president," Leo observed, "and I will be doing what I am doing, God willing, long after."[33]

The process of crafting the list of potential Supreme Court justices took far more time than Trump had anticipated because the final version was delayed by internal "bickering," as one adviser put it, over who would make it on and who would be left off. The hastily assembled list of foreign policy advisers Trump had released to the *Washington Post* the day of the Jones Day meeting—including such nonentities as Carter Page and George Papadopoulos—had been met with widespread derision. That kind of scorn infuriated Trump, and he was determined that it not be repeated with his Supreme Court list. "If we're going to do this, we can't fuck it up," Trump told McGahn. "We can't have anybody angry with me when this list comes out. I want everybody to be happy." Assembling the list, McGahn lamented to one friend, was like "juggling chain saws."

McGahn later made the point that his candidate, in assembling the list, had rejected the conventional political advice to move in a more moderate direction after securing the nomination. "It was not done in the primary season to get people to think he was more conservative than he was," McGahn said. "It came out after he was the presumptive nominee, at which point every person in Washington said, 'It's over; can't do that; got to move to the middle. It will scare people.'"[34]

That account is more than a little self-serving. Assembling, and publicizing, a list of full-throated conservatives was not an act of political foolhardiness on Trump's part or a demonstration of damn-the-torpedoes conservative bravado. It was a calculated— and long-planned—maneuver to reassure the base. After calling Trump a "pathological liar," "narcissist," and "serial philanderer," Ted Cruz had dropped out of the race a few weeks before the list was finally unveiled.[35] But as the harshness of his language about the putative nominee indicated, the fears the Texan had fomented about Trump among the conservative base lingered. Cruz remained a lurking irritant to the Trump campaign, which feared a convention challenge.

It took an additional nudge from McConnell to get the list unveiled two months later. Meeting with Trump later that spring, McConnell suggested that the candidate finally put "pen to paper," and that "there would be great satisfaction in the conservative community if he made his list public," said McConnell strategist Josh Holmes.[36]

In the end, the list, released on May 18, consisted of six federal appeals court judges named by President George W. Bush and five state supreme court justices appointed by Republican governors. It was heavy on social conservatives, including the two Trump had mentioned on the night of Scalia's death, Sykes and Pryor. "We did what we had to do," McGahn told one associate. "It's not the Bible. It's a list." The list, said social conservative activist Gary Bauer, "was huge . . . It was a list full of people that we that work in this field know of, and know about."

The first list was not the final one. In September, the campaign issued a second roster, with ten additional names. If the point of the first list was to reassure conservatives in general, the second was designed to reassure one conservative in particular—Cruz. The Texas senator had declined to endorse Trump at the Republican convention in Cleveland, urging listeners instead to "vote your conscience."[37]

By September, Cruz was prepared to make the endorsement, but he had a price, consisting of two list-related parts. The first was a tighter commitment that Trump would limit himself to the list in choosing a replacement for Scalia. Trump's original language, back in May, was more loosey-goosey. The list, he said then, was "representative of the kind of constitutional principles I value" and would serve as "a guide to nominate our next United States Supreme Court justices."[38] Cruz wanted Trump to nail things down, so he did. "This list is definitive, and I will choose only from it in picking future justices of the Supreme Court," Trump proclaimed. Cruz's second requirement was that Trump put Mike Lee, Cruz's Senate colleague from Utah—who had, notably, refused to back Trump—on the list.[39]

Within hours after the second list was released, Cruz posted his endorsement of Trump on Facebook, citing the addition of Lee and Trump's promise to select only from that expanded roster. "This commitment matters, and it provides a serious reason for voters to choose to support Trump," he argued.[40] Two other additions were notable: Amul Thapar, a forty-seven-year-old Kentucky district court judge and McConnell favorite, and Gorsuch. So was the continuing omission: no Kavanaugh.

Releasing the list was not the end of the campaign's efforts to calm conservative nerves. A month after the first list was unveiled, at a closed-door gathering of leading religious and social conservatives, Trump sought to provide additional reassurance. At a news conference, eight evangelical leaders who attended the session were asked if they were ready to endorse Trump; none raised a hand.[41] "I know a lot of people who are holding their nose," said Marjorie Dannenfelser, president of the antiabortion Susan B. Anthony List. But she also approvingly cited Trump's vow to appoint a "pro-life Supreme Court justice."[42]

On the campaign trail, Trump hammered home the point that Republicans could trust him on judges. In fact, they needed him. The message was delivered with typical Trumpian subtlety. "If you really like Donald Trump, that's great, but if you don't, you have to vote for me anyway. You know why? Supreme Court judges, Supreme Court judges," Trump said at a rally in Cedar Rapids, Iowa, in July. "Sorry, sorry, sorry. You have no choice."[43]

Whereas previous Republican candidates had been coy about applying litmus tests, Trump was explicit: overturning *Roe v. Wade* would "happen automatically," he said in the third and final presidential debate with Clinton, "because I am putting pro-life justices on the court."[44]

In rally after rally, Trump warned voters: their Second Amendment rights were at risk. So was their religious liberty. "You pick the wrong people, you have a country that is no longer your country," Trump said at the Values Voter Summit in September. "This will determine whether or not we remain a constitutional republic, frankly."[45] In Waukesha, Wisconsin, a few weeks later, Trump urged the crowd, "Don't let it slip away. We have one chance. This is it. We don't have four more years . . . They'll start appointing justices of the Supreme Court. Remember that, Supreme Court—we lost a great one, Judge Scalia. We can't let it slip away."[46]

Although Kavanaugh himself does not vote—he decided to abstain shortly after becoming a judge—he gave more credence than most to the possibility that Trump might win.[47] Still, he was already beginning to think ahead to life under a second President Clinton. "He thought Trump was a buffoon, like everyone else," one friend said. Kavanaugh's stints in private practice had been brief; he hadn't had the years to amass the wealth some of his peers were enjoying. He was beginning to muse to friends about feeling bored and talking about leaving the bench to make some money.

Trump's unexpected win changed all that. It meant that what once seemed like a theoretical problem for Kavanaugh—not being on Trump's list—was now a serious impediment. He had a Bush problem with Trump and a conservative problem with Leo. Both needed to be resolved if he were to have any chance of becoming a justice.

CHAPTER TWO

Making the List

I f Kavanaugh faced obstacles in making his way onto Trump's list, he also had a not-so-secret weapon: the new White House counsel, Don McGahn. Leonard Leo, with his Federalist Society seal of approval, had been in the ascendancy during the campaign; once Trump was sworn in, McGahn was the one with the power, and the access that only a West Wing office can bring. At the urging of Mitch McConnell, who had helped get him named to the Federal Election Commission, McGahn consolidated the judge-picking power in the White House, where he could control it closely, and made judicial selection his top priority.

First on McGahn's agenda, once Gorsuch was confirmed, was adding Kavanaugh's name to the list. Leo was not thrilled at this prospect—he felt like the list was his baby, and he didn't especially want to see it messed with. During the Gorsuch nomination he and McGahn had clashed, and Leo had felt excluded, frozen out from key meetings. Since influence was his stock-in-trade—a key to his ability to reel in the seven-figure checks—maintaining that access was paramount, and that meant staying on McGahn's good side. If McGahn wanted Kavanaugh, Leo needed to take that seriously. Trump wasn't generally a fan of his White House counsel, to say the least, but when it came to judge picking, McGahn had proved himself to Trump with his work on Gorsuch.

In the meantime, Kavanaugh and his allies did not rely on McGahn alone. Kavanaugh considered a career change that might help put him in Trump's good graces. His supporters made the case for Kavanaugh to Leo and other key players. And Kavanaugh did what he could to sell himself to Leo and other wary conservatives.

At his confirmation hearings, Kavanaugh was asked how he finally made it onto Trump's list. He responded with fuzzy understatement that nonetheless made clear the avidity with which his allies pursued—and Kavanaugh monitored—the addition of his name. "A lot of judges and lawyers I know made clear to, I think, various people that they thought I should at least be considered based on my record for the last twelve years," he said. "And colleagues of mine thought I should be considered."[1]

This was an astonishingly mild description of what became an intense behind-the-scenes campaign for Kavanaugh's inclusion on Trump's roster of potential nominees. Kavanaugh's absence from the list "was the talk of the town" after Election Day, said one influential Republican lawyer. "People were chatting, and to a person . . . there was a sense that something went wrong, something went awry, and that now needs to be corrected." Kavanaugh "knew he needed to get on these lists," said one well-placed observer. "I remember Leonard telling me people were calling him making the case for why Brett should be put on."

One possible route onto the list was taking a job with the new administration. Rod Rosenstein, the incoming deputy attorney general, who had worked with Kavanaugh on Kenneth Starr's Whitewater investigation, called to see if Kavanaugh might be interested in becoming Trump's solicitor general, the government's chief lawyer before the Supreme Court. As Kavanaugh well knew, that move hadn't worked so well for Starr, who had left the D.C. Circuit to become solicitor general under George H. W. Bush, only to see his high hopes for becoming a justice dashed. On the other hand, taking the job did the trick for Elena Kagan, who left the deanship of Harvard Law School to become Obama's solicitor general before he tapped her for the high court. Maybe the solicitor general's job would bolster Kavanaugh's credentials with Trump, or maybe it would be too risky, requiring Kavanaugh to endorse legal positions that could cause difficulties in the event of a Supreme Court nomination. He weighed seeking the position, despite the concern of some friends who advised him against throwing in his lot with the Trump crowd, and spoke with Jeff Sessions about it.[2]

The problem was, others had their eyes on that prize, one of the plum legal jobs in the federal government. Maybe Kavanaugh could prevail in the end, but it was going to take mounting an effort. Kavanaugh decided it would be better to stay put on the appeals court. He liked being a judge and was in line to become chief judge of the circuit in February 2020.

That spring, shortly after Gorsuch was confirmed, a delegation of Kavanaugh clerks went to see Leo at the Federalist Society, where a telling nameplate sits on his bookshelf: THE REAL BOSS, it says. The clerks' mission was twofold: make the positive case for Kavanaugh and, more important, assuage what they understood were the concerns of Leo and some of his fellow conservatives.

The biggest hurdle was Kavanaugh's 2011 opinion in *Seven-Sky v. Holder*, one of the early constitutional challenges to the Affordable Care Act. The majority in the case voted to uphold the law against a claim that Congress had gone too far by requiring individuals to obtain health insurance. Notably, the two judges voting to sustain the law included not only liberal Harry Edwards, a Jimmy Carter appointee, but also Laurence Silberman, a Reagan nominee and conservative stalwart who wrote the opinion. The individual mandate was a stretch, Silberman concluded, but the Supreme Court's precedents made clear that Congress had the power under its broad authority to regulate interstate commerce.

Kavanaugh took a different tack. He dissented but refrained from opining on the law's constitutionality, for or against. Instead, he said, it was premature to decide that issue, citing an obscure 1867 law known as the Tax Anti-Injunction Act, which prevents taxpayers from challenging the legality of a tax until the bill is due. Kavanaugh concluded that the penalty imposed on individuals who failed to obtain coverage was a tax—after all, it was paid through tax returns. Therefore, the suit had to wait until the fine was actually imposed. Better to avoid the issue and see how things played out than to have the courts intervene unnecessarily, Kavanaugh observed. "You know, we're courts of judicial restraint," he commented at the oral argument in the case. "It's a delicate act to declare an act of Congress unconstitutional."[3]

This was, in a sense, a conservative position, but it did not endear Kavanaugh to conservatives. He had the chance to vote to strike down Obama's signature achievement, and he balked—not only balked but also did so in a way that suggested he might have lined up with what conservatives viewed as the chief justice's eventual treachery in saving the Affordable Care Act, which relied in a different way on the notion that the penalty was a tax. Kavanaugh's dissent, said Josh Blackman, a conservative law professor who has written extensively about the Affordable Care Act, "was being too cute by half. It really read like someone who was trying as hard as he could to avoid the most easy opinion, which was Silberman's," upholding the statute.[4]

Another supposed black mark against Kavanaugh involved a second Obamacare case, about the law's requirement that employers include contraception as part of workers' insurance packages. Recognizing that some religious groups objected to being forced to provide contraception, the Obama administration had allowed such entities to avoid the requirement by simply filing a form stating their objections. But a group called Priests for Life and other nonprofit organizations affiliated with the Catholic Church claimed that even having to submit this form required them to violate their religious convictions and therefore represented an unconstitutional infringement on religious freedom. A three-judge panel of the D.C. Circuit rejected that argument, concluding that "the opt-out mechanism imposes a *de minimis* requirement on any eligible organization." All the objecting organization had to do, the majority said, was file "a single sheet of paper."[5]

When the full appeals court declined to rehear the case, Kavanaugh issued a lengthy dissent, saying he would have ruled for the religious groups. Submitting the form on threat of being fined represented a "substantial burden" on their free exercise of religion, Kavanaugh said. It triggered the process of providing alternative coverage and thereby made the groups, as they understood it, "complicit in wrongdoing in contravention of their religious beliefs."[6] This position was remarkably—if anything, unduly—protective of religious liberty. Indeed, seven other appeals courts that considered the issue joined the D.C. Circuit in agreeing that having to file the form did not rise to the level of a substantial burden.

Yet Kavanaugh's language nonetheless concerned conservatives and posed a problem for his potential Supreme Court candidacy. In his dissent, Kavanaugh cited Kennedy's concurrence a year earlier in the *Burwell v. Hobby Lobby* contraceptive-coverage case, a similar dispute that involved privately held corporations rather than religiously affiliated organizations. "In short, even if the Court did not formally hold as much," Kavanaugh wrote, "*Hobby Lobby* at least strongly suggests that the Government has a compelling interest in facilitating access to contraception for the employees of these religious organizations." Indeed, Kavanaugh went on, it would make sense to find such an interest: "It is commonly accepted that reducing the number of unintended pregnancies would further women's health, advance women's personal and professional opportunities, reduce the number of abortions, and help break a cycle of poverty that persists when women who cannot afford or obtain contraception become pregnant unintentionally at a young age."[7]

This argument made logical sense, it was in keeping with precedent—and it infuriated some conservatives, who bristled at Kavanaugh's suggestion that contraceptive access was a compelling government interest. Their critique of Kavanaugh in the *Priests for Life* case was almost the converse of their complaint about him in the individual mandate case. In that case, conservatives were unhappy about Kavanaugh's bottom line or, more precisely, his avoidance of one. In *Priests for Life*, conservatives were fine with Kavanaugh's conclusion, which backed their position, but were unhappy about the language, seemingly supportive of a right to contraception, that he used along the way. It was anathema to suggest that the Constitution protected contraceptive access or even to express sympathy for the need to obtain birth control.

As his clerks and other allies lobbied on his behalf, Kavanaugh himself made the rounds of the conservative legal lecture circuit, delivering speeches that could not help but have a salutary effect on conservative jitters.

In February 2017, Kavanaugh gave the keynote address at a Notre Dame Law School symposium in honor of Scalia. "I loved the guy," Kavanaugh said. "Justice Scalia was and remains a judicial hero and role model to many throughout America. He thought carefully about his principles, he articulated those principles, and he stood up for those principles. As a judge, he did not buckle to political or academic pressure from the right or the left."[8]

Kavanaugh took care to phrase this buckling as a risk in either ideological direction, but his comments addressed one of conservatives' deepest fears about Supreme Court nominees—that once on the court, they would temper their conservative beliefs under the glare of attention from a liberal-leaning media and legal intelligentsia. This tendency was commonly known as the "Greenhouse effect," after Linda Greenhouse, the Pulitzer Prize–winning *New York Times* Supreme Court correspondent, and conservatives were apoplectic that so many Republican-appointed justices had succumbed to it. Scalia was his hero, Kavanaugh assured conservatives, because the late justice had not been among them. The suggestion was implicit: pick me, and I'll be strong, too.

Notably, Kavanaugh took the opportunity, while lauding Scalia, to differ with him—although he did not advertise it as a difference— on a key question of regulatory law. Scalia had generally been a defender of what was known as *Chevron* deference, after a 1984 decision (*Chevron U.S.A., Inc. v. Natural Resources Defense Council, Inc.*) involving the Environmental Protection Agency. Although the ruling favored industry interests at the time, *Chevron* has come to be a tool for regulators and a thorn in the side of big business. The case instructs judges, when reviewing a regulation, to defer to the agency that wrote the rule, as long as the underlying law is ambiguous and the agency's interpretation is reasonable. Modern conservatives increasingly chafed under *Chevron*'s restrictions, believing that the approach cedes too much power to agencies and encourages excessive regulation. Indeed, Gorsuch's attack on *Chevron* had been a key factor in helping him secure the nomination.

Now Kavanaugh, who had previously expressed his concerns about *Chevron*, weighed in again, with gusto. "The *Chevron* doctrine encourages agency aggressiveness on a large scale," he said. "Under the guise of ambiguity, agencies can stretch the meaning of statutes enacted by Congress to accommodate their preferred policy outcomes. I saw this firsthand when I worked in the White House, and I see it now from the other side as a judge."[9] *Chevron* deference, Kavanaugh concluded, effectively rigged the legal system in favor of regulators. His remarks were music to modern conservatives' ears.

There was more to follow. In September 2017, Kavanaugh, asked to give a Constitution Day lecture at the American Enterprise Institute, chose as his subject "The Constitutional Statesmanship of Chief Justice William Rehnquist." Kavanaugh focused on the late chief justice, he told the group, because "it pains me that many young lawyers and law students, even Federalist Society types, have little or no sense of the jurisprudence and importance of William Rehnquist to modern constitutional law. They do not know about his role in turning the Supreme Court away from its 1960s Warren Court approach, where the Court in some cases had seemed to be simply enshrining its policy views into the Constitution, or so the critics charged." During Rehnquist's tenure, Kavanaugh said, the court "unquestionably changed and became more of an institution of law, where its power is to interpret and to apply the law as written, informed by historical practice, not by its own personal and policy predilections."[10]

In the speech, Kavanaugh went about as far as a sitting lower-court judge could go to signal where he would come down on the constitutional right to abortion. He noted that Rehnquist, one of the two dissenters in *Roe v. Wade*, had criticized the majority in that case for creating a right not only unstated in the Constitution—unenumerated rights, as the court called them—but also inconceivable to the framers. The better approach, Kavanaugh suggested, was the one outlined by Rehnquist in a 1997 assisted-suicide case, *Washington v. Glucksberg*. Writing for a five-justice majority that rejected the idea of a constitutional right to assisted suicide, Rehnquist reiterated his view that such unenumerated rights would be recognized by the courts only if they were "deeply rooted" in the nation's history and tradition.

"Of course, even a first-year law student could tell you that the *Glucksberg* approach to unenumerated rights was not consistent with the approach of the abortion cases such as *Roe v. Wade* in 1973—as well as the 1992 decision reaffirming *Roe*, known as *Planned Parenthood v. Casey*," Kavanaugh observed. This comment did not reveal whether Kavanaugh was prepared to overrule *Roe*, but it did make clear how little he thought of the case on its own merits. Rehnquist may have lost the abortion battle, but, Kavanaugh noted approvingly, he succeeded "in stemming the general tide of free-wheeling judicial creation of unenumerated rights that were not rooted in the nation's history and tradition. The *Glucksberg* case stands to this day as an important precedent, limiting the Court's role in the realm of social policy and helping to ensure that the Court operates more as a court of law and less as an institution of social policy."[11]

Having influential advocates weigh in was good for Kavanaugh, as was giving speeches to shore up his conservative credentials. But having Don McGahn on his side was even better. McGahn was an unusual choice for White House counsel. His training was in the hard-edged trenches of campaign finance law, one of the most partisan and street-fighting specialties in the profession. A former general counsel to House Republicans' campaign arm, McGahn had been handpicked by Mitch McConnell, an ardent foe of campaign finance regulation, to serve on the Federal Election Commission beginning in 2008. He was sworn in by a young federal appeals court judge, Brett Kavanaugh, and his presence in the Trump administration would be key to Kavanaugh's ultimate elevation.

McGahn arrived at the Federal Election Commission as a man on a mission. Like his sponsor, McConnell, McGahn saw campaign finance rules not as legitimate efforts to limit the corrupting influence of money in politics but as unconstitutional incursions on freedom of speech. So McGahn's goal was to rein in—his critics would say neuter—the very agency he oversaw. He swiftly commandeered his two Republican colleagues and, blockading progress on even the most inconsequential actions, made the notoriously ineffective commission even more dysfunctional.

Robert Bauer, a leading Democratic election lawyer who became Obama's White House counsel, described McGahn as "the most significant commissioner to ever serve," adding, "He set the tone and a relentlessly ideological direction and went about this very aggressively."[12] The norm among Washington bureaucrats is to take steps to placate the opposition and dampen its squealing. When campaign finance reform advocates protested that he had brought the agency to a standstill, McGahn reacted with a characteristic doubling down. "The criticism backfired on them in many ways," he said in 2013, shortly after his departure. "I think they figured I would see this stuff in the newspapers and start moving to the middle. Actually, it pushed me to the flank and it made me stronger. And the more they screamed, the more I knew I was doing the right thing."[13]

As Trump toyed with running for president, he was introduced to McGahn by David Bossie, a campaign aide and president of Citizens United, the group that had provoked the campaign finance ruling of the same name. Their mutual willingness to engage in brash behavior and disrupt the status quo was an obvious point of connection between Trump and McGahn. But Trump's iconoclastic brand of conservatism did not necessarily fit with McGahn's libertarian perspective. And McGahn, a graduate of Widener University Delaware Law School, in the bottom tier of law school rankings, lacked the Ivy League credentials that were so key to winning Trump's respect.

Even at the top pinnacles of government, McGahn had never shed his sense of aggrievement at being an outsider, looked down on by others because of his less-than-stellar résumé, notwithstanding the fact that he had ended up with a partnership at Jones Day, where he reported handsome compensation of $2.4 million in the year before joining the White House. Speaking to the Federalist Society, McGahn recalled being snowed in one year at a Federalist Society student conference in Boston. "Nobody talked to me because I didn't go to Harvard," he observed tartly. "I remember all of you, though."[14]

The counsel's job, one of the most important in the White House, tends to go to a lawyer who shares a close personal bond with the president or is steeped in the kinds of constitutional questions about separation of powers, executive privilege, and national security that the president's chief lawyer is called on to navigate. McGahn possessed neither qualification. In a particularly baroque bit of palace intrigue, Reince Priebus, Trump's incoming chief of staff, had pushed for a well-known Republican lawyer, Bobby Burchfield, in that spot. But Ivanka Trump and Jared Kushner were feuding with Priebus and, as a consequence, sided against Burchfield and for McGahn.

The Trump-Kushners and McGahn later grew to detest one another, in particular over McGahn's role in handling their security clearances; Jared and Ivanka angled to have McGahn replaced by White House staff secretary Rob Porter until the stories appeared that Porter had physically abused his ex-wives. For the moment, though, it was enough, in the knives-out atmosphere of the incoming Trump White House, that McGahn was not Priebus's preferred candidate.

So he landed the counsel's job and, with it, the ability to be of immense help to Kavanaugh—even more than an ordinary White House counsel. In most administrations, the responsibility for judicial selection is divided—exactly how is a function of each individual presidency—between the White House and the Justice Department. McGahn centralized the function in the White House, and in his own office, to an unusual degree. In a more traditional administration, the attorney general would have at least played a key advisory role, certainly on Supreme Court nominations. But Jeff Sessions had been excluded from the start from judicial selection and was increasingly at odds with the president. The White House chief of staff could ordinarily be expected to weigh in on choices of this magnitude as well. But John Kelly, who had replaced Priebus in July 2017, was a military man who had little interest in the topic and was happy to delegate that portfolio to McGahn. So McGahn became by far the dominant player on questions of judicial selection.

Shortly after the Gorsuch confirmation—the Gorsuch triumph, as Trump saw it—McGahn pursued the opportunity to get Kavanaugh onto the Supreme Court list. He had bristled at the notion that judge picking had been outsourced to the Federalist Society, and this was the opportunity to put his own stamp more firmly on the list. His pitch to Trump was simple: a list with Kavanaugh on it would be a comfort to Justice Kennedy, an inducement to retire. Without Kavanaugh on the list, that was less likely to happen. Much as the first list was aimed at calming social conservatives and the second was the price of Cruz's endorsement, this third list had an audience of one—Anthony Kennedy.

As it was being finalized, Trump brought up Kavanaugh's name in conversations with aides: Do you know this guy? What do you think of him? McGahn had encouraged colleagues who knew Kavanaugh to make the pitch for him if the opportunity arose. As one White House official recalled, Trump would ask, "Why didn't anyone tell me he was on the court for twelve years? Why didn't anybody tell me he clerked for Kennedy and went to Yale and said these nice things about executive power?" One entry on Kavanaugh's résumé particularly appealed to Trump: his work for Starr. The president liked the idea of Kavanaugh as a fighter, especially as a fighter against Bill and Hillary Clinton.

As preparations were under way to unveil the list at the upcoming annual meeting of the Federalist Society, October 2017 brought an unexpected test—as much of a danger for Kavanaugh as an opportunity. He was assigned to hear a case that directly involved abortion, an unusual departure from the D.C. Circuit's ordinarily arid docket of regulatory appeals. Most abortion cases present challenges to state laws and end up being heard by one of the regional federal appeals courts. But this one concerned a dispute over the action of a federal agency, so it landed at the D.C. Circuit. The case, *Garza v. Hargan*, involved a pregnant seventeen-year-old who was being held in detention after illegally crossing the Mexican border into Texas. The teenager, identified as J.D., or Jane Doe, sought an abortion over the objection of Trump administration officials, who argued that they did not want to be forced to "facilitate" the procedure. Kavanaugh found himself part of the three-judge panel assigned to hear the case on an emergency basis. Along with another Republican-appointed judge, he voted to prevent the abortion from proceeding. The full appeals court then took the unusual step of intervening and reversed that ruling, allowing the abortion to take place.

For someone in Kavanaugh's position—that is, someone with an eye on the Supreme Court—the case presented a delicate challenge, which could not have been lost on a person so sophisticated at navigating the politics of judicial nominations. A judge could go an entire career on the D.C. Circuit without being called on to decide an abortion case, and if you were interested in higher office, that was probably a good thing: supporters and opponents might try to deduce where you stood on the issue, but no one could claim to know for certain.

Now this especially emotional dispute—abortion, a young girl, a migrant—had landed in Kavanaugh's lap. However he decided, his conclusion and his language would be flyspecked by both sides as a window into his views on *Roe v. Wade*. As a matter of sheer politics, there were risks either way. If Kavanaugh demonstrated hostility to the right to abortion, that could jeopardize his ability to win the kind of swing votes necessary for confirmation—including pro-choice Republican senators such as Susan Collins of Maine and Lisa Murkowski of Alaska—if the opportunity arose. On the other hand, if he seemed too willing to abide by the abortion-rights status quo, even as a lower-court judge obliged to follow precedent, he risked being targeted as a squish by right-to-life groups and perhaps never getting nominated at all.

The random composition of the three-judge panel assigned to hear the case made Kavanaugh the judge in the middle. Patricia Millett, an Obama appointee, argued that the case law was clear. The pregnant teen had followed the Texas procedure for a minor seeking an abortion. She had received approval from a Texas judge, who decided that she was mature enough to make the abortion decision on her own.[15] That right was being illegally denied her by the Trump administration. Meanwhile, the other judge on the panel, Karen LeCraft Henderson, a George H. W. Bush appointee, asserted that J.D., as an "alien minor" who had entered the United States illegally, had no constitutional right at all to obtain an abortion.[16]

Kavanaugh did not go nearly as far—a reticence that eventually generated criticism from some antiabortion advocates as the scramble was on to fill Kennedy's seat. Instead, Kavanaugh seized on a solution the government had not asked for and didn't seem to consider feasible: giving authorities additional time to find the teen a "sponsor"— effectively a foster parent—who could take over responsibility for J.D.'s care before she would have to make that "momentous life decision" on her own. Waiting a bit longer, he said, would not constitute an undue burden so long as the hunt for a sponsor was "expeditious."[17] As Millett pointed out, however, Kavanaugh's approach would give the government only eleven extra days to complete a task it had failed to accomplish in the seven weeks the teen had been in its custody. Meanwhile, the clock was ticking: by the time the case made its way to the appeals court, J.D. was fifteen weeks pregnant, and Texas law bars most abortions after twenty weeks.

Kavanaugh's opinion, dissenting from the full appeals court's determination, was studded with what many took as signals about his own inclinations on abortion rights. Three separate times he used a particularly loaded phrase—accusing the majority of creating a right to "immediate abortion on demand"—to criticize what he described as the appeals court's "radical extension of the Supreme Court's abortion jurisprudence." Citing the fervent disagreement about whether the Constitution protects the right to abortion, Kavanaugh noted, "As a lower court, our job is to follow the law as it is, not as we might wish it to be," which raised, none too subtly, the question of what Kavanaugh might wish the law to be. He referred repeatedly to "existing Supreme Court precedent," an odd phrasing that at least raised the possibility that such rulings could be discarded. Richard Blumenthal, the Connecticut Democrat, noted that language at Kavanaugh's confirmation hearing. "It's a little bit like somebody introducing his wife to you as my current wife," he said. "You might not expect that wife to be around for all that long."[18]

The abortion case had fallen into Kavanaugh's lap at a particularly precarious time, with McGahn preparing to unveil the list. He had handled it in trademark Kavanaugh fashion, with an opinion that managed not to show too much of his hand but also served to deepen the suspicions about him on both sides.

For those who closely followed the process, Kavanaugh's addition to the list in November 2017 was no surprise. For months, the word in the conservative legal community had been that Kavanaugh had a leg up on the nomination if and when another vacancy arose. His addition was a formality, albeit a crucial one.

The expanded list was painstakingly curated, lest the roster become overly swampy. It ended up with five new names. The other four seemed a bit of a stretch, too young and green to be taken seriously, but they had two characteristics in common—beyond, of course, their Federalist Society credentials: they were not Beltway candidates, and they had no ties to Bush. Former Oklahoma solicitor general Patrick Wyrick, only thirty-six, had been named just nine months earlier to the Oklahoma Supreme Court and would be confirmed in 2019 for a federal district judgeship. Britt Grant, thirty-nine, had a similar profile: a former Kavanaugh clerk and Georgia solicitor general, she, too, had been named to the state supreme court earlier in the year and would be confirmed for an Eleventh Circuit federal appellate judgeship in 2018. Kevin Newsom, forty-five, had been solicitor general of Alabama and was nominated to the Eleventh Circuit federal appeals court just that May. And Amy Coney Barrett, forty-five, a former Notre Dame law professor, had been on the Seventh Circuit just fifteen days when the list was released, although she later emerged as a strong competitor for the Kennedy seat.[19]

But the others were largely cover—a feint at regional and gender diversity to obscure what was obvious: the ultimate D.C. insider was being added to the list. Kavanaugh, at fifty-two and with eleven years on the bench, was by far the heavy hitter of the group. The notion of an expanded list was technically inconsistent with Trump's pledge to voters to choose only from the names he had proffered during the campaign: Cruz's tightened language had Trump promising that the list was "definitive, and I will choose only from it in picking future justices." In the end, McGahn simply declared that the list was being "refreshed."

At the Federalist Society that November night, McGahn ticked off the additions to a standing-room-only crowd. Kavanaugh's name drew raucous cheers. "He's winning on the applause meter," McGahn ad-libbed.[20]

Later, after Kavanaugh was nominated, McGahn confided to one senator, "You have no idea how hard it was for me to get Brett on the list, and no idea how hard it was to get him to the top of the list."

The last part of that work was yet to come.

CHAPTER THREE

The Swing Justice Departs

Brett Kavanaugh e-mailed his wife and told her to go ahead and put down the deposit on the beach house in Rehoboth. It was June 27, 2018, the final day of the Supreme Court term. Like every court watcher in Washington, but with more at stake than perhaps any other, Kavanaugh had been keeping an eye out for an announcement from the bench that morning, as was customary in the case of a retirement. Well, that was that, Kavanaugh figured when the chief justice gaveled the term to a close with no such word. Knowing that Anthony Kennedy might be leaving—more to the point, knowing that if he left, Kavanaugh had a decent shot at the nomination—the Kavanaughs had held off making vacation plans they might have to cancel. Now it looked like Brett, Ashley, and the girls—Margaret, twelve, and Liza, ten—would have a relaxing summer.

A few hours later, everything changed. The moment the White House had been waiting for, that it had been trying to engineer since Trump took office, had arrived. The opportunity that Kavanaugh had been preparing for his entire adult lifetime was finally here. He didn't think it was likely Trump would choose him, not with his ties to Bush, but if there was a chance, this was it.

The White House had expected Kennedy's departure the year before, although Don McGahn had worried that the president's hotheaded behavior would alienate the staid justice. At one point early on, McGahn came barreling into Steve Bannon's office, lamenting that Trump's attacks on the "so-called" judges who had blocked his travel ban would disrupt the plan for a summer retirement by Kennedy.[1] Watching the travel ban making its way through the courts, seeing Trump's intemperate tweets, Kennedy would decide to stick around, McGahn predicted.

Indeed, there were portents of Kennedy's unhappiness and concern with the new administration. In February 2017, he made an unmistakable reference to the travel ban at an eightieth birthday celebration for him at the Bel Air mansion of Julie Chrystyn Opperman, widow of the founder of Westlaw, the legal research service. Kennedy quoted to the assembled crowd from the words engraved at the base of the Statue of Liberty: "Give me your tired, your poor, / Your huddled masses yearning to breathe free, / The wretched refuse of your teeming shore." It was a not terribly veiled swipe—and a signal that Kennedy might be nervous about leaving his seat in the hands of this erratic new president.[2]

In the Kennedy worldview, civility was one of the paramount values, respect for the rule of law another. Trump, with his provocative, belligerent tweets, was no Kennedy Republican. "He was repelled by Trump, but he didn't want Hillary Clinton to be president," said one person who knows Kennedy well. Repelled or not, Kennedy wanted to be replaced by a Republican. "Justice Kennedy is a creature of politics," said another friend. "And he understood that his moral obligation—whatever he thought of the president—that he owed it to our system for the president of his own party to have the benefit of the nomination."

As the court prepared to finish its term in June 2017 and attention turned to the prospect of a Kennedy retirement, the Supreme Court rumor mill was in high gear. With Kennedy, one supposed clue was that his clerk reunion, traditionally held every five years, was accelerated a year ahead of schedule, to June 2017. The proffered explanation for the change was that the reunion would mark Kennedy's eightieth birthday, which would have been more convincing were it not for the fact that the justice had reached that landmark eleven months earlier. At the event, held the weekend before the court's term concluded, Kennedy himself had some teasing fun with the subject. "There has been a lot of speculation about . . . a certain announcement from me tonight," he told the room. "And that announcement is: the bar will remain open after the end of the formal program!"[3]

The end of the term came and went with no news from Kennedy. McGahn's prediction turned out to be correct, at least for the time being. But if the administration was disappointed about the failure of a second vacancy to materialize, it was assiduous in seeking to create an environment conducive to a Kennedy retirement. Trump nominated three former Kennedy clerks to federal appeals courts. Most significant of all, of course, was the expanded list of potential Supreme Court nominees, including Kavanaugh at long last.

Having counted on Kennedy's retirement and been disappointed in 2017, administration officials thought they had another shot early the next year. In December 2017, Trump told a friend that he thought Kennedy would resign by February—and, tellingly, asked what his friend thought about Kavanaugh. When nothing happened, White House officials began to think Kennedy wasn't leaving after all.

By then, with midterm elections looming, the pressure was on Kennedy—from both sides. From the liberals came desperate entreaties to Kennedy not to quit. In April, the *New York Times* editorial board wrote a "Dear Justice Kennedy" open letter to that effect, asking, "Did you spend a lifetime honoring and upholding the Constitution and the values of civility and decency in American public life only to have your replacement chosen by Donald Trump?"[4]

From conservatives, there was a scarcely disguised shove: time to go, Mr. Justice. In early May, the Republican chairman of the Senate Judiciary Committee, Charles Grassley of Iowa, put it bluntly on conservative pundit Hugh Hewitt's radio show. "My message to any one of the nine Supreme Court justices, 'If you're thinking about quitting this year, do it yesterday,'" Grassley said.[5]

At the White House, as the weeks passed without any move from Kennedy, some officials gave up hope of filling a second vacancy before the midterms—and, with them, the threat, however remote, of losing the Senate. "By the end of the Supreme Court session we assumed he wasn't retiring, that if he was going to do it he would have done it sooner to provide the space to get a confirmation completed," recalled Marc Short, then the White House legislative director.[6]

That assessment proved unduly pessimistic. Anthony McLeod Kennedy, the 104th justice of the United States Supreme Court, was indeed thinking about it—if not exactly on Grassley's preferred timetable, then close enough.

Kennedy would say later that he had only made the final decision, and told Mary, his wife of fifty-five years, the night before.[7] That may have been technically true, but it omitted a major fact: the day before, Kennedy had reached out to a former clerk, Steven Engel, now head of the Justice Department's Office of Legal Counsel, to pass the word to McGahn that he was expecting to leave and to make arrangements for him to see the president. McGahn, tellingly, opted not to inform the president for fear that Trump would blab the news.[8] And even earlier, although he kept other White House officials in the dark, McGahn had reason to believe that Kennedy would be leaving. He was barely on speaking terms with the president that spring, and the report by special counsel Robert Mueller, for whom he had been a key witness about whether the president had obstructed justice, could land at any minute. The prospect of being able to fill a second vacancy gave McGahn the incentive to stick it out despite the unpleasant situation.

In private, Kennedy had been talking for some time about retiring. South Carolina senator Lindsey Graham had a few conversations with the justice that spring as he mulled over his options. Kennedy had been open about his desire to spend time with his grandchildren in New York and with his wife. She had spent decades sitting by as he immersed himself, night after night, in reading briefs and cases; she deserved more of his time now, Kennedy told friends. But there were also other concerns. At eighty-one, Kennedy had slowed down, and he seemed to recognize it. Former clerks noticed that the justice would repeat himself even within the space of a short conversation. The buzz among clerks was that it was better to get his attention in the morning, when his mind was still fresh. The speculation within the court was that Kennedy's decidedly conservative tilt in his final term had been the product of conservative clerks holding more sway than usual over the justice.

On the morning of Kennedy's announcement, Trump spoke with McConnell, musing about a Kennedy retirement. I'll believe it when I see it, was McConnell's response; he'd been hearing those rumors for years. In fact, Trump had known something was up. By then, McGahn had told the president that Kennedy had asked to see him. Trump asked the obvious question: Is he going to tell me he's stepping down? McGahn's response was circumspect but unmistakable. He's got to tell you that, not me.

The day before Kennedy announced his retirement, he had voted to uphold Trump's travel ban but went out of his way to issue a mournful four-paragraph concurrence in *Trump v. Hawaii* that seemed to signal, once again, his unhappiness with the president and to implicitly lecture Trump about the failure to live up to his constitutional responsibilities. "It is an urgent necessity that officials adhere to these constitutional guarantees and mandates in all their actions, even in the sphere of foreign affairs," Kennedy wrote in what would be among his last words as a justice. "An anxious world must know that our Government remains committed always to the liberties the Constitution seeks to preserve and protect, so that freedom extends outward, and lasts."[9]

That made Kennedy's decision to travel to the White House in person to deliver his retirement letter all the more striking. It was little noted at the time, but this was a departure from customary practice. For retiring justices to give the White House a private heads-up about their plans was not at all uncommon. Sometimes the White House would have just a few days' notice, sometimes just a few minutes; in some cases, the news would be conveyed privately months in advance. An in-person visit, justice to president, however, was unusual, although not unprecedented.[10] But the setting, meeting with the president in the White House residence, chatting for some time before handing over a letter floridly addressed to "My dear Mr. President," offered Kennedy another chance to make his pitch for a replacement. "I asked him if he had certain people that he had great respect for that potentially could take his seat," Trump said immediately afterward.[11] In fact, Kennedy did, and his recommendation came as no surprise to the president. Kennedy had lobbied to get Brett Kavanaugh on the president's list. Now he recommended his former clerk as a worthy successor.[12]

To grasp the significance of Kennedy's retirement, it helps to return to the moment that brought him to the court, three decades earlier. On that late June day in 1987, a different swing justice, Lewis Powell, was departing. At the time, the impact of Powell's retirement seemed apocalyptic. The court was closely divided: Powell, although a Nixon appointee and generally solid conservative, held the key vote on the most contentious issues of the day. He was, as *Washington Post* Supreme Court reporter Al Kamen put it at the time, "the justice who almost single-handedly stymied the Reagan judicial revolution, consistently voting against the administration in close cases involving abortion, affirmative action and separation of church and state."[13]

For the Reagan administration, that revolution was a top priority. Reagan and his senior lieutenants had made installing a cadre of conservative judges a central element of their administration's governing philosophy and political strategy. Reagan's California confidant, White House counselor, and, by the time of Powell's retirement, attorney general, Edwin Meese, had used a series of speeches to champion what he called a "jurisprudence of original intention." As Meese declared in the opening salvo of this effort before the American Bar Association in July 1985, four months after being sworn in as attorney general, "It has been and will continue to be the policy of this administration to press for a Jurisprudence of Original Intention. In the cases we file and those we join as amicus, we will endeavor to resurrect the original meaning of constitutional provisions and statutes as the only reliable guide for judgment." Any other method, Meese added, "suffers the defect of pouring new meaning into old words, thus creating new powers and new rights totally at odds with the logic of our Constitution and its commitment to the rule of law."[14]

The notion that the Constitution should be interpreted according to what came to be called its "original public meaning" seems today like a staple of legal debate. But at the time, it was viewed as an outlier—an almost wacky method of constitutional decision-making. Justice William Brennan, the court's liberal stalwart, responded to Meese's provocation in a speech several months later, terming the hunt for original intent "little more than arrogance cloaked as humility." As Brennan argued, "It is arrogant to pretend that from our vantage we can gauge accurately the intent of the framers on application of principle to specific, contemporary questions."[15]

This was no mere academic debate. Meese and a group of like-minded conservative lawyers worked to stock the federal bench with adherents of their vision of constitutional interpretation. Reagan's nomination of O'Connor was an early, and significant, exception; he had pledged during the presidential campaign to name the first female justice, and considerations of gender trumped matters of ideology. But Scalia's selection—first for the federal appeals court in the District of Columbia in 1982 and then for the Supreme Court in 1986—marked the beginnings of the effort to transform originalism from academic theory into judicial practice.

Powell's retirement offered an opportunity to significantly further that mission—especially with Reagan's choice of federal appeals court judge Robert Bork, an early leading proponent of originalism, to replace the courtly Virginian. Bork's nomination set off a confirmation battle of previously unimaginable intensity, a struggle that ended with his defeat and, ultimately, Kennedy's confirmation by a unanimous Senate, 97–0.

In hindsight, the court Powell left looks decidedly moderate in contrast to its present-day version. Its conservatives were less conservative and its liberals more liberal. The conservative wing, such as it was, consisted of Rehnquist and Scalia on the furthest right reaches, augmented by O'Connor and Byron White, a John F. Kennedy appointee who often voted with the conservative bloc. Its left wing was occupied by Brennan and Thurgood Marshall, who were far more liberal than any of the current justices.

By the time of Kennedy's departure, after decades of determined effort, the court had become an immeasurably more conservative body. Anchoring the right wing were Clarence Thomas and Samuel Alito, O'Connor's significantly more conservative successor, along with Neil Gorsuch, who in his first full term on the court was shaping up to be a vigorous addition to those two conservatives. Slightly to the left of that trio was Chief Justice John Roberts, whose solicitude for the court as an institution and concern about its being perceived as just another partisan actor occasionally led him to try to restrain his conservative colleagues.

Roberts's chief perfidy, in the view of his conservative critics, was engaging in legal contortions to avoid striking down the Affordable Care Act in 2012. "Justice Roberts turned out to be an absolute disaster, he turned out to be an absolute disaster because he gave us Obamacare," Trump charged during the campaign.[16] But this focus on an exceptional case or two was misguided. To imagine a court in which Roberts would operate, on rare occasions, as the swing vote was to misconstrue the already remarkably conservative composition of the institution.

Still, there was no doubt—for liberals or conservatives—that Kennedy's departure would make a striking difference. After a start that signaled his opposition to abortion rights, he had turned out to be a grudgingly reliable vote to uphold the right to choose. In 1992, when it appeared that there were five votes on the court to overrule *Roe v. Wade*, Kennedy shocked court watchers—and infuriated fellow conservatives—by joining with O'Connor and Souter to reaffirm the "essential holding" of *Roe*, that the Constitution protects a woman's right to decide whether to terminate a pregnancy.[17] Twenty-four years later, Kennedy again surprised observers by siding with the court's four liberals in another abortion ruling, striking down parts of a Texas law that would have made it impossible for most abortion clinics to operate in the state.[18]

As he did with abortion, Kennedy posed an unexpected obstacle to conservatives' drive to undo affirmative action programs. After voting against affirmative action in a 2003 case involving the University of Michigan Law School, Kennedy in 2016 voted with the court's liberals in a 4–3 decision (Justice Elena Kagan was recused, and Scalia had died) to uphold an undergraduate affirmative action program at the University of Texas.[19]

Most notably, Kennedy was instrumental in charting a new direction for the court—and a new reality for the country—on gay rights. In a series of cases that emphasized his central theme of treating all citizens with equal "dignity," Kennedy led the court to overrule its repugnant 1986 decision upholding the constitutionality of a Georgia law that criminalized private homosexual conduct. The Constitution's framers, Kennedy wrote, "knew times can blind us to certain truths and later generations can see that laws once thought necessary and proper in fact serve only to oppress. As the Constitution endures, persons in every generation can invoke its principles in their own search for greater freedom."[20] That case, *Lawrence v. Texas*, created the doctrinal foundation for the court to declare in 2015 that the Constitution protects the right of gays and lesbians to marry. "The limitation of marriage to opposite-sex couples may long have seemed natural and just, but its inconsistency with the central meaning of the fundamental right to marry is now manifest," Kennedy wrote in *Obergefell v. Hodges*. "With that knowledge must come the recognition that laws excluding same-sex couples from the marriage right impose stigma and injury of the kind prohibited by our basic charter."[21]

The main dissenting opinion in *Obergefell* was authored by

Roberts, who accused the majority of substituting its policy views, however laudable, for constitutional analysis. "Stealing this issue from the people will for many cast a cloud over same-sex marriage," Roberts warned, "making a dramatic social change that much more difficult to accept."[22]

That did not make Kennedy a liberal justice by any stretch. He was the author of the decision in *Citizens United*, the campaign finance ruling reviled by liberals for helping to usher in a new era of unlimited campaign spending. He sided with fellow conservatives to declare that the Constitution protects an individual's right to bear arms, to award the presidency to George W. Bush in *Bush v. Gore*, and to disembowel the Voting Rights Act. According to a database maintained by the Washington University in St. Louis School of Law, Kennedy took the conservative side in 71 percent of close cases (those decided by a five-justice majority) through the 2016 term.[23]

His final term was even more dramatically conservative: Kennedy did not side with the liberal justices in a single 5–4 ruling. Rather, he voted to uphold Trump's travel ban, to prevent states from requiring so-called crisis pregnancy centers to inform patients about the availability of abortion services, to uphold Ohio's voter-roll purges, and to overturn a forty-year-old precedent protecting public-employee unions. The term that concluded in 2018, said liberal law professor Erwin Chemerinsky, was "the most conservative since October 1935," at the height of the Supreme Court's resistance to the New Deal.[24]

Nonetheless, the swap of Kennedy for a justice to be named augured a momentous change. Not since Powell's retirement was the shift of a single seat poised to move the court so firmly to the right. Bork's defeat and Kennedy's eventual confirmation had turned Powell's departure into a missed opportunity. Conservatives were committed to ensuring that would not happen again. This was their chance to seize control, at long last. As Thomas Goldstein, founder of SCOTUSblog.com, put it, "An already right-leaning Supreme Court is poised to become the most conservative institution in the entire history of America's government."[25]

Liberals had little hope of halting that transformation. Republicans controlled the Senate, although just barely, with a two-vote Senate majority. The biggest procedural constraint on the majority, the filibuster, had been eliminated, meaning that Republicans could confirm a nominee with just fifty votes and Vice President Pence on deck to break the tie. Nonetheless, the stakes were so high and the liberal base so inflamed that Democratic leaders were determined to try—or, to be more precise, to try so long as the effort to defeat the nominee did not imperil the party's chances in the election just four months away.

The battle over Bork had ushered Anthony Kennedy onto the high court. The impending fight over his successor was even more consequential and, as it turned out, would be even more ferocious.

If there was one man prepared to carry on that battle with maximum ferocity, it was Addison Mitchell McConnell Jr., the Senate majority leader. McConnell was not a judge picker so much as a judge maker. He created the space for Trump to transform the federal judiciary, first by preventing Obama from filling scores of judgeships, then by ensuring that the new Republican president and Republican-controlled Senate would not squander the chance to fill those seats and more. Thanks to McConnell, seventy-four at the time of Trump's election, the new president inherited 107 judicial vacancies—nearly double the fifty-four openings that awaited Obama at the start of his first term. And thanks to McConnell, of course, Trump had the Scalia seat to fill.[26]

With Trump's election, McConnell could pivot from defense to offense, from blocking Democratic judges to stocking the courts with Republican ones. "We are going to move judges like they are on a conveyor belt," McConnell told his then chief of staff, Brian McGuire, in the days after the election. McConnell soon put that plan into action, calling McGahn to talk judges. This was an opportunity to remake the federal judiciary, McConnell said, but the new administration needed to be disciplined about generating nominees.

For his part, McConnell would work to speed up the Senate process.[27] Unaccompanied by staff, McConnell made a postelection trip to see the president-elect. He had a single item on his agenda: emphasizing to Trump the critical importance of filling judgeships, even at the expense of other presidential priorities. Taking the time to confirm judges might slow things down for executive-branch nominees, but it would be worth it, McGahn assured the president-elect. "The thing that will last the longest," McConnell noted later, "is the courts."[28]

That assessment was the key to understanding McConnell. The senator titled his memoir *The Long Game*, and that was what he played, with a tenacity and patience forged in childhood. In the summer of 1944, ten years before Jonas Salk invented the polio vaccine, two-year-old McConnell contracted polio. The disease kept him off his feet and forced him to endure painful strengthening exercises for two excruciating years. But his mother, overseeing the rehabilitation, vowed he would be able to walk again, and so McConnell did, with a limp perceptible only as he climbed stairs. Such determination remained on display throughout his political career as he methodically made his way to the only job he had ever really wanted, that of Senate majority leader.[29]

Serving in that role during a Trump presidency was a particular challenge for McConnell, who had endorsed Trump only belatedly and with gritted teeth. "I have committed to supporting the nominee chosen by Republican voters, and Donald Trump, the presumptive nominee, is now on the verge of clinching the nomination," he choked out in a written statement in May 2016.[30] The two men could not have been more different, except that both enjoyed the acquisition and exercise of power. McConnell was disciplined and calculating where Trump was impulsive and freewheeling. McConnell was prepared where Trump winged it; he was reserved and careful where Trump was volatile. But for all the strains that developed in their relationship in the coming months—Trump lashed out at McConnell, "Mitch, get back to work," after the Senate failed to repeal the Affordable Care Act in 2017—judgeships were one area of unalloyed synergy.[31] Each man was essential to helping construct the other's legacy.

This symbiosis also included present-day politics, a subject never far from McConnell's mind. For McConnell, as for Trump, it was extraordinarily helpful to have a slate of confirmed conservative judges to dangle before voters like a fisherman displaying his catch. Now, with Kennedy's retirement, there would be a second justice on the line.

In his third-floor chambers at the federal courthouse in Washington, Kavanaugh got the news just as everyone else did. He had been given no heads-up, either by Kennedy or McGahn; they were too smart to offer inside information that might create an uncomfortable situation if Kavanaugh were to be questioned about it down the road. But as his reluctance to make summer plans illustrates, the prospect of a vacancy wasn't far from his mind, and the same was true of others around him.

The night before, Kavanaugh's Bush administration colleague, Joel Kaplan, now a senior executive at Facebook in Washington, was making calls to influential conservative lawyers: If Kennedy were to step down, would they be with Kavanaugh? Now that the news was out, it didn't take long for the phone to ring in Kavanaugh's chambers. The White House counsel was on the line. We need to talk, McGahn told Kavanaugh. This was Wednesday; could he come by Kavanaugh's chambers on Friday? It was to be no casual chat, as Kavanaugh understood, having been on the other end of this transaction in his role as a White House lawyer. It was a vetting conversation that would stretch to three hours and touch on anything Kavanaugh might have done that could cause embarrassment—or endanger his possible confirmation. McGahn left the session confident that there would be no such problem.

CHAPTER FOUR

The Not-So-Invisible Primary

The twelve days between Kennedy's retirement announcement and Kavanaugh's selection were as intense as any Supreme Court campaign in history. This jockeying was at once invisible and in unprecedented public view—not surprising given that the ultimate target of the lobbying was a president fixated on television and on one network in particular.

Other presidents would deliberate behind closed doors over their Supreme Court nominees. Some would dither. In 1993, cycling through potential nominee after potential nominee, Clinton took eighty-seven days before settling on Ruth Bader Ginsburg. Trump, ever the showman, set the stage for a big, and swift, reveal. Two days after Kennedy's announcement, he declared that he would name the winner on July 9.[1]

The identities of the contestants dribbled out as the finalists trooped to the White House for interviews with the president—Kavanaugh; Amy Coney Barrett, the newly minted Seventh Circuit judge; federal appeals court judge Raymond Kethledge of Michigan; and Kethledge's new colleague on the Sixth Circuit, McConnell protégé Amul Thapar. Thomas Hardiman of the Third Circuit, who had interviewed in person with the president for the Scalia seat, spoke with him again by phone. It was Supreme Court nomination as reality show, with a target date for the series finale.

As with all things Trump, this primary was different from what had come before it, more public and more random. The president demonstrated an unusual propensity to reach out to assorted, not necessarily expert, friends to get their reads on various contenders— Steve Wynn, the casino magnate and Republican National Committee finance chair; New York real estate buddies such as Richard LeFrak and Tom Barrack; old friends such as Christopher Ruddy of Newsmax Media; influential social conservatives such as Tony Perkins of the Family Research Council; and outside advisers such as former New Jersey governor Chris Christie, former New York mayor Rudy Giuliani, and Fox News host Sean Hannity.

Kavanaugh would be widely derided as a suck-up for saying of Trump, on the night that his nomination was announced, "No president has ever consulted more widely, or talked with more people from more backgrounds, to seek input about a Supreme Court nomination."[2] In fact, although his own aides asked Kavanaugh if he really wanted to go that far, there was a certain truth to that claim. It was just that Trump's amalgam of consultants was different from that of an ordinary president. He was the ultimate crowdsourcer. Only hours before Kavanaugh was offered the nomination, Trump, lunching at his golf club in Bedminster, New Jersey, solicited advice not only from Giuliani, Hannity, and Ruddy but also from a Pennsylvania dentist and a Florida car tycoon who happened to be part of the president's group that day.

Along the way to filling his two Supreme Court vacancies, Trump attracted a *Star Wars* bar-scene cast of unlikely contenders. Among those who considered themselves in the running, at various points, were Fox News legal commentators Jeanine Pirro and Andrew Napolitano. Pirro, as the administration was staffing up, secured a secret weekend meeting with incoming attorney general Jeff Sessions to discuss her interest in becoming his number two— deputy attorney general. That wasn't going to happen, but Pirro was offered the rather significant—and, given her television performances, unsettling—consolation prize of being U.S. attorney for

Brooklyn. She demurred, observing that she thought she would be a better fit as a Supreme Court justice.

Similarly, Andrew Napolitano, who served eight years as a judge on the New Jersey Superior Court, a midlevel trial court, let it be known not only that he was available but also that he considered himself on the short list for both the Scalia and Kennedy vacancies. Trump outed Napolitano's lobbying for a seat after the commentator said Mueller's report had "laid out at least a half-dozen crimes of obstruction committed by Trump."[3] Tweeting angrily in response, Trump said, "Ever since Andrew came to my office to ask that I appoint him to the U.S. Supreme Court, and I said NO, he has been very hostile!"[4] Napolitano replied that he and Trump had two ninety-minute meetings to discuss the Scalia replacement, during which Napolitano pitched Gorsuch and Trump asked Napolitano to make the case for himself. "Who would turn that down?" Napolitano asked. "I gave him the spiel, so to speak."[5]

Neither Pirro nor Napolitano was ever seriously contemplated. "He's complicated," one associate said of Trump. "But he's not *that* crazy."

In the arena of judges, at least, Trump seemed more canny than crazy. The official list notwithstanding, Trump asked Ted Cruz not once but twice—at the point of the Scalia vacancy and again when Kennedy retired—whether he was interested in the nomination. The idea didn't go anywhere, but as a matter of crass politics it was not a bad plan. A Justice Cruz could get a potential political rival out of the way and please the base, all at once.

The president's choice of Gorsuch and the progress of his confirmation battle would serve as a useful template for Kavanaugh in the days before his selection and in the weeks to follow. The Gorsuch experience showed that with Trump, nothing was done until it was announced: the president's advisers had settled on the Coloradan early on as their top pick, but Trump was tempted until close to the end by Hardiman, the Third Circuit judge and favorite of the president's sister, who had been urging him on Trump for months. Hardiman's blue-collar background and potential electoral benefit were attractive; the first in his family to attend college, he had grown up working for the family taxi business and lived in Pennsylvania, a state that had voted for Trump in 2016 and was key to his reelection. The ultimate selection of Gorsuch instead illustrated what sold Trump on picking a justice—having a classy Ivy League résumé and looking the part, among other qualities. It also underscored what not to do once the nominee was announced. Looking in any way disloyal to the president could be fatal, as Gorsuch had nearly discovered. Kavanaugh would not repeat that mistake.

When it came to filling the Scalia seat, Leonard Leo had pushed hard for William Pryor, the conservative judge the president had mentioned on the night of Scalia's death. That was a nonstarter. Politically, there wasn't anything to be gained by choosing an Alabaman; the president had just won that state by twenty-eight percentage points and had already chosen its senator, Sessions, to be his attorney general. Pryor's slashing criticism of *Roe*—he called the ruling "the worst abomination of constitutional law in our history"—guaranteed a brutal confirmation fight.[6] And, in any event, Trump didn't like his southern accent.

Instead, Gorsuch quickly emerged as the choice of Trump's advisers—Pence, his counsel Mark Paoletta, incoming chief of staff Priebus, and McGahn—as they met in the secure facility in the basement of the Trump transition office. McGahn issued an edict at one of the first sessions that took some of those present aback. "There can never be another Sandra Day O'Connor," he said. The first female justice, in the view of social conservatives, had turned out to be a disaster, voting to uphold abortion rights and leave affirmative action programs in place.

A more predictable rallying cry for the group assembled at the transition headquarters would have been "no more Souters," given that retired justice David Souter, George H. W. Bush's supposed "home run for conservatives," had instead tended to side most often with its liberal wing.[7] Bush himself had a premonition that Souter might disappoint on that score. On July 23, 1990, the day he interviewed Souter for the job, Bush took careful notes on a yellow legal pad, outlining two columns of comments about Souter, "+" and "−." In the minus column, Bush wrote of Souter, "Earl Warren—though no one thinks so—only that he hasn't written on Fed Law."[8] The president's prescient reference was to Earl Warren, the Republican governor of California who was tapped by Republican Dwight Eisenhower to be chief justice—and became the liberal leader of a newly activist court. Bush was choosing between Souter and Edith Jones, a conservative Texan nominated to the Fifth Circuit by Ronald Reagan. "Souter is more of a gamble on issues," Bush noted in a handwritten memo comparing the two.[9]

The Souter debacle still weighed on conservatives. There would be no more gambling, not if McGahn could help it. From now on, after the twin disappointments of O'Connor and Souter, Supreme Court nominees would have a paper trail attached. No more "stealth" nominees, as Souter had been described. The Trump judges would come bearing significant, and unmistakably conservative, judicial records. Written opinions were the best, most reliable predictor of future judicial performance. No longer would a compelling personal narrative or demographic considerations alone determine the nominee, as they did with O'Connor. Not again would the pick be a politician—O'Connor had been majority leader of the Arizona state senate—inclined, as politicians tend to be, toward crafting compromise solutions instead of standing firm on ideological principle.

The Trump judge pickers' focus during those early discussions was not on prospective nominees' positions on the hottest-button social issues, abortion and same-sex marriage. Instead, it was on the less sexy but—to the assembled lawyers and, as significantly, to the wealthy donors who financed the Republican party—even more important matter of what Steve Bannon would later call the "deconstruction of the administrative state." Priebus laid it out: the social conservatives who had helped elect Trump might focus on abortion and same-sex marriage, but the donors cared about regulation. They were eager to undo what they viewed as the out-of-control regulatory apparatus that had been assembled since Franklin Roosevelt's New Deal.

As McGahn later told the Federalist Society, "The greatest threat to the rule of law in our modern society is the ever-expanding regulatory state, and the most effective bulwark against that threat is a strong judiciary."[10] Overturning *Chevron* would help with Bannon's promised deconstruction. And that, for all evangelical voters' focus on the Supreme Court and social issues such as abortion, was the real goal. The emphasis on social conservatism and its associated hot-button issues ended with Scalia, McGahn said at the first meeting after the election to discuss the justice's successor. It was now all about regulatory relief. On that score, McGahn said, Scalia "wouldn't make the cut."

On this front, Gorsuch had a big leg up on the competition—and so would Kavanaugh, with his extensive record on administrative law. Ironically, the *Chevron* case involved an Environmental Protection Agency regulation issued during the tenure of Gorsuch's mother, Anne Gorsuch Burford, as head of the agency. In that case, deferring to the EPA operated to the benefit of the oil company and against the environmental group that had challenged the regulation. Nonetheless, over the years, *Chevron* deference had worked more often against business interests and, in the view of legal conservatives, offended the constitutional separation of powers by transferring too much authority from elected, and therefore accountable, lawmakers to agency bureaucrats.

Gorsuch was among these conservatives. Shortly before the election, he wrote an opinion decrying the way *Chevron* and later cases "permit executive bureaucracies to swallow huge amounts of core judicial and legislative power and concentrate federal power in a way that seems more than a little difficult to square with the Constitution of the framers' design." The opinion—a jurisprudential oddity, a concurrence to his own majority ruling—happened to come after Gorsuch was absent from Trump's first list but before the candidate released the second version.[11] For cynics watching the process, it was the judicial equivalent of a job application for the high court in what then seemed like the implausible event of a Trump election.

Yet for all the wonky focus on regulatory considerations, what won the day with Trump, the ultimate decision-maker, were Gorsuch's good looks—his strong jaw and silver hair—and his academic pedigree, which included not just Columbia University and Harvard Law School but also a stint at Oxford on a Marshall scholarship. This was Trump's idea of a nominee from central casting. The original plan for the Gorsuch unveiling had placed the judge alone on stage with Trump. When the president met Gorsuch's wife, Louise, he decided that she, too, looked the part and should be called up to stand beside her husband. The next year found Kavanaugh, his wife, and two young daughters on the East Room stage, an adorable, camera-friendly tableau.

To outside observers, the progress of the Gorsuch nomination looked remarkably well executed, a striking departure from the turmoil then plaguing the infant administration. Behind closed doors, however, tensions simmered that had implications for the Kavanaugh nomination. In addition to the friction between Leo and McGahn, the White House counsel was not getting along with Gorsuch. The nominee bristled at being handled and at being told how to answer particular questions. More than once, he threatened to get on a plane and return to Colorado. White House aides didn't take that terribly seriously—it was a release valve for a nominee exhausted by making the rounds of senatorial courtesy calls—but Pence was deployed to help calm matters. He instituted a weekly lunch with Gorsuch and gently reminded the judge that he was the president's nominee, not a solo actor.

The biggest flare-up came a week into the nomination, as Trump was on a Twitter tear over "disgraceful" federal judges ruling against his travel ban. Meeting with Connecticut senator Richard Blumenthal, a Democrat, Gorsuch termed Trump's comments "demoralizing" and "disheartening," an assessment that was promptly, and predictably, reported.[12] In fact, that had been the plan. Trump's attacks on the judiciary were, back then, so shocking from a sitting president, so outside the norm of previous behavior, that some comment from the nominee was in order, Gorsuch and his confirmation team recognized. Over lunch in the Senate earlier that day, Gorsuch described the language he intended to use to the group, which included McGahn, legislative affairs director Marc Short, communications adviser Ron Bonjean, and Kelly Ayotte, the former New Hampshire senator serving as Gorsuch's "sherpa," or guide, through the confirmation process. Everyone agreed.

There was one problem. McGahn had neglected to—or, perhaps knowing that the president would be displeased, chose not to—inform Trump. And the president, watching television coverage of Gorsuch's remarks that night, blew up, threatening to yank the nomination. With remarks like that, Trump wondered, could he count on Gorsuch being "loyal"?[13] McGahn and Priebus were terrified that the president might actually follow through. They managed overnight to redirect Trump's ire. Bonjean, the administration's official spokesman on Gorsuch, had confirmed the nominee's remarks to Blumenthal. But that didn't stop Trump from attacking the Connecticut Democrat. "Sen. Richard Blumenthal, who never fought in Vietnam when he said for years he had (major lie), now misrepresents what Judge Gorsuch told him?" Trump tweeted at 7:57 a.m.[14] Although Gorsuch was no longer the primary target of the president's rage, the judge was himself angry. He had executed an agreed-on plan.

Even after Trump backed down from the threat to pull the Gorsuch nomination, his fury continued to simmer. In a meeting with McConnell and House Speaker Paul Ryan, he complained that Gorsuch is "probably going to end up being a liberal like the rest of them."[15] That prediction did not pan out—far to the contrary, judging by Gorsuch's initial performance. The justice's assessment of Trump did not improve, either. Once at the Supreme Court, he would privately describe the president's behavior as "appalling."

For Kavanaugh, the Gorsuch episode was a cautionary tale. The president doesn't simply nominate a judge, he also signs the judicial commission at the end of the process. As Kavanaugh knew well from his White House years and his own earlier confirmation battle, it remains critical throughout to have the president fully on board in case a nomination runs into political headwinds and needs a presidential push. It was important to handle any president, this one in particular, with care. You never knew what might happen.

The Gorsuch vote also set the political contours for the choice of Kennedy's replacement. No nominee was likely to do better. Gorsuch had imagined, naively, that he could secure as many as seventy votes in his favor, but in the aftermath of the Merrick Garland blockade that was a mirage. In the end, Gorsuch was confirmed by a vote of 54–45. (Republican senator Johnny Isakson of Georgia was absent, recovering from back surgery.) Three red-state Democrats—Joe Donnelly of Indiana, Heidi Heitkamp of North Dakota, and Joe Manchin of West Virginia—broke ranks to support Gorsuch. As it happened, all three were up for reelection in 2018, as the Kennedy seat was being filled. They constituted the political playing field, along with pro-choice Republicans Susan Collins of Maine and Lisa Murkowski of Alaska.

There was almost no room to spare. Losing any among that group of five could be disastrous. With senator John McCain suffering from brain cancer and back home in Arizona, the GOP's fifty-one-vote majority could be effectively narrowed even more, meaning that a single vote against the nominee could sink him or her. (In the end, McCain would pass away before the confirmation vote, to be replaced by former Arizona senator Jon Kyl, giving Republicans extra breathing space.) So Trump's calendar the day after Kennedy's announcement was no surprise: he invited Donnelly, Heitkamp, and Manchin to the White House Thursday night, along with Republicans Collins, Murkowski, and Grassley.

The two Republican women had demonstrated their willingness to break from the pack on occasion, most recently voting against confirming education secretary Betsy DeVos and against repealing the Affordable Care Act. Collins in particular made clear that the eventual nominee's view on abortion rights would be central to her decision. "I would not support a nominee who demonstrated hostility to *Roe v. Wade* because that would mean to me that their judicial philosophy did not include a respect for established decisions, established law," Collins said.[16]

Even before going to the White House, she had received a call from McGahn and urged the White House counsel to have Trump look beyond his preexisting list, a position she reaffirmed in her meeting with the president. "I think the president should not feel bound by that list," Collins said that weekend. Indeed, she said, "there are people on that list whom I could not support."[17] In conversations with White House officials, Collins was more direct, signaling her particular discomfort with Pryor, whose name Trump had floated on the night Scalia died, and proposing a name who had appeared on Trump's original Supreme Court list—Joan Larsen, a former Michigan Supreme Court justice who was named to the federal appeals court by Trump in 2017 and who had, after some delay, obtained the support of Michigan's Democratic senators. White House officials recalled Collins being inclined in Kavanaugh's direction—"She told the president in the White House that he was the top choice," said one—but Collins said that was not correct. "I cannot recall having any discussion of Brett Kavanaugh at that meeting," she said.[18]

The Democrats were a more mixed bunch. All three faced difficult races but slightly different dynamics. Donnelly and Manchin described themselves as pro-life, which gave them, at least in theory, more flexibility to back a Trump nominee. Heitkamp, who had perhaps the toughest race of all, supported the right to choose. From the moment her campaign began, the one thing she feared was another Supreme Court vacancy and the accompanying social issues a confirmation battle would stir up. Now that had happened. The night of Kennedy's announcement, Trump had flown to North Dakota to campaign for Heitkamp's opponent, arguing that "we need Kevin Cramer to replace liberal Democrat Heidi Heitkamp in the Senate."[19] Here he was, the next day, soliciting her help with the court seat. "It was a little awkward," Heitkamp recalled. "The message clearly was, look, we're going to advance a nominee. This puts you in some political peril given the favorabilities of the president in North Dakota."[20]

"Some political peril" was, as Heitkamp had understood from the start, an understatement.

Each of the short-list contenders had his or her squad of supporters, with former clerks lined up to place supportive op-eds and troop to television studios to make the case for their judges. Conservative radio host and *Washington Post* columnist Hugh Hewitt weighed in for Kethledge, declaring the Michigan appeals court judge "the best choice" to be "Gorsuch 2.0," a formulation certain to appeal to the president.[21] Hardiman had backing from former Pennsylvania senator Rick Santorum, but his cheerleader in chief remained Trump's sister, who had served with Hardiman on the Third Circuit and had been touting him to her brother even before Scalia's death. "The president doesn't trust a lot of people in the world, but one person he does trust is his sister, and she had recommended him highly," said one Trump friend.

Amy Coney Barrett, still in her first year on the bench, had not assembled enough former clerks to constitute a personal lobbying squad, yet she turned out to be perhaps Kavanaugh's leading competitor. She had a compelling personal and legal story that proved irresistible to social conservatives. She was the mother of seven— five biological children, including one with Down syndrome, and two adopted from Haiti. She was a deeply committed Catholic, part of a tightly knit, mostly Catholic group called People of Praise, whose female advisers were called handmaids before that term was dropped because it had become too charged in the aftermath of the popular television series based on Margaret Atwood's book.[22]

Barrett had been cast as a victim of Democrats' seeming religious intolerance thanks to a tone-deaf comment at her confirmation hearing for the appeals court the previous year by California senator Dianne Feinstein, the ranking Democrat on the Senate Judiciary Committee. Feinstein, questioning whether Barrett's religious faith might overtake her judicial responsibilities, observed, "The dogma lives loudly within you."[23] That oddly phrased remark instantly made Barrett a judicial rock star among social conservatives, who viewed it as an offensive assault on faith—and promptly had it emblazoned on coffee mugs and T-shirts.

Barrett, one of Scalia's favorite clerks, had conservative legal credentials to match her personal ones. Her academic writings made clear that she did not believe *stare decisis*, the legal doctrine that instructs judges to be reluctant to overturn precedent, should stand in the way of jettisoning rulings that are clearly incorrect. "I tend to agree with those who say that a justice's duty is to the Constitution," Barrett wrote in 2013, "and that it is thus more legitimate for her to enforce her best understanding of the Constitution rather than a precedent she thinks clearly in conflict with it."[24] It wasn't hard to make the leap, given Barrett's other writings, and figure out the precedents she might have in her sights. Still, there was some conservative uneasiness about Barrett, in particular on the issue of gun rights. She had no record on Second Amendment issues, a lapse that was a cause of concern for the National Rifle Association.

Throughout the maneuvering, conservatives kept close tabs on the shifting fortunes of the contenders through private e-mail listservs that circulated news reports and shared inside information. One such group, led by Republican judiciary staffer Barbara Ledeen, was called Bravoure—French for "bravery"—and one member was Ginni Thomas, the conservative activist and wife of the Supreme Court justice. Bravoure's secrecy was underscored by the all-caps warning at the bottom of messages: "PLEASE DO NOT FORWARD EMAILS WITHOUT FIRST REMOVING THE LISTSERV HEADING."

"Any insight on where things stand folks," Matthew Boyle of the conservative news site *Breitbart* queried the group on Saturday, July 7, two days before Trump was scheduled to make his announcement. "POTUS has not decided," replied Jonathan Bunch of the Federalist Society. "Four people under consideration, in alphabetical order: Barrett, Hardiman, Kavanaugh, Kethledge."

For all the grassroots excitement about Barrett, no one had a lobbying operation more serious, more focused, and, ultimately, more effective than Kavanaugh's. Joel Kaplan, a Bush administration veteran and Facebook vice president of global public policy, helped quarterback the Kavanaugh campaign. The day-to-day work fell to a volunteer squadron of former clerks, including Travis Lenkner, a Kansas-born lawyer who clerked for Kennedy, and Roman Martinez, a Washington lawyer who had also clerked on the Supreme Court for Chief Justice Roberts. Lenkner, who had joked at the Kavanaugh reunion about his absence from Trump's list, flew in from Chicago, where he practiced law, the day Kennedy announced his retirement and remained for what turned out to be the three-month duration of the confirmation effort.

The Kavanaugh push came even before the primary season officially opened. "I have never seen the amount of support expressed for any potential nominee as I saw for Kavanaugh in terms of people reaching out to make the case for him, and that was not just when Kennedy retired, it was not just when Scalia died—it was for years preceding that," said Ramesh Ponnuru, a senior editor at *National Review* who is particularly well plugged in among legal conservatives and went on record favoring Barrett.[25] "Kavanaugh had the most intense lobbying campaign inside and outside the White House," said one White House official. "He had the biggest batch of fierce defenders I've ever seen in any kind of political fight in my life."

Although Kavanaugh had gained his judge-picking experience in the more orderly world of the George W. Bush administration, he understood how Trump would go about his decision-making and tailored his approach accordingly. As one close associate described it, Kavanaugh knew that "Trump is going to call a lot of people, people who know nothing about the Supreme Court, all his developer buddies and a bunch of other stupid people. Brett's plan is, he's got to reach out to all those people so when Trump calls they'll say Kavanaugh."

Because one of the chief raps on Kavanaugh was that he was "too Bushie," veterans of that administration were careful to tread lightly in making the case for their former colleague. What would be a benefit with a more run-of-the-mill Republican president in office could be a major liability with Trump. So, for example, Ohio senator Rob Portman, a Bush White House veteran and Kavanaugh friend, held off speaking to the White House on his behalf.

Instead, one key supporter who could bridge the two worlds, Bush and Trump, was Matt Schlapp, chairman of the American Conservative Union, which put on the annual CPAC convention at which Nunberg had buttonholed Leo so many months before. Schlapp was the unusual figure, a Bushie—he served as political director in the George W. Bush White House, where he got to know Kavanaugh—who also had close ties to Trump, not only through CPAC but also through his wife, Mercedes Schlapp, another Bush 43 veteran who had joined the Trump White House.

On July 5, Matt Schlapp published an op-ed in *The Hill* touting Kavanaugh's conservative credentials. "I want to hit the critics head-on," Schlapp wrote. "A few conservatives have raised concerns that Judge Kavanaugh will be 'another John Roberts,' who sounds great but lets down conservatives in the end. Other than the fact that both sat on the D.C. Circuit (where Justices Scalia and Thomas also sat), the Kavanaugh-Roberts comparison is completely misplaced. When Roberts was nominated to the Court, he had a short judicial record that included few significant opinions. Kavanaugh's 12-year record includes dozens of textualist and originalist opinions. Kavanaugh is not another Roberts; he's another Scalia, Alito, or Gorsuch. In fact, on issues such as reining in the administrative state, he is arguably more conservative than even those three highly regarded justices."[26]

Karl Rove, Bush's top political adviser, spoke with Brad Parscale, Trump's 2020 campaign manager, and made the case for Kavanaugh. Forget about the Bush thing, Rove advised—anyone you'd consider was named to the federal bench by Bush. Where do you think Gorsuch came from? Trump himself tracked down Rove, then aboard a friend's boat in Europe, to discuss Kavanaugh by phone. What can you tell me about him? the president asked Rove. You have three other good choices, Rove replied. But Barrett's only been on the bench a short while; you don't know how she's going to evolve or whether she'll be able to handle the fire of a confirmation hearing. The other two, Kethledge and Hardiman, are good guys. But with Kavanaugh, Rove said, you've got someone who has compiled the longest record, dealt with the widest range of issues, and possesses the demonstrated intellectual firepower. The last thing you want is to have people look back and say you had the chance to appoint someone who is a strong conservative, and instead he flipped and flopped. Rove got off the phone with the impression that Trump was interested in Kavanaugh but hadn't finally decided.

To appeal to a television-and-Twitter-focused president, it was important for potential nominees to enlist television personalities on their side. For Kavanaugh, one such supporter was Ann Coulter, the conservative commentator whose first book, *High Crimes and Misdemeanors: The Case Against Bill Clinton*, was a subject that Kavanaugh knew well from his work in the independent counsel's office. At a critical moment, when conservatives were questioning Kavanaugh's bona fides, Coulter emerged as an important validator. (This was before Coulter and Trump diverged over his supposed weakness on immigration and Trump derided her as a "Wacky Nut Job.")[27]

Coulter was tireless in promoting Kavanaugh—and going after the opposition. "Who is pushing Kethledge for the S. Ct?" she tweeted on July 4. "Answer: Same people who swore by Souter."[28] It was a busy day for Coulter. "Hardiman & Kethledge are open borders zealots," she followed up a few minutes later, although this assessment had scant basis in their actual records.[29] And, that same day: "Kavanaugh's record on 2d amt is EXCELLENT, just like his record on everything else."[30] On July 7, referring to Harriet Miers, Bush's White House counsel and ill-fated first choice for the O'Connor seat: "I was a lonely voice in the woods warning you about Judge Roberts. Also opposed Miers—while being attacked for it on Fox News. Now, I'm telling you Kavanaugh is stellar."[31]

The Kavanaugh clerk network, which included several well situated inside the White House itself (staff secretary Derek Lyons, Claire Murray in the counsel's office, and Zina Bash, until recently on the domestic policy staff), was poised to leap into action to rebut any criticism—and did so, at times, in language that would be used against Kavanaugh once he was selected. Much as presidential candidates must appeal to the base in order to win the primary, then can move to the center in the general election, the immediate goal for Kavanaugh's backers was securing the nomination. Thus, when social conservatives started to tout Barrett and sow doubts about Kavanaugh, citing his ruling in the migrant abortion case as supposed evidence of inadequate opposition to abortion rights, Sarah Pitlyk, who clerked for Kavanaugh from 2010 to 2011, took to *National Review* online to attest to his conservative fortitude.

"This is no time for a gamble," warned Pitlyk, special counsel to the Thomas More Society, which describes itself as a "public interest law firm dedicated to restoring respect in law for life, family, and religious liberty." In an oblique jab at Barrett, who had been on the bench for just eight months, Pitlyk added, "As social conservatives know from bitter experience, a judicial record is the best—really, the only—accurate predictor of a prospective justice's philosophy on the issues that matter most to us. On the vital issues of protecting religious liberty and enforcing restrictions on abortion, no court-of-appeals judge in the nation has a stronger, more consistent record than Judge Brett Kavanaugh."[32]

Likewise, Pitlyk and another clerk, Justin Walker, countered conservative criticism of Kavanaugh as "Roberts lite" for his ruling in the Affordable Care Act case. "Although [Kavanaugh] ultimately determined that a challenge to Obamacare had to be brought later, he left no doubt about where he stood," Pitlyk wrote. "No other contender on President Trump's list is on record so vigorously criticizing the law. He called the individual mandate 'unprecedented on the federal level in American history' and said that upholding it would 'usher in a significant expansion of congressional authority with no obvious principled limit.'"[33]

On *The Federalist*, a conservative website, Walker went even further, responding to a critique that accused Kavanaugh of handing the justices "a roadmap for saving Obamacare."[34] Kavanaugh's "thorough and principled takedown of the mandate was indeed a roadmap for the Supreme Court—*the Supreme Court dissenters*, justices Antonin Scalia, Anthony Kennedy, Clarence Thomas, and Samuel Alito, who explained that the mandate violated the Constitution," Walker wrote. "I am very familiar with that opinion, because I served as Kennedy's law clerk that term. I can tell you with certainty that the only justices following a roadmap from Brett Kavanaugh were the ones who said Obamacare was unconstitutional."[35]

These assessments from Pitlyk and Walker, both of whom were later nominated by Trump for district court judgeships, contained more than a bit of cherry-picking. Although Kavanaugh did not address the merits of the health care law's constitutionality, he signaled that the individual mandate might pass muster as part of Congress's taxing power, even going so far as to outline a fix that might do the constitutional trick. He called the question of whether the mandate violated Congress's power under the Commerce Clause "extremely difficult and rife with significant and potentially unforeseen implications for the Nation and the Judiciary." Notwithstanding the risks of unduly expanding congressional power, he warned against "prematurely or unnecessarily *rejecting*" that power, noting that the Affordable Care Act was passed "after a high-profile and vigorous national debate. Courts must afford great respect to that legislative effort and should be wary of upending it."[36]

In fact, Kavanaugh was neither the flag-waving Obamacare opponent of the Pitlyk-Walker depiction nor the Obamacare lover of conservative opponents' caricature. But none of that mattered, not at this point. In order to get to the general election, first you had to win the primary.

CHAPTER FIVE

A Thorn in the Flesh

Brett Kavanaugh had impeccable credentials, an impressive lobbying operation, and the fervent support of the White House counsel. Still, as the date for the president's big reveal drew closer, his prospects were threatened on multiple fronts. Some White House staffers, chafing at McGahn's efforts to control the process, advocated for other candidates, primarily Amy Coney Barrett. Kavanaugh's Bush ties still rankled. The social conservatives' campaign against Kavanaugh and in favor of Barrett gained steam—a development that was partly organic and partly the product of a rogue anti-Kavanaugh effort being run by the Senate Judiciary Committee's chief nominations counsel, Mike Davis.

And as Republican leaders began to grapple with the reality of the mountain of documents that a Kavanaugh nomination would entail, they began to express their misgivings to the president and suggest that he might be wiser to look elsewhere. The day before Trump offered the nomination to Kavanaugh, the judge's team thought all was lost. Even when the signals improved, in the final hours, they remained uncertain. After all, this was Donald Trump, notoriously mercurial. For some of Kavanaugh's closest allies, it was not until late Monday afternoon, July 9, when an e-mail arrived from the White House social secretary inviting them to the East Room announcement that night, that they were fully convinced they had prevailed after all.

· · ·

Notwithstanding McGahn's efforts to exert tight control over the selection process, and notwithstanding his staunch backing of Kavanaugh, not everyone inside the White House, or among Trump's circle of outside advisers, was on board. Having centralized judge picking in the counsel's office, McGahn jealously guarded that prerogative, much to the displeasure of others not only in the Justice Department but also elsewhere in the White House. They chafed at what they viewed as McGahn's prickly, insecurity-fueled efforts to elbow others out of the way, controlling the process and steering it in his desired direction.

"This was something Don thought he owned and tried to push anybody else out," said one former White House official. Said another, "There's no doubt Don wanted to be more possessive of this and I think pushed Brett Kavanaugh on the president."

That did not stop other administration officials from weighing in. The aides debated: Should Trump please the base with a social conservative like Barrett? Did picking a woman make sense this time around, given Trump's polling deficit with female voters? Or should he hold Barrett in reserve so that she could obtain more seasoning on the appellate bench and be at the ready in case Ginsburg left the court?

Short, the legislative director, senior adviser Kellyanne Conway, and press secretary Sarah Huckabee Sanders made the case for Barrett. With an election looming, they argued for going bolder and generating excitement among voters, not making a safe but boring pick. They saw a path to confirmation for Barrett. She might lose the votes of pro-choice Republicans Collins and Murkowski, but Republicans could lure Democrats Manchin and Donnelly instead. Both had voted for Barrett for the appeals court, and Donnelly was from Barrett's home state of Indiana.

Jared Kushner and Ivanka Trump were not especially visible, but given Ivanka's special access to her father, they didn't need to be. Ivanka Trump urged her father to pick a woman. Kushner and Ivanka didn't like Kavanaugh. He was a Bushie and therefore suspect. And if McGahn was for Kavanaugh, the reflexive response of the pair was to be against him. Although they had helped McGahn get the counsel's job to begin with as a way of getting back at Priebus, by this point McGahn had interfered with Kushner's efforts to obtain a security clearance. He was in the couple's crosshairs.

The irony of the situation, and McGahn's first-among-equals position when it came to the selection of a Supreme Court justice, was that by this point Trump, too, loathed his counsel. McGahn had never been a particular Trump favorite, even stretching back to the campaign. Once in the White House, he found himself in a position of having to say no, repeatedly, to a president heedless of ordinary rules of ethical conduct. The Mueller report offered a window into the Trump-McGahn dysfunction. It described McGahn's refusal to comply with Trump's order that he instruct the Justice Department to fire Mueller over supposed conflicts of interest, and detailed how Trump called his counsel a "lying bastard" after news reports of the showdown surfaced months later.[1]

Now, a year after that episode, McGahn was still on the job, and the president and his counsel remained so at odds that Trump was reluctant to meet with McGahn alone. At the same time, the fact was—and Trump knew—that McGahn had overseen perhaps the single most successful aspect of Trump's presidency: the effort to fill the federal courts with conservative judges. Trump was proud of the Gorsuch pick as something that went beyond mere base pleasing—it would burnish his legacy. So notwithstanding his dislike for McGahn, Trump "trusted Don" when it came to the Supreme Court, said one adviser. "He really was infatuated with what he perceived as his success at Gorsuch."

McGahn's argument to Trump and others was that Kavanaugh would be the safest choice. This second vacancy, he knew, was harder to fill because of the higher stakes involved with Kennedy's departure. More than anything, Trump needed to ensure that mainstream Senate Republicans were comfortable with the pick. Kavanaugh was the most reputable candidate, credentialed and experienced. "He checks every box," McGahn kept saying. "Everybody will love him." The president "was told this would

be an easy win," one adviser said. "There were people who were
risk averse who, ironically, said, 'Let's go Kavanaugh,'" said one
White House official. "And that ended up being the biggest circus
you could imagine."

As McGahn pushed for Kavanaugh, one astonishing locus of anti-
Kavanaugh activity was in the office of the Senate Judiciary Committee chairman, Charles Grassley. The Iowa Republican's chief
nominations counsel was Mike Davis, a former Gorsuch clerk who
had helped steer Gorsuch through the confirmation hearings. Davis,
himself a Bush 43 alumnus, told pretty much anyone who would
listen that Kavanaugh was "too Bushie, too swampy, too Chiefy"—
that is, too similar to Roberts in his supposed squishiness. Most
mere staffers would not take it on themselves to try to sink a prospective nominee, certainly not without their boss's approval. But
Grassley had a tendency to give his staff wide berth, and the pug-
nacious Davis, who understood the brass-knuckle aspects of confirmation battles from his time in the political affairs shop at the Bush
White House, was no ordinary staffer. Joined by communications
aide Garrett Ventry, on leave from CRC Public Relations, effectively the PR arm of the Federalist Society, Davis mounted a not-
so-stealthy campaign to deny Kavanaugh the confirmation.

It did not help Kavanaugh's prospects that Davis had a less-
than-warm relationship with McGahn. They had clashed frequently
during the Gorsuch nomination. Now Davis was in an even more
critical position as Grassley's chief nominations counsel. As White
House officials saw it, Davis was acting well beyond his authority.
If Kavanaugh, with his lengthy paper trail, were to be the nominee,
Davis kept telling them, Grassley was committed to getting documents disclosed and working with the minority to accomplish that
task. The chairman would hold up the nomination until after the
election if need be, Davis threatened. Fine—if it comes to that, our
boss will call your boss, White House officials thought. Still, this
was a problem, and it wasn't the only one.

Anthony Kennedy had announced his retirement on Wednesday, June 27. That same day, an Alabama lawyer named Phillip Jauregui, president of a little-known entity called the Judicial Action Group, circulated a memorandum to fellow conservatives comparing Kavanaugh unfavorably to Barrett and citing Kavanaugh's decision in the *Garza v. Hargan* abortion case to demonstrate "why Kavanaugh is not the best available Supreme Court prospect."[2] Jauregui was the longtime lawyer for former Alabama Supreme Court justice and Senate candidate Roy Moore. His Judicial Action Group was not any kind of major player on nominations; its 2017 tax forms disclosed a paltry $287,337 in revenue.[3] Who was this guy? Kavanaugh's team wondered.

They didn't know, but they watched in astonishment as Jauregui's critical memo whizzed around the conservative ecosystem. (By Friday, July 6, Jauregui had gotten himself spun up even further, saying on a conservative monthly prayer call that Barrett was "the one that God has chosen," while Kavanaugh was Absalom, the usurper.)[4] Over the next several days, the conservative angst about Kavanaugh ramped up, focused in significant part on the *Garza* case. The leaders of three socially conservative groups—the American Family Association, the American Principles Project, and Liberty Counsel—joined with Jauregui to send a letter to the president pushing for Barrett. "It is better to have a vacancy until next year than to fill the seat with a weak nominee who will betray your legacy and the constitution for the next forty years," they warned.[5] These weren't the most influential or most powerful of the social conservatives, but they were the public face of mounting conservative anxiety over a Kavanaugh selection.

Behind the scenes, the criticism of Kavanaugh was more pointed. At a meeting McGahn held with conservative activists just after Kennedy's announcement, Tom McClusky, vice president of government affairs at March for Life, the annual protest on the anniversary of the *Roe v. Wade* ruling, expressed misgivings about Kavanaugh. So did Marjorie Dannenfelser of the Susan B. Anthony List, which works to elect candidates opposed to abortion rights. Dannenfelser, after her initial unease over Trump, had taken a chance on the candidate. As her official biography on the organization's website described it, she agreed to serve as chair of the Trump campaign's Pro-life Coalition "after securing four pro-life commitments from the nominee during the 2016 campaign."[6] Dannenfelser was wary of being too vocal with her worries about Kavanaugh—perhaps not surprisingly, given that the Leo-affiliated Judicial Crisis Network had dispensed nearly $800,000 to her group over the previous two years—but she made her concerns clear.[7]

Some of the conservative griping about Kavanaugh arose naturally; some was attributable to behind-the-scenes stoking by Davis. "Anti-abortion rights groups and activists have been quietly lobbying . . . against possible Supreme Court nominee Brett Kavanaugh," Tara Palmeri reported on ABCNews.com in a story posted at 9:24 p.m. on July 2.[8] MOVEMENT CONSERVATIVES FUME AT TRUMP SCOTUS FAVORITE, read a July 3 headline in the *Daily Caller*. Columnist Benny Johnson quoted an unnamed senior administration official who termed Kavanaugh the "low-energy Jeb Bush pick"—a phrase that was a favorite Davisism. Johnson quoted American Family Association president Tim Wildmon, warning, "We've seen this movie before. A conservative president compromises with the left on our nominees. What do we get? A court packed with Kennedy, O'Connor, Souter and Roberts."[9]

That same day, conservative commentator Glenn Beck tweeted along the same skeptical lines: "I cannot get excited about someone who recommended Roberts to Bush, wrote an opinion upholding Obamacare, and has hired throngs of liberal law clerks and fed them to liberal justices."[10] The *National Law Journal* reported that James Bopp, the longtime general counsel of the National Right to Life Committee, had written to Trump and Vice President Pence urging Trump to choose Barrett over Kavanaugh.[11]

Given that this was friendly fire—after all, one of the short-list candidates would become the president's nominee—the attacks on Kavanaugh took on a notably ugly edge. One of them involved Kavanaugh's relationship with Alex Kozinski, the Ninth Circuit judge for whom he had clerked and with whom he had worked closely helping select clerks for Kennedy. Kozinski had recently been forced off the bench after reports of inappropriate and abusive behavior toward female clerks and lawyers, which raised the obvious question of whether Kavanaugh had been aware of his problematic behavior, including an e-mail list known as the "Easy Rider Gag List" on which Kozinski distributed sexually explicit jokes. *Politico* reporter Eliana Johnson, whose background as Washington editor of *National Review* equipped her with particularly good connections in the conservative community, was given a six-page opposition research document—"#MeToo and the Kavanaugh-Kozinski Collaboration"—circulated to make the case that Kavanaugh must have known. An agitated Kavanaugh himself called Johnson to try to quash the story.

Johnson did not quote directly from the document, which came from proponents of another candidate, but it was a remarkably nasty piece of work.[12] Among the bullet-pointed "key concerns" were that "Judge Kavanaugh has been so close to Judge Kozinski for so long that ignorance of 'open secrets' about sexual abuse is highly unlikely," that at "Kavanaugh's last confirmation hearing, he was accused of lying under oath by Senators Leahy and Durbin, both of whom still serve on the Judiciary Committee," and that "[a]ny denial of knowledge about Judge Kozinski's widely known misconduct will likewise appear to be false."

The document made the kind of unsupported leaps that might not have been surprising in an opposition research paper circulated by liberal opponents of a potential nominee. But from fellow conservatives? This was staggering.

It was not the only sign of trouble for Kavanaugh, who also faced a boomlet in favor of Utah senator Mike Lee. Cruz, who had maneuvered Lee onto the list, termed Kavanaugh "unreliable" and relayed his reservations to the president, as did Arkansas senator Tom Cotton. Cruz aides also circulated criticism of Kavanaugh for hiring liberal law clerks and sending them on to liberal justices—a practice that Scalia had privately derided, not from Kavanaugh but in general, as "credentialing the opposition." Jim DeMint, who had helped Trump with the original list and by then had left the Heritage Foundation for a group called the Conservative Partnership Institute, called Trump to lobby for Lee and wrote an op-ed for the conservative *Daily Caller* endorsing the Utah senator.[13] Radio host Mark Levin described Lee as "the gold standard" for a Supreme Court nominee. "Mike Lee is a perfect pick," tweeted conservative columnist Erick Erickson.[14] On July 6, a group of conservative leaders and lawmakers signed a letter announcing support for Lee. They included DeMint; Beck; Adam Brandon, president of FreedomWorks, a conservative-libertarian group affiliated with the Tea Party; conservative megadonor Rebekah Mercer; and, most ominously, a sitting senator—Kentucky senator Rand Paul.[15]

Paul had already demonstrated his willingness to break with Trump. Just that spring, he had voted against the president's choice for CIA director, Gina Haspel, although his vote did not sink the nomination, and he had made noises about defecting on secretary of state nominee Mike Pompeo as well. Paul would probably fall in line, but with the slim Senate margin, he could be a problem. There was little room for error, and at this point he was threatening not to vote for Kavanaugh.

Paul's concerns—again, stirred up in part by Davis—centered on whether Kavanaugh, with his roots in the Bush White House in the aftermath of 9/11, would be too supportive of mass surveillance programs and too dismissive of privacy concerns. Paul focused on Kavanaugh's 2015 opinion in a case challenging the government's bulk collection of telephone metadata, the surveillance program exposed by former National Security Agency contractor Edward Snowden. A panel of the appeals court had allowed the collection to continue while the case was being litigated, and the full appeals court declined to intervene.

Kavanaugh weighed in with a short, and legally unnecessary concurrence, volunteering his view that the surveillance "is entirely consistent with the Fourth Amendment." The metadata program, he said, "serves a critically important special need—preventing terror- ist attacks on the United States," which "outweighs the impact on privacy occasioned by this program."[16] For a libertarian like Paul, these were fighting words that displayed disregard for fundamental constitutional rights.

McGahn went to work on Paul. At least keep an open mind, he argued; don't express outright opposition. Trump put in a pre- selection call. It ultimately took until the end of July, after a meet- ing with the nominee, for Paul to endorse Kavanaugh. For the moment, Paul was a problem to be managed, if not solved.

The conservative revolt, such as it was, reflected the unantic- ipated downside of the Trump list. The list had helped to reas- sure conservatives about Trump the candidate. Now it served to embolden them about Trump the president. He had produced a set menu of Supreme Court choices, and some of the selections, to con- servative eyes, looked far more enticing than others. Since Trump had promised to make his choice only from that list, the downside of sinking a nominee was more limited than it would have been other- wise. It wasn't Kavanaugh or some unknown quantity who might be even worse; it was Kavanaugh or one of twenty-four others, none of whom would be a disaster from the conservative perspective.

Trump was rattled by the conservative opposition to Kava- naugh. "The president was really confused by that, and he was putting a lot of pressure on Don," said one Trump adviser. For McGahn, it was a constant fire drill: every time Trump mentioned a conservative who had called him to complain about Kavanaugh, he hurriedly arranged for a countervailing call from a Kavanaugh supporter.

Meanwhile, as Davis's talk about Grassley's commitment to trans- parency indicated, another element of the case against Kavanaugh, nonideological but perhaps even more dangerous, was emerging. A Kavanaugh nomination, thanks to his years of service in the Bush administration, would come with a mammoth paper trail—millions of pages of documents that Democrats would inevitably demand.

This cumbersome reality posed two distinct problems. First, time was running out. Kennedy had taken so long to announce his retirement that reviewing all the documents could bump up against the coming midterm elections and the prospect, however unlikely, that Democrats might retake control of the Senate. Second, no one knew what material might be contained in those pages or whether it could be used by Democrats, fairly or not, as ammunition. Depending on who was making this argument about Kavanaugh's extensive paper trail, it was either a convenient excuse or a problematic reality. Either way, it was an issue that Kavanaugh's advocates had to contend with. He would be the first real nominee of the digital age.

The documents provoked conference calls and tense meetings in McConnell's office between the administration and Senate staff. McGahn's deputy, Annie Donaldson, argued that denying Kavanaugh the nomination because the documents posed a problem would amount to penalizing him for having devoted his career to public service. When Trump solicited Grassley's views on the nomination, Grassley said he would be supportive of whomever the president selected. But, he observed, it might be easier not to choose Kavanaugh.

George W. Bush had pushed the Senate to approve Kavanaugh's appeals court nomination a dozen years earlier. Now he once again lent a hand. It would be terrible for Kavanaugh's chances to be ruined over the documents issue, he said. Through staff, Bush conveyed assurances to the White House that his presidential library would do whatever it took—and spend whatever money was necessary—to make certain that the Kavanaugh documents housed there would be made available in time to get the nomination done before the election.

On the documents front, Kavanaugh was, once again, perfectly positioned. The "personal representative" designated by Bush for approving releases of documents from his administration was a

Washington lawyer named William Burck. As it happened, Burck had been Kavanaugh's deputy as staff secretary. And in the Mueller probe, the ubiquitous Burck represented Steve Bannon, Reince Priebus, and, even more pertinent, Don McGahn.

As the president pondered his choice, the Bush library conducted an initial computerized sweep, looking for any Kavanaugh time bombs—racial epithets or sexist terms. As expected, nothing turned up. Still, everyone understood that if the document production were to be conducted in the regular manner, through the National Archives, it would take months to complete. One solution was to hire outside law firms to speed up the process, utilizing the computerized search tools common in modern litigation. So Burck lined up three major firms—his own, Quinn Emanuel Urquhart & Sullivan; Kirkland & Ellis, where Kavanaugh had once been a partner; and Texas-based Baker Botts. It would cost millions—the precise figures were confidential—to get the work done, but Bush was committed. He had envisioned this moment, Kavanaugh elevated to the high court, long before and wanted to see it happen.

Still, the documents issue loomed large. On Saturday evening, July 7, the *New York Times* posted a story by Maggie Haberman and Jonathan Martin. They reported that Mitch McConnell had advised Trump and McGahn that either Kethledge or Hardiman would be easier to confirm, citing the documents problem. "While careful not to directly make the case for any would-be justice," the story said, McConnell "made clear in multiple phone calls" with Trump and McGahn that Kavanaugh's "lengthy paper trail . . . would pose difficulties for his confirmation."[17]

The story landed like a grenade in the Kavanaugh camp, marking, for them, the lowest point of the long twelve days. Opposition from social conservatives was one thing—that could be handled. But if McConnell was gunning for them, that was a real problem. And the clock was ticking. Trump had promised to announce his choice Monday. Maybe they were sunk. It was time for a last-ditch effort to salvage the nomination.

Burck, the documents guy, was tasked with damage control. He called John Abegg, McConnell's chief counsel. He delivered the same message to Davis, the Grassley staffer who had been orchestrating the Kavanaugh opposition. "If you guys don't get this done, trust me, Grassley is blaming you," Davis warned Burck. "You guys fucked this up, not us."

The Kavanaugh team was despondent. "Over the weekend," said one person closely involved in the process, "we thought he was sunk."

Sunk or not, there was work to do. On Saturday, the White House had asked the leading contenders to draft acceptance remarks, seven minutes maximum, and assemble guest lists, just in case. Trump was capable of changing his mind at the last moment; it was better to be prepared. Indeed, Trump was having a hard time deciding. He called one outside adviser: "People are really pushing me on Kavanaugh here—what do you think?" he asked. Hardiman was a better story, this adviser said—more difficult for Democrats to attack and no less conservative than Kavanaugh. "I know Bush 43 loves him," the adviser said of Kavanaugh, hoping that the faux praise would serve to turn Trump off, "but Hardiman is the better choice."

Other advisers weighed in with conflicting advice. Lindsey Graham had been speaking with Trump frequently throughout. "I kept saying this is your legacy," Graham recalled. "Of all the things you'll do, this is at the top." Graham pointed out to Trump that one seeming Kavanaugh disadvantage was actually a benefit. "One thing about the Bush pick: you have all the Bush people helping you," Graham said. "And they did. I said, 'With the environment in Washington you're gonna need all the help you can get.' I remember telling him, having no idea it'd be the way it was."[18]

As Trump deliberated that final weekend, he called a friend. It was coming down to the wire. What did his friend think about

Kavanaugh? Kavanaugh, Trump said, was like Classic Coke—you know what you're getting: a traditional, solid choice. The friend talked up Kavanaugh. He has a consistent voting record. And with his Irish Catholic background, the friend told Trump, Kavanaugh would be loyal—always a key selling point with Trump. Still, the president didn't sound entirely convinced. What about Hardiman? he asked. Don't you think he would be pretty good?

Meanwhile, the revolt of the social conservatives was beginning to get to Leonard Leo. The Federalist Society official had been assuring skeptics that Kavanaugh's writings had been thoroughly scrubbed—but now he was having second thoughts. "He was never a big Brett fan, so anytime there was a little hiccup, Leonard would get nervous," said one observer. Leo called Kellyanne Conway, expressing concern about Kavanaugh. You should tell the president that Barrett is a great choice, he suggested. Conway had no patience for this last-minute wavering. By that point, the president's position was becoming clear, and even though she would have preferred Barrett, she was too skilled a bureaucratic player to get crosswise with the president at this late stage. If Kavanaugh was the direction that Trump wanted to go in, Conway could use the choice to help prove her favorite point—that the media was wrong. Some commentators had questioned whether Trump would ever pick a Bushie. Kavanaugh's selection would be proof of his open-mindedness and the unreliability of the commentariat. Conway wasn't the only one with whom Leo shared his eleventh-hour concerns. "Leonard's going squishy on me," McGahn told friends.

Trump spent the weekend at his golf club in Bedminster, soliciting advice. Sunday morning, he called Kavanaugh to reassure him. Don't worry about the *Times* story, the president said. He was still thinking things through. It was a remarkably thoughtful act from the ordinarily self-involved Trump.

After that morning's round of golf, Trump had lunch with Fox

News's Sean Hannity and Rudy Giuliani. Christopher Ruddy, who ran the conservative website Newsmax, was driving from Washington to New York with Justin Lilley, a telecommunications consultant who did lobbying work for Ruddy and was a friend of Kavanaugh; they were planning to stop off at Bedminster for lunch.

For Ruddy to have become a Kavanaugh booster was the ultimate surprise. When Kavanaugh was a young prosecutor working for Kenneth Starr and assigned to investigate Vincent Foster's suicide, Ruddy had been the chief proponent of theories that Foster had been the victim of foul play, perhaps involving the Clintons themselves. In his 1997 book, *The Strange Death of Vincent Foster*, Ruddy blasted Starr as "a patsy for the Clintonites." For his part, Kavanaugh had dismissed Ruddy as a kook. "Most of the conversation involved Ruddy ranting and raving about various matters," he advised Starr in a May 1995 memo.[19] Now the job Kavanaugh had craved for so long was on the line—and Ruddy, of all people, was in a critical position to help.

Trump's looming choice was the major topic of the lunch. Hannity made the case for Barrett. She would be really good for conservatives, rallying the base in the midterms, he argued. Also, she would make for great television. Giuliani was for Hardiman. Ruddy and Lilley made the case for Kavanaugh. Meese, Reagan's former attorney general, believed that Kavanaugh was a true conservative, Ruddy reported. Trump peppered Lilley, though he had never before met him. Who do you think would be best? Kavanaugh's the choice, Lilley argued. He's the best qualified, and will be a reliable conservative. As the lunch concluded, it seemed as if Trump was inclining in Kavanaugh's direction.

As Trump lunched in Bedminster and prepared to return to the White House, Kavanaugh and his clerks were in his chambers, drafting an acceptance speech that might never be delivered. It was Kavanaugh's custom to attend the 5:30 Mass at the Shrine of the Most Blessed Sacrament, and it was his assigned Sunday to do the reading. But at this point reporters were following Kavanaugh everywhere, and he didn't want to look showy, like he was advertising his faith.

Kavanaugh glanced at the church bulletin. "Wow, the second reading today—that is pretty bizarre; that is right on point," he told the clerks. It was 2 Corinthians 12:7–10, in which the apostle Paul relates, "That I . . . might not become too elated because of the abundance of the revelations, a thorn in the flesh was given to me, an angel of Satan, to beat me, to keep me from being too elated."[20] Indeed, this was not the moment to get too elated.

The federal marshals who now accompanied him everywhere drove Kavanaugh to Blessed Sacrament. On his way to church, the White House called: could he come see the president? But there was a problem. Kavanaugh was in khakis and a dress shirt—not appropriate for a presidential meeting. He needed a way to get a suit. With reporters camped outside her house, Ashley Kavanaugh managed to smuggle a suit to Kavanaugh's car for what was arguably the most important meeting of her husband's life.

Kavanaugh attended Mass, then headed to the White House to meet in the residence with Trump and First Lady Melania Trump.[21] The conversation was more a casual chat than intense grilling. The First Lady didn't say much, but her presence was a sign of her little-appreciated influence with Trump. As the discussion drew to a close, Trump told Kavanaugh he would like him to be the nominee. That night Trump called Graham, saying he had settled on Kavanaugh.

Kavanaugh, poker-faced, arrived back in his chambers around nine that night. He wasn't telling the clerks anything, either way. But it was time to get back to work on the speech. The acceptance remarks were a nominee's best shot at shaping public opinion; after that, the nominee would have to remain silent for weeks. These fights, Kavanaugh observed, are won or lost in the first forty-eight hours. Kavanaugh knew this firsthand. He had been through this drill before, watching the Roberts and Alito nominations succeed, seeing Harriet Miers blow up.

On Monday morning, President Trump called Bush. The forty-third president had let it be known he did not vote for his Republican successor, adding that Trump "doesn't know what it means to be President."[22] Trump had not been any more flattering to Bush; in a speech to Republican donors just that March, he sarcastically termed Bush a "real genius" whose decision to invade Iraq was "the single worst decision ever made."[23] But Trump always looked for the opportunity to get a chit in the favor bank. I'm picking your guy, he told Bush. The White House staff was pleased. Perhaps this could be a turning point in a frosty relationship.

Kavanaugh himself remained mum. Some of his closest friends weren't completely certain he was the pick until they received their invitations to the announcement. And Grassley, whose top nominations aide had labored in secret to deny Kavanaugh the nomination, the Judiciary chairman to whom Kavanaugh's fate was now entrusted, did not learn who the choice would be until the president announced it in the East Room that night.

For all the feverish jockeying over filling the Kennedy seat, for all the social conservatives' private and public hand-wringing about Kavanaugh's reliability, Republican troops largely fell in line once the president made his selection. The outcome, although not guaranteed, was not much in doubt—unless some problem emerged, unknown to the White House, undiscovered by the vetters.

Just such an issue was already brewing across the country. A Palo Alto psychology professor named Christine Blasey Ford was telling friends that she had been sexually assaulted by Kavanaugh and a high school friend at a party in suburban Maryland on a summer night thirty-six years earlier. By the evening of Trump's prime-time East Room announcement, Ford had already reached out to her local congresswoman, Democrat Anna Eshoo, and, for good measure, the *Washington Post*'s tip line. Her story would not surface for nine more weeks, after Kavanaugh's hearings had concluded and he appeared on the cusp of confirmation.

When it erupted into public view, it imperiled Kavanaugh's nomination and irrevocably changed both their lives—the justice whose reputation was forever marred; the shy professor and reluctant witness whose name became a household word. And it plunged the country into yet another anguished, angry national conversation: about how, in the midst of the #MeToo movement, to deal with allegations of sexual misconduct both serious and decades in the past. About the nature of memory, whether fallible or indelible. About the proper application of presumptions of innocence and burdens of proof, not in the staid confines of a courtroom but in the pitched, partisan context of a Supreme Court confirmation battle.

CHAPTER SIX

No Rebel, No Cause

From the modest brick home on a quiet cul-de-sac in suburban Bethesda, Maryland where Brett Kavanaugh grew up, to
the gray-shingled bungalow in Chevy Chase where he now
lives with his family is a scant three miles, and that short distance
explains a good deal about Kavanaugh. Perhaps because he was
the only child of doting parents, perhaps because his professional
interests happened to be geographically compatible with his childhood home, this is a man who never had the urge to rebel or even
to roam far from the familiar confines of his early years. Kavanaugh traveled up the East Coast to Connecticut for college and
law school; he ventured as far as California for the clerkship that
set him on the road to legal stardom. Yet there was little doubt, in
the end, that he would return home to practice law and to inhabit
a particular subset of suburban Washington: Catholic, Republican,
and traditional.

In a region of transients that changed from administration to
administration, the community in which Kavanaugh was raised and
remained as an adult was stable and tightly knit to the point of
being tribal. It was a comfortable life, insular and orderly, going
to the Mater Dei School and then Georgetown Prep, playing in
Catholic youth league basketball and attending Sunday Mass up
Massachusetts Avenue at the Church of the Little Flower, where
Kavanaugh served as an altar boy. Like Kavanaugh, the friends of
his childhood, the Molloys and McCalebs and the Kanes, did not
stray far—in these circles a big move was going from Little Flower

parish to Blessed Sacrament, off Chevy Chase Circle, which the Kavanaughs now attend. This is the world in which Kavanaugh had been immersed for a lifetime and that produced the loyal band that fiercely defended him at his moment of greatest need.

It is possible to look back at the lives of some Supreme Court justices and trace the indicia of greatness, to show a consistent path of intellectual curiosity and academic excellence. The arc of Kavanaugh's early years tells a less obvious story, of a boy and young man who was smart, certainly, but perhaps more diligent than obviously brilliant, more interested in watching and playing sports than engaging in intellectual discourse—yet with a particularly useful knack for forging bonds with older men. As his ambitions grew and his chances to grasp the top rung of the legal profession flourished, these men, up to and including the president of the United States, for whom he worked, became his mentors and ultimately his ardent champions.

No one who attended college or law school with Kavanaugh imagined that they had a future Supreme Court justice in their midst—or if they did, that it was Kavanaugh. Nor, although they vaguely understood him to be quietly Republican, an affable ideological outlier within their liberal ranks, did Kavanaugh's peers consider him to be an ardent movement conservative of the sort that was emerging under the auspices of the still young Federalist Society.

It is telling that, even when he managed to join the elite ranks of Supreme Court law clerks, his peers did not envision a future Justice Kavanaugh. In the clerks' year-end predictions, a story Kavanaugh himself shared at his investiture as a federal appeals court judge a dozen years later, they voted him among the most likely to become managing partner of a law firm—an assuredly comfortable, eminently respectable establishment outcome.[1] The building blocks of Kavanaugh's ambition were assembled in these early years; the Yale-Yale résumé that so impressed Trump was a foundational part of his eventual success. But the smoldering drive and the commitment to a conservative legal philosophy that ultimately

secured him a spot on the high court would take some time to manifest themselves.

Kavanaugh and his allies later bristled at the notion that his childhood was rich and entitled, and they had a point. The money came
later, around the time Brett was ready to graduate from high school,
and by then it was more than ample. From his position as head
of the Cosmetic, Toiletry, and Fragrance Association, the lobbying arm of the cosmetics industry, Ed Kavanaugh earned as much
as $5 million a year, enough to join multiple country clubs and
buy a vacation place on three acres in Easton, on Maryland's East-
ern Shore. When he retired, in 2005, his compensation package
reached $13 million. But Ed Kavanaugh didn't rise to the lobby-
ing group's top job, and the money that accompanied it, until 1983,
when Brett was a senior in high school.

In an atmosphere where some of his peers enjoyed significant
wealth—his friend Don Urgo's family, with their hotel holdings,
had a lavish spread in Potomac—the Kavanaughs were, for most
of Brett's childhood, comfortably middle class, not wealthy. Their
1,320-square-foot colonial, on a corner lot in Bethesda just past the
District line, had three bedrooms, and, during Kavanaugh's childhood, just one full bath—enough for a family that, unusually in the
Catholic community that the Kavanaughs inhabited, had only one
child. At one point, Kavanaugh's father considered taking a second
job to pay his son's tuition at Mater Dei, the Catholic elementary
and middle school that Kavanaugh attended; it made a big difference to the family budget when Brett won the headmaster's award
and, with it, free tuition for a year.

Likewise, for all the leafy elegance of Georgetown Prep's
North Bethesda campus, for all the school's vaunted exclusivity,
in the social architecture of privileged Washington the Georgetown
Prep boys were looked down on by those who went to even tonier
schools, such as St. Albans and Sidwell Friends. They were viewed
as less academic, more focused on sports and drinking. Getting into

Yale was no big deal for St. Albans grads; it was for a kid from Georgetown Prep. "People lump it together with the private-school culture writ large, and that's not who he is," said one Kavanaugh friend. "He's the only child of quite Catholic parents who are nice people, but their world was somewhat limited. It's a very white world. They weren't hanging out with Jews; they weren't hanging out with blacks. That's not what the milieu was."

Everett Edward Kavanaugh Jr. met Martha Gamble Murphy in the fall of 1962. Ed Kavanaugh was from Connecticut, the son of a Yale graduate who had become a manager at the local telephone company. Martha Murphy was the oldest of five children of a prominent Washington psychiatrist. Both were college seniors, he at Georgetown, then all male; she at all-female Trinity College, across town. They married not long after, in February of their senior year.

Brett arrived almost exactly two years later. Being an only child meant that Brett was, throughout his life, particularly close to his parents and adept at dealing with other adults. Not having brothers or sisters also seemed to instill in Kavanaugh a lifelong capacity to create and nurture friendships, as if to make up for the absence of actual siblings. Kavanaugh was the energetic participant in, and often organizer of, outings and activities, from Beach Week with his Georgetown Prep buddies to the annual reunions of his law school roommates; from a field trip to Orioles stadium with Chief Justice Rehnquist and his fellow clerks to the purchase of Washington Nationals season tickets.

From his father, Kavanaugh derived valuable lessons about the ways of Washington—the importance of forging bipartisan relationships and how socializing can yield political benefits. Ed Kavanaugh's relationships crossed political boundaries; decades later, his son had carefully—some said strategically—amassed a similar amalgam of friends across the ideological spectrum. Ed Kavanaugh played golf with then House Speaker Tip O'Neill, the Massachusetts Democrat; Illinois Republican Bob Michel, who became House minority whip and later minority leader, was so close to the

Kavanaughs that he would be introduced years later, almost as a guest of honor, at Brett's wedding. "We all know Ed," Utah Republican senator Orrin Hatch said at Kavanaugh's first confirmation hearing to be an appeals court judge in 2004.[2]

On the appeals court, Kavanaugh bridled at the seemingly unfettered power of regulatory agencies, and the Trump White House promoted the nominee as a judge who "protects American businesses from illegal job-killing regulation."[3] Perhaps the roots of that skeptical attitude can be traced to Ed Kavanaugh's experience at the helm of the trade association as it sought to fend off additional regulation, in particular a requirement that it obtain government approval of new ingredients before they could be put on the market. "Self-regulation" was enough to protect consumers, the group argued. As animal rights activists pressured cosmetics manufacturers to end animal testing, Ed Kavanaugh expressed exasperation with their hard-line position. "We are not dealing with rational opponents," he wrote in a 1989 letter seeking to raise $1 million for a campaign against state bans on animal testing. "We are dealing with zealots who cannot comprehend that a child's life is more important than a dog's."[4]

Ed Kavanaugh's lobbying activities enjoyed an unwelcome prime-time moment in 1990, the fall after Kavanaugh's graduation from law school, when ABC reported on a taxpayer-paid "fact-finding" trip to the Caribbean taken by nine members of Congress, their spouses, and staff. Members of the tax-writing House Ways and Means Committee, including chairman Dan Rostenkowski, were joined in Barbados by lobbyists, including Kavanaugh, who underwrote rounds of golf, Jet-Skiing, and fine dining, all caught on ABC's hidden cameras. "The delegation is invited to a private party hosted by a long-time friend of Congressman Rostenkowski, Washington lobbyist Ed Kavanaugh," ABC's Sam Donaldson reported.[5]

Over the years, Brett Kavanaugh was more likely to point to his mother as a career role model. She had received a master's degree in teaching in 1968, when Brett was three, and gone on to teach history at two predominantly African American public schools in

Washington, H.D. Woodson and McKinley Tech. "I vividly remember days as a young boy sitting in the back of my mom's classroom as she taught American history to a class of African American teenagers," Kavanaugh testified at his confirmation hearings, a half century after Martha Kavanaugh began her teaching career. "Her students were born before *Brown versus Board of Education* or *Bolling versus Sharpe*," the Supreme Court case that extended the holding of *Brown* to the District of Columbia.[6]

Ed Kavanaugh had started night law school at American University in 1974, and Martha Kavanaugh followed the next year. She attended during the day, Ed Kavanaugh at night, which meant they graduated the same year. Martha liked to tease Ed that she got the better grades; Ed would point out that he had a full-time job in addition to studying law.

The 1970s was a decade when the number of women in the legal profession skyrocketed, from 4 percent of lawyers in 1970 to 12.4 percent in 1980.[7] Still, Martha Kavanaugh's career path was unusual even for those early days. She joined the Montgomery County prosecutor's office after graduating from law school, part of the first wave of female assistant district attorneys hired. It was not always easy. In 1983, she was finishing jury selection in a case involving a home break-in when the judge asked jurors if there were any reasons they should be excused. One panel member, a sixty-two-year-old man, approached the bench to confide that he was sexually attracted to the prosecutor and might find it hard to concentrate. "I thought it was a legitimate excuse," the judge told the *National Law Journal*.[8] It was more than a little humiliating and a story of sexism in the profession that stuck with Brett Kavanaugh, one that he brought up over the years, talking with his clerks about the obstacles faced by female lawyers.

Martha Kavanaugh's career was unusual in the Kavanaughs' social circle as well. Growing up, Kavanaugh was the only one of his friends with a mother who worked. On the days it was her turn to do the car-pool pickup, Martha Kavanaugh arranged for a Barwood cab, with its trademark light blue color, to collect the boys from Mater Dei. Kavanaugh would let himself into the house with the spare key hidden underneath the planter, then get on his bike and pedal over to Westbrook Elementary, a half mile away, to shoot baskets with his friends until dinnertime.

"My introduction to law came at our dinner table when she practiced her closing arguments," Kavanaugh recalled on the night he was nominated to the high court. "Her trademark line was: 'Use your common sense. What rings true? What rings false?'"[9] After fifteen years as a prosecutor and in private practice, Martha Kavanaugh became a district judge in 1993. She was elevated to the circuit court, which handles more serious cases, two years later.[10]

Politically, the Kavanaughs' was a slightly mixed marriage. Ed Kavanaugh was a registered Republican, although in those days a rather moderate one. Martha officially switched her registration in 1976, in the aftermath of Watergate, to become a Democrat, yet even before then, she voted for liberal Democrat George McGovern over Richard Nixon in 1972. But despite Kavanaugh's upbringing inside the Beltway, despite his father's relationships with some of the capital's most prominent lawmakers, politics was not a focus, or even much of a subject, of Kavanaugh family life. On the night that Nixon resigned, when Kavanaugh was nine, Brett's parents pulled him away from watching a summer football game to view the speech, but that was an unusual moment when politics intruded.

What dominated instead was sports, playing and watching. For Kavanaugh, sports was an early and enduring obsession: playing Wiffle ball in the yard with his dad; learning to shoot baskets on a jerry-rigged low hoop in the garage; keeping baseball and football stats with his father on a yellow legal pad as they watched television. At his confirmation hearings years later, Kavanaugh could still recite the precise location of his father's Redskins season tickets at RFK Stadium: upper deck, section 503, row 3, seats 8 and 9.

Childhood friends point to Ed Kavanaugh as the source of his son's work ethic and to Martha Kavanaugh as the wellspring of his affability. "The source of that discipline and drive I think is in part fear of failure. And when I say that, I'm really focused on fear of failure in the eyes of his parents," said one friend. "He held his parents in the highest esteem . . . For a lot of kids that age, they're like, 'I don't ever want to be in the room with my parents alone.' Brett was the opposite."

Kavanaugh, the friend said, "was always the guy who if we were out somewhere on a Saturday night . . . would say, 'I'm going to go home a little bit early' so that he'd be prepared to study in the morning. He excelled academically and athletically, and a lot of it was not native. A lot of it was the product of really, really hard work."

Kevin Dowd, who coached Kavanaugh on the Georgetown Prep junior varsity and varsity basketball teams, remembered Kavanaugh staying behind at the gym to hone his foul shot after the ninety-minute practice was over. "Brett was from the beginning different from the other boys," said Dowd, whose sister is the *New York Times* columnist Maureen Dowd. "He was very quiet—just did his work, listened, didn't fool around."

But of course, being a high school student, he did fool around, and with a certain juvenile zest. "Prep was a school positively swimming in alcohol, and my class partied with gusto—often right under the noses of our teachers," Kavanaugh's friend Mark Judge wrote in his memoir, *God and Man at Georgetown Prep*.[11] In a 1983 letter outlining the plans for a "beach week" getaway in Ocean City, Maryland, an eighteen-year-old Kavanaugh warned, in a childish print, "The danger of eviction is great and that would suck because of the money and because this week has big potential. (Interpret as wish.)" He added, "P.S. It would probably be a good idea on Sat. the 18th to warn the neighbors that we're loud obnoxious drunks with prolific pukers among us."[12] Kavanaugh's now infamous yearbook page cited his role in the "100 Kegs or Bust" club and his status as "Beach Week Ralph Club—Biggest Contributor."

Was Kavanaugh's behavior excessive or out of line with that of his classmates? That question would come front and center at Kavanaugh's confirmation, when Christine Blasey Ford described an impromptu summer gathering where, she said, a drunken Kavanaugh grabbed her at a party and sexually assaulted her. Kavanaugh himself vigorously denied those allegations but acknowledged, "I think all of us have probably done things we look back on in high school and regret or cringe a bit."[13] At the investiture ceremony when he became an appellate judge, in 2006, Kavanaugh referred ruefully to his high school days with a formulation that would become familiar: "Fortunately, my friends also adhere to another good motto of Georgetown Prep, which is, what happens at Georgetown Prep stays at Georgetown Prep."[14]

One way to put Kavanaugh's high school behavior in perspective is to compare him to Gorsuch, who was, coincidentally, just two years behind Kavanaugh at Georgetown Prep. Gorsuch's rather pompous self-presentation in the school's yearbook, *The Cupola*, strikes a markedly different tone from Kavanaugh's boisterous jockiness. Gorsuch identifies himself as, among other things, "President of the Yard" (the student government), national champion of "Forensics 1, 2, 3," cofounder of the International Relations Club, and president and cofounder of the apparently fictitious "Fascism Forever" forum, which *The Cupola* describes as determined to battle the views of the school administration, dominated by liberal Jesuits. "In political circles, our tireless President Gorsuch's 'Fascism Forever' forum happily jerked its knees against the increasingly 'left-wing' tendencies of faculty," said the yearbook. One photo showed Gorsuch, in collar and tie, ostentatiously reading William F. Buckley's 1959 conservative classic, *Up from Liberalism.*

Kavanaugh's photos portrayed him playing basketball, suited up for football, and at the beach. When he applied to Yale, both of his required essays focused on his love for basketball.

Kavanaugh arrived in New Haven in the fall of 1983 to a campus riven by politics, from the still-boiling antiapartheid campaign to an emerging movement for the rights of gays and lesbians. Among the issues in the news that fall was alcohol, in particular how to adjust to the state's move to raise the drinking age to twenty effective that October. The fall's first edition of the *Yale Daily News*, published on September 8, greeted students with an alarming headline: COLLEGE MASTERS ABOLISH ANNUAL TANG COMPETITION, referring to the notorious beer-drinking relay race that pitted Yale's residential colleges against one another, with teams that practiced for the big event weeks in advance.[15]

Some students were already organizing for the presidential election the next year, forming groups such as Yalies for Gary Hart; Yale College Republicans was preparing to support Ronald Reagan's reelection. A newly created student group was pressing the Yale Corporation to divest itself of stock in companies that did business in South Africa, and three students were arrested protesting the launching of a Trident nuclear submarine in nearby Groton. On campus, the union representing clerical workers was threatening to strike and would do so the following year.[16]

This politically charged, liberal-leaning environment was not Kavanaugh's Yale. All campuses have competing subcultures: Kavanaugh immersed himself almost immediately among the jocks, even though he was not in their most elite ranks, having failed in his dream of walking onto the varsity basketball team. Kavanaugh settled for junior varsity basketball, plus intramural football, softball, and, in junior and senior years, basketball. And, on an alcohol-soaked campus, Kavanaugh gravitated toward a hard-drinking crowd, which was congruent with the jock circles he frequented. Sophomore year, joining his friend Chris Dudley, a basketball star later to play for five NBA teams, he pledged one of Yale's fraternities, Delta Kappa Epsilon. Known as DKE (pronounced "deke"), the frat, although it lacked an actual house, had an Animal House–ish reputation, complete with would-be members describing themselves as "buttholes" and engaged in juvenile pranks such as filching female students' underwear.[17] The *Yale Daily News*'s warnings to the contrary, the Tang competition survived, and Kavanaugh, beer drinker that he was, played for his residential college team.

Classmate Lynne Brookes remembered Kavanaugh, as part of the DKE initiation ritual, standing outside Sterling Memorial Library wearing a superhero cape and an old-fashioned leather football helmet, jumping on one foot, and reciting a silly rhyme: "I'm a geek, I'm a geek, I'm a power tool. When I sing this song, I look like a fool."[18] If Kavanaugh looked like a fool, he retained some affection for the getup. According to Brookes, he would often wear the football helmet on nights out. "He called it his drinking helmet," she said.[19]

Drinking was a big part of Kavanaugh's campus life, although that did not make him unique. Warren Sams, a DKE fraternity brother, recalled the pledge class of fourteen boys being locked in a squash court with a full keg, at least three liters of hard liquor, and a giant trash can to hold their vomit. They couldn't leave until they had drunk it all. DKE was "for guys to get together and drink," Sams said. "Drinking was the point."[20] In the spring of junior year, Yale's senior societies, such as Skull and Bones or Scroll and Key, offered membership to some of the most accomplished members of the class; Kavanaugh joined a less elite group called Truth and Courage, all male and, like DKE, dominated by athletes.

Alcohol brought out an otherwise unseen belligerence in the young Kavanaugh, one that included an undertone of misogyny, according to numerous college and law school classmates. "It was part of Brett's shtick—the more he got drunk, the more expletives [would] come out about women who didn't want to sleep with him and the men he deemed not masculine enough," said Chad Ludington, a basketball player who knew Kavanaugh early in their college years.[21] Kavanaugh, said Sams, "had a really smart mouth. He was a counterpuncher with the cutdowns. You didn't throw a diss Brett's way and expect to come away unscathed."[22]

One night after a concert by the English pop band UB40, Kavanaugh went to Demery's, a popular bar known for its cheap beer and generous pizza slices, with his close friend Dudley. They thought one patron looked like the UB40 lead singer; the customer told them to stop staring at him. The situation escalated from there, with Kavanaugh throwing an ice cube at the guy, a fight breaking out, and police being summoned.[23]

An affidavit submitted to the FBI in the aftermath of the Ford allegations offered another example. One of Kavanaugh's fellow members of Truth and Courage, who said he was a registered Republican, described an evening in the fall of 1986 when, after a meeting of the senior society, a group of the drunken revelers was heading toward a different part of campus. As they walked, they passed the man's blue Ford Courier pickup truck, and he saw that someone was pounding on it. "I yelled and moved toward the truck, and the person began smashing the black cargo box in the bed of the pickup," the Truth and Courage member wrote. "As I came closer to the truck, I noticed the person had broken it open and was trying to reach into the box for something." At that point, he realized it was Kavanaugh. "I stopped Brett from further damaging my vehicle and asked him repeatedly what the hell he was doing (using some even more colorful language). His response was quite remarkable: He just looked at me with a blank expression, turned, and walked away down College Street." At the next society meeting, the student raised the matter of the damage to his vehicle. "I was looking directly at Brett as I was saying it," he wrote. "Brett's response was again quite remarkable: Not a single word, nothing." The writer said he had seen Kavanaugh drinking "to the point of incoherence" on other occasions but that this one particularly stood out because of "his lack of personal responsibility in the days following."[24]

The drinking, sometimes to excess, persisted even after college. "He was a partier and he was a drinker and frankly he was not a very nice guy in a lot of ways when he was drunk," said one law school classmate. "He would say pretty outrageous things and be pretty cutting to people." Said another law school classmate, "If you had asked me who was the biggest drinker in our class I would have said Brett." In a speech to the Yale Federalist Society in 2014, Kavanaugh described episodes of drinking in law school, including organizing a trip to Boston for a Red Sox game and a night of bar-

hopping that featured "group chugs from a keg" on the ride home
and "falling out of the bus onto the front steps of Yale Law School
at about 4:45 a.m." Once again, Kavanaugh summed up: "Fortunately for all of us, we had a motto. What happens on the bus stays
on the bus."[25]

One of the attractions of Yale for Kavanaugh was its top-tier
history department, and Kavanaugh took some of the most popular
courses: Gaddis Smith on American foreign policy, Edmund Mor-
gan on colonial history, Wolfgang Leonhard on Russian history,
Brad Westerfield in the political science department on intelligence
policy (better known as "spies and lies"). But Kavanaugh left little
in the way of an academic footprint on campus. He won no academic prizes, was awarded no prestigious fellowships.

Indeed, as graduation approached, classmates were surprised to
discover that Kavanaugh had managed to win admission to Yale
Law School. "The common refrain was, 'Brett Kavanaugh got into
Yale Law School?'" one friend recalled. Given Kavanaugh's academic record, his admission to Yale Law School was somewhat
of a surprise. Notwithstanding President Trump's claim that Kavanaugh was "number one in his class at Yale," he graduated only
cum laude, a distinction shared by nearly half the class. "If you
had asked anybody in our Yale class who was going to be the most
famous person in the class of '87, nobody would have said Brett
Kavanaugh," said Dan Levy, sports editor of the *Yale Daily News*.[26]

If Kavanaugh did not arrive at Yale Law School with the most
impressive résumé among his peers, he seemed to try to compen-
sate by working harder. Yale Law School is a paradoxical environment: it is at once the most selective law school in the country and
a place where trying too hard is considered uncool. Kavanaugh was
the guy who came to class with his casebooks highlighted in multiple colors, the subject of some ribbing from classmates. While
other students killed time hanging out in the law school courtyard,
Kavanaugh was at his usual place in the law library, planted in a
carrel near the middle of the main reading room. "He spent more
time in the library than anyone I can think of," said one classmate.

"He worked at times of the week when other people didn't work . . . Thursday evening at 8:30, the library's empty but for Brett." Still, Kavanaugh was not an outspoken presence. Members of his small section—first-year law students are divided into small-group seminars of around eighteen for one of their required courses—recall him saying little in class.

Kavanaugh joined the Federalist Society, according to the questionnaire he later filled out for the Senate Judiciary Committee. But those involved in the Federalist Society at the time have scant recollection of Kavanaugh attending the chapter's weekly dinners or traveling to its annual student seminars. More broadly, if Kavanaugh was a conservative on an overwhelmingly liberal campus, he was not a particularly outspoken one—so much so that some law school friends wondered, as Kavanaugh skyrocketed through the conservative legal ranks, how much of his conservatism was the product of conviction and how much was a matter of career convenience.

"Certainly there's some people who were very politically conservative all along, and this is who they've always been, and I'm not saying he was a Democrat—he wasn't," said one law school friend. "But his views were much less formed, and he was happy to have them formed by people along the way—particularly if that meant he could then rise. I don't mean it in this purely opportunistic way, but I think there is some opportunism probably along the way. And that's true with each successive position a little bit." Said another law school friend, "I had a general sense that Brett was conservative but no sense at all that he was about to become professionally conservative, that he would become deeply partisan or even deeply ideological for purposes of his career. I guess if you asked me I probably would have been able to say he likely votes Republican. Really just likely. It wasn't something we talked about much, and I don't think he talked about it with anybody."

The fall of Kavanaugh's first year of law school, the campus was transfixed by the Senate Judiciary Committee hearings under way for Bork, who had taught at Yale for years. If Kavanaugh had strong feelings about Bork's treatment and whether the Senate was overstepping its constitutional bounds, no classmates remember his sharing them.

Kavanaugh's main circle was a group known as the "tall boys," although at five feet eleven Kavanaugh was not, technically, in those ranks. They played basketball at the Payne Whitney Gymnasium and hosted parties in their ramshackle turn-of-the-century house, divided into apartments, at 61 Lake Place, behind the gym. "I never considered him to be political one way or the other in law school," said Jonathan Franklin, who served with Kavanaugh as a notes editor of the *Yale Law Journal*. "He was more of a sports fan than a fan of any political agenda."[27]

Indeed, the student note that Kavanaugh wrote for the *Yale Law Journal* betrayed none of the conservatism that propelled him to the Supreme Court. On the contrary, Kavanaugh chose a surprising topic for a Federalist Society member: combating racial discrimination in jury selection. The Supreme Court had recently decided a case condemning racial discrimination in peremptory challenges, the tool given to prosecutors and defense lawyers to get rid of potential jurors without having to explain why. In practice, peremptory challenges often served as a way for prosecutors to keep African Americans from deciding cases involving black defendants, and the court in *Batson v. Kentucky* ruled that it violated the equal protection clause for prosecutors to behave this way. The question the case left open—and that Kavanaugh tackled in his note—was how, exactly, defendants would go about showing that prosecutors had been motivated by racial considerations.

Two of the court's most conservative members, Chief Justice Warren Burger and William Rehnquist, whom Kavanaugh later described as his judicial hero in law school, had dissented in the case. But Kavanaugh's note betrayed no disagreement with the ruling. Instead, he advocated for giving defendants extensive rights to prove that prosecutors had used their peremptory challenges in a manner motivated by improper racial considerations. Relying "solely on the good faith of prosecutors is misguided in light of the history of peremptory challenges," Kavanaugh cautioned. He even highlighted the need to root out instances of subtle or unknowing bias, "since arguably much racism and racial stereotyping is lodged in the subconscious and will stay there unless forced into the open."[28]

This was hardly the work of a budding movement conservative.

After graduation, Kavanaugh headed to a clerkship with Walter Stapleton, a federal appeals court judge for the Third Circuit, which covers Pennsylvania, New Jersey, and Delaware, where Stapleton was based. Any position working for an appeals court judge is prestigious, a useful line in a young lawyer's résumé. But in the rarefied milieu of Yale Law graduates, the Stapleton clerkship was nothing special. Stapleton was not one of the "feeder" judges whose clerks had a shot at working for a Supreme Court justice, the most sought-after position for ambitious law graduates; in fact, Kavanaugh was to be the only Stapleton clerk ever to move on to a high court clerkship. Nor was Stapleton, despite a solid Republican pedigree—he was named to the district court by President Richard Nixon in 1970 and elevated to the appeals court by President Ronald Reagan in 1985—considered especially ideological. He was not part of the new cadre of committed originalists whom Reagan had begun appointing to the federal bench, nominees who pledged to hew to the original meaning of the Constitution and avoid substituting their policy preferences for the intent of the framers.

As it happened, this was to be a particularly significant year in Stapleton's chambers, because a challenge to Pennsylvania's abortion law—a case widely seen as a potential death knell for the right to abortion—had arrived at the appeals court. Stapleton was assigned to the three-judge panel, along with Judge Collins Seitz and the court's newest member, a forty-one-year-old former federal prosecutor named Samuel Alito.

It was a pivotal—and, from the point of view of abortion-rights supporters, treacherous—moment for the right to choose. Just two years earlier, in *Webster v. Reproductive Health Services*, the justices had rejected the Bush administration's entreaty to use a Missouri abortion case to overrule *Roe v. Wade*. Yet the splintered nature of that decision and the court's newly enhanced conservative majority made clear that the right to abortion was hanging by a thread. "A chill wind blows," Harry Blackmun, the author of the majority opinion in *Roe*, had warned in his *Webster* dissent.[29] Anthony Kennedy had voted with the majority in that case, and in October 1990, a new justice, David Souter, had taken the place of the liberal William Brennan. *Roe* appeared ready to fall.

The Pennsylvania law that landed in Stapleton's chambers imposed informed-consent obligations on women seeking abortions, requiring them to hear information about the risks of and alternatives to abortion, the probable gestational age of the fetus, and the availability of prenatal care, then wait twenty-four hours to obtain the procedure. Married women had to inform their husbands that they were seeking abortions. The lower court that heard the case found the law unconstitutional in its entirety. The appeals court was just a way station. "Everybody knew it was going to go to the Supreme Court," Stapleton recalled.

He assigned the case to his star clerk, Kavanaugh. "Brett and I really sweated over that for long hours," Stapleton said.[30] It was a complicated situation because, in the most recent abortion rulings, no five justices had agreed on the proper standard of review for judging abortion laws. That presented a puzzle: what should an appeals court do when there was no longer a clear majority approach from the high court to guide it? One potential answer was that the justices had considered almost identical provisions in 1983 and 1986 and found them unconstitutional. Those decisions hadn't been overruled; therefore, their results were controlling.

Stapleton, joined in the majority by Seitz, took a different, more aggressive stance. His opinion said that where the law was in flux, the appeals court was obliged to tease out and apply the controlling legal standard. Automatically following a precedent that might have been overtaken by later cases, he said, was illogical.

Stapleton determined that the new, binding test for judging abortion restrictions had been laid out by Sandra Day O'Connor, the deciding vote in the most recent case. Under O'Connor's test, abortion would no longer be considered a "fundamental" constitutional right. As a consequence, laws governing abortion would no longer be reviewed under the toughest available standard, known as "strict scrutiny." Instead, abortion restrictions would be allowed as long as they did not impose an "undue burden" on a woman's access to abortion.

As a consequence, Stapleton wrote in the majority opinion, provisions such as Pennsylvania's twenty-four-hour waiting period, once unconstitutional, now passed constitutional muster. The wait, he wrote, "does not prevent any woman from having an abortion." And, even if forcing women to wait didn't make sense in every case, he added, that "does not render it irrational, especially given the serious and irreversible consequences of a hasty and ill-considered abortion decision."[31]

By contrast, Stapleton found, the state's requirement that a pregnant woman notify her husband of her decision to terminate the pregnancy went too far. Stapleton and Kavanaugh had consulted with the judge's sole female clerk that year, Yale Law graduate Frances Ruml Beckley, who told them that being forced by the state to tell her husband would make her feel like chattel, or property. Perhaps inspired by her view, the opinion offered a sensitive discussion of "the real-world consequences of forced notification." Stapleton outlined the various ways in which a husband opposed to his wife's abortion could interfere with her right, from physical violence to economic coercion.[32] Alito dissented from the majority's decision to strike down the spousal notice provision. He argued that the Pennsylvania legislature "could have reasonably" concluded that requiring women to inform their husbands would "properly further a husband's interests in the fetus in a sufficient percentage of the affected cases to justify enactment of this measure."[33]

Alito's position was far more extreme than that of the Stapleton majority. But abortion-rights advocates were nonetheless outraged by the majority's leap to declare that abortion was no longer a fundamental constitutional right and to anticipate the substitution of a more lenient standard for weighing abortion restrictions. "For the first time since 1973, a federal court of appeals has directly said that *Roe v. Wade* is no longer the law of the land," Kathryn Kolbert, the lawyer for the American Civil Liberties Union's Reproductive Freedom Project who argued the case for Planned Parenthood, said at the time.[34]

In the end, the Supreme Court, in *Planned Parenthood v. Casey*, agreed with the Stapleton majority and formally adopted the "undue burden" test that Stapleton said was the new governing standard. Still, it had been a leap for the appeals court to anticipate where the justices would end up. And the "undue burden" standard that the appeals court laid out was more accommodating to antiabortion laws—only those that imposed a "severe" or "drastic" impact would constitute an undue burden—than what the justices ultimately settled on when they decided the case.

Judges, not their law clerks, are responsible for their rulings. Still, had Kavanaugh's work on *Planned Parenthood v. Casey* been known at the time of his nomination, it would have provoked an interesting set of questions—not just from the left, about whether he was overly eager to curtail abortion rights, but potentially from the right as well. As with his abortion and contraceptive rulings years later as an appeals court judge, when he differed with an even more conservative colleague, Kavanaugh's involvement in a position to the left of Alito's might have raised alarm bells among social conservatives and deepened their preexisting jitters. But his role in that case was a subject that Kavanaugh deftly avoided as he made the rounds of senators in advance of his hearings.

As he was finishing up his clerkship with Stapleton, Kavanaugh received a phone call that changed the trajectory of his life—a call without which he would likely not be sitting on the Supreme Court today. At the other end of the line was Yale Law School professor

George Priest. Kavanaugh had been a student in Priest's insurance law class, but the professor knew him better from the Payne Whitney Gymnasium, where he had recruited Kavanaugh to play on his intramural basketball team. Now he was phoning with an unexpected offer. Alex Kozinski, a rising young conservative judge on the Ninth Circuit in California, had a sudden opening in his chambers. Might Kavanaugh be interested?

While still in law school, Kavanaugh had applied for the Kozinski clerkship and traveled to California for an interview. But Stapleton made him an offer before he heard back from Kozinski, and he had accepted immediately. Kozinski took no clerks from Yale that year.

Kozinski was then renowned for two things: demanding that his law clerks work punishing hours and helping them secure Supreme Court clerkships. "I'm looking for amazingly intelligent Supreme Court clerk wannabes eager to slave like dogs for an unreasonably demanding boss," Kozinski wrote in his clerkship job posting for 1990, the year Kavanaugh graduated from law school.[35] But putting up with Kozinski's excesses was viewed as a reasonable price to pay for a high court clerkship. He was regularly sending a few clerks every year on to the justices, mostly conservatives such as Scalia, O'Connor, and Kennedy, for whom Kozinski himself had served as one of the first clerks when Kennedy was a newly minted judge on the federal appeals court in California.

Alex Azar, a year behind Kavanaugh at Yale and later to become Donald Trump's secretary of health and human services, had pursued the Kozinski clerkship almost from the moment he arrived in New Haven. Now, with a Supreme Court clerkship for Scalia already in hand, Azar was leaving, a scant six weeks after arriving. This was an unusual development, and the precise circumstances of Azar's departure were a subject of both gossip and mystery in the elite, close-knit community. Azar told friends he was exasperated with Kozinski's unreasonable demands and quit; Kozinski, as Priest recalled, said he had fired Azar. Either way, he needed a replacement and looked to Priest, who had recommended Azar, to solve the problem. "It was a pretty good clerkship, but under the circumstances, it was difficult," Priest said. "There weren't a lot of candidates, to be honest with you."[36]

Kavanaugh came to mind, not so much for his legal expertise as his social skills. In his class, Kavanaugh "was a good student, not a great student," Priest recalled. "He wasn't very active . . . He didn't talk that much in class." Neither was Kavanaugh "a rabid conservative or a rabid Federalist Society member," said Priest, who served as faculty adviser to the group. "I didn't know he was a conservative, to tell you the truth." Azar was more of an academic star, Priest figured, but Kavanaugh could help soothe a bad situation. "This is obviously a chambers that was in some trouble. It's very unusual for a judge to fire a clerk, so I tried to think of somebody that was decent and smart and could kind of calm the turmoil."[37]

The previous summer, Kavanaugh had made it as far as an interview with Rehnquist but didn't receive an offer. Now, working for Kozinski presented another chance at the golden ticket of a Supreme Court clerkship. If that didn't happen, there was little harm, besides enduring a year of twenty-hour days. Afterward, Kavanaugh could always come home to Washington and start back up at Williams & Connolly, where he had worked the previous summer. But if Kozinski opened the door to a Supreme Court clerkship—well, that was a life changer.

In the world of law, a Supreme Court clerkship is a credential like no other. Of all the brilliant law students at all the top-tier law schools in the country, only thirty-six or so each year manage to secure that opportunity. Accurately or not, it marks them for life as something special. Top law firms pay eye-popping bonuses— today, they have climbed as high as $400,000, in addition to six-figure salaries—to lure high court clerks. And, increasingly, the ranks of the federal judiciary and the high court itself are populated with former Supreme Court clerks. Kavanaugh's ascension to the high court marked the first time that a majority of justices were themselves former clerks.

Kavanaugh's decision offered a glimpse of the drive that had been previously buried underneath the sports-talking, jump-shot-shooting bonhomie that had drawn Priest to him. This ambitious side of Kavanaugh wasn't always evident. "If you had asked him back then: 'You have the option of becoming a Supreme Court justice or having a six-year career in the NBA,' I think he would have picked the NBA," Rusty Sullivan, a fellow sportswriter at the *Yale Daily News*, would recall after Kavanaugh's nomination.[38]

Kavanaugh had been planning to start that fall at Williams & Connolly, a highly regarded Washington litigation firm. Founded by the legendary trial lawyer Edward Bennett Williams, who also owned the Washington Redskins and Baltimore Orioles, Williams & Connolly was a good fit for a sports-loving hometown Irish Catholic boy like Kavanaugh. An additional circuit court clerkship would be an unusual step. Kavanaugh told Priest he would think it over. He called back the next day to say yes.

The Kozinski clerkship opened doors, which opened additional doors. Instead of returning to Williams & Connolly, Kavanaugh secured a one-year fellowship in the office of the solicitor general at the Justice Department. The office, which makes the government's arguments before the Supreme Court, was headed at the time by a former federal appeals court judge named Kenneth Starr, a conservative luminary who seemed destined for the high court. Starr's principal deputy was a bright young conservative lawyer named John Roberts.

Next, courtesy of the Kozinski connection, came the clerkship with Kennedy, and with it the lifelong cachet of having been one of the elite of the legal elite. Kennedy took a particular shine to Kavanaugh, a pride that only swelled as Kavanaugh became one of the justice's greatest success stories. "This is where Brett sat," Kennedy would tell his clerks years after Kavanaugh had worked for him. "I think Kennedy looked at Brett and saw an idealized version of his own younger self," said one former Kennedy clerk. Some clerks maneuver to move their justices to their preferred ideological result; Kavanaugh was more inclined to be an honest channeler of the justice's own views. "Kennedy looked out and saw Brett as the one who was most about Kennedy," the clerk said. "Brett is very good at working for other people. He's good at serving bosses."

That Supreme Court term—October Term 1993, in Supreme Court parlance—was largely devoid of blockbuster cases; in fact, the court decided fewer cases than it did in any term since 1955. That was a welcome respite from previous years, which had seen the court riven by issues like the death penalty and abortion, including the *Planned Parenthood* case on which Kavanaugh had worked for Stapleton. The year marked Justice Ruth Bader Ginsburg's first term, but it also signaled the emergence of Kennedy, alongside O'Connor, as the court's swing vote. "Justice Kennedy occupied the gravitational center of the court," the *New York Times*'s Linda Greenhouse wrote in her end-of-term roundup. "He was never on the losing side in a 5–4 decision, and he dissented in only five of the term's 84 cases."[39]

There remained clear ideological divisions between the clerks— the liberals called the group of ultraconservative clerks the cabal— but Kavanaugh was notable for his ability to maintain friendships across those divides. "Out of the movement folks, Brett was by far the most normal," recalled one clerk for a liberal justice. "Out of all of them, Brett was the one who was the most able to socialize with people of different ideologies." Kavanaugh, said Stephen Smith, a Clarence Thomas clerk, "was by no means one of the conservative bomb throwers."[40]

Kennedy made it a point to hire clerks with an array of viewpoints, generally two liberals and two conservatives. But whereas Kennedy's other conservative clerk, Nate Forrester, was ideologically unyielding in a way that seemed to make Kennedy uneasy, Smith said, "Brett was always the guy who just had a way with Justice Kennedy, who could make the conservative arguments to him but do it in a way that he wouldn't recoil." Kavanaugh, he said, "could reach conservative results without upsetting the apple cart."

One of Kennedy's liberal-leaning clerks that year, Gary Feinerman, said that what was more memorable than Kavanaugh's ideology was his round-the-clock schedule. "We all worked ridiculous hours," Feinerman said. "His degree of ridiculousness was slightly higher than the rest of us."[41] Years later, with future clerks, Kennedy himself liked to reminisce about Kavanaugh's work ethic. "He would point to the chair where Justice Kavanaugh had been a clerk and would say, 'Well, Brett was always at his desk,'" one Kennedy clerk recalled the justice saying. "I'd come in in the morning and he'd be there and I'd leave at night and he'd be there, and I'd say, 'Brett, go home.' Then I'd come in the next morning and he'd be there again."

One decision that Kavanaugh worked on that year was an important securities law case, *Central Bank of Denver, N.A. v. First Interstate Bank of Denver, N.A.*, which highlighted the tension faced by courts between hewing to the precise language of the legislative text and avoiding upsetting existing practices and expectations. The court had previously ruled that federal securities law could be used by private parties to sue those responsible for fraud in the course of securities transactions, even though the statute didn't specifically provide for such lawsuits. For years, private plaintiffs had assumed—and the lower courts had agreed—that those who aided and abetted such fraud could also be sued. Indeed, the bank being sued in this case had not even contested that assumption.

But prompted by O'Connor, the justices decided on their own to raise that question.[42] The first, tentative votes in the case, following oral argument, suggested that the court would stick with the status quo and allow such suits to proceed.[43] A few months later, Kennedy switched his vote, joining the four other conservative justices to find that the law did not go that far.[44] "The issue," Kennedy wrote for a five-justice majority, "is not whether imposing private civil liability on aiders and abettors is good policy but whether aiding and abetting is covered by the statute."[45] Justice John Paul Stevens, dissenting, noted that all eleven appeals courts to have considered the issue had disagreed, along with the Securities and Exchange Commission. He and the other liberal justices criticized the majority for reaching out "to overturn a most considerable body of precedent" that had "become a part of the established system of private enforcement."[46]

Another Kavanaugh case, *Holder v. Hall*, involved the even more contentious issue of voting rights. The case came from a rural county in Georgia that had a 20 percent African American population and was governed by a single elected county commissioner, who had always been white. A group of black residents sued, claiming that the single-member commission violated the federal Voting Rights Act and that the county should be required to shift to a multimember commission in order to give African Americans a shot at representation. Internal memoranda show that the case was a mess, with the justices switching votes and the majority in doubt until almost the last moment.[47]

In the final days of the term, the conservative justices prevailed, and Rehnquist assigned Kennedy to recast what had been his dissent into the lead opinion for a fractured court, with five other concurrences and dissents.[48] Kennedy's bottom line was firm: the voting rights law could not be used to argue that the size of a government body violated the rights of minority voters by diluting their political power. "There is no principled reason why one size should be picked over another as the benchmark for comparison," Kennedy wrote.[49]

The liberal justices, in a dissenting opinion written by Harry Blackmun, noted that the most egregious forms of disenfranchisement, such as poll taxes and literacy tests, had been eliminated. "But subtler, more complex means of infringing minority voting strength—including submergence or dispersion of minority voters—are still present and indeed prevalent," Blackmun wrote. "We have recognized over the years that seemingly innocuous and even well-intentioned election practices may impede minority voters' ability not only to vote, but to have their votes count. It is clear that the practice of electing a single-member county commission can be one such dilutive practice."[50]

On the surface, the two cases, securities fraud and voting rights, seemed to have little to do with each other. But the approach in both was to consider a law that was intended to have a broad remedial purpose—protecting investors in one case, empowering minority voters in the other—and construe it narrowly. Judges need to stick close to the text of the laws they are interpreting. It isn't the court's business to right every wrong. These were Kennedy's opinions, but they also dovetailed with Kavanaugh's emerging, increasingly conservative worldview and would become a familiar theme for Kavanaugh in the years ahead.

CHAPTER SEVEN

Right Turn

The whole thing will take maybe six months, Ken Starr assured Kavanaugh over lunch at Cactus Cantina, a Mexican restaurant in northwest Washington, D.C.

Kavanaugh had just finished up his clerkship with Kennedy, and Starr, for whom he had worked at the solicitor general's office, was trying to lure the promising young lawyer to sign on with Kirkland & Ellis. The Chicago-based firm was building up its appellate and Supreme Court practice, not just with Starr but also with conservative hotshots of Kavanaugh's generation.

History intervened. Once again, the element of chance—this time, the unexpected selection of Starr to head an investigation into the Arkansas business dealings of Bill and Hillary Clinton—would alter Kavanaugh's career trajectory. Once again he seized the opportunity to further polish what was turning into a golden and distinctly right-leaning résumé. Kavanaugh's clerkships had helped develop and sharpen a legal conservatism that had lain rather dormant in law school. Now the Starr years served to awaken his political conservatism. If the embers of political partisanship had been smoldering in Kavanaugh, the Starr investigation was the bellows that seemed to make those instincts catch fire. Kavanaugh had chosen his team.

But far from the six-month stint of Starr's imagining, the probe overseen by the former solicitor general stretched past four years, wandered astray from the Whitewater real estate investment that was its original trigger, and resulted in the first impeachment of a president since Andrew Johnson in 1868. During the course of the probe, Kavanaugh developed a deep-seated and intense dislike of both Clintons, which would alarm his liberal friends at the time and emerge, to even greater alarm, at his confirmation hearings years later.

Starr was an accidental independent counsel. By January 1994, as Whitewater, the Clintons' failed Arkansas real estate development, became a political millstone for the year-old administration, the independent counsel law had lapsed. Attorney General Janet Reno instead turned to an internal Justice Department regulation that allowed her to appoint a special counsel, Robert Fiske, a highly regarded Republican former U.S. attorney, to conduct an investigation. When Congress reinstated the independent counsel law in July 1994, all expectations—consistent with Reno's recommendation— were that the three-judge court in charge of overseeing independent counsels would simply tap Fiske to remain in place. Instead, the next month, the panel—over the vociferous but privately stated objections of its lone Democrat—named Starr.[1]

The move was controversial: Starr was a more partisan figure than Fiske, and he lacked prosecutorial experience. Starr had been passed over by George H. W. Bush in 1990 for the Supreme Court vacancy created by William Brennan's retirement. Then solicitor general, he was vetoed by attorney general Richard Thornburgh and William Barr, then deputy attorney general, who considered him too squishy. Starr was "unacceptable," Thornburgh declared, and went so far as to threaten to resign if he were chosen.[2] (The spot went to David Souter, who turned out to be far more liberal.) Now, at forty-eight, Starr was still young enough to have another shot at the high court, if circumstances and another Republican president permitted. "I sensed that investigating Clinton, our youthful new president, was not likely to be a career-enhancing move," Starr wrote years later.[3]

For ambitious young conservative lawyers, however, the prospect of being part of such a high-profile investigation was too tempting to pass up. Alex Azar, the Kozinski clerk whose precipi-

tous departure had created a spot for Kavanaugh, signed on. So did
Rod Rosenstein, then a young Justice Department lawyer and later
to become deputy attorney general.

So did Kavanaugh. Within his social circle of many liberal
friends who counted themselves Clinton supporters, it was a surprising, somewhat jarring, move. Joining forces with Starr to investigate the president was stepping firmly into the role of "partisan
warrior," as one friend put it. For years, Kavanaugh had talked
about wanting to be a judge, like his mother. Friends worried he had
signed on to an enterprise that might build loyalty with a particular
conservative contingent but might taint him and interfere with his
judicial ambitions down the road. "It looked to me like a calculated
risk: 'I am going to place myself very firmly in one camp, and I'm
going to do the hard work of proving myself and doing the "right"
thing for that camp,'" one friend said of Kavanaugh's decision to
follow Starr to the independent counsel's office. "His calculation
came out right for him."

The picture of Kavanaugh that emerges from his years with
Starr—he was in the office for its first three years, left briefly to
join Kirkland & Ellis, and returned several months after the Monica Lewinsky allegations came to light—is one of a hardworking
young lawyer who was at times judicious and tempered and at other
times aggressive, helping to stretch the limits of the law in probing a president he viewed as corrupt, dishonest, and disgraceful.
Kavanaugh was not the most hard-charging of the bunch—Starr
had brought on board some particularly aggressive and partisan
prosecutors—but at key moments, on matters of how far to take the
investigation and whether to bring charges against peripheral players, he came down on the assertive side.

One example involved whether to pursue criminal contempt
charges against Susan McDougal, one of the Clintons' Whitewater
business partners. Starr's office considered McDougal's testimony
crucial to figuring out whether President Clinton had committed
perjury when he testified at the trial at which Susan and her former
husband James were convicted of fraud and conspiracy charges.

But Susan McDougal refused to cooperate, instead serving eighteen months in jail for civil contempt. When that sentence was completed, Starr's office faced the decision of whether to charge McDougal with criminal contempt as well. Some prosecutors said that would be too heavy-handed. Kavanaugh's position was that McDougal should not be let off the hook. Her refusal to testify before the grand jury risked allowing disrespect for the legal system to go unpunished.

"If she would agree to testify—even to prosecutors not now affiliated with our Office—then I would drop the case," Kavanaugh wrote in a December 1998 memo, as he was preparing to leave the office. "If she does not, then we have to go forward, however unpleasant it might be."[4] Unpleasant it was: the jury eventually deadlocked 7–5 in McDougal's favor on contempt charges while finding her not guilty on a related count of obstructing justice.[5]

At other, arguably more important moments, Kavanaugh counseled restraint. One example involves the handling of documents taken out of the office of deputy White House counsel Vincent Foster after his death and the issue of whether to seek criminal charges against Hillary Clinton's chief of staff, Maggie Williams, adviser Susan Thomases, and Clinton herself for obstructing justice or giving false testimony about the Foster documents. In a still-secret three-hundred-page memo, Kavanaugh recommended against prosecution; Starr's report concluded that, despite "circumstantial evidence" of efforts to tamper with the Foster documents, there was "simply insufficient evidence" to bring such charges.[6]

The Clintons' conduct, and that of some of their advisers, did not always inspire trust, to put it mildly. Words were parsed to the point of inviting perjury prosecutions. Lost billing records mysteriously resurfaced. So if Starr's prosecutors privately vented about the Clintons, that was understandable. But Kavanaugh did not keep such thoughts to himself or within the safe confines of the independent counsel's office. Instead, he was at times remarkably, and unprofessionally, indiscreet about his animus toward the Clintons. Colleen Covell, at the time a federal prosecutor in the District, was set up on a date with Kavanaugh by a mutual friend, his law school classmate Jeb Boasberg, during his stint with Starr. She was stunned by Kavanaugh's willingness to vent about the subjects of his investigation. "He was fanatical about the Clintons," she recalled. "He was kind of ranting and raving about 'how could you have voted for them' . . . The personal animosity was so apparent."[7]

Others who had known Kavanaugh longer were similarly surprised at what they saw as his transformation into a partisan who viewed the independent counsel's work as righteous and considered both Clintons liars. Speaking of the Clintons, Kavanaugh would raise his voice and sound genuinely angry, railing about their dishonesty. For some friends, the Kavanaugh of the Starr years offered an unsettling precursor to the Kavanaugh they saw at the close of his Supreme Court confirmation hearings, when he erupted over "a calculated and orchestrated political hit fueled with apparent pent-up anger," including anger about the 2016 election and "revenge on behalf of the Clintons."[8]

One of Starr's most significant early decisions—and Kavanaugh's initial assignment—involved the death of Foster, a close friend of the Clintons. A former law partner of Hillary Clinton's at the Rose Law Firm in Little Rock, Foster, forty-eight, was among the group of Arkansans who came with the Clintons to the White House. He almost immediately found himself embroiled in a series of controversies, including the failed nominations of Zoe Baird and Kimba Wood to be attorney general and the firing of seven employees of the White House Travel Office. The *Wall Street Journal* launched a series of blistering editorials focused on the otherwise obscure deputy counsel, the first one entitled "Who Is Vincent Foster?"

The last of the *Journal* editorials was published on July 19, 1993. The next day, six months into the new administration, Foster attended the president's Rose Garden announcement of Louis Freeh's appointment as FBI director. Foster asked an assistant, Linda Tripp—the same Linda Tripp who would later alert Starr's office to Clinton's dalliance with Lewinsky—to get him lunch from the White House mess. Then, around 1:00 p.m., Foster stopped by the desks of Tripp and another assistant to announce he was leaving. "I'll be back," he said.

Five hours later, U.S. Park Police found Foster's body in Fort Marcy Park, in McLean, Virginia, a gunshot wound through the back of his head and a .38 caliber revolver in his right hand, which contained gunshot residue.

From the start, it appeared highly likely—indeed, a near certainty—that Foster had killed himself. He had confided to friends that he was considering resigning but could not tolerate the "humiliation" of having been driven from the White House. Foster told his sister four days before his death that he was depressed; the day before he died, he called a family doctor, seeking antidepressant medication. After his death, a torn-up paper was found in the bottom of a briefcase in his West Wing office. In it, Foster defended his handling of the travel office matter and lamented that "the WSJ editors lie without consequence," concluding: "I was not meant for the job or the spotlight of public life in Washington. Here ruining people is considered sport."[9]

From the start, too, conservative conspiracy theorists conjured dark suggestions that Foster had been murdered. The bullet was never found; skull fragments were missing; carpet fibers of unknown origin were found on Foster. Foster's body had been moved, the theorists insisted. Foster was the keeper of the Clintons' secrets about Whitewater: perhaps, they speculated, the Clintons had him murdered. Chief among the conspiracists was Christopher Ruddy, who alleged that the Park Police falsified reports and staged a cover-up of the actual crime scene. Years later, the Foster conspiracy theories made their way into the 2016 presidential campaign, when then candidate Trump, a longtime Ruddy friend, told the *Washington Post* that Foster's death was "very fishy," adding, "I will say there are people who continue to bring it up because they think it was absolutely a murder."[10]

Ruddy's theorizing notwithstanding, the weight of the evidence was strongly against him. The Park Police concluded that "the condition of the scene, the medical examiner's findings and the information gathered clearly indicate that Mr. Foster committed suicide."[11] Two congressional investigations ended with the same result. In August 1994, shortly after Starr's appointment, a report by Representative William Clinger, the ranking Republican on the House Government Operations Committee, found that "all available facts lead to the undeniable conclusion" that Foster committed suicide. A bipartisan report issued by the Senate Banking Committee in January 1995 agreed.

Most pertinent was special counsel Fiske's conclusion in June 1994. The investigation, directed by Roderick Lankler, a veteran homicide prosecutor in the Manhattan district attorney's office, featured 125 interviews, including with Foster's colleagues, friends, and family members, and employed a four-member panel of experienced pathologists, who concluded that the gunshot wound was self-inflicted and occurred in Fort Marcy Park. Fiske's fifty-eight-page report found that "the overwhelming weight of the evidence compels the conclusion" that Foster committed suicide and that there was "no evidence" that the Whitewater investigation or "other personal legal matters" involving the Clintons factored into Foster's suicide.[12]

Nevertheless, Starr decided that he was duty bound to start again, from scratch. "Unfortunately, Fiske's report was dismissed in various quarters as unconvincing at best and a whitewash at worst, raising more questions than it answered," he wrote in his memoir. Starr had learned about the dangers of rushing a report that failed to convincingly debunk conspiracy theories from a friend who had served as counsel to the Warren Commission, which investigated the Kennedy assassination. "I decided the investigation into Foster's death would begin anew," he wrote. "I was stepping into Fiske's shoes, but I would not simply retrace his path."[13] That was Starr's call to make as independent counsel, although, as Trump's "something fishy" comment illustrates, nothing was ever going to satisfy the most die-hard Foster conspiracy theorists. In pursuing the Foster investigation, Kavanaugh was following Starr's orders. But there is no evidence that Kavanaugh disagreed with Starr's second-look approach, and there is ample indication that he carried out the assignment with maximum aggressiveness. Combined with Kavanaugh's prosecutorial inexperience—Yale Law School and Supreme Court clerkships offer little instruction in how to handle a homicide probe—that willingness to investigate to the maximum extent possible helped stretch out the length of an investigation that had already taken an emotional toll on Foster's grieving family.

In a March 1995 memo to Starr, Kavanaugh noted that the White House had "informally questioned our jurisdiction" to investigate Foster's death, which he described as an effort to determine "whether he was murdered in violation of federal criminal law." (The body had been found on federal property.) Kavanaugh acknowledged that the grant of authority for Starr's probe did not specifically mention Foster's death. Nonetheless, he noted, the independent counsel had power to investigate any potential federal crime "relating in any way" to Whitewater or Madison Guaranty Savings and Loan, the thrift owned by the Clintons' Whitewater investment partner, James McDougal, or "connected with or arising out of that investigation."

In the Foster case, Kavanaugh observed, "we have received allegations that Mr. Foster's death related to President and Mrs. Clinton's involvement with Madison [and] Whitewater"—either that Foster "was murdered because of the President or Mrs. Clinton's involvement with those entities" or that Foster committed suicide "because of his involvement in or awareness of potential violations of federal law in connection with President or Mrs. Clinton's involvement with those entities." In conclusion, Kavanaugh said, "We have a very strong argument that, in order to investigate these allegations in a thorough manner, it is necessary for us to conduct a full-fledged investigation of Mr. Foster's death."[14]

Kavanaugh made no mention of the fact that Fiske had found zero evidence that Foster was murdered—indeed, Fiske had found no evidence that Foster's apparent suicide had anything to do with Whitewater or Madison Guaranty. Another memo, from March 1995, underscores Kavanaugh's aggressiveness: "We should discuss whether to issue subpoenas to Foster's mother, Lisa Foster [his wife], Foster's siblings, and Foster's friends for documents that might shed light on Foster's state of mind or their perceptions of Foster's state of mind (e.g., letters from Foster, letters to each other before or after Foster's death, notes, personal diaries, etc.)," he wrote. "I would be uneasy issuing such subpoenas, but I would be more uneasy making definitive conclusions about Foster's state of mind without reviewing these relevant documents."[15] Among the steps that Kavanaugh recommended were having the Internal Revenue Service conduct a "full financial analysis" of Foster, "track[ing] down all of Foster's foreign travel" and investigating "an alleged Swiss bank account that was in Foster's name." No Swiss bank account was ever found.

All this came at a stage when Kavanaugh himself had already concluded, according to a memo in the files, that "Foster was sufficiently discouraged or depressed to commit suicide."[16] A month later, an FBI agent assigned to the investigation, Chuck Regini, advised Kavanaugh that, "In my personal opinion, we have established beyond a reasonable doubt that the death was caused by a self-inflicted gunshot wound at Ft. Marcy Park by the weapon that was found in [Foster's] hand."[17]

Still, Kavanaugh persisted, at times with Javert-like intensity. "Let there, then, be no mistake about our intentions: We do not plan to halt this investigation until we are confident that we have obtained the full story about Mr. Foster's thoughts, words and activities in the days and weeks preceding his death," Kavanaugh wrote in a December 1995 draft of a letter to be sent to Foster's lawyer, James Hamilton. "We are fully prepared to deal with any criticism by you or others that may be directed at our Office for the time and effort spent in pursuing that goal, so any veiled threats in that vein do not affect us."[18] The missive was toned down by Kavanaugh's supervisor, John Bates.

When Hamilton advised the office that he would allow access to Foster's personal diary, but only by Starr himself, Kavanaugh bristled at what he considered an insult. "An implicit attack on my integrity and credibility," Kavanaugh wrote in an October 21, 1995 memo.[19] It was an early glimpse of an episodic truculence that contrasted with Kavanaugh's ordinarily genial demeanor but that surfaced at various points throughout his career.

Handed the Foster assignment, Kavanaugh pursued every available angle. He obtained carpet fiber samples to rebut suggestions that Foster's body had been wrapped in a carpet and moved from a different location (the fibers were consistent with samples from Foster's home) and, at one point, even pressed for obtaining a hair sample from Foster's daughter to see if it matched two blond hairs found on Foster's clothing. Likewise, Kavanaugh did not shy away from investigating some of the most salacious allegations about Foster. "I note that we have asked numerous people about Foster's alleged affair with Mrs. Clinton, but have received no confirmation of it," Kavanaugh wrote to Starr and other lawyers in June 1995. "If we want to pursue this line of investigation further, however, we should ask Mrs. Clinton about the alleged affair at her next interview."[20] In the end, Clinton was not questioned on the subject.

Fiske's probe took less than six months. Starr's "second look" consumed three years, part of that because one of the other prosecutors in the office had become obsessed with the notion that Foster had been murdered and needed to be assuaged. On October 10, 1997, more than four years after Foster's death, the independent counsel released its conclusion: "[B]ased on all of the available evidence, which is considerable, the OIC agrees with the conclusion reached by every official entity that has examined the issue: Mr. Foster committed suicide by gunshot in Fort Marcy Park."[21]

With the Foster investigation finished, Kavanaugh finally headed to Kirkland & Ellis—only to be lured back less than a year later, after the Lewinsky story broke. During that interim period, even

Kavanaugh questioned whether the Lewinsky matter might be better resolved by Congress, which had shown little inclination to deal with it. "From the country's perspective, it is absurd that Congress is doing nothing," Kavanaugh told the author in a story for the *Washington Post*. "The way to avoid a long, drawn-out process is for Congress to gather the relevant evidence, hold a hearing and ask [Clinton friend Vernon] Jordan, Ms. Lewinsky and the president to provide testimony. Then Congress and the people can determine directly and quickly what the facts are and whether any sanction should be imposed against the president, which are clearly the most important questions for the country."[22]

For Kavanaugh, returning to Starr's office held two attractions— not just being part of the Lewinsky investigation but also the chance to argue his first, and what turned out to be his only, case before the Supreme Court. The case involved the independent counsel's effort to gain access, as part of its investigation into the travel office firings, to confidential notes taken by Foster lawyer James Hamilton, shortly before Foster's death.

The case, which Kavanaugh had argued and won before the federal appeals court that he later joined, represented another example of the aggressive stance of the independent counsel's office. The Starr team's argument was that attorney-client privilege, a lawyer's duty to protect a client's secrets, could be breached after the client's death. The American Bar Association and other legal groups filed friend-of-the-court briefs opposing Starr's position, and the justices, dividing 6–3, ruled against the independent counsel. "It has been generally, if not universally, accepted, for well over a century, that the attorney-client privilege survives the death of the client in a case such as this," Rehnquist wrote for the majority.[23]

But it was the Lewinsky investigation that especially revealed Kavanaugh's willingness to push the limits in pursuing the president— this president, anyway. Some lawyers inside Starr's office advocated for a degree of delicacy in questioning the sitting president about his sexual activities. Not Kavanaugh. In a memorandum to fellow prosecutors entitled "Slack for the President?," Kavanaugh

endorsed a no-holds-barred approach. "After reflecting this evening, I am strongly opposed to giving the President any 'break' in
the questioning regarding the details of the Lewinsky relationship—
unless before his questioning on Monday, he either (i) resigns or
(ii) confesses perjury and issues a public apology to you," he wrote
to Starr and other office attorneys on August 15, 1998, two days
before Clinton was to be questioned at the White House. "I have
tried hard to bend over backwards and to be fair to him and to think
of all reasonable defenses to his pattern of behavior. In the end, I
am convinced that there really are none. The idea of going easy on
him at the questioning is thus abhorrent to me."[24]

The memo throbbed throughout with a sense of Kavanaugh's
moral indignation at Clinton's conduct. "The President has dis-
graced his Office, the legal system, and the American people by
having sex with a 22-year-old intern and turning her life into a
shambles—callous and disgusting behavior that has somehow gotten lost in the shuffle." Clinton, he said, "has lied to his aides. He
has lied to the American people. He has tried to disgrace you and
this Office with a sustained propaganda campaign that would make
Nixon blush."[25]

Clinton's grand jury testimony, Kavanaugh argued, offered the
opportunity to expose all that. "It may not be our job to impose
sanctions on him, but it is our job to make his pattern of revolt-
ing behavior clear—piece by painful piece," he wrote. Yes, Kavanaugh said, he was "mindful of the need" to respect the office. But
the interests of the office, and the country, "would be best served
by our gathering the full facts regarding the actions of this President so that the Congress can decide whether the interests of the
Presidency would be best served by having a new President." Consequently, Kavanaugh proposed a series of uncomfortably explicit
questions. "If Monica Lewinsky says that you inserted a cigar into
her vagina while you were in the Oval Office area, would she be
lying?" "If Monica Lewinsky says that on several occasions in the
Oval Office area, you used your fingers to stimulate her vagina and
bring her to orgasm, would she be lying?" "If Monica Lewinsky

says that on several occasions you had her give . . . oral sex, made her stop, and then ejaculated into the sink in the bathroom off the Oval Office, would she be lying?"[26]

Bob Bittman, a more senior prosecutor in the office who pushed for less explicit questioning, recalled that Kavanaugh, by the next morning, had expressed regrets about his strident tone. "That memo was a complete aberration . . . completely atypical of Brett," Bittman said. "He was always a moderating voice and influence in the office on issue after issue. So it was very unusual for it to have come from him . . . I made of it what he said, that he was up late and that was a weak moment."[27]

But the memo was consistent with the way Kavanaugh spoke about the Clintons in private. And if he regretted the tone, Kavanaugh clearly remained on the side of those who believed that Clinton needed to be confronted with the distasteful specifics of his sexual encounters with Lewinsky. When the prosecutors returned from the White House after the questioning was concluded, Kavanaugh gave prosecutor Sol Wisenberg a pat on the back and congratulated him for asking the "sex questions."[28]

Still, as Bittman and others noted, there were other times when Kavanaugh was among those who counseled restraint. He was particularly adept at seeing around corners in ways that served to protect Starr's reputation. As Starr prepared to send his impeachment referral to Congress, one question was how explicitly to treat the lurid details of Clinton's behavior with Lewinsky. This time, Kavanaugh found himself on the opposite side of his position on the Clinton questioning, arguing for discretion. The lengthy narrative that prosecutors had been writing, he contended, wasn't necessary. As Susan Schmidt and Michael Weisskopf described it in their book on the investigation, "Kavanaugh contended that the narrative gave the impression that this was a sex tale, not a serious legal matter." Kavanaugh and another lawyer in the office, Bill Kelley, "urged Starr to scrap it, subordinate it to the grounds section of the referral, or put it in an appendix." The ordinarily prissy Starr disagreed. The narrative remained.[29]

Then, in September 1998, with the report transmitted to Congress and poised for release before any of the lawmakers had read the document and therefore recognized its salacious nature, Kavanaugh, joined by Bittman and another prosecutor, Jackie Bennett, urged Starr to warn Congress that the contents of the referral he had just sent them were, as Schmidt and Weisskopf wrote, "highly sensitive and might never be suitable for public dissemination."[30] Kavanaugh drafted a letter from Starr—"an emergency warning letter," Kavanaugh later said—expanding on the independent counsel's note to House leaders in his initial referral to Congress, which had merely cautioned that it contained "information of a personal nature."[31]

Starr demurred. It wasn't his job to tell Congress what to do. Characteristically, Kavanaugh later defended his former boss against criticism of the way the unsavory details of Clinton's conduct had spilled into public view. "I recall no one thinking or saying . . . that Congress was likely to simply dump the whole thing into the public domain without even reviewing it beforehand," he wrote to present and former lawyers in the office in February 1999. "For these reasons, I believe we should *never* express any regret over the contents of the [impeachment] referral itself," only "regret over how Congress handled the referral."[32]

In October 1998, the month after Congress received the impeachment referral, Kavanaugh argued that the Starr probe, by then more than four years old, needed to be brought to a close. "In my view," he wrote, "we cannot responsibly enter 1999 without fishing or cutting bait on most matters within our jurisdiction."[33] Preparing to leave the independent counsel's office, he wrote a Christmas Eve 1998 memo that touched again on this point. "At some point, this Office has to close," Kavanaugh wrote. "There needs to be a plan for how to get from here to there." Significantly, although Starr's outside adviser, Ronald Rotunda, had told Starr that Clinton could be indicted while in office, Kavanaugh was unwilling to push that constitutional envelope. Instead he urged that the decision be left to the next administration.[34] (In the end, the matter was settled in the final moments of the Clinton presidency by Starr's successor,

Robert Ray, with Clinton agreeing to accept a five-year suspension of his law license, pay a fine, and acknowledge that he had committed a breach of conduct.)[35]

For Kavanaugh, as much as he believed that Clinton had abused the powers of his office to conceal his affair with an intern, there were also moments of doubt about the enterprise. In his book on the Starr investigation, Michael Isikoff wrote about a conversation he had with Kavanaugh in September 1998, after the probe was finished, in which Kavanaugh described the way, in Isikoff's words, "the tawdriness of the case ate at him." As Kavanaugh said, "Sometimes I wake up in the middle of the night and wonder to myself, what am I doing? There are a lot of mixed emotions about this."[36]

CHAPTER EIGHT

White House Years

Brett Kavanaugh's road to the White House began in Volusia County, in east-central Florida, in the chaotic aftermath of the 2000 election. A minuscule 537 votes in Florida, out of nearly six million cast in the state, separated Al Gore and George W. Bush. The recount that ensued would not only decide the state's twenty-five electoral votes, it would also determine the presidency. Republican lawyers, hungry to regain the White House, raced to Florida to help count ballots and examine chads. Kavanaugh, who had been regional coordinator for Lawyers for Bush Cheney 2000 during the campaign, was deployed to Democratic-leaning Volusia, which would end up conducting a hand recount of all 184,019 ballots.

There, Kavanaugh met a Texas lawyer named Stuart Bowen, who had worked for Bush's future White House counsel, Alberto Gonzales, in the Texas governor's office. After the whirlwind thirty-six-day postelection battle, after a bitterly divided Supreme Court settled the outcome late one December night, Bowen was helping Gonzales staff up the counsel's office. When he received Kavanaugh's résumé from a mutual friend, the fit was obvious. Hiring Kavanaugh was "sort of a no-brainer," Gonzales recalled. "I interviewed Brett and offered him a job."[1]

After eight years out of power, Kavanaugh and the other Republican lawyers of his generation were eager to sign on with the new administration. "There was pent-up demand among young Republican lawyers waiting for a Republican president," Gonzales said.[2]

One of Kavanaugh's particular selling points, in Gonzales's estimation, was his experience with Starr. He figured that Kavanaugh,
having investigated one president, could be helpful in making certain that the new one would not find himself in similarly perilous
circumstances.

The next five years charted the course for Kavanaugh's future,
personal and professional. It was at the Bush White House
that Kavanaugh met Ashley Estes, a pretty young woman from
Abilene who was the president's personal secretary. It was at the
Bush White House that Kavanaugh learned the intricacies of governing, policy making and legislative strategizing, cutting brush
with Bush on his Crawford ranch and traveling the world with the
president as his staff secretary. It was at the Bush White House
that Kavanaugh, once willing to relentlessly investigate if not
indict a sitting president, began to moderate his position, coming
to appreciate, especially in the aftermath of 9/11, the overwhelming demands of the office and the imperative of protecting presidential authority.

Perhaps most important, it was at the Bush White House that
Kavanaugh witnessed the judicial nominating process up close and
learned what it took to become a federal judge—competing for the
slot, marshaling advocates in support, coaxing key senators. He
worked closely with—and learned the influence and importance
of—Leonard Leo, the Federalist Society official who would play
an even more prominent role for the next Republican president.
Kavanaugh first applied those lessons to help select and confirm
other judges; he then deployed that skill set on his own behalf as
he was tapped for the judgeship that he had long wanted—not just
any judgeship but a coveted slot on the D.C. Circuit, considered
the second most important court in the country. It took three years,
two hearings, and, not for the last time, a personal assist from Bush
himself for Kavanaugh finally to be confirmed to the appeals court.
A dozen years later, he would be selected by a very different president for an even more important court, this time despite Bush rather
than because of him. But it was his years in the Bush White House

that firmly put Brett Kavanaugh on the path to becoming Justice Kavanaugh.

Kavanaugh's portfolio in the counsel's office ran the gamut from the mundane nuts and bolts of how to safely navigate the ethical lines between government and politics—could political counselor Karl Rove use a corporate jet to get to a political event?—to more elevated issues such as the scope of religious liberty, the future of affirmative action, and, in the wake of September 11, the varying legal ramifications of the war on terror. September 11 was a searing day for everyone in the relatively new White House, but for Kavanaugh, September 10 was equally if not more life-altering: it was the day of his first date with the twenty-six-year-old Estes— dinner at the Cafe Deluxe restaurant in northwest D.C. Several weeks later, on October 6, 2001, Kavanaugh would take Estes— along with a rowdy bunch of his high school friends, as he ruefully remembered at their rehearsal dinner three years later—to watch Cal Ripken play his final Orioles game. After studying journalism at the University of Texas, Estes had worked for Bush as governor and during the presidential campaign and followed him from Austin to Washington.

Kavanaugh, by then thirty-six, had dated a series of women, mostly lawyers, both liberal and conservative. During his clerkship years, he was serious about Tracy Thomas, a fellow clerk at the Ninth Circuit, in California, a liberal who went on to teach the feminist foundations of family law at the University of Akron School of Law. When he served on Starr's staff, Kavanaugh was involved with Dabney Friedrich, who later worked with him in the counsel's office and was named to the district court in D.C. by President Trump. Estes and Kavanaugh seemed an unexpected match to some of those who watched the romance blossom at the White House. "I kind of watched it happen as it was happening, and I was surprised because Ashley was so Texas, Texas, Texas," recalled White House chief of staff Andrew Card. "She kept longing to go

back to Texas. I was surprised she was paying attention to somebody who was Washington, D.C."[3]

Kavanaugh alluded to those Texas ties during his swearing-in
to the appeals court in 2006. "Ashley," he said, "likes to remind
me that true love is a Texas girl who is willing to marry a guy with
a lifetime appointment in Washington, D.C."[4] Kavanaugh's connection to Estes took his own relationship with the president to a
different level. "She was kind of like family to George W. Bush,"
Card said, "and when she and Brett discovered each other's love
it brought him into a little tighter circle."[5] Bush, who loved knowing gossip about his staff, encouraged the budding relationship.
"I think Bush really pushed it," said one friend. "He [Kavanaugh]
wanted to please him." The Bushes doted on Estes as if she were
a surrogate daughter. After the couple's engagement, the president and First Lady hosted a seated dinner for them in the Rose
Garden, and attended their wedding ceremony at Christ Church in
Georgetown.

In the counsel's office, Kavanaugh helped craft an executive order
restricting release of presidential papers under the Presidential
Records Act, the law that would govern the release of his own
records when he was nominated to the Supreme Court years later.
After 9/11, he worked on issues of airline liability, victim compensation, and terrorism insurance. For the most part, he did not
become involved in the most contentious legal issues at the heart of
the new war on terror, such as warrantless wiretapping, torture, and
detention of enemy combatants. Still, when the administration was
debating whether citizens could be declared enemy combatants and
held without access to counsel, Kavanaugh advised colleagues that
Justice Kennedy would never accept that argument.[6] His assessment was reported by the *Washington Post* in 2007, sparking a
request from Senate Democrats that the Justice Department investigate whether Kavanaugh had testified truthfully at his confirmation
hearings for the circuit court when he said he was "not involved" in

"questions about the rules governing detention of combatants." But Justice said it had "reviewed this matter and determined there was not sufficient basis to initiate a criminal investigation."[7]

One of the most intense disputes of Kavanaugh's time in the counsel's office involved affirmative action—specifically, what position the Bush administration should take in a pair of cases pending at the Supreme Court in 2003, one involving undergraduate admissions at the University of Michigan, the other at Michigan's law school. E-mails from earlier in the administration depict Kavanaugh as hostile to affirmative action. In a March 2001 exchange with Courtney Elwood, another lawyer in the counsel's office, Kavanaugh bristled at her suggestion that a potential nominee's Jewish background might be a "plus factor" among equally qualified candidates. He derided "this entirely disgusting bean-counting process," adding that taking religion into account was "too dangerous in practice and too un-American in principle for me."[8] In August 2001, assessing the constitutionality of a Transportation Department program to favor minority enterprises, Kavanaugh observed, "The fundamental problem in this case is that these regulations use a lot of legalisms and disguises to mask what in reality is a naked racial set-aside."[9]

As the Bush administration weighed how to deal with the Michigan cases, Kavanaugh was tasked with a delicate middleman role in which his responsibility to adhere to the wishes of the chief executive seemed to clash with his own inclinations. The fundamental question was whether ensuring racial diversity on campus could justify taking race into account in admissions, as Justice Powell had suggested in his concurring opinion in the 1978 case *Regents of the University of California v. Bakke*. As Gonzales later related in his memoir, conservative groups were eager to seize the moment "to eliminate affirmative action once and for all, to strike down Powell's opinion in *Bakke*, and to prohibit any future consideration of race in university admissions decisions."[10] Attorney general John Ashcroft and solicitor general Ted Olson wanted to state flatly that racial diversity was not a compelling government interest.

Bush balked at being so explicit. "I don't want to be known as the president who did away with affirmative action," he told Gonzales.[11] Meanwhile, Olson was threatening not to sign the government's brief—a major statement from the government's top lawyer at the high court. The president wanted to duck the fundamental question of whether race could be considered but say that the Michigan programs failed to pass constitutional muster because the university had neglected to try race-neutral approaches first.

Gonzales tapped Kavanaugh to try to work things out with Olson's top deputy, Paul Clement, with whom he had clerked on the Supreme Court. It did not go well—to the extent that Vice President Dick Cheney, who had aligned himself with the Justice Department's more conservative position, called Gonzales at one point, inquiring, "Do you have a Brett Kavanaugh working for you?" Why, Cheney wanted to know, was a White House lawyer interfering with the normally independent work of the solicitor general?[12] It was an odd position for Kavanaugh. Not only did his e-mail musings suggest his own opposition to race-conscious affirmative action programs, in private practice he had also taken on, as a pro bono project, a challenge to a Hawaii law that allowed only those of native Hawaiian ancestry to vote for trustees of an agency that distributed benefits to the natives' descendants. In a friend-of-the-court brief filed at the Supreme Court with none other than Robert Bork, Kavanaugh had attacked the program as "infused with explicit racial quotas, exclusions and classifications," and he wrote a *Wall Street Journal* op-ed decrying what he termed the state's "naked racial-spoils system."[13] The evidence suggested strongly that Kavanaugh, left to his own devices, would have been more comfortable with the hard-line anti–affirmative action position that the Justice Department was advocating. But he had a job to do and a president to represent.

The e-mail records from Kavanaugh's White House days are both informative and incomplete. Much of the most interesting back-

and-forth remains shielded from public view. Nonetheless, snippets emerge to give a glimpse of Kavanaugh's personality and legal views.

In September 2001, as Gonzales's assistant set a daily morning staff meeting for 8:15, Kavanaugh tried to head off the eager beavers in the office who kept showing up early. "Given the new real-time rule, can we agree not to have a race to the door at 8:05 or so?" he wrote. "Not to micro-manage, but at this point, there is surely no need for anyone to get there 10 minutes early to demonstrate their commitment to punctuality, which simply encourages a few others to do the same, which simply moves the meetings back earlier and earlier because the Judge invites everyone in when a critical mass gathers rather than waiting until the appointed time to call people in. So I would say that we ALL try to arrive no earlier than 8:10 and no later than 8:14. Any disagreements?"[14]

Other e-mails reveal Kavanaugh's sarcastic brand of humor. When a *National Journal* reporter was trying to fact-check the résumés of the lawyers in the counsel's office, Kavanaugh e-mailed colleagues: "Yes, I also just confirmed the basics for her—that I clerked for [liberal judges] Harry Edwards and John Stevens and have worked at Public Defender Service for the last 9 years."[15] As office lawyers debated the relative merits of two poems, "Invictus" and "My Captain," Kavanaugh weighed in: "As my esteemed former colleague Jackie Bennett would say (and did say) when caught in a conversation like this, 'Anyone seen Caddyshack lately?'"[16] One 2002 e-mail featured a photograph of Kavanaugh shaking hands with Chuck Schumer staffer Jeff Berman at an American Bar Association event. "A proud moment, you ABA gladhander, you," teased fellow counsel Brad Berenson. "[W]as trying to break his hand," Kavanaugh replied.[17]

Kavanaugh was simultaneously inclined to reach across the ideological divide and to take umbrage at what he considered mistreatment by colleagues. In June 2001, Kavanaugh encouraged a reluctant colleague to "show the Bush flag" at a Yale Law School dinner, observing, "I generally think it is good when working in a high-profile office like this to socially engage (rather than avoid) the critics. In this instance, I tend to think it's good for the libs to know that 2 normal people (or at least one normal person, you) work here in this office for the President."[18]

Several months later, in November 2001, he angrily e-mailed Gonzales and deputy counsel Tim Flanigan about David Addington, Cheney's lawyer, who had criticized Kavanaugh over the proposed wording of the executive order on presidential records. Addington "was grossly out of line and unprofessional in his comments to me at staff meeting this morning," Kavanaugh wrote his superiors. "I neither deserve nor appreciate that kind of crap in a staff meeting. No need to respond to this; just did not want to let that incident pass unstated."[19] Letting an insult pass unstated was not the Kavanaugh way.

Some of the e-mails touched on Justice Kennedy, his former boss, sometimes admiringly, sometimes less so. "Way to go, Justice Kennedy," Kavanaugh wrote in an officewide e-mail on March 30, 2001.[20] That day, newspapers reported that Kennedy, in testimony before Congress, defended the court's intervention in *Bush v. Gore*, saying the case posed "constitutional issues of the gravest importance" that the court had a "responsibility" to resolve.[21]

Other times, he seemed more bemused by Kennedy and his florid prose. In February 2001, when Kennedy issued a typically loftily worded concurrence in a disability rights case, Kavanaugh e-mailed the office: "All of you AMK fans will want to read his concurrence today." "Uh-oh," responded Berenson, another former Kennedy clerk. "What did he say? Are you referring to the classic AMK rhetoric on the first page about the law as a teacher?" Kavanaugh replied, "Yes, the whole concurrence is a classic, esp the reference to law as a teacher."[22]

The following year, Bowen e-mailed Kavanaugh an excerpt from a Kennedy ruling in a child pornography case concerning the constitutionality of a law that barred the use of sexually explicit images that appear to depict minors but are produced without using real children. "The right to think is the beginning of freedom, and speech must be protected from the government because speech is the beginning of thought," Kennedy wrote for the majority in striking down the law as a violation of the First Amendment.[23] "No doubt a line straight out of the former boss' word processor," Kavanaugh observed. Bowen: "So actually word processing is the beginning of thought . . ." Kavanaugh: "In this case, I fear . . ."[24]

Kavanaugh could also be an astute observer of Supreme Court politicking. In March 2002, one lawyer in the counsel's office circulated a link to opinions by Michael Luttig and J. Harvie Wilkinson, two judges on the Fourth Circuit federal appeals court based in Richmond, who were viewed as leading contenders, and rivals, for a high court vacancy. The case involved the then cutting-edge issue of criminal defendants' rights to DNA testing. A three-judge panel had rejected a convicted rapist's request for testing, and the full Fourth Circuit declined to review that decision. But Luttig seized the moment to write a lengthy opinion that, in the first such ruling by a federal appeals court judge, found that the inmate had a constitutional right to examine the DNA evidence. Wilkinson responded by agreeing that the inmate should have access to the DNA material but chided Luttig—"my good colleague"—for jumping in ahead of state courts.[25] "Are these guys running or what," Kavanaugh observed.[26] Some of his own appeals court colleagues would wonder the same about him, not many years later.

Of interest in light of the role it played in his own Supreme Court nomination is that one recurring theme in the e-mails involves the Federalist Society; one recurring correspondent is Leonard Leo. Early on, as reporters were starting to focus on the influence of the Federalist Society in the new administration, Kavanaugh recommended aggressive pushback: "While you cannot possibly respond to every false statement in the press reports, you may want to (or at least have the press office do so) point out obvious whoppers," he advised Gonzales. For example, he said, "this may seem technical, but most of us resigned from the Federalist Society before starting work here and are not now members of the Society." Berenson, his colleague, advocated restraint. "I think it's far better to simply give that 'accusation' a shrug of the shoulders," he recommended. "I don't think we should cede ground to the left by appearing to be at all embarrassed or concerned about it." Kavanaugh pushed back. "True, but the stories are still factually inaccurate . . . The reason I (and others) resigned from Fed Society was precisely because I did not want anyone to be able to say that I had an ongoing relationship with any group that has a strong interest in the work of this Office."[27]

The e-mails suggest precisely such an ongoing relationship, with Kavanaugh solicitous of the Federalist Society in general and of Leo in particular. In November 2002, Kavanaugh arranged a meeting for "some leading members of Fed Society" with senior White House officials, including Gonzales. "I think it would be great if Karl also popped in for a few minutes," Kavanaugh wrote, referring to senior adviser Karl Rove. "Leonard tells me that about 65 people want to come."[28] In May 2003, as the White House put on an event to publicize the long list of Bush judicial nominees stalled in the Senate, Kavanaugh took pains to make certain that Leo, along with fellow conservatives Jay Sekulow of the American Center for Law and Justice and George H. W. Bush White House counsel Boyden Gray, were among those accorded "VIP seating."[29] But he also expressed exasperation with Federalist officials for overstepping their proper boundaries and inviting people from the Senate and the administration itself to the White House event. "Federalist Society should NOT be calling people in government (Justice and Senate) to invite them," he lectured Leo.[30] The next month, Kavanaugh tried, unsuccessfully, to get Bush to address the Federalist Society's annual meeting. "Can we talk about President possibly speaking at Federalist Society National Convention in November?" he wrote. "The Vice President spoke last year."[31]

Kavanaugh's involvement with Leo and the Federalist Society is no surprise. One early and continuing focus of the counsel's office—one that consumed around half of Kavanaugh's time—was to resume the Republican project, interrupted by two terms of the Clinton administration, of filling the federal courts with conservative judges. One of Kavanaugh's particular port-folios was the D.C. Circuit, where he was tapped to serve not many years later. Among the early candidates he championed were John Roberts, whose original nomination had languished in the Democratic-controlled Senate at the end of the first Bush administration; Miguel Estrada, a promising young Hispanic law-yer whose confirmation would end up being filibustered by Dem-ocrats in the second Bush's first term; and Janice Rogers Brown, an African American California Supreme Court justice whose extreme views—she advocated a return to the *Lochner v. New York* era, when the court struck down worker protection laws on the grounds that they interfered with freedom of contract—would lead to a showdown over judicial filibusters.

Almost all Kavanaugh's substantive assessments of the judicial nominees remain shielded from public view. But documents released in conjunction with Kavanaugh's nomination offer glimpses of an industrious young lawyer understandably eager to make a good impression on the president. In March 2001, as the counsel's office prepared for its first meeting with the president to present its slate of proposed judicial nominees, Kavanaugh suggested adding an extra planning session before the big event. "Maybe this is overkill, but because this meeting is our first with the President and because our anxiety levels therefore likely will be high," Kavanaugh sug-gested, the team should add "a dry run rehearsal" to another pre-meeting scheduled for later that day. "I would not want anyone to be winging it or trying something out for the first time in the meet-ing with the President, so an earlier session may help iron out any kinks," he said. Gonzales gently demurred. "It never hurts to be prepared, but we need to calm down," he replied. "The President is very personable, he will want to make a good first impression on his lawyers. This is just another client—the most powerful man on the planet." Kavanaugh backed off. "Sorry," he wrote. "I can be a bit obsessive."[32]

One of Kavanaugh's projects, ultimately unsuccessful, was getting Estrada confirmed—although Estrada's eventual withdrawal from the judicial nomination battle arguably helped pave the way for Kavanaugh's own confirmation to the same court. Even as the Estrada nomination stalled, the D.C. Circuit faced another vacancy: Judge Laurence Silberman had taken senior status in November 2000. Kyle Sampson, another lawyer in the counsel's office, raised the possibility of Kavanaugh going for the spot himself. When Kavanaugh was circumspectly silent, Sampson raised the possibility directly with Gonzales. One e-mail from the time reflects some tension between Kavanaugh and Estrada over their potentially competing judicial prospects. "Why is it that half of washington knows you want to get out soon, Not helpful for you or others if Ds find that out," Kavanaugh e-mailed Estrada on May 7, 2003, by which point Estrada's nomination had been pending for two years. Estrada responded with some asperity, "Don't razz me about. Why is it half the town thinks you are next at bat?"[33]

In fact, Kavanaugh's own nomination was beginning to germinate. Originally, he had been talked about for a seat on the Fourth Circuit, which included his home state of Maryland, but the state's two Democratic senators balked on the grounds that he did not have enough legal ties there. As Kavanaugh told the Senate Judiciary Committee in 2004, he met "at length" in 2002 with Paul Sarbanes, the state's senior senator, who "made it clear that he would not support a nominee for that seat on the Fourth Circuit unless the nominee was a Maryland lawyer, maintained an office in Maryland, and practiced regularly in the Maryland courts."[34] So attention shifted to the D.C. Circuit, which was, ironically, both more prestigious and less politically difficult, without home-state senators to insert themselves and block nominees. A week after Estrada jabbed him for being "next at bat," Kavanaugh was, in fact, at bat.

The fact that Kavanaugh was dating the president's secretary—they were engaged just before Christmas 2003—didn't hurt Kavanaugh's standing with Bush, and the degree to which it helped secure Kavanaugh's nomination was the subject of some snarky commentary even among colleagues. The selection was almost certain to be controversial—given Kavanaugh's young age, his political activities, and his role as Starr's right hand during the Clinton investigation—but any nomination to the D.C. Circuit was going to run into some flak. Kavanaugh was popular in the White House; maybe the nomination would get through, maybe not, but in any event there was no harm, including to Kavanaugh's reputation, in trying. Look at how long it had taken for Roberts.

Even as Kavanaugh's nomination to the appeals court made its way through the White House process—he was formally nominated on July 25, 2003—he moved into a new White House position, as staff secretary. Kavanaugh had lost out on a different promotion at the end of 2002, to become deputy counsel, but the staff secretary job was even more of a plum. Along with his relationship with Estes, this job brought him into daily contact with the president and forged a close bond between the two that would only strengthen over the next three years.

Bush could be a demanding, even brusque, taskmaster— Kavanaugh himself told friends that Bush was the toughest boss he ever had, a surprise given the Kozinski clerkship—but the forty-third president took a shine to Kavanaugh. The young lawyer was quiet, meticulous, and a straight shooter with the documents that he was responsible for funneling to the president; he was a useful foil for Bush's sometimes cutting teasing and a good partner for his penchant for sports talk. Kavanaugh logged hours traveling the world with Bush and staying at Bush's Crawford ranch, living out of the double-wide trailer that housed the traveling staff and heading out with the president and his ranch hands to cut back cedar with a chain saw after the paperwork was done.

Condoleezza Rice, the national security adviser, witnessed the Bush-Kavanaugh relationship flourish at close range. "I think from a very early phase he saw Brett as someone who was going to have a brilliant future, maybe on the court," Rice said of the president.

"It made him a little tougher on Brett. It made him have really high expectations of him, but I think it was like a father who had high expectations for a son."[35]

Kavanaugh later described his three years as staff secretary as the most informative for his later role as judge. "I saw regulatory agencies screw up. I saw how regulatory agencies try to comply with congressional mandates. I saw how agencies try to avoid congressional mandates. I saw the relationship between agencies and the White House and the president. I saw the good and the bad sides of a president's trying to run for reelection and to raise money while still being president," Kavanaugh recalled. "I was involved in the process for lots of presidential speeches. I traveled almost everywhere with the president for about three years. I mostly recall the massive decisions that had to be made on short notice."[36]

Two of those massive decisions—three, as it turned out, because Bush botched one of them and had to try again—involved nominating Supreme Court justices. It had been fourteen years since a Republican president had been able to fill a seat on the high court (George H. W. Bush's selection of Clarence Thomas), and Bush was determined not to repeat his father's mistake with Souter the year before Thomas was nominated. The first vacancy came on July 1, 2005, with the retirement of O'Connor, who wanted to care for her ailing husband. Bush's advisers were divided: Cheney and Gonzales backed Luttig, the Fourth Circuit judge they considered the most solid conservative; Harriet Miers, by then White House counsel, was for Samuel Alito, the Third Circuit judge; Card and Rove favored Roberts, who had only been on the appeals court for two years. In his memoir, Bush recalled how he leaned on Kavanaugh's advice in making the choice. "I solicited opinions from others, including some of the younger lawyers in the White House," he wrote. One was Kavanaugh, still awaiting his own confirmation to the appeals court on which Roberts sat. "Brett told me that Luttig, Alito, and Roberts would all be solid justices," Bush wrote. "The tiebreaker question, he suggested, was which man would be the most effective leader on the Court—the most capable of convincing his colleagues through persuasion and strategic thinking."[37]

As Roberts's nomination to O'Connor's seat was pending, an even more important vacancy opened. Rehnquist, the ailing chief justice, died on September 3 of thyroid cancer. Bush, coping with the aftermath of Hurricane Katrina—"one of the worst weeks of the Bush presidency," Kavanaugh called it—quickly moved to nominate Roberts to take Rehnquist's place. That reopened the O'Connor vacancy, and Bush, under pressure to name a woman—from, among others, First Lady Laura Bush and O'Connor herself—seized on the idea of picking Miers.[38] A prominent Texas lawyer, Miers, a graduate of Southern Methodist University and its law school, had been head of the Texas Lottery Commission and Bush's personal lawyer before following him to Washington. Though Kavanaugh had kept his counsel during the selection of Roberts, some colleagues believed he was privately disposed toward Alito as the most reliable conservative choice. Now he weighed in to make the case for Alito, whom he knew from the Stapleton clerkship.

Bush went instead with Miers—"a pit bull in size six shoes," he called her.[39] The selection was a terrible blunder. Miers not only lacked judicial experience, she also had little familiarity with the nuances of constitutional law, a deficit that became painfully clear as she began senatorial courtesy calls. In the meantime, conservatives began to mutiny. Kavanaugh joined the team that tried to help prepare Miers for the hearings and had to deliver the awkward news to the chief of staff: getting Miers through the hearings was going to be a challenge. Three weeks after she was nominated, Miers, under pressure, asked Bush to withdraw her nomination. Four days later, Alito was nominated in her place, and was, as Kavanaugh had predicted, confirmed without great difficulty.

For Kavanaugh, the nominations offered an inside glimpse at a process he would next experience from the other side, and with a very different president. He had witnessed two nominees succeed and one go up in flames. Thirteen years later, at Kavanaugh's formal investiture, Roberts presided over the ceremony, administering the judicial oath in which Kavanaugh pledged to "do equal right to the poor and to the rich," as Alito watched from the bench. Miers, along with a bevy of Kavanaugh's colleagues from the Bush White House, looked on from the crowded chamber.

CHAPTER NINE

Auditioning

From the moment Brett Kavanaugh was nominated to serve on the United States Court of Appeals for the District of Columbia Circuit—from the moment, really, when the news of his nomination first surfaced—friends and foes alike, not to mention Kavanaugh himself, had the prospect of a different court in mind. This ambition did not require any leap of the imagination. By the time of Kavanaugh's nomination, the D.C. Circuit had become a well-trodden stepping-stone to the Supreme Court. Scalia and Thomas had been elevated from there; two other members of the appeals court, Bork and Douglas Ginsburg, had been tapped for the seat that Kennedy eventually took. As Kavanaugh's nomination was pending, Roberts was promoted from the circuit to the Supreme Court. Roberts had been forced to wait eleven years from his first nomination to the D.C. Circuit until his eventual confirmation, to a different seat under a different president Bush, and that delay was no accident. Everyone understood: confirming a nominee to the D.C. Circuit, particularly one so young and so well credentialed, meant confirming a potential future justice.

That prospect was not lost on Kavanaugh, nor was he particularly shy about expressing such ambitions. "He was telling everyone for the longest time he's going to be on the Supreme Court," said one person who has known Kavanaugh for years. "He was telling people before he was on the appeals court that was his ultimate goal." Said John Yoo, who was two years behind Kavanaugh at Yale Law School and served in the Justice Department while Kavanaugh was at the White House, "He's been running for the Supreme Court since he's been 25 years old."[1]

Kavanaugh's wait for the appeals court was shorter than the future chief justice's, but the opposition to Kavanaugh was far more intense. And while the majority of Kavanaugh's service on the appeals court—eight years out of twelve—would be during the tenure of a Democratic president, the potential for future elevation, when a Republican finally regained the White House, seemed never far from mind. Kavanaugh displayed a penchant for unnecessary concurrences and showy dissents that would lead some of his colleagues to shake their heads and mutter, "There he goes again." They had a snarky term for what they suspected the ambitious young judge was up to. They called it auditioning.

The headline in the New York *Daily News* on June 6, 2003—the first to report Kavanaugh's possible nomination—helped explain, in classic New York journalese, why his selection would be so controversial. MULL BILL PROBER FOR FED BENCH, it read, a reference to Kavanaugh's fraught history with the Clintons. The story quoted a Democratic source predicting a bumpy future for a Kavanaugh nomination. Tapping Kavanaugh, the source said, would "be viewed as a ratcheting up of the confrontation with Senate Democrats" over Bush's court nominees.[2]

"Happy to be a ratchet," Kavanaugh wrote a White House official who forwarded the report. "But the other nom will be even more of a ratchet."[3] Kavanaugh was referring to Janice Rogers Brown, who was eventually nominated on the same day. As controversial as she was, Brown ended up being confirmed almost a year before Kavanaugh. "Web blogs are already going crazy," Kavanaugh e-mailed Joel Kaplan, his close friend and White House colleague, at 11:40 p.m. on June 18, as the *Washington Post* published a story about the planned nomination.[4]

In the coming days, congratulations would begin to pour in—some illustrating the tight-knit, almost incestuous world of conservative Washington, some tinged with a discernible touch of professional jealousy. "It's good to see yet further confirmation of this President's excellent judgment, and it is a most deserved honor," wrote Neil Gorsuch, Kavanaugh's former Georgetown Prep classmate and Kennedy clerk, then in private practice in Washington.[5] "Let me know if I can be of any help," offered Rod Rosenstein, Kavanaugh's former colleague in the Starr office and then at the Justice Department.[6] Jay Apperson, a House Judiciary Committee staffer, could not help but note Kavanaugh's home-court advantage. "Not since Dick Cheney headed the search for Vice President has a better selection been made!" he wrote.[7] Ted Cruz weighed in from Texas, where he was serving as solicitor general. "Terrific news," Cruz wrote, his envy of Kavanaugh's success not terribly well disguised. "Given Miguel's and John's recent experiences, you may, alas, have a long road ahead, but you'll make one hell of a judge . . . 38 years old and named to the D.C. Circuit. Jeez, what do you do for an encore?"[8]

Cruz's assessment was prescient. Although Republicans controlled the Senate, it took until the following April for Kavanaugh to have a hearing, at which Democrats came out with guns blazing. "The nomination seems to be as much about politics as it is about ideology," New York Democrat Charles Schumer said at Kavanaugh's confirmation hearing. "While the nominations of William Pryor and Janice Rogers Brown and Priscilla Owen may be among the most ideological we have seen, the nomination of Brett Kavanaugh is among the most political in history."

Kavanaugh had sterling credentials, Schumer acknowledged, but they were overly partisan. "Some might call Mr. Kavanaugh the Zelig of young Republican lawyers, as he has managed to find himself at the center of so many high-profile, controversial issues in his short career, from the notorious Starr Report to the Florida recount, to this President's secrecy and privilege claims, to post-9/11 legislative battles . . . to controversial judicial nominations," Schumer went on. "In fact, Mr. Kavanaugh would probably win first prize as the hard-right's political lawyer . . . Brett Kavanaugh's nomination to the D.C. Circuit is not just a drop of salt in the partisan wounds, it is the whole shaker."[9]

Schumer's ferocity was both genuine and strategic. Kavanaugh, as he saw it, lacked the legal experience to leapfrog onto the appeals court; at thirty-eight, he was the youngest person nominated to the D.C. Circuit since Starr, who had been thirty-seven. But Schumer was not as worried about Kavanaugh on the D.C. Circuit as he was about what might happen next—Kavanaugh on the Supreme Court. Schumer did not want to see that happen, and that fear helped explain the intensity of his opposition.

As Kavanaugh's nomination languished in the Senate, it became tangled in a broader dispute over judges. In an unprecedented move, the Democrats had deployed the filibuster to block Bush's most controversial judicial nominees, in effect imposing a sixty-vote threshold. Republicans were threatening to retaliate with what was termed the "nuclear option," changing Senate rules by a simple majority vote—rather than the usual two-thirds—to eliminate the filibuster for judges. The issue was defused in the spring of 2005, when a bipartisan group of senators known as the Gang of 14 agreed that the filibuster would only be used against judicial nominees in "extraordinary circumstances." What precisely rose to the level of "extraordinary" was left undefined. The Gang explicitly provided for some contested nominations to move forward by majority vote, even as others were quietly withdrawn. Ronald Weich, then senior counsel to Senate minority leader Harry Reid, recalled trying unsuccessfully to get Kavanaugh's name on the list of nominations that would not proceed.[10] But Democrats on the Gang were unwilling to push that hard. Instead, Kavanaugh's fate remained deliberately unclear. He was left in limbo, neither approved to move ahead nor killed outright.

When the new Congress convened, in January 2006, Bush promptly resubmitted Kavanaugh's nomination. By this point, however, Democrats already hostile to Kavanaugh were further infuriated by his failure to submit answers to written questions for seven months after his first hearing, a move they said was disrespectful and evasive. They seized on the revelation of warrantless wiretapping of American citizens, controversies over the detention of suspects in the war on terror, and even an unrelated lobbying scandal to demand that Kavanaugh return for additional questioning.[11] In the early months of 2006, it looked as if a fight over Kavanaugh might push the Senate to go nuclear after all.[12]

Senate Judiciary Committee chairman Arlen Specter was furious over the mess, which had him caught between Democrats insisting on another hearing and conservative groups that pegged him as weak for considering capitulating to the minority. The Pennsylvania Republican was no particular fan of Kavanaugh's; he did not think the young lawyer was anywhere near ready to be on the appeals court. But Specter found himself under unusual pressure from the president to get the nomination done. Bush called Specter personally to say that he wanted Kavanaugh confirmed—an unusual presidential intercession on behalf of a lower-court nominee. Even so, Bush himself was not optimistic about Kavanaugh's prospects. He questioned aides about Kavanaugh's confirmation chances and expressed doubt that Democrats would let him through.

"Bush obviously loved the guy to death," one former Senate staffer recalled of Kavanaugh. As a result, the staffer said, "the president was all over [Specter]. The president and Specter talked about it several times. The president really wanted to get this done and made it a big priority." It was not the last time that Bush's personal intervention helped Kavanaugh win confirmation.

Kavanaugh's cause was also helped by controversy over another of the president's nominees. Terrence Boyle, a North Carolina district judge who had originally been nominated to the Fourth Circuit by the first President Bush, had been among the first batch of nominees sent up by George W. Bush, back in May 2001. Boyle was already controversial because of his views on civil rights and his connection to former North Carolina Republican senator Jesse Helms. Then, five years after his renomination, news reports questioned whether Boyle had ruled in cases involving companies in which he held stock. As the Gang of 14 was reconstituted to defuse yet another threat to use the nuclear option, the deal was evident: Democrats would get their second hearing on Kavanaugh, then the nomination would move forward.[13] Meantime, Boyle's prospects were dead. His nomination languished until January 2007, at which time the White House would announce that it did not intend to renominate him.

As the committee prepared to hold its second hearing on Kavanaugh, leading newspapers were split on the nomination. "A wise president would have chosen someone utterly above partisan objection," the *Washington Post* editorial board wrote about Kavanaugh in May 2006. "Democrats can perhaps be forgiven for balking." Still, the *Post* concluded, Kavanaugh should be confirmed.[14] The *New York Times*, more editorially inclined to oppose presidential prerogatives on nominees, adopted the opposite view. "Mr. Kavanaugh was unqualified then, and he is unqualified now," the newspaper wrote in an editorial. Kavanaugh's résumé, it said, "screams political partisanship."[15]

Meanwhile, the American Bar Association downgraded its assessment of Kavanaugh. It had initially rated the nominee well qualified, the highest category, with a minority considering him qualified. After interviewing additional lawyers and judges familiar with Kavanaugh's work, the ABA lowered its assessment to qualified, with a minority considering Kavanaugh well qualified. In a statement to the Judiciary Committee, New Hampshire lawyer Stephen Tober, who chaired the bar's assessment committee, said the new interviews raised "additional concern over whether this nominee is so insulated that he will be unable to judge fairly in the future." One interviewee found Kavanaugh "immovable and very stubborn and frustrating to deal with on some issues." The ABA also raised new worries about Kavanaugh's lack of experience. One judge "commented that the nominee was 'less than adequate' before the court, had been 'sanctimonious' and demonstrated 'experience on the level of an associate,'" Tober reported. "A lawyer who had observed him during a different court proceeding stated: 'Mr. Kavanaugh did not handle the case well as an advocate and dissembled.'"[16]

For his second hearing, Kavanaugh arrived with reinforce-
ments. Eight-month-old Margaret sat on her mother's lap. Without
a home-state senator to introduce him, he brought in Stapleton and
Kozinski, the judges for whom he had clerked, to do the honors.
Five former attorneys general, nine former White House counsels
or deputy counsels, and three former solicitors general signed letters on Kavanaugh's behalf. Yet Kavanaugh's testimony at the second hearing was wooden and grudging. One exchange, about his
failure to submit answers to written questions after his first hearing,
was illustrative of what Democrats saw as Kavanaugh's maddening
evasiveness and arrogance.

> Leahy: "Why did you take seven months to answer the written
> questions you were given after your hearing last time?"
>
> Kavanaugh: "Senator, I take responsibility for that, and I'm happy
> to answer any additional questions."
>
> Leahy: "Why did you take seven months?"
>
> Kavanaugh: "Senator, again, I take responsibility for that, and—"
>
> Leahy: "Of course you take responsibility for it. Obviously, they
> are your answers. But why seven months?"
>
> Kavanaugh: "Senator, if there was—I take responsibility for that.
> I think I had a misunderstanding, which is my responsibility. I'm
> happy to answer additional questions today that you may have, or
> other members of the Committee may have. Again, I take—"
>
> Leahy: "What was the misunderstanding?"
>
> Kavanaugh: "Senator, I take responsibility for that."
>
> Leahy: "Mr. Kavanaugh, we are not playing games. I am just
> asking you a question."[17]

Republican supporters of Kavanaugh dismissed this as play-
acting on the part of Democrats. Kavanaugh hadn't filed the answers
promptly because there didn't seem to be any rush; there was no

expectation that his nomination would be acted on that Congress. Still, one Republican staffer called it "the worst hearing I've ever seen for a court of appeals nominee, period."

Senate Democrats, however, didn't have a real hook for opposing Kavanaugh. At that point, with the partisans on both sides dug in and the Republicans in the majority, the outcome was guaranteed. There would be a party-line vote in the committee for Kavanaugh, then he would move on to the Senate floor and confirmation to the position he had been awaiting for nearly three years.

Kavanaugh was finally confirmed by a vote of 57–36. Only four Democrats crossed party lines in support, a partisan achievement that came about in part because of lobbying from the junior senator from New York, Hillary Clinton.[18] She had once been the target of Kavanaugh and his colleagues in the Starr office, and even though he was receiving a lifetime appointment, there was some grim satisfaction in the nearly solid Democratic vote against him.

For most appeals court judges, being sworn in is a low-key affair. For Kavanaugh, the event took place in the White House Rose Garden, overseen by two men who had played such a pivotal role in Kavanaugh's arrival at that moment and who would help him rise even higher. As Ashley Kavanaugh held the Bible, Justice Kennedy administered the oath of office. President Bush looked on, beaming like a proud parent. Vice President Cheney, with whom Kavanaugh had tangled over affirmative action, was in attendance, as was attorney general Alberto Gonzales and his predecessor, John Ashcroft. So was Kavanaugh's infant daughter, as Bush observed. "Margaret has her mother's good looks and her dad's preference for hearings that do not last too long," he said.[19]

The day before, Bush, "with mixed emotions," had penned a handwritten letter to his trusted aide. "Who knows?" Bush mused. "Some future president may be wise enough to name you to the Supreme Court."[20]

·   ·   ·

The D.C. Circuit that Kavanaugh joined was decidedly conservative: he would make the seventh Republican nominee among the
ten active judges. His more liberal appeals court colleagues found
him affable but unyielding. He would engage but rarely, if ever,
change his mind—the general assessment was that Kavanaugh was
a great colleague except in the cases where it mattered. Kavanaugh
also soon displayed a propensity for filing separate concurrences
and dissents, actions that some colleagues took as judicial grandstanding and, more to the point, an effort to position himself for a
Supreme Court seat. A report by the Congressional Research Service after Kavanaugh's Supreme Court nomination found that he
filed concurrences or dissents in more than 15 percent of cases,
more frequently than any colleague. By contrast, Merrick Garland
wrote separately in fewer than 2 percent of cases.[21] Kavanaugh, the
liberal group People for the American Way found in an analysis,
dissented more each year on the bench than any of his D.C. Circuit
colleagues, whether Republican or Democratic appointees.[22]

Kavanaugh quickly became popular among the trial court judges
for frequently joining them for lunch in the judges' dining room—
not all the appeals court judges deigned to mingle with the lower
ranks. Kavanaugh, by contrast, seemed eager to soak up their on-
the-ground experience. Having little courtroom experience before
taking the bench, he talked so often about presiding over a trial—
appeals court judges have that flexibility, if they so choose—that it
became something of a running joke at the courthouse, with some
of Kavanaugh's colleagues wondering privately whether he was
nervous about taking that plunge. After all, trial judges can find
themselves overruled on appeal.

Kavanaugh's chambers were distinctive for their relatively
large number of female and African American clerks. It is possible
to see this as canny advance planning for a Supreme Court nomination, and some in the courthouse viewed Kavanaugh's performance
in this cynical light. Certainly Kavanaugh was not shy, when that
moment arrived, about touting the fact that more than half his law

clerks—twenty-five of forty-eight—had been women. Yet the fact remains: Kavanaugh produced in an area where many of his colleagues, on the Supreme Court as well as the D.C. Circuit, fell short. He took pains, on trips to New Haven, to meet with Yale's Black Law Students Association to solicit clerkship applicants.

And he showed flexibility in accommodating female clerks with children. Sarah Pitlyk, who clerked for Kavanaugh after graduating from Yale Law School, recalled receiving a call from the judge. "He just put it out there: 'You're a mom coming to clerk. Let's figure out what we need to do to make the clerkship just as rewarding for you as it would be otherwise and also to make it possible for you to be a mother while you're doing it,'" she said.[23] Several years later, when one of his female clerks needed to leave the office by six in order to care for her child, Kavanaugh relaxed the general rule in his chambers, that clerks were expected to be there from nine to seven. Incoming Kavanaugh clerks were warned—don't refer to your female colleagues as girls, or the judge will flip out.

Kavanaugh the judge developed into a clear, well-organized, sometimes even sparkling writer, particularly good at translating obscure legal language into accessible prose. He opened one 2017 opinion about preventing fax advertisements with this punchy sentence: "Believe it or not, the fax machine is not yet extinct."[24] In a 2012 case involving an arbitration award against the government of Belize, Kavanaugh wrote a dissent taking the majority to task for issuing a writ of mandamus, a remedy generally reserved for extraordinary situations. "Mandamus for this case," Kavanaugh wrote, "is akin to using a chain saw to carve your holiday turkey."[25] Dissenting in a 2017 case concerning a man accused of securities fraud for sending e-mails his boss had written, Kavanaugh structured his opinion as a drama in three acts.[26]

Because of its location in the nation's capital, the caseload of the D.C. Circuit skews toward complex issues of administrative law. As mind-numbing as this docket may sound, for Kavanaugh the regulatory issues evoked larger questions about the division of constitutional responsibilities among Congress, the executive branch, and the judiciary. "Every case is a separation of powers case," he liked to tell his clerks.[27] Several Kavanaugh rulings help illuminate that approach. In a 2017 decision, the full appeals court declined to review a ruling that upheld the Federal Communications Commission's net neutrality rule, which barred Internet service providers from slowing down or otherwise discriminating against content delivered on their networks. Kavanaugh dissented, noting that the net neutrality rule "is one of the most consequential regulations ever issued by any executive or independent agency in the history of the United States" and asserting that the FCC had overstepped its proper boundaries. First, he said, Congress had not explicitly empowered the agency to issue the rule, and for rules of this importance, the Supreme Court required "clear congressional authorization." This "major rules" doctrine, Kavanaugh said, "helps preserve the separation of powers and operates as a vital check on expansive and aggressive assertions of executive authority." Second, he said, the net neutrality rule violated the First Amendment rights of Internet service providers to decide what content to carry or to favor.[28]

Kavanaugh's position—his colleague Janice Rogers Brown dissented on narrower grounds—drew a particularly sharp rebuke from two Democratic-appointed colleagues, Sri Srinivasan and David Tatel. They began by noting that it would be especially unwise for the appeals court to intervene at that point because the FCC was in the midst of replacing the challenged rule with a different one. Then they took on Kavanaugh's legal analysis. Even assuming the Supreme Court had established a "major rules" doctrine of the kind that Kavanaugh posited, they said, the FCC's authority to regulate Internet service providers had already been decided in a 2005 Supreme Court case. The FCC's power in this area was so clear, they noted, that none of the parties in the case, no member of the appeals court panel, and none of the dissenting FCC commissioners had even raised the issue flagged by Kavanaugh as a problem. Similarly, they said, none of the main parties in the case had challenged the net neutrality rule as an infringement on free speech.[29] The judges were too polite to put it this way, but it was not hard to read between the lines of what they were saying: Kavanaugh was not only wrong on the law, he was also showboating.

Another high-profile Kavanaugh dissent came in a 2018 case involving the Consumer Financial Protection Bureau, the Obama-era agency first conceived by Elizabeth Warren when she was a professor at Harvard Law School. The issue in the CFPB case involved whether its unusual structure—an independent agency headed by a single director with a five-year term, subject to removal by the president only for good cause—impermissibly infringed on presidential authority. This dispute might sound arcane and picayune—it was anything but. Rather, the case was part of a long-running campaign by conservatives against the power of independent agencies, which they consider a "headless fourth branch" of government in contravention of the constitutional scheme establishing a powerful, or "unitary," executive.

Conservatives had lost this argument during the New Deal, in a 1935 case, *Humphrey's Executor v. United States*, which upheld the constitutionality of the independent Federal Trade Commission. As judge Nina Pillard, an Obama appointee, noted in upholding the constitutionality of the CFPB, the court in *Humphrey's Executor* "approved the very means of independence Congress used here; protection of agency leadership from at-will removal by the president." The organizational difference between the two agencies—a five-member FTC and a single-director CFPB—did not carry constitutional significance, she added.[30] Pillard did not mince words about what was at stake in the case, *PHH Corporation, et al. v. Consumer Financial Protection Bureau*, which involved a mortgage lender fined $109 million for allegedly giving kickbacks to insurers in exchange for customer referrals. "Ultimately," she wrote, "PHH makes no secret of its wholesale attack on independent agencies—whether collectively or individually led—that, if accepted, would broadly transform modern government."[31]

Kavanaugh dissented. He didn't go as far as another conservative colleague, Karen LeCraft Henderson, who would have struck down the agency in its entirety. Instead, he found the structure unconstitutional but said, in an opinion joined by Raymond Randolph, that the constitutional problem could be cured by allowing the president to remove the CFPB director at will. What was striking about the Kavanaugh opinion was both its thundering rhetoric, with repeated invocations of the need to prevent tyranny and protect individual liberty, and its all but explicit suggestion that *Humphrey's Executor* should be overturned. "This is a case about executive power and individual liberty," Kavanaugh began his dissent.[32] "Because of their massive power and the absence of Presidential supervision and direction," he wrote, "independent agencies pose a significant threat to individual liberty and to the constitutional system of separation of powers and checks and balances."[33] The CFPB's "concentration of enormous power in a single unaccountable, unchecked Director poses a far greater risk of arbitrary decision-making and abuse of power, and a far greater threat to individual liberty, than a multi-member independent agency does."[34]

Then Kavanaugh dropped a lengthy footnote that essentially said he would be delighted to overturn *Humphrey's Executor* if only he held a job that would let him do so. *Humphrey's Executor* was "inconsistent" with a prior Supreme Court ruling and "in tension with" more recent ones, he noted. It "has received significant criticism" in the legal academy. Doing away with the ruling wouldn't be the end of the world; agencies would still exist, just subject to the president's direction. "In any event, it is not our job to decide whether to overrule *Humphrey's Executor*," Kavanaugh acknowledged. "As a lower court, we must follow Supreme Court precedent."[35] For conservatives eager to rein in independent agencies, there could have been no stronger signal. Kavanaugh would be their man.

Not all Kavanaugh's concurrences were aimed, to the extent that they had an objective, at appealing to conservatives. In one 2013 case heard by Kavanaugh, Garland, and Thomas Griffith, a fellow George W. Bush appointee, the court ruled for an African American man who sued Fannie Mae for racial discrimination and sent the case back to the lower court for a full trial. The man, Placide Ayissi-Etoh, claimed that his supervisor, a vice president, had used the *n* word in ordering Ayissi-Etoh out of his office. As a legal matter, one of the questions was whether that incident, standing alone, was bad enough to show that Ayissi-Etoh had been subjected to a hostile working environment. The unanimous panel concluded as much. Kavanaugh wrote a separate concurrence, as he explained, to "underscore" that determination.

The concurrence cited Langston Hughes, Alex Haley's *Roots*, and Harper Lee's *To Kill a Mockingbird*; to this day, Kavanaugh keeps a tattered copy of his sixth-grade edition of the Harper Lee novel in his chambers. "No other word in the English language so powerfully or instantly calls to mind our country's long and brutal struggle to overcome racism and discrimination against African-Americans," Kavanaugh wrote.[36] Perhaps he was so outraged by the use of the epithet that he felt compelled to write a separate concurrence. There is a less flattering interpretation, one that did not escape notice when the opinion was released: this concurrence was one for the confirmation hearings, a convenient way to illustrate racial sensitivity in the event of a promotion. Indeed, when Kavanaugh submitted his Senate Judiciary Committee questionnaire listing his ten most significant cases, he cited nine in which his position was later upheld by the Supreme Court—and the *Ayissi-Etoh* concurrence, because, he said, "of what it says about anti-discrimination law and American history."[37] During the hearings, Idaho Republican senator Mike Crapo helpfully questioned Kavanaugh about the decision. "This case to my mind was one case with one person arguing one claim of one incident, but to me the whole history of the country . . . on race relations and racial discrimination was represented in that one case," Kavanaugh testified.[38] If the opinion was not written with a future confirmation hearing in mind, it certainly served a useful purpose once that moment arrived.

Unmentioned on Kavanaugh's Judiciary questionnaire, but assuredly not unnoticed by the National Rifle Association, which backed him over Amy Coney Barrett when the time came, was Kavanaugh's 2011 dissent in a gun-rights case, *Heller v. District of Columbia*. In a 2008 case between the same parties, *District of Columbia v. Heller*, the Supreme Court decreed that the Second Amendment protects an individual's right to keep and bear arms. This case, a follow-up challenging the District's ban on assault weapons and high-capacity magazines, was argued before a three-judge panel that included Kavanaugh and two other Republican appointees: Douglas Ginsburg and Karen LeCraft Henderson. The majority, in an opinion by Ginsburg, upheld the ban—and then added a nine-page "Appendix: Regarding the Dissent" to take apart Kavanaugh's reasoning.[39]

That step was extraordinary, but then again, so was Kavanaugh's dissent finding the ban on semiautomatic rifles unconstitutional. In determining the constitutionality of particular laws, courts ordinarily apply differing levels of "scrutiny"—from merely asking whether the law has a "rational basis" to imposing "strict scrutiny"—depending on the significance of the right that is involved. Kavanaugh said that Scalia, writing for the majority in the *Heller* case, had junked that approach. Instead, according to Kavanaugh, the correct test involves looking to "text, history and tradition." Courts, he said, should simply ask whether the weapons at issue are like those that have been traditionally restricted and whether they are in common use. "Semi-automatic rifles have not traditionally been banned and are in common use today, and are thus protected under *Heller*," Kavanaugh concluded.[40]

The conservative judges in the majority rejected that reasoning. "If the Supreme Court truly intended to rule out any form of heightened scrutiny for all Second Amendment cases, then it surely would have said at least something to that effect," Ginsburg noted tartly. "The Court did not say anything of the sort; the plaintiffs in this case do not suggest it did; and the idea that *Heller* precludes heightened scrutiny has eluded every circuit to have addressed that question since *Heller* was issued."[41]

Finally, the Kavanaugh case that received the most scrutiny during his confirmation hearing was, unsurprisingly, *Garza v. Hargan,* the abortion-rights case involving the pregnant teenage migrant being held in a government shelter. Kavanaugh ruled against the teenager, J.D., as part of a three-judge panel. The full appeals court took up the case on an emergency basis and allowed the abortion to proceed. As in the CFPB case, Kavanaugh was outflanked by Henderson, who asserted that the teenager, as an illegal alien, had no constitutionally protected right to obtain an abortion and who angrily took the Trump administration to task for failing to raise that issue.

But once again, Kavanaugh also sent comforting signals to the right. "The majority's decision represents a radical extension of the Supreme Court's abortion jurisprudence," he wrote. "It is in line with dissents over the years by Justices Brennan, Marshall, and Blackmun, not with the many majority opinions of the Supreme Court that have repeatedly upheld reasonable regulations that do not impose an undue burden on the abortion right recognized by the Supreme Court in *Roe v. Wade.*"[42]

Particularly galling for some of his colleagues was a footnote chiding the full court for having "unwisely" intervened in the case. In an e-mail to colleagues that weekend, Kavanaugh had said he understood why the full court might want to take the unusual step of taking up the emergency appeal. Then his dissent zinged the court for doing precisely that—and in a footnote added so late in the already hurried process that the majority had no chance to respond.

What did Kavanaugh's opinion in *Garza* suggest about how he would weigh abortion rights as a justice? The Kavanaugh-Henderson dichotomy is illustrative of his approach, which often features a judicious reluctance to avoid reaching ultimate conclusions in the hope that the problem at hand will resolve itself. Whereas Henderson was willing to say explicitly that the teenager had no claim, Kavanaugh wanted to see if time, and the successful hunt for a sponsor, could make the problem go away.

At the same time, it is fair to read his ruling and wonder what burden on the abortion right would Kavanaugh ever find to be undue. The teenager had already waited more than seven weeks to obtain the abortion to which he agreed she was constitutionally entitled and which, under Kavanaugh's proposed timetable, would have had to be delayed at least eleven days more. Perhaps he was moved by the fact that this case involved a pregnant minor alone in a strange country: the government, Kavanaugh argued, was "merely seeking to place the minor in a better place when deciding whether to have an abortion." But Patricia Millett's concurring opinion made clear that his "better place" argument had no place in the Supreme Court's abortion jurisprudence, which gives minors the right to choose to have abortions if they satisfy state procedures, as J.D. had. And she put Kavanaugh's contention that a little more delay would be no big deal into legal and medical context, underscoring "the irreparable injury to J.D. of postponing termination of her pregnancy—the weekly magnification of the risks to her health and the ever-increasing practical barriers to obtaining an abortion in Texas."[43]

The next time Kavanaugh was called on to intervene in an abortion case, he would be on the Supreme Court, and his position bore striking similarities to his approach in *Garza*.

PART TWO

The Fight

CHAPTER TEN

An Impending Sense of Doom

I t took twenty-three minutes from the moment that Trump unveiled his selection of Brett Kavanaugh for Senate minority leader Chuck Schumer to declare all-out war on the nomination. The next morning, joined by the Democratic members of the Senate Judiciary Committee, the New York senator trooped across the street from the Capitol to reiterate the point—this time in the camera-friendly setting of the Supreme Court steps. "The ramifications of this battle will last a generation or more," he proclaimed, tortoiseshell reading glasses perched on the bridge of his nose, bouncing on the balls of his feet. "I'm going to fight this nomination with everything I've got."[1]

The problem, as Schumer well knew, was that he and his fellow Democrats didn't have all that much ammunition to fight with—nor was it clear, as the coming weeks demonstrated, that Democrats were willing to fully deploy what ammunition they had. Republicans controlled the Senate. The filibuster was gone, a casualty of the Gorsuch confirmation. And while Schumer certainly did not want to see Kavanaugh on the high court—he had fought the judge's confirmation to the appeals court in the hope of averting this very moment—defeating him was a long shot at best, and Schumer had endangered incumbents to worry about in the midterm elections just four months away. A pitched campaign against Kavanaugh could help rally the base that fall and, although this was unlikely, make Schumer majority leader. But the paradox was that it could also undermine that goal by hurting Schumer's most vulnerable members, the Democrats running for reelection in Trump states. Meanwhile, much like a military campaign, every nomination battle requires a committed and even ruthless commander. As Schumer understood, and as became painfully evident as the nomination fight proceeded, the ranking Democrat on the Senate Judiciary Committee, California senator Dianne Feinstein, was miscast for that role. She was a relic of a kinder, gentler era in the Senate, and at eighty-five, if she had once been up for a battle like this, that was no longer the case. Schumer could do work-arounds, dispatching trusted aides to monitor the proceedings, but he was a leader without the right general in place to conduct this war.

For Kavanaugh, all this boded well. Confirmation wasn't a lock, and there was a lot of work ahead. Some Republicans who had been lukewarm at best on Kavanaugh, such as Ted Cruz and Mike Lee, needed tending to; Rand Paul was not yet on board and required some reassuring. Then, of course, there were the two most at-risk Republicans, Collins and Murkowski, plus the three Democrats who had voted for Gorsuch and were therefore in play. But securing the nomination had been, or so it appeared, the hard part. Now the burden was on Democrats to try to pull off a feat that the numbers suggested was doubtful if not impossible. They were not only in the minority but also faced an opposition, led by McConnell, that had already proved itself willing to discard any norms of bipartisanship. Republicans would do whatever it took to get Kavanaugh confirmed, and the legislative arithmetic was on their side. To defeat Kavanaugh, Democrats would have to peel off two Republican votes and keep their own fractious ranks unified as the midterms approached. "You had this impending sense of doom from moment one," said Democratic strategist Ronald Klain, who had worked on the selection or confirmation of eight justices and provided advice on Kavanaugh.[2]

Democrats had an undoubtedly bad hand—and they proceeded to play it badly, at least if the aim was beating Kavanaugh. Their leaders were either conflicted over goals (Schumer) or unsuited to the task (Feinstein). Their message was muddled; they lurched from tactic to tactic. They were divided internally not only over small-bore issues (how quickly to come out against Kavanaugh, for example) but also over more fundamental matters of strategy. Was the goal of Senate Democrats really to defeat the nominee? Or was it simply to do enough to look like they were trying their best and avoid losing Senate seats? The answer was unclear, and Kavanaugh was the beneficiary.

If, as Klain feared, Democrats were doomed from the start of the Kavanaugh nomination, one reason was a fateful decision they had made fifteen months earlier: to filibuster Gorsuch. As Democrats fully expected, that move provoked Republicans into triggering the nuclear option to eliminate the filibuster entirely when it came to judicial nominations. This change gave the president vast new leeway in filling Supreme Court seats: without having to surmount the sixty-vote hurdle, a nominee could be more extreme and still make it through. Schumer's predecessor as Democratic leader, Nevada senator Harry Reid, had set this change in motion in 2013 when he deployed the nuclear option to eliminate the filibuster for executive branch nominees and lower-court judges. It was clear then that it was only a matter of time before the threshold was lowered in the case of Supreme Court nominees.

The question facing Democrats in the spring of 2017 was whether that time had arrived with Gorsuch's nomination. The immediate politics suggested that they had little choice but to force McConnell to act. With Trump newly elected and the wound of Merrick Garland's treatment at McConnell's hands still raw, Democrats were in no mood for restraint. The base wanted a fight, which meant a filibuster. If they didn't press the point then, or so the argument went, McConnell would certainly go nuclear the next time, which made waiting politically perilous and hopelessly naive.

The counterargument, made by some moderate Democrats, was

that it made sense to hold fire and wait to force the Republicans' hand in a more difficult circumstance. The next vacancy was likely to be more consequential, which would make it harder for McConnell to marshal a majority to change the rules. As ruthless as the Republican leader was, some of his moderate, more institutionalist members were going along only reluctantly. They might balk in a different circumstance. Democrats "didn't have the discipline to play it strategically," said Michael Bennet, the moderate Colorado Democrat who had tried to forestall the change. "And as a result, when Kavanaugh got there, Democrats could do nothing except pretend to our base that we were fighting."[3]

That view looks even more convincing in hindsight than it did at the time. If Democrats had allowed the Gorsuch nomination to proceed with a majority vote, the filibuster rule would have still been in place for the Kavanaugh confirmation. As things turned out, McConnell would have had the difficult task of persuading a majority to go nuclear and change the Senate rules just as his members were reeling from the sexual assault allegations against the nominee. Changing the rules, said McConnell adviser Holmes, wasn't easy to do the first time, with Gorsuch. "Knowing what we know now about the way the Kavanaugh nomination was ultimately decided, can you imagine trying to change the rules of the Senate in order to do that? It would have provided the perfect excuse for anybody who didn't want to vote for him in the first place. I don't think he [McConnell] could have gotten it done."[4]

Of course, there is no way to know what would have happened had the filibuster remained in place when Kennedy retired. Would a nominee as provocative as Kavanaugh been nominated? Almost certainly, given Trump's list. Would Republicans have been willing to go nuclear in the face of the allegations against him? Probably, given the imperative of getting him confirmed. But eliminating the filibuster in advance meant that Republicans were never put to that test. Without much to show for it—Gorsuch had been confirmed, after all—Democrats had eliminated their best hope for defeating the next nominee. As a result, Kavanaugh needed only a simple majority—and in the summer of 2018, as the nominee began his rounds of Senate courtesy calls, that target seemed well within reach.

The Gorsuch experience helped shape Kavanaugh's fate, but there was another, even more momentous confirmation fight on the minds of Democrats as they prepared to battle Kavanaugh. Schumer's bellicose language after Kavanaugh's nomination echoed the ferocious attack launched against Bork three decades earlier, when Massachusetts Democrat Edward Kennedy took to the Senate floor less than an hour after President Ronald Reagan announced his nomination. "Robert Bork's America," Kennedy charged in language so unsparing that its aftershocks would reverberate years later, "is a land in which women would be forced into back-alley abortions, blacks would sit at segregated lunch counters, rogue police could break down citizens' doors in midnight raids, schoolchildren could not be taught about evolution."[5]

With Kennedy's retirement, the stakes for the court and the country were even higher than with Bork's nomination because of the court's already significant conservative drift. But as much as the Bork episode was on the mind of Schumer and the Democrats, it was going to be difficult to turn Kavanaugh into a Bork-like figure or replay the Bork scenario to a similarly triumphant conclusion. Liberals might disagree vehemently with Kavanaugh and dread the impact of a reinforced conservative majority. Yet Kavanaugh lacked the record of demonstrably extreme views that brought down Bork, who had argued against the constitutionality of the 1964 Civil Rights Act and been unequivocal in his opposition to abortion rights.[6] Kavanaugh was no Borkean fire-breather; it was more difficult to draw a compellingly scary picture of Brett Kavanaugh's America. He was, literally, a more attractive candidate than Bork, whose scruffy beard had a tendency to make him look weird and slightly demonic. And for all Trump's excesses, Kavanaugh was the kind of nominee who would have been the logical choice of a more run-of-the-mill Republican, a Mitt Romney or a Jeb Bush. "The country certainly could have expected worse from President Trump," the *Washington Post* observed in its initial editorial on the selection.[7]

Moreover, the political landscape was tilted against Democrats in a way that it had not been during the Bork battle. Then, Democrats controlled the Senate, with a fifty-four-vote majority. Now Democrats had just forty-nine votes, including the two independents who caucused with the party. In addition, party lines had calcified so much that significant defections were unimaginable. In 1987, six Republicans had voted against Bork. That was not going to happen in 2018; there were only a few senators in play on either side. And Republicans had internalized the painful lesson of the Bork defeat: they were not going to suffer another such loss, and, thanks to Leonard Leo and the Federalist Society, they had created the political and financial infrastructure to prevent it. If anything, getting Supreme Court justices confirmed was more of an electoral imperative for Trump and Republicans in 2018 than it had been for Reagan three decades earlier. Republicans would not let Kavanaugh lose.

Kavanaugh's advisers and the White House were taken aback—in an odd way, they were rather pleased—by the speed and intensity of Schumer's attack. To the extent that it immediately put moderate incumbents in a tough spot, that was fine from the White House's perspective. The fact that allied groups were ready with fill-in-the-blank press releases opposing the nominee—the Women's March released a statement that first night denouncing Trump's "nomination of XX to the Supreme Court"—served to underscore that this fight was not about Kavanaugh himself but about anyone whom Trump might nominate. Collins might end up on Kavanaugh's side in any event, but this kind of automatic slashing opposition didn't seem to be the right way to convince her to oppose him.

Some Democrats had similar misgivings about what they considered premature opposition. In a lunch with Senate Democrats, Virginia senator Tim Kaine argued for withholding judgment. His point was not only that opposing the nominee before even hearing from him would make Democrats look reflexively partisan, although that was true as well. It was also that a nominee with Kavanaugh's credentials would be defeated only if some character issue were to emerge. Being open-minded—or, perhaps more accurately in the case of most Democrats, appearing to be open-minded—would help buy time as the nominee trudged his way through rounds of courtesy calls. In the interim, maybe something would come to light.

Unlike the Bork nomination, which unfolded in an odd-numbered year, the Kavanaugh nomination was overshadowed by the reality of the looming election. If everything fell into place, the midterms could give Democrats control of the chamber and, with that, elevate Schumer to majority leader. That outcome was remote, but whatever happened, Schumer had vulnerable incumbents to worry about and protect, if at all possible. Senators such as Manchin, Donnelly, Heitkamp, and Missouri's Claire McCaskill faced tough races to retain their seats in red states that had voted overwhelmingly for Trump. There was no path to defeating Kavanaugh without their votes, yet a vote against Kavanaugh could risk their reelection. It was going to be hard enough for them to win in any event. This vacancy, with the unpalatable choice it would force, was the last thing they needed—it was, as McCaskill would later say, an "oh, shit" moment in the campaign.[8] As a consequence, Schumer monitored the Kavanaugh confirmation with a constantly watchful eye on the needs of his caucus, not to mention his own political ambitions.

Meantime, the party base, with a newly energized left still inflamed by what it viewed as the theft of the Scalia seat, was itching for—and demanding of Senate Democrats—an all-out fight. These activists were in no mood for sober withholding of judgment or even for granting Schumer's endangered red-state Democrats some breathing space to see how the nomination fight developed. They wanted all-out opposition to Kavanaugh, and they wanted it now. Their needs required attending to as well. Even if Kavanaugh couldn't be defeated, it was important to make the case against him, to keep the base motivated for the election ahead.

Schumer was torn between clashing constituencies and competing imperatives. He wanted to see the battle prosecuted in a way that would not end up with the worst of all possible worlds: Kavanaugh confirmed and vulnerable incumbents defeated.

There was another set of challenges for Democrats as well. Dianne Feinstein was not the person you would pick to oversee a knives-drawn confirmation fight. Over the course of a storied career, she had displayed an undisputed capacity for toughness. She had risen to national prominence in the wake of a tragedy, the 1978 assassination of San Francisco mayor George Moscone and supervisor Harvey Milk. Then president of the city's board of supervisors, Feinstein had heard gunshots and raced into Milk's office, where, feeling for a pulse, she put her finger into a bullet hole in the wrist of the dying supervisor. The shooting made Feinstein mayor—and spurred her lifelong commitment to gun control.[9] During her second year in the Senate, Feinstein insisted that a ban on assault weapons be included in the 1994 crime bill, over the objections of, among others, Delaware Democrat Joe Biden, and she fought to have the ban reinstated after it lapsed a decade later. "Show some guts," she lectured her colleagues after the massacre of schoolchildren at Sandy Hook Elementary School, as the Senate failed even to summon the votes to overcome a filibuster.[10]

As chair of the Senate Intelligence Committee from 2009 to 2015, Feinstein, for the most part a reliable defender of the intelligence community, did not flinch from doing battle with the CIA—and the Obama administration—over the panel's 2014 report on the torture of terrorism detainees in the wake of the September 11 attacks. In the face of warnings from secretary of state John Kerry that releasing the details could spark unrest in the Middle East, Feinstein fought to ensure that as much of the report was released as possible. "Nobody wants to do something that is going to bring on any kind of attack," Feinstein said. "But I came to the conclusion that America's greatness is being able to say we made a mistake and we are going to correct it and go from there."[11]

Yet by the time of Kavanaugh's nomination, Feinstein was also a throwback to a more civilized era in the Senate, an age before nuclear options and blockades of vacant Supreme Court seats. A moderate in an increasingly liberal party, she believed in the virtues of comity and bipartisanship, which, in the view of many colleagues and staff, were fusty artifacts of the past. She nurtured her relationships with Republican colleagues with courtly charm. When Chuck Grassley and his wife celebrated their sixty-fourth wedding anniversary in August 2018, the month before the hard-fought hearings, Feinstein sent the couple a white orchid.[12]

She had not accommodated herself to the brutal new realities of Trump's Washington and McConnell's Senate. "I think my greatest strength is finding a solution when there are opposing sides," she told the *San Francisco Chronicle* in 2012.[13] Washington in 2018 was not a place for splitting differences. "Moderation is not obsolete," the *Chronicle*'s editorial board wrote in endorsing Feinstein's bid for reelection in April 2018, but that was, perhaps, more wish than reality.[14]

And, at eighty-five the Senate's oldest member—Grassley, her Republican counterpart, was the second oldest—Feinstein was, to be blunt, not at the top of her game. More junior colleagues on the Judiciary Committee—"down dais" members, in Senate parlance—had whispered for a few years that Feinstein was fading. She could still perform well on a Sunday show, but sometimes she seemed less than fully present, protected by a staff that served as a buffer to prevent her deficits from manifesting themselves. She could read prepared speeches and ask prewritten questions, but she did not seem prepared, emotionally or cognitively, to oversee the kind of brutal fight that lay ahead—not if there was any hope of defeating Kavanaugh. Her colleagues had been privately chagrined when Feinstein decided to seek reelection in 2018. Now they worried among themselves, and in private conversations with

Schumer, about her capacity to oversee a pitched confirmation fight—worries that would only mount and, eventually, explode. "Nobody thought she should run again," said one longtime colleague. "She is not nearly who she was."

On occasion, as the Kavanaugh fight progressed, Feinstein's deficits were on public display. During Kavanaugh's testimony about Ford, Feinstein seemed slightly befuddled when she was quizzed by Texas senator John Cornyn about whether her staff had leaked the allegation. "Oh, I don't believe my staff would leak it," she said. "I have not asked that question directly, but I do not believe they would." At that point, Jennifer Duck, Feinstein's top aide on the committee, stood to whisper in her boss's ear. "The answer is no," Feinstein said. "Have you asked your staff or other staffers on the Judiciary Committee?" Cornyn persisted. "I just did," Feinstein replied. At this point, Duck's comments were audible. "You've asked me before," she told Feinstein. "Well, Jennifer reminds me I've asked her before about it, and that's true," Feinstein said.[15] It was an uncomfortable moment, but a telling one.

Even so, Democrats thought, there might be a path to defeating Kavanaugh. Some, especially veterans of Kavanaugh's rocky previous confirmation, were surprised that Trump had picked what they saw as an unnecessary fight by choosing Kavanaugh, with his lengthy record and partisan background. They wondered, why pick a wolf with such sharp teeth when a different wolf in sheep's clothing would be so much easier to confirm? Kavanaugh's protracted path to the appeals court, and his unimpressive performances at his two previous confirmation hearings, augured some vulnerability. His dozen years on the bench meant there would be something in the record for everyone to dislike. At least Trump had given Democrats something to work with.

To win, though, they would need more. Some critical early days were wasted as advocates bandied about fanciful Garland-inspired scenarios such as holding off a vote until after the midterms by shutting down the Senate Judiciary Committee and refusing to participate in hearings. That was never going to work, yet it frittered away valuable time. The only way to beat Kavanaugh was to amass votes, and the best way to do that was exactly what McConnell and others had warned Trump about: the documents. There had to be something in all that paper—if only it could be dislodged.

As the struggle over access to Kavanaugh's Bush-era records developed, Republicans argued that the best guide to a nominee's performance on the Supreme Court is his or her judicial rulings, and they had a fair point. Democrats had made that very case when Republicans were demanding documents in advance of the confirmation hearings for then appeals court judge Sonia Sotomayor in 2009. "Judge Sotomayor's mainstream record of judicial restraint and modesty is the best indication of her judicial philosophy," Vermont Democrat Patrick Leahy, then chairman of the Judiciary Committee, said at the time. "We do not have to imagine what kind of a judge she will be because we see what kind of a judge she has been."[16] Opinions, especially from a nominee with a lengthy judicial record, certainly offer the most relevant information. Yet there are limits to what can be gleaned from those rulings. Because lower-court judges are duty bound to abide by Supreme Court precedent, it is not possible to study their decisions and know with precision how they would behave with that constraint removed.

In addition, especially after Bork's relative candor had helped sink him, nominees have been unwilling to offer much if any insight into how they view existing precedent. As a consequence, questioning about nominees' legal views has become a maddening exercise in evasion. Even before Bork, Scalia famously dodged answering whether he agreed with *Marbury v. Madison*, the iconic 1803 case establishing the principle that the courts are empowered to review the constitutionality of acts of Congress. Other justices have been only slightly more forthcoming. Gorsuch, asked about *Brown v. Board of Education*, the landmark 1954 case declaring separate-but-equal schools unconstitutional, would allow only that it was "a correct application of the law of precedent."[17]

As a result, documents become—depending on which side is doing the asking—either an invaluable potential window into a nominee's unfiltered views or a way for the opposition to play "gotcha." In reality, the quest for documents tends to be far more the latter, less a disinterested quest for truth than a partisan political tactic. Democrats considering the nominee of a Republican president—or Republicans considering the nominee of a Democratic president—aren't interested in documents because they are searching in good faith for a deeper understanding of the nominee's jurisprudence. Rather, they are hunting for ammunition. Maybe the documents will turn up an unwise offhand remark that exposes the nominee's true views on a hot-button issue—a scrawled comment about abortion, say, on an otherwise routine briefing paper. Or perhaps a set of documents will emerge that, as Democrats would contend in Kavanaugh's case, call into question the nominee's previous candor under oath. The gun doesn't have to be smoking to be useful. Mere wisps of vapor will suffice.

At the same time, any documents fight is arcane and dreary. There is a saying in Washington that if you are arguing about process, you are losing, and that proved true with the Kavanaugh confirmation. As Democrats found, it is hard to achieve traction, to get the masses riled up enough to make a difference, by emphasizing issues of dry procedure rather than red-meat substance—even if the procedure is the key to getting at the meat.

Experience with previous nominees—in particular, Kagan and Roberts, both of whom had served in the White House counsel's office—offered some guidance and precedent in the battle over documents. But figuring out how to handle Kavanaugh's documents posed particular challenges, as the Trump administration and Senate Republicans had already realized. For Roberts's nomination, the National Archives, the custodian of presidential papers and the entity ordinarily responsible for producing them to the Senate, had released seventy thousand pages of documents. For Kagan's, the documents totaled more than double that—170,000 pages. The potential page count of the Kavanaugh documents, depending on how the request was phrased, ran into the several millions.

The scope of document requests sent to the Archives is always the subject of negotiations—sometimes tense, often self-serving—between the majority and the minority. The competing imperatives for speed and transparency have a tendency to be weighed differently depending on the party of the president doing the nominating and that of the senators clamoring for documents. Who is doing the squawking depends in large part on who is doing the withholding.

During the Kagan nomination, for example, Alabama Republican senator Jeff Sessions, then the ranking member of the Senate Judiciary Committee, complained bitterly that the hearings were being scheduled to start too soon, without adequate time for senators to review Kagan's record. "We're heading toward what could be a train wreck," he lamented a month before Kagan's hearings were scheduled to start. "The public record of a nominee to such a lifetime position as Justice on the Supreme Court is of such importance that we cannot go forward without these documents."[18]

But the way the Kavanaugh documents fight proceeded was different, both in intensity and in outcome, from what had come before—as the preselection jousting had illustrated. Two days after the nomination, Bush called Grassley to reassure him: the library was committed to doing whatever necessary to get the papers reviewed in time.

One threshold question was whether senators were entitled to see any documents from Kavanaugh's three years as Bush's staff secretary. At a Senate Judiciary Committee meeting on July 19, ten days after Kavanaugh's nomination, Republicans seemed to recognize that it would be reasonable to request at least some staff secretary records. Demanding documents that Kavanaugh had merely shuttled on to the president would be irrelevant and burdensome, they said. However, as John Cornyn, the Republican whip, acknowledged, it "just seems to be common sense" to seek documents that Kavanaugh had "generated," "authored," or "contrib-uted to" as staff secretary.[19]

On July 24, Don McGahn met privately with Republican sen-ators to discuss the documents issue. Afterward, Cornyn shifted his language about the staff secretary documents. Those were now deemed "a bridge too far," Cornyn said. As staff secretary, he said, Kavanaugh "was just a traffic cop."[20] Three days later, Grassley sub-mitted the official documents request. Whereas other such requests had been bipartisan, this one was sent without Feinstein's signa-ture. Grassley sought only documents relating to Kavanaugh's time in the counsel's office.[21] The staff secretary records would remain entirely shielded from senators'—and the public's—view.

That was just the start of a process that Democrats viewed as unprecedented and unfair and that Republicans countered gave Democrats more documents than had ever been previously released.

One striking—and, to Democrats, unsettling—difference from earlier nominations was that the documents were not produced by the National Archives itself. Archives general counsel Gary Stern reported back to Grassley on August 2 that the requested docu-ments, estimated at more than nine hundred thousand pages, would take until the end of October to produce—well after Republicans expected to hold hearings and after the start of the Supreme Court term.[22] As the documents dispute made its way onto cable news, Trump once again erupted at McGahn and Leo. No hearing date had yet been set. Trump demanded to know why he hadn't been aware of the documents problem (he was—McConnell and Grassley had raised the issue, rather fervently, before Kavanaugh's selection) and insisted that he never would have picked Kavanaugh had he known that might result in delay. Leo in particular came in for presiden-tial ire. Trump "was basically saying to Leonard, 'That's what I'm counting on you to avoid, is stuff like this,'" said one adviser.

Republicans came up with—imposed, as Democrats viewed it—an alternative. Instead of leaving document review to the Archives, it would be overseen by William Burck, the former Kava-naugh deputy who was Bush's designated representative for document release. His team of fifty lawyers had already been plowing through the material. Under the terms of the Presidential Records Act, Burck, as Bush's representative, had the right to review any documents to determine if they should be withheld on grounds of executive privilege. Letting Burck's group conduct the initial screening as well, Republicans contended, would simply speed up the process.

The National Archives issued a news release describing the Burck review as "something that has never happened before," adding pointedly, "This effort by former President Bush does not represent the National Archives or the George W. Bush presidential library."[23] It was not hard to read between the lines: this was a highly irregular process, and the professionals at the Archives were none too happy about it.

Neither were Democrats. As Burck examined the documents to see what should be kept secret and what should be turned over, they argued, he was not a neutral arbiter: he wanted to see Kavanaugh, his friend and former boss, confirmed. Over the coming weeks, Democrats' unhappiness only mounted. First, a significant share of the records that Burck provided—38 percent of the 458,000 pages eventually turned over to the committee—were deemed "committee confidential."[24] That label meant that senators were not permitted to use them in public without obtaining advance approval—approval that would, of course, tip the Democrats' hand about the scope of their planned questioning. During previous confirmation hearings, the committee-confidential designation had been employed, with bipartisan agreement, to shield documents that contained personal information, and it applied to a much smaller universe of documents. Now it was being used to keep from public view a large amount of information, not only for reasons of personal privacy but also because the documents involved supposedly confidential communications among the president's advisers.

Second, while the Obama White House had waived any claims of executive privilege relating to the Kagan documents, Burck, just four days before the hearings were to begin, invoked a newly minted claim, "constitutional privilege," to block release of another 102,000 pages. The assertion of constitutional privilege allowed Republicans to keep the Kavanaugh material from prying eyes without having to go through the bother of invoking executive privilege, which requires a formal assertion from the president and, in theory at least, is subject to being challenged. These documents were potentially the most significant—although it was impossible to tell, because Grassley didn't insist that Burck supply any specifics about what he was withholding. Instead, Burck just informed the committee that "the most significant portion" of the withheld documents involved discussions about judicial nominations, along with documents involving "advice submitted directly to President Bush" and consideration of executive orders.[25] In other words, if it was interesting or might be, it was likely to remain secret. Yet without a Republican willing to join with the minority to subpoena this material, there was no way of obtaining the documents. In fact, there was no way of even knowing what, exactly, was being hidden.

Grassley defended the Kavanaugh document production as "the most expansive and transparent confirmation process in history," with senators receiving "more pages of executive branch documents than we did for any Supreme Court nominee ever."[26] That latter point was true in terms of gross numbers. But it did not account for the far greater volume of Kavanaugh material in existence. Nor did it address the use of the committee-confidential designation and the claim of constitutional privilege to keep documents from the public and the Senate.

Still, Republicans had a useful talking point in the sheer amount of pages provided and in the argument they continued to make: Democrats who had already announced their opposition to Kavanaugh weren't involved in a good-faith search for information to guide their decision-making. They were hunting for something to use against him or hoping that a deluge of document requests would delay the hearings. "They would like to bury the Senate in mountains of irrelevant documents to delay the confirmation as long as possible," Grassley said in an angry floor speech on July 31. "I won't allow them to abuse the process."[27]

The majority staff was perfectly happy to let Democrats froth over documents. It was an inside fight, and no one outside the Beltway understood it, much less cared about it. Some of the most liberal groups made much the same point. "Chuck Schumer is bringing a FOIA request to a knife fight," Elizabeth Beavers, associate policy director of Indivisible, the grassroots Trump-resistance group, said in August. "Most ordinary constituents are not enraged and spurred to action by process."[28]

No organization better typified the emerging strains between the Democratic leadership and more radical activists than the newest group on the progressive block, Demand Justice. Created in the angry aftermath of the Garland blockade, Demand Justice was run by Brian Fallon, a former aide to Hillary Clinton's presidential campaign and, more pertinent to the Kavanaugh fight, a six-year veteran of Schumerworld. The New York senator, known for his love of matchmaking among members of his staff, had flown to Cleveland to celebrate the 2011 wedding of Fallon, then his communications director, to a senior Schumer staffer, Katie Beirne, giving a ten-minute toast and leading the band in a rendition of "New York, New York."

Before the Kavanaugh confirmation was over, Fallon and Schumer would not be on speaking terms. Where other organizations that were a traditional part of the judicial nominations process took a more conciliatory approach, Fallon and Demand Justice were unrelenting in insisting that, in a post-Garland, postfilibuster environment, Democrats needed to start playing hardball.

Demand Justice launched in May 2018 and kicked off its first campaign in mid-June, in anticipation of a Supreme Court vacancy, with a simple, preemptive message: #DitchTheList. Anyone on Trump's list, given his announced outsourcing to the Federalist Society and flagrant litmus test on overturning *Roe v. Wade*, should be automatically off-limits, Demand Justice argued. In Fallon's assessment, the converse of Kaine's, Democrats had too often made a strategic mistake by choosing to hold fire on a nominee. They wanted to seem open-minded and judicious when, in fact, their reticence simply ceded the playing field to the other side. Instead of wasting time assessing the retiring justice and withholding judgment to see who the nominee might be, Fallon said, Democrats should define the debate early. "Our point was, react forcefully right out of the gate," Fallon said. "That if he picks anybody from this list, it's going to be an all-out fight."[29]

This was a controversial and, as a historical matter, an unusual tactic, although these were, assuredly, unusual times. Back in the day, after Powell's retirement, Joe Biden and Senate majority leader Robert Byrd, of West Virginia, had reached out to Reagan's chief of staff, former Tennessee senator Howard Baker, with their own preemptive message: anyone but Bork. It was advice that the White House ignored at its peril. Now, instead of the microtargeting of one unacceptable nominee, Fallon and other Democrats were advocating a broad-brush strategy. No one, not a single judge, on Trump's list of twenty-five would be an acceptable nominee. Animating this approach was the conviction that Democrats had for too long been complacent in the judicial nominations wars. The left's problem, in this view, wasn't just Republicans being nasty—it was also Democrats being weak. Yes, it was important to try to take back the Senate, but what would it gain Democrats to recover the majority if they failed, as Fallon put it, to "do unto the Republicans what they did unto us"?[30] It was time for Democrats to tap into their inner McConnells, Fallon believed. If Democrats were to win the Senate majority, he argued, they should simply refuse to act on any Supreme Court nominee until the 2020 election. It was past time for Democrats to allow themselves to indulge in what he termed "romantic notions" of senatorial courtesy and bipartisan cooperation.[31]

Demand Justice acted early. In mid-June, well before Kennedy's announcement, it launched a digital advertising campaign skewering Amy Coney Barrett over her opposition to rulings upholding the Affordable Care Act. It also targeted McConnell favorite Thapar over campaign finance rulings favoring Trump's "billionaire friends" and Kavanaugh over whether his writings on presidential power would lead him to favor Trump in any fight with the special counsel.

"Imagine you were President Trump and you wanted to be sure that someone would have your back in a constitutional crisis. What would you do?" the Kavanaugh ad asked. "You'd start by nominating someone like Brett Kavanaugh to the Supreme Court."[32] The digital advertising did not require a big investment, but the spots conveyed the message: there was a new group on the block, and it wasn't waiting to attack.

In the hours after Kennedy's retirement, Schumer ended up going even beyond the Demand Justice position. He was exquisitely aware of the potential pressures from the left. Just the day before, twenty-eight-year-old Alexandria Ocasio-Cortez had shaken the Democratic establishment by defeating incumbent Joe Crowley in the primary for a New York congressional seat.

Schumer chief of staff Mike Lynch spoke to Fallon before Schumer went to the floor. You'll be happy with what he has to say, Lynch assured Fallon. Schumer made the Demand Justice point about not confirming anyone on Trump's list, but he also, much to Fallon's surprise, went further, suggesting that the Scalia precedent meant the Senate should hold off on filling the Kennedy vacancy until after the election. "Our Republican colleagues in the Senate should follow the rule they set in 2016 not to consider a Supreme Court justice in an election year," Schumer said. "Millions of people are just months away from determining the senators who should vote to confirm or reject the president's nominee, and their voices deserve to be heard now, as Leader McConnell thought they should deserve to be heard then."[33]

Feinstein—surprisingly, given her innate cautiousness—agreed. "We're now four months away from an election to determine the party that will control the Senate," she said. "There should be no consideration of a Supreme Court nominee until the American people have a chance to weigh in."[34] Feinstein, too, may have had political considerations in mind. Up for reelection, she was facing a challenge on the left from state senator Kevin de León, who had criticized Feinstein for not fighting back hard enough against McConnell in 2016, when Garland was nominated. The next month, de León won the endorsement of the state Democratic party.

Whatever the reason, this impromptu position against confirming any nominee quickly evaporated—in Fallon's view, muddling what should have been a clear argument about the list. It was an early warning sign that Democrats might not be exactly organized or ready for the fight ahead.

In the following days, Fallon was unsparing, on Twitter and in real life, in going after fellow Democrats he considered wavering or spineless. Demand Justice not only targeted Republicans Murkowski and Collins, it also launched ads urging Heitkamp, Donnelly, and Manchin, the trio of Democrats who had voted for Gorsuch, to oppose Kavanaugh, warning that he would undermine the health care law's protections for people with preexisting conditions.[35] That was relatively mild, but when Kaine—Clinton's running mate in the campaign for which Fallon had served as national press secretary—tweeted shortly after Kavanaugh's selection that he had questions about whether the nominee would uphold the Affordable Care Act or protect abortion rights, Fallon was biting in response. "We already know the answers to these questions, Tim Kaine," he tweeted. "Stop playing political games and help us #StopKavanaugh."[36] After the first round of hearings, in September, when Democratic senator Chris Coons of Delaware said that the Senate should have a "real conversation about restoring" the filibuster for judges, Fallon tweeted back, "We would be better off if the witch had won," a reference to the 2010 election in which Coons's Republican opponent, Christine O'Donnell, was lampooned for insisting, "I'm not a witch."[37]

This approach did not exactly win Fallon friends in the Democratic caucus. In late August, Demand Justice and other progressive groups launched a campaign, #WhipTheVote, targeted at the two dozen Democrats who had not yet announced opposition to Kavanaugh. The campaign's website offered a suggested script for calling senators and pressuring them to take a stance on Kavanaugh. Fallon's group was abruptly disinvited from the weekly strategy sessions that the Democratic leadership held with outside groups.

But Fallon was convinced this was no time to hold fire. Having Democratic senators say they were undecided on Kavanaugh was not consistent with the notion that Kavanaugh posed a dire threat to Americans' rights. If Democrats like these were going to withhold judgment, how would opponents ever generate enough pressure to persuade Republicans Collins and Murkowski to oppose the nominee? Fallon went so far as to prepare ads to run against the three endangered Democrats, showing them to Schumer chief of staff Lynch so the leader would have a heads-up about what was coming. Schumer was enraged by what he viewed as Fallon's disloyalty. He buttonholed leaders of other groups involved in combating the nomination, pulling them aside to complain about Fallon.

Fallon wasn't alone, however. His assertiveness was part of a larger unrest on the left of Schumer's party. As the hearings got under way, an array of groups on the far-left flank of the organizations opposing Kavanaugh sent a scathing letter to the minority leader. "Your strategy to sacrifice the Supreme Court in order to hold Democratic Senate seats is not only strategically and morally wrong, it will fail," they warned. "The Democratic Party's progressive base expects nothing less than all-out resistance to Trump's dangerous agenda . . . And they know that anything less than 49 Democratic votes against Kavanaugh would be a massive failure of your leadership."[38]

This blast at Schumer did not reflect the majority position of the outside groups battling the Kavanaugh nomination. But even among more mainstream advocates there was impatience with what some saw as the inadequately muscular approach of Schumer and the Senate Democrats' leadership. "They weren't fighting," said one advocate. "They were saying the right things—'We will win'—but honestly I don't think that . . . they believed that they could win."

One problem Democrats faced in fighting Kavanaugh was that they couldn't agree on the right message. Was it that Kavanaugh would overturn *Roe v. Wade*? Or was it that he would be more hostile to health care coverage generally? Was it that he would help Trump in his fight against Mueller? Or was it Kavanaugh's broader views on presidential power? The message seemed to shift from moment to moment, which made it less likely that any particular argument would break through. That changing approach reflected a strategic disagreement, in part about how much to focus on the threat to abortion rights. Abortion was a double-edged sword, at once a mobilizer and a turnoff. NARAL Pro-Choice America in particular pressed for an undiluted message that *Roe* was in jeopardy: that was the way, the group argued, to generate the grassroots alarm that would be needed to win this uphill battle. But the organization faced resistance from Schumer and others who worried about the impact that emphasizing abortion would have on vulnerable incumbents. Focusing on abortion made the "Joes"—Manchin of West Virginia and Donnelly of Indiana—especially uncomfortable.

Another approach, perhaps more effective, might be to emphasize the threat Kavanaugh supposedly posed to the Affordable Care Act, although this argument entailed an intellectual leap from his health care rulings. Still, Collins and Murkowski had recently broken with their party to save the Affordable Care Act. Now another legal challenge to the law was making its way through the courts. Perhaps health care reform might work with the pair this time, too. So the two issues were lumped into one clunky package—abortion plus the Affordable Care Act—even if it didn't fit on a bumper sticker.

Over the summer, the polling showed a country both nearly evenly divided on and not overly attuned to the Kavanaugh nomination. From the time of Kavanaugh's selection through the third week of August, Gallup found, the share of those supporting and opposing his nomination remained almost flat. In mid-July, 41 percent wanted to see him confirmed, compared to 37 percent opposed and 22 percent with no opinion. By late August, with the hearings about to get under way, that was essentially unchanged. Republican support for Kavanaugh actually dipped slightly, from 76 percent to 72 percent.[39]

The polling contained both worrying and comforting indications for Kavanaugh. The bad news was that he was a remarkably unpopular nominee. As Gallup noted, "Kavanaugh's four-point margin in favor of confirmation is one of the smallest measured to date, leaving him less of a cushion in public support should any problematic issues arise in the hearings." The only other nominees besides Kavanaugh to enjoy a margin in favor of confirmation of less than ten percentage points had been Bork and Miers, hardly reassuring precedents.[40]

The good news for Kavanaugh was there was no indication that the country was poised to revolt against his confirmation. Nominees' approval numbers tend to drop after their selection—by an average of six points—as critics mobilize and fewer people remain undecided. For Kavanaugh, both support and opposition held steady; meanwhile, more people said they were undecided in August than had said so the month before, and nearly half said they had no strong opinion on the nominee.[41] During the Bork battle, by contrast, the numbers showed a far more heated and engaged audience. Opposition to Bork rose by ten points and support for him by seven points during the summer of his nomination.[42] The Kavanaugh confirmation, for now, was not a fight that was capturing public attention. That augured well for the nominee.

The hearings were set to start September 4, the day after Labor Day, and on the Democratic side, a revolt was brewing over Feinstein's leadership, both among outside groups and among her own Democratic colleagues on the committee. It had been building for weeks. She insisted on reading every word in every news release that went out from committee Democrats, which dramatically slowed Democrats' ability to respond in a rapid-fire news environment. She was, as they saw it, letting Republicans run roughshod over the minority in the documents fight—a few stern letters and floor speeches weren't sufficient to convey what Democrats viewed as the outrage of the Republicans' stonewalling on documents. In particular, although the painful cost of this approach would not become evident for some time, she was reluctant to authorize a full-scale investigation of Kavanaugh, even knowing, thanks to the letter she received from Christine Blasey Ford on July 30, what was still a secret from her colleagues—that there was a serious allegation of sexual misconduct by the nominee.

"One of the original sins was she refused to sign off on allowing investigators on the judiciary committee to go out and investigate Kavanaugh," said one Democratic aide closely involved in the process. "The rule became that the committee was not allowed to reach out to anyone who didn't reach out to us first or who we didn't have an existing connection with. Senator Feinstein thought it was unseemly for us to be investigating him. The nominations team didn't do any investigating except for the people who came to us. It was astonishing." Said another aide, "There's just a lot of investigation that could have been done that wasn't done . . . I thought the investigative piece would be an integral part of what we were doing, but there was no investigation . . . The explanation I was always given was that Feinstein, that's not her way of behaving."

Feinstein's staff would strenuously dispute this assessment. As they saw it, they did what they could, but they faced limitations, with rumors and tips that were fuzzy at best. They couldn't simply cold-call Kavanaugh's classmates or law-firm colleagues for fear of being accused of trolling for dirt on the nominee. But some veteran Democratic staffers believe this was a massive abdication of responsibility. They would commonly make such calls, asking about temperament and experience, for even the most minor district court nominee.

Investigations aside, Democrats and their outside allies were increasingly alarmed that there seemed to be no plan for the hearings. While Democratic counsels held weekly sessions, Feinstein had yet to convene the members to craft anything approaching a common strategy. Maybe they wouldn't be able to stop Kavanaugh, but this didn't even look like they were giving it a serious try.

A group of civil rights leaders staged what they privately described as an "intervention" with Feinstein. Derrick Johnson of the NAACP, Vanita Gupta of the Leadership Conference on Civil and Human Rights, and the Reverend Al Sharpton of the National Action Network met with Feinstein and other Democratic senators in her office, with Sherrilyn Ifill of the NAACP Legal Defense Fund joining by phone. Feinstein needed to be more aggressive, they argued. She was defensive in response. She was issuing sharply worded letters to the Republicans, Feinstein told them. Back in the '90s, Feinstein said, the groups would have been sending more letters themselves, making more noise in the media. Letters? Really? It felt like an argument from a bygone era.

Everything came to a head in the last few weeks before the hearings over the handling of the documents designated "committee confidential." On August 20, Democratic senator Sheldon Whitehouse of Rhode Island asked Grassley to make publicly available the documents relating to Kavanaugh's relationship with Leo and the Federalist Society.[43] Two days later, Grassley turned him down. The request "is unreasonable in its present form," he instructed Whitehouse. If Whitehouse wanted to use any such documents, he needed to inform the majority about which ones, precisely, and keep the request "reasonable both in size and scope," Grassley advised.[44]

Democrats had had enough. Grassley was promoting himself as the champion of transparency, but he expected Democrats to effectively reveal their questions in advance—if they were permitted to use the documents at all. Democratic staffers debated how to proceed. Since, as they saw it, there was no actual rule mandating the committee-confidential procedure, should they simply release these documents themselves?

Schumer, under mounting pressure from outside groups to do something about the document situation, convened a meeting of the Democratic committee members and staff. He more or less announced the plan: Connecticut senator Richard Blumenthal would release the committee-confidential documents on his own, joined by others on the committee in later waves of document release. Republicans might contend that this disclosure violated Senate rules and was, in theory at least, punishable by expulsion. Fine, the Democrats decided: let them try. As the discussions continued, it became clear that Feinstein was having no part of it; she wouldn't participate, but neither would she stop her colleagues from proceeding.

But as Blumenthal's counsel Sam Simon and others worked around the clock to get the documents into proper shape to release— everyone agreed, for example, that personal information would have to be scrubbed—some Democrats began to express qualms and dropped off the disclosure plan. New Jersey senator Cory Booker at least was with the program, but he argued that Democrats should wait until the hearing. It was the end of August, the Senate was in recess, no one was paying attention. Releasing the documents before the hearings started would end up burying the story, Booker said. For anyone who had been through a previous hearing—Booker was new to the committee—this made little sense; the drama of the hearings would crowd out whatever news was contained in the documents. In the end, the plan quietly fizzled. Even once the hearing started, there was no mass release of documents. Some came out, instead, in dribs and drabs, to little effect.

With or without the documents, the issue remained, on the eve of the hearings: What was the plan? What was the message? Where was the leadership? Where, not to put too fine a point on it, was the ranking member? Her fellow committee members were agitated, in particular Booker and California senator Kamala Harris, both preparing to run for president. They called on Schumer to intervene. Joined by Feinstein, Schumer convened the unhappy Democratic members on a boisterous conference call the evening of September 3. This hearing could not be allowed to proceed as if it were business as usual, senator after senator said. They had already considered, then dropped, the notion of walking out of the hearings in protest. All that would mean was that Republicans would proceed without them.

They came up with an alternative and sketched out the precise plans for it that night. As Grassley began his opening statement, Democrat after Democrat would interrupt, seeking a delay in the proceedings to obtain the withheld documents. Harris, the most junior Democrat on the panel, volunteered to go first. Others would follow. Feinstein didn't oppose the interruption—she, too, was angry about the documents—but once again, she made clear she wasn't going to take part. Disruption was not the Feinstein way. Her members could do what they had to, but she was the senior person on the dais. Her role was to deal directly with Grassley, not talk over him.

Later that night, Burck, on behalf of the Bush library, released another 42,000 pages of documents—with instructions that these, too, be treated as committee confidential.[45] The Democrats had already planned to disrupt the start of the hearing. This development reaffirmed their instincts and galvanized their sense of outrage. How could the hearing proceed when this many documents had been dumped on the panel just fifteen hours before it was to start?

CHAPTER ELEVEN

Nothing About This Is Normal

The opening moments of a Supreme Court confirmation hearing tend to unfold with the stately cadence of a meticulously choreographed minuet. The committee chair gavels the room to order, welcomes the nominee, offers him or her the chance to introduce family members, then proceeds to opening statements.

Day 1 of the Kavanaugh hearing was less regular order than senatorial roller derby, with Kavanaugh as bystander to the fury erupting around him.

Grassley, in a red-and-blue striped tie and an American flag pin in his lapel, was just six seconds into his first sentence when, from the far end of the dais, Harris interjected, complaining about the latest document dump and seeking a postponement. Grassley rapped his gavel. "You're out of order," he said. "I'll proceed."[1]

Harris continued, speaking over him. "We cannot possibly move forward, Mr. Chairman, with this hearing," she said. Then Minnesota senator Amy Klobuchar weighed in. Then Blumenthal moved to adjourn, generating whoops from the audience. Then Booker. Then Mazie Hirono of Hawaii. Then Whitehouse. Then Leahy, the Senate's most senior member.

"What are we trying to hide?" asked Leahy, who had chaired the committee for ten years. "Why are we rushing?" The Kavanaugh episode, he said, had produced "the most incomplete, most partisan, least transparent vetting for any Supreme Court nominee

I have ever seen, and I have seen more of those than any person serving in the Senate." As Leahy would say later in the day, ticking through his objections to Republicans' handling of the documents, "Nothing about this is normal." Ranking member Feinstein, weighing in after her more junior members had spoken, offered mildly, "I really regret this, but I think you have to understand the frustration on this side of the aisle."[2]

And so it went, for nearly ninety minutes, an astonishing display of anger—or, from the Republicans' point of view, insolence—by the minority. At one point Davis, Grassley's lawyer, leaned over to Duck, the Feinstein aide: was the ranking member going to tolerate this kind of disrespect to the chairman? The revolt on the dais was mirrored by outbursts from protesters in the room, mostly women. "This is a mockery and a travesty of justice," shouted one. "Cancel Brett Kavanaugh," yelled another. "We dissent! Vote no! Vote no!" said another. One by one, they were dragged out of the hearing room, where women dressed in scarlet *Handmaid's Tale* outfits thronged the hallways.

Through it all, Kavanaugh sat stone-faced, hands clasped on the table, as if oblivious to the senators squabbling in front of him and the protesters yelling in back. Seated just behind Kavanaugh to his right were his wife and two young daughters, alongside his parents. Behind the nominee and to his left was McGahn, the man who had worked so hard to get him to this moment. The morning's spectacle—the screaming demonstrators, the bickering senators—was not judiciary business as usual, but it was of no huge concern. Kavanaugh just had to survive the next three days of ritualized thrust-and-parry and he would, in all likelihood, be seated by the start of the new Supreme Court term on the first Monday in October.

Republicans used the disorder to their advantage, accusing Democrats of descending into "mob rule," as Cornyn put it. His fellow Texan, Cruz, seized on the protests to offer a treacly apology to Kavanaugh. "I'm sorry that your daughters had to endure the political circus of this morning," he said. If anything, the protests from the audience were more disturbing to many of the Democrats on the dais. That the senators interrupted the chairman at the start of his opening statement was a shocking, if understandable, breach of decorum. Combined with the screaming audience members being forcibly removed, it made Democrats look like a single unruly, even unhinged, pack. Feinstein, beginning her questioning of Kavanaugh the next day after a renewed round of audience protests, apologized to the nominee. "I'm sorry about the circumstances," she said, "but we'll get through it."[3]

For Kavanaugh, that was the goal: to get through it. Notwithstanding his experience preparing judicial nominees for confirmation hearings during the Bush administration, Kavanaugh had been a less-than-stellar witness on his own behalf during his appeals court hearings, arousing the concerns of Democrats such as Leahy and Dick Durbin instead of allaying them. His Supreme Court hearings represented a higher-stakes sequel. Accompanied by McGahn, he had trudged through sixty-five courtesy calls with senators over the summer, boning up on each senator's peeves and interests. He worked through binders of material on legal issues, from environmental law to gun rights, separation of powers to substantive due process; then, like a law student cramming for an exam on material he already knew, held study sessions with former clerks and other advisers on potential questions. He had subjected himself to several practice sessions designed to be even more grueling than the real thing—murder boards, they were called. The hearings were the final hurdle to achieving his decades-long dream. If it took sitting through a little yelling, so be it.

For all the hours of preparation, there wasn't much that could be gleaned from Kavanaugh's testimony, except that, like his recent predecessors, he was adept at displaying familiarity with doctrine without tipping his hand about any of his own views. Any nominee to the high court must tread a delicate line between angering senators by coming off as slippery and endangering his or her confirmation by saying too much. The lesson of Bork, with his extensive discussion of his legal philosophy, was that it was better to err on the side of caution.

And err the nominees did, in what became known as the Ginsburg rule, after the justice who, at her 1993 hearing, vowed "no forecasts, no hints" of how she might vote.[4] Kagan, who had signed on to work for Biden as an adviser during the Ginsburg hearing, offered a cogent, if depressing, analysis of how the process had been degraded. "The Bork hearings presented to the public a serious discussion of the meaning of the Constitution, the role of the Court, and the views of the nominee; that discussion at once educated the public and allowed it to determine whether the nominee would move the Court in the proper direction," Kagan wrote in a 1995 law review article. "Subsequent hearings have presented to the public a vapid and hollow charade, in which repetition of platitudes has replaced discussion of viewpoints and personal anecdotes have supplanted legal analysis."[5] Unsurprisingly, a different, cagier Kagan turned up before the committee as a nominee in 2010.

So Kavanaugh was not the first witness to irritate senators seeking answers the nominee was unwilling to provide. And he could hardly be blamed if he viewed the hearing less as an exercise in disinterested fact-finding than as partisan warfare by opponents who would leap at any excuse to take him down. As the nominee, his role was essentially Hippocratic—to do no harm to his own cause. Still, Kavanaugh's innate caution, his tendency to look for the potential trap lurking behind every question from a Democratic senator, seemed at times to cross the line into evasiveness and disingenuousness. Perhaps that didn't matter—it wasn't as if Kavanaugh was going to win over any Democratic senators with his testimony. The vote on the committee itself was all but guaranteed to split along party lines. But for Democrats, Kavanaugh's performance at the hearings reinforced a lingering sense of distrust about the nominee. No one predicted it at the time, but the doubts about Kavanaugh's honesty evoked at the hearings would come to the fore in the next pivotal weeks.

•   •   •

Throughout the Democrats' protests, Grassley, a taciturn eighty-four-year-old who grew up on his family's farm and was serving his sixth term in the Senate, maintained his cool. "If people wonder why the chair is so patient during this whole process," he observed, "I have found that it takes longer to argue why you shouldn't do anything than let people argue why they want it." Still, he noted at one point, "This is something I've never gone through before in fifteen Supreme Court nominations . . . since I've been on here."[6]

By the time of the Kavanaugh hearing, Grassley was in his sixtieth year in elective office, having spent sixteen years in the Iowa legislature before being elected to the U.S. House in 1974 and, in 1980, to the Senate. Grassley liked to refer to himself as "a pig farmer from Iowa." As one profile early in his Senate career put it, "on first sighting he looks like the sort of Central Casting character who comes in from the sticks and gets his clock cleaned in the big city."[7]

But Grassley's opponents had learned not to be fooled by his slow-talking midwestern manner. He had made a name for himself in the Senate as a champion of whistle-blowers, willing to take on both Republican and Democratic administrations when he thought they were withholding documents or impeding his efforts at oversight. As the documents fight unfolded, Democrat after Democrat appealed to Grassley's vaunted reputation for fairness and dedication to transparency. Their blandishments had little discernible effect. Before the nomination, Grassley and his staff had worried about balancing Kavanaugh's lengthy paper trail with the Iowan's commitment to transparency. Once Trump made his choice, Grassley—along with Davis, his sharp-elbowed, short-tempered nominations counsel—was fully committed to getting Kavanaugh across the finish line.

As the Democrats bemoaned the withholding of documents, Grassley countered numbers with numbers, precedent with precedent. Leahy pointed to the small percentage of Kavanaugh documents they had been permitted to see; Grassley cited the raw number of pages, more than had been produced for any nominee in history. Harris complained about inadequate time to review the material, including the just-released documents; Grassley noted that his staff had set up 24-7 work stations for all one hundred senators to review the committee-confidential documents. Whitehouse and Klobuchar questioned the invocation of "constitutional privilege"; Grassley retorted that the Obama administration had refused to release Kagan's documents from her time in the solicitor general's office. This point omitted the fact that such documents had traditionally been withheld—John Roberts's memoranda from that period were also not disclosed. But these niceties tended to be lost in the furious, partisan posturing.

The chief substantive issue in the hearings was, predictably, abortion and the related question of what factors the court should take into account in deciding whether to overturn a case. For Kavanaugh, the discussion proceeded along the path of avoidance well-trodden by previous nominees. Naturally, judicial propriety prevented him from sharing his thoughts on *Roe v. Wade* and whether the Constitution protects a woman's right to choose, he said.

Then, much as Gorsuch did the year before, he ticked through the relevant considerations of *stare decisis*, the principle that the court should not overturn decisions lightly. *Roe* was not only a long-standing precedent, Kavanaugh noted, it was also one that had been repeatedly reaffirmed, reinforcing its claim against being overturned "It's not as if it's just a run-of-the-mill case," he said, adding, "I live in the real world. I understand the importance of the issue."[8]

Was Kavanaugh saying that he understood how disruptive it would be for millions of women across America if the constitutional right to abortion were eliminated? Was he saying that he grasped how strongly millions of other Americans who believe that abortion is the taking of a human life feel about the issue? If you were inclined in Kavanaugh's direction but worried, like Collins, that he might overturn *Roe*, you could choose to take some solace from his testimony. If you were mistrustful, you might note that nothing Kavanaugh was saying would tie his hands once he was on the court. After all, just the year before, Gorsuch had sat in that very hearing room assuring senators of his dedication to *stare decisis*. "You start with a heavy, heavy presumption in favor of precedent in our system," he told the committee.[9] Then, in his first full term on the court, he voted to jettison a forty-one-year-old ruling letting public-sector unions require nonmembers to pay for the costs of collective bargaining. "Rarely if ever has the Court overruled a decision—let alone one of this import—with so little regard for the usual principles of *stare decisis*," Kagan wrote in dissent in the case, *Janus v. AFSCME*.[10]

With Kavanaugh, senators had a little more to go on than they did with Gorsuch in probing the nominee's views on abortion rights. There was the *Garza* case, involving the pregnant teenage migrant. In that situation, Kavanaugh told the senators, he had done his best to apply what he considered the most relevant precedents—the Supreme Court's rulings on minors' access to abortion—to a new situation. The justices had already countenanced brief delays for minors seeking abortions, he said, and he was merely applying that approach to a different circumstance. "It was a delay, undoubtedly, but a delay consistent as I saw it with the Supreme Court precedent on parental consent provisions," Kavanaugh said. As Democratic senators noted, the pregnant teenager had already complied with Texas's procedure for minors and obtained a judge's assessment that she was mature enough to make her own decision.[11] The discussion was interesting but inconclusive. Kavanaugh was not going to budge, or show his cards on *Roe*.

Another opportunity to press Kavanaugh on abortion involved an e-mail from his days in the White House counsel's office, showing the notes he had made on a draft op-ed defending the nomination of Priscilla Owen. The draft asserted that it is "widely understood . . . by legal scholars across the board that *Roe v. Wade* and its progeny are the settled law of the land." In the e-mail, originally among those deemed committee confidential, Kavanaugh took issue with that assessment. "I am not sure that all legal scholars refer to *Roe* as the settled law of the land at the Supreme Court level," he observed, "since [the] Court can always overrule its precedent, and three current Justices on the Court would do so."[12]

Questioned about the e-mail by Feinstein, Kavanaugh said he was simply trying to ensure that the op-ed was "technically accurate." Then he pivoted to the "broader point." *Roe* "is an important precedent," he said. "It's been reaffirmed many times." One useful analogy, he suggested, was Chief Justice Rehnquist's 2000 ruling in *Dickerson v. United States*, declining to overrule the landmark case of *Miranda v. Arizona*. Rehnquist had long inveighed against the 1966 ruling in which the court required that criminal suspects be advised of their constitutional rights. Still, he not only voted to uphold it but also wrote the decision himself, Kavanaugh noted.[13] By that point, Feinstein was ready to move on.

Democrats were similarly unable to make much progress in pinning down Kavanaugh's views on executive power. That had been another focus of Democratic criticism over the summer, as the Mueller investigation dragged on. The pendency of the Mueller probe raised any number of questions that could wend their way to the high court. Could a sitting president be indicted? Did Trump have the authority to fire Mueller? Could the president be compelled to testify?

These questions would be relevant for any nominee, but they were of particular importance in the case of Kavanaugh, given his extensive writings on the subject. The young prosecutor who once took such an aggressive stance on investigating the president in Starr's office had developed a different view of subjecting a president to such inquiries after his stint in the Bush White House.

In a 2009 article for the *Minnesota Law Review*, Kavanaugh proposed that Congress enact legislation that would make sitting presidents immune from civil suits and, in the criminal realm, immune not only from indictment but also from any investigation whatsoever while serving. "Looking back to the late 1990s," he acknowledged, "the nation certainly would have been better off if President Clinton could have focused on Osama bin Laden without being distracted by the Paula Jones sexual harassment case and its criminal-investigation offshoots."[14] This was a policy proposal, not a matter of legal interpretation, but there were indications that it also fit within Kavanaugh's constitutional vision of broad presidential authority. And during a 1998 discussion on the independent counsel law, Kavanaugh had been among the panelists who raised their hands when the moderator asked whether they believed that a sitting president was immune from indictment.[15]

The following year, at a discussion on attorney-client privilege, Kavanaugh suggested that perhaps *United States v. Nixon*, the 1974 case in which a unanimous Supreme Court ordered the president to turn over Oval Office tapes to the Watergate special prosecutor, had been "wrongly decided—heresy though it is to say so . . . Maybe the tension of the time led to an erroneous decision." At another point he suggested that perhaps the court shouldn't have inserted itself in the case at all. "Should *U.S. v. Nixon* be overruled on the ground that the case was a nonjusticiable intra-branch dispute?" Kavanaugh asked. "Maybe so."[16]

In 2016, asked about what Supreme Court case he would like to see overturned, Kavanaugh at first demurred, then cited *Morrison v. Olson*, the 1988 case that upheld the constitutionality of the independent counsel statute and that has long been among the most reviled by conservatives. "It's been effectively overruled, but I would put the final nail in," Kavanaugh said.[17] This assessment did not have direct bearing on the legitimacy of Mueller's probe— the independent counsel law upheld in *Morrison* had long expired, and Mueller had been appointed under a less controversial internal Justice Department regulation. But Kavanaugh's views about the case were illustrative of a broader adherence to what conservatives describe as the "unitary executive," envisioning a president in full control of executive power.

Delaware Democrat Chris Coons, who had been at Yale Law School with Kavanaugh, was the one to question him most extensively about his views on presidential power. Kavanaugh insisted that his comments about whether *United States v. Nixon* had been wrongly decided had been "mischaracterized." He had been arguing with lawyers for Clinton about whether Starr's office had weakened the presidency, Kavanaugh noted. His point was that the fault did not lie with Starr but with the *Nixon* case itself. "The tone of voice there makes the printed words look much different from how they were intended," he said. This was unconvincing, but it was also clear that Kavanaugh had repeatedly praised *Nixon* years before being nominated. He did so, extravagantly, at the hearing, even as he avoided any answers about how the holding in *Nixon* might apply in the Mueller probe.[18]

The rest of the discussion proceeded along the same lines. Questioned about *Morrison v. Olson* and the unitary executive, Kavanaugh repeatedly cited a stray remark by Kagan as evidence that their views were the same. During a 2015 event at Stanford, the justice had called Scalia's solo dissent in the case "one of the greatest dissents ever written, and every year it gets better."[19] Kavanaugh seized on Kagan's offhand comment as conclusive evidence that she agreed with him about the merits of the case. Kagan, Kavanaugh said, "seemed to be saying, at least I think this is the only reading of it, that the *Morrison v. Olson* decision was wrong." That was a vast overreading of Kagan's comment, which had come during a conversation about examples of excellent legal writing, and an inaccurate description of her views. In fact, as Coons noted, Kagan had written a law review article that rejected the unitary executive theory at the core of Scalia's dissent and cited *Morrison* as "accepted constitutional doctrine."[20]

Coons was a smart questioner with the capacity to read the cases and law review articles that Kavanaugh was citing and to match wits with him. He was correct that Kavanaugh was taking Kagan's words too far. That didn't matter much. The issues of presidential authority were as abstruse as they were important. It was almost impossible to translate these esoteric debates to the public in a way that would have much real-world impact.

As the hearings proceeded, presidential ambitions were not difficult to detect.

Late in the evening of Kavanaugh's first full day of testimony, Harris, a former prosecutor, seemed to violate the first rule of cross-examination—never ask a question to which you don't know the answer—when she went hard at Kavanaugh in her opening question: "Judge, have you ever discussed Special Counsel Mueller or his investigation with anyone?"[21]

The exchange got weirder from there. Harris acted as if she had some goods on Kavanaugh, but they were never revealed. Meanwhile, the nominee, perhaps out of an abundance of lawyerly caution, came off as evasive. Harris asked Kavanaugh whether he had discussed the Mueller probe "with anyone at Kasowitz, Benson and Torres, the law firm founded by Marc Kasowitz, President Trump's personal lawyer," adding ominously, "Be sure about your answer, sir."

Kavanaugh demurred—"Well, is there a person you're talking about?"—and he and Harris kept circling. The squirrelier he sounded, the more her prosecutorial instincts were aroused.

Kavanaugh: "I'm not sure I know everyone who works at that law firm."

Harris: "But I don't think you need to. I think you need to know who you talked with. Who did you talk to?"

And so it went, for almost eight uncomfortable minutes, until Harris moved on. "I think you're thinking of someone and you don't want to tell us," she said.[22]

The next day, Harris returned to the topic, telling Kavanaugh that she had received "reliable information that you had a conversation about the special counsel or his investigation with the law firm that has represented President Trump." Again, Kavanaugh was an uncooperative witness, either careful or elusive, depending on your perspective.[23]

> Harris: "I'm asking you, were you a party to a conversation that occurred regarding special counsel Mueller's investigation, and a simple yes or no would suffice."
>
> Kavanaugh: "About his investigation, and are you referring to a specific person?"
>
> Harris: "I'm referring to a specific subject, and the specific person I'm referring to is you."
>
> Kavanaugh: "Who was the conversation with? You said you had information."
>
> Harris: "That is not the subject of the question, sir . . . The subject of the question is you and whether you were part of a conversation regarding special counsel Mueller's investigation."
>
> Kavanaugh: "The answer—the answer is no."
>
> Harris: "Thank you. And it would have been great if you could've said that last night."[24]

It required mop-up questioning from a friendly interlocutor, Republican senator Thom Tillis of North Carolina, to clarify the mystery, at least somewhat. Tillis asked Kavanaugh if he knew any lawyers at the Kasowitz firm, and Kavanaugh finally volunteered a name. "I know Ed McNally: he used to work in the White House counsel's office." Kavanaugh then said that the two had never discussed the Mueller probe.[25]

It was far from a Perry Mason moment, and veterans of confirmation hearings were left scratching their heads about what Harris was trying to achieve and whether she had erred in raising the topic without the evidence to back it up. But perhaps such concerns were outmoded in a hyperpartisan, hyperconnected world. By the afternoon following the original Harris questioning, a C-SPAN video of the exchange had been viewed nearly five million times.

Then came Booker's self-proclaimed Spartacus moment. After the plan to release the committee-confidential documents before the hearings fell apart, senators began simply using the documents. Some, such as Klobuchar, obtained permission. Others, such as Whitehouse, Blumenthal, and Hirono, just began quoting from them.

Cory Booker found the spotlight. On the second evening of Kavanaugh's testimony, he read aloud from e-mails that touched on racial profiling, affirmative action, and set-aside programs for minority-owned businesses. The next day, without going through Grassley's approval mechanism, he released the e-mails in their entirety.

"I knowingly violated the rules that were put forth," Booker acknowledged as Republicans sputtered angrily. "I come from a long line, as all of us do as Americans, who understand what that kind of civil disobedience is, and I understand the consequences . . . I openly invite and accept the consequences of my team releasing that e-mail right now," Booker said.[26]

Grassley drily interjected. "Can I ask you how long you're going to say the same thing three or four times?" Booker responded, "I'm saying I'm knowingly violating the rules." Grassley: "Okay. How many times do you want to tell us."

Cornyn turned up the heat. "Running for president is no excuse for violating the rules of the Senate or of the confidentiality of the documents that we are privy to," he lectured, comparing Booker's move to the unauthorized release of classified information. "That is irresponsible and outrageous. And I hope that the senator will reconsider his decision, because no senator deserves to sit on this committee or serve in the Senate, in my view, if they decide to be a law unto themselves and willingly flout the rules of the Senate."

Cornyn went so far as to accuse Booker of "conduct unbecoming a senator," a weighty charge to lodge against a colleague, even one from the other party. Cornyn invoked the Senate rule—the one Democratic senators had discussed as they weighed releasing the committee-confidential documents en masse—that exposes senators to expulsion if they "disclose the secret or confidential business" of the Senate or its committees. "Bring it," Booker replied.

Booker's colleagues, up to and including Feinstein, came to his defense, agreeing with his assessment of the irregularity of the committee-confidential process. "This is about the closest I'll probably ever have in my life to an 'I am Spartacus' moment," Booker observed, referring to the famous scene in the 1960 Kirk Douglas film in which the Roman slave is protected from exposure by his fellow captives as they, too, proclaim themselves to be Spartacus.[27]

As it turned out, unbeknownst to Booker, Grassley had lifted the confidentiality restrictions earlier that morning for those very documents, meaning that he was not actually in ethical jeopardy. It became a Republican talking point that Booker had engaged in an unnecessary and embarrassing bit of theatrics, even though, as Cornyn's threats of expulsion illustrated, Republicans themselves were also unaware that the documents' status had changed. Still, Booker's performance, and the unavoidable fact of his looming presidential ambitions, exposed him to inevitable criticism for grandstanding. "One couldn't help wondering," observed *Washington Post* columnist Kathleen Parker, "whether the 'I am Spartacus' bumper stickers and 'Break Rules' T-shirts were already being printed."[28]

For Kavanaugh, a more damaging series of exchanges—to the extent anything was damaging at this stage—involved questions about whether he had been truthful with the committee at his appeals court confirmation hearings. This focus was linked to, and helped explain, the Democrats' insistence on access to documents. Being able to see material that had been shielded from view when Kavanaugh was up for the appeals court could confirm Democrats' suspicions that he had, at a minimum, been less than forthcoming about his work in the Bush counsel's office.

One set of issues concerned Kavanaugh's testimony about controversial judicial nominees, in particular whether he had been truthful about his work on their confirmations. These included William Pryor—the judge whom Trump cited, on the night of Scalia's death, as an example of the kind of justice he would choose—whose nomination to the Eleventh Circuit had been one of the most controversial of the Bush administration. At his appeals court hearing in 2004, Kavanaugh downplayed any involvement with Pryor. "That was not one of the people that was assigned to me," Kavanaugh said then. "I am familiar generally with Mr. Pryor, but that was not one that I worked on personally."[29]

That was true in the sense that Kavanaugh was not the specific attorney assigned to shepherd the Pryor nomination. In answers to written questions back then, Kavanaugh noted, "It is fair to say that all of the attorneys in the White House Counsel's office who worked on judges . . . participated in discussions and meetings concerning all of the President's judicial nominations."[30] But the newly released documents revealed that Kavanaugh's account of his role was disingenuous at best. They showed that Kavanaugh in fact suggested that Pryor be considered for the appeals court vacancy, that Kavanaugh may have interviewed him for the job, that he participated in a "working group" on the Pryor nomination, and that he was invited to participate in a conference call and an "emergency" meeting about the nomination.

The records demonstrate that Kavanaugh was in frequent contact with others in the Bush administration, as well as with outside groups, about the Pryor nomination. "Hatch's staffer just told DOJ there would be a hearing on Pryor next week," he advised colleagues on June 4, 2003.[31] Two days later, a Justice Department lawyer sent Kavanaugh a document called "Pryor paper." Benjamin Powell, the White House lawyer primarily assigned to Pryor, followed up several hours later, asking whether Kavanaugh had a chance to read the document. "I did send around to groups," Kavanaugh responded.[32] On June 12, the day after Pryor's confirmation hearing, Kavanaugh e-mailed Benjamin Wittes, then an editorial writer at the *Washington Post*, "Did you watch pryor hearing?" and circulated an e-mail "from a prominent Catholic conservative" about Pryor.[33] The next month, Kavanaugh wrote an e-mail to Powell with the subject line, "I would tell Pryor . . . " The rest of that e-mail was withheld.[34] This was hardly the minimal involvement with Pryor's nomination that Kavanaugh had testified to under oath.

An even more emotional question was whether Kavanaugh, as a White House lawyer, realized—or should have—that a Republican Senate staffer was hacking into Senate Judiciary Committee files to obtain inside information about Democrats' tactics on judicial nominees. This subject, which also first arose during Kavanaugh's appeals court hearings, involved a Republican staffer named Manuel Miranda, who between 2001 and 2003 worked for then Judiciary ranking member Orrin Hatch and later became chief nominations counsel to Senate majority leader Bill Frist. Miranda piggybacked on the work of a clerk in the Judiciary Committee's nominations unit, Jason Lundell, who discovered that he could access the computer files of Democratic committee staffers and repeatedly did so at Miranda's direction, hunting for information about Democrats' tactics to fight some of the Bush administration's most controversial judicial nominees. A Senate investigation found that the pair had accessed 4,670 files. Miranda was never prosecuted, but this was an unforgivable breach of trust, one that still stung committee veterans such as Illinois Democrat Richard Durbin and Leahy, the chairman at the time, who called the hacking a "digital Watergate."

Miranda said he never told Kavanaugh he was sharing stolen information, and Kavanaugh insisted, at his appeals court hearings and again when tapped for the high court, that he had no clue there was anything amiss with the information that Miranda was funneling to the White House. "There was nothing out of the ordinary of what Senate staffs would tell us or what we would hear from our legislative affairs folks," Kavanaugh told Durbin in 2004.[35] Two years later, Durbin raised the issue again, asking Kavanaugh whether he had worked with Miranda. "We talked about this last time," Kavanaugh said, again insisting that all the detailed information Miranda was sending around had struck him as completely normal. "He was part of the staff, of course, that worked on judicial nominations."[36]

By the time of Kavanaugh's Supreme Court nomination, Leahy and other Democrats had the benefit of something they had lacked in the earlier rounds: some, at least, of the e-mail traffic between Miranda and Kavanaugh. Those documents demonstrated repeated contact between the two, involving, among other things, the contested nomination of Priscilla Owen to the Fifth Circuit, one of Kavanaugh's responsibilities in the counsel's office. In a July 18, 2002, e-mail headlined "Highly confidentail" [sic], Miranda informed Kavanaugh that Biden's staff "is asking him not to attend the hearing" and noted that a critical article "is being distributed by the Leahy staff."[37] The next day, Miranda shared with Kavanaugh two questions that appeared to have been drafted by Leahy's staff: "What is the connection between Owen and Texans for Lawsuit Reform (larger issue) and the Texas Civil Justice League (smaller)? Is their [sic] any coincidence in her donors and theirs?" Miranda reaffirmed the focus of Democrats' planned attack two days later, writing, "Intel suggests that Leahy will concentrate on all things Money."[38]

Later that month, Miranda emphasized even more strongly that the information he was providing about the Owen nomination needed to be kept secret. "It is important that it be confidential to the recipients of this e-mail and up your chains of authority only," he wrote to a group that included Kavanaugh and several Justice Department officials who worked on nominations. Miranda's tip concerned a confidential letter that had been circulated by Leahy's staff to other Democratic committee staff. It came from a Texas lawyer, Collyn Peddie, who criticized Owen's handling of abortion cases involving pregnant minors as a Texas Supreme Court justice. "According to either the letter or the Leahy staff Ms. Peddie sent this letter in the strictest confidence because she is up for partner, and believes she will be fired if it is publicized," Miranda wrote.

"Several members of her firm are lead supporters of the Owen nomination. Leahy's staff is only sharing with Democratic counsels."

Miranda said he had not seen the letter—then proceeded to quote directly from it, noting that Peddie criticized Owen for "appalling insensitivity" to the pregnant teens and for publishing "dissents and concurrences in which paragraph after paragraph of confidential testimony was quoted in great detail."[39] Two days later, Miranda again contacted Kavanaugh with inside information. "I have it on 100% info that Leahy is trying to convene the Dems this afternoon after Policy Lunch to check on where they stand on Owen . . . refer only to rumor, not to me."[40] This hardly seemed like the kind of run-of-the-mill information-sharing of Kavanaugh's mild depiction.

Likewise, in a March 2003 e-mail marked "for use and not distribution," Miranda shared a lengthy internal Democratic memo about the Miguel Estrada nomination and Democrats' efforts to obtain documents from Estrada's service in the solicitor general's office.[41] As Leahy nominations counsel Lisa Graves, who authored the memo, later wrote, "We would never have provided that information—key to our strategy to try to block what we considered extremist judicial nominations—to Miranda or to the White House."[42] Kavanaugh, she said, "would know exactly what this was, that this was secret research from the Democrats, from a Democratic lawyer, on the most important fight they were having, in the middle of that fight, on the most important issue that fight was about."[43]

Leahy drilled down on these e-mails at the hearing—but he was constrained, in his first round of questioning, by the fact that some of the documents remained committee confidential and could not be quoted directly. Did Miranda "provide you with highly specific information regarding what I or other Democratic senators were planning in the future to ask certain judicial nominees?" he asked Kavanaugh. As in the appeals court hearings, Kavanaugh demurred. It was "very common," he said, for administration officials working on nominations to try to figure out what senators from the opposite party were planning to focus on. And he described a collegial, cooperative process in which it was a matter of course for staffs of opposite parties to work together. "It's not always the case, at least my understanding, that the people on, for example, your staff and Senator Hatch's staff were necessarily working at odds," he said.[44]

Leahy returned to the subject in his second round of questioning the next day—after securing, at three o'clock that morning, the public release of committee-confidential documents. Leahy quoted from the documents—about the confidential Peddie letter distributed to Democratic counsels and about Leahy's strategy for when to hold the Owen vote. "Did any of this raise a red flag in your mind?" he asked.

Kavanaugh: "It did not Senator, because it all seemed consistent with the usual kinds of discussions that happened . . . People have friends across the aisle who they talk to—at least this was my experience back then; maybe it's changed. And there was a lot of bipartisanship on the committee. There was a lot of bipartisanship among the staffs."[45]

This was a lovely sentiment but, as Leahy noted, not an accurate portrayal of the deeply felt and fiercely fought nominations wars of the period. It was not, in fact, normal for a staff member of one party to have precise details about the planned questioning from a senator of the opposing party or drafts of the other side's talking points. Kavanaugh might have at least conceded, in the glare of hindsight, that the Miranda information had a suspect quality to it, whether or not he realized something was amiss at the time.

The *Washington Post*'s Fact Checker awarded Kavanaugh's testimony on Miranda three Pinocchios, meaning "significant factual error and/or obvious contradictions." (The maximum is four, reserved for "whoppers.") Kavanaugh's claims "defy logic," wrote fact-checker Salvador Rizzo. "An elite Republican lawyer who was immersed at the time in Washington's inside baseball, Kavanaugh strains credulity by claiming this extraordinary window he had into Democrats' thinking seemed aboveboard . . . The best-case scenario is that Kavanaugh, who is up for a seat on the nation's highest court, has a glaring lack of curiosity or a superficial level of discernment. The worst-case scenario is that he has been feigning ignorance since his first confirmation hearing."[46]

Leahy opted for the worst case, writing a *Washington Post* op-ed under the headline BRETT KAVANAUGH MISLED THE SENATE UNDER OATH. I CANNOT SUPPORT HIS NOMINATION. During his forty-four years in the Senate, Leahy wrote, "it has never been normal to obtain sensitive, inside information from the opposing party, conveyed in secret and in real time involving the most contentious issues before our committee. A smart political operative on the frontlines of these battles would have seen these glaring red lights for what they were: clear evidence of nefarious acts."[47]

The op-ed was, in its own way, a sign of the times, the seniormost Democratic senator asserting that Kavanaugh was disqualified not because of his views but because he had repeatedly misled the Senate. It was another indication of how poisonous the atmosphere around Kavanaugh had become and how much the Democrats' distrust of the likely new justice had deepened.

CHAPTER TWELVE

Paddling In

For a surfer, one of the most shameful events is having to "paddle in"—to face a big wave and balk at catching it. That was the thought that haunted Christine Blasey Ford during the long summer of 2018. Would she end up having to paddle in? Would she never tell her story, after all the anguish about whether to come forward with her account of how a seventeen-year-old Brett Kavanaugh had sexually assaulted her at a high school party on a summer night on another coast more than three decades earlier?

By profession, Ford is a professor of psychology, with a particular expertise in biostatistics and how to measure the aftermath of trauma. But by avocation she is a passionate surfer. She spends summer days, from dawn to sunset, on the beach in Santa Cruz, around forty-five miles away from Palo Alto; she and her husband, Russell, dream of saving up for a condo in Hawaii and retiring to surf there.

"I kept trying to explain that metaphor to my team, because they hadn't surfed a wave," Ford recalled, sitting in the February chill outside a Stanford museum four months after Kavanaugh's confirmation. All that summer, as Ford debated whether to go public, as her team of advisers warned about the life-changing consequences of doing so—their metaphor of choice was a freight train bearing down on her—Ford thought about the humiliation of having to paddle in.[1]

"I said, 'You just have to go. You can't paddle in once you've paddled out' . . . I said to them at one point, 'You just have to go on a wave.' Maybe I'm going to wipe out, and maybe I'm going to get hurt. But I have to at least try it and take a wave to the beach. I'm not going to paddle in."[2]

Ford had moved away from the East Coast, from the Maryland suburbs where she grew up and the Delaware beach where she spent summers with her family, in part to get away from memories of Kavanaugh. It was, in her telling, an encounter that she remembered with a combination of piercing detail and frustrating haziness, one she had taken pains to keep hidden from her parents and classmates. She had mentioned it occasionally over the years—to a friend coping with the aftereffects of a sexual assault, and in conversation with another friend in shared outrage over the light sentence imposed on Stanford swimmer Brock Turner for sexually assaulting an unconscious woman. It had come up in therapy sessions, including couples therapy with Russell, trying to explain her puzzling insistence that as they remodel their modest Palo Alto home they install a second front door to exit the master bedroom.

Chrissy Blasey was the youngest of three, with two older brothers. Her father was a businessman, her mother a housewife. It was a strict upbringing: talking back was not tolerated, and, as the only girl, Chrissy was subject to the strictest rules of all, a double standard that chafed even then. At 9:00 p.m., when she was talking away on the phone with her girlfriends, her parents would pick up the phone and announce summarily that Chrissy needed to go. She had a curfew—sophomore year it was 11:00—that was strictly enforced. A minute late, and she was grounded.

Ford went to public elementary school—Carderock Springs, out past the Beltway in Bethesda—before transferring to the all-girls Holton-Arms in seventh grade. The Holton girls wore green, blue, and white plaid pleated skirts, as far above the knee as they could get away with, except on Fridays, when the dress code was relaxed enough to permit blue corduroy slacks. In Ford's retelling, she was a sassy, even annoying student, "immature and problematic," the youngest in her class of sixty girls and prone to getting into trouble with her teachers for mouthing off and passing notes. Ford was a cheerleader, soccer player, and manager of the basketball team; one year she earned a medal in Latin, her favorite class, and had it not been for her parents' insistence that she find a career, she imagined that she might have been a classics major in college. "Chrissy is a very sunny personality," her friend Samantha Guerry recalled. "She was laid back, she was funny; my impression is she was somebody who was always goofing around, laughing."[3] Every high school divides itself into cliques, and Ford's place was with the popular crowd. "We were the girls who went out to parties," she recalled. "We were the girls that were out and about."[4]

The episode with Kavanaugh was, in Ford's view, "the gas on the fire" of her bad behavior. "I was a sweeter person before then," she said. Afterward, in junior and senior years, she became more of a screw-up. One day, maybe at the end of junior year, one of her favorite teachers, a former Marine, pulled her aside. He was fond of Chrissy, but the teacher said she needed "to know how badly you're screwing up. The teachers think very poorly of you; you're not doing well, and when you apply to college those are the people that write the letter." For years Ford avoided Holton reunions because she was so ashamed that her behavior had been rude, that the teachers disliked her.[5]

The summer of her encounter with Kavanaugh was a typical upper-middle-class suburban idyll—sunny days by the pool at Columbia Country Club, occasional rounds of golf with her friend Leland Ingham (who took the last name Keyser when she married), a gifted golfer. Every night, they were in search of a party, looking for somebody's house to hang out at. There would be some drinking, maybe a keg of beer, maybe people sitting on couches and making out, but not much more than that, certainly not before junior or senior year.

Before the party that night, Ford had run into Brett Kavanaugh and Mark Judge at parties with their Georgetown Prep classmate Chris Garrett. She had met Garrett on the boardwalk in Rehoboth Beach, Delaware, where her family vacationed, and they dated, briefly, in tenth grade. Judge, she thought, was "fun and funny"—

Leland had a bit of a crush on him—while Kavanaugh seemed "more intense." She couldn't remember exactly where the house was but thought, vaguely, it had been borrowed from someone's friend or a relative; they had to be careful not to mess it up. When Kavanaugh and Judge arrived, "they were really, really drunk, louder than they were supposed to be."[6]

Then, maybe an hour into the gathering, Ford went up the stairs to use the bathroom, at which point, she said, Kavanaugh and Judge pushed her into a bedroom. She thought, at first, it was a prank. "They're just joking, this is going to stop, because they were friends," she recalled. "Then I was like, 'Oh, my God, why are they pinning me down?' . . . Rapidly, like, 'Oh, my God, they're not going to let me up.'" It ended when Judge jumped on Kavanaugh and knocked them all off the bed. "I jumped up and got out of there," Ford said. "I went into the bathroom, and I was scared, but then I heard them hitting the walls, trying to get back downstairs . . . and I was like, well, I'm never going to get out of there because I have to walk past them."

Ford does not have a clear recollection of how she got home that night, but she believes it was with Leland, in her mom's blue station wagon with wood-grain panels. "Nobody believes that I wouldn't tell my friend, but back then the calculation is popularity," Ford said. "I don't want to be less popular." Even more motivating was the need to avoid telling her father that anything bad had happened. It was early—well before her curfew—and he would wonder why she was home so soon. She had to find a way to shut down any questioning.

When she returned home that night, she said, "my entire focus is, I have to get past my father, and I don't want him to look at me," she recalled. "I don't want him to see that there's something wrong with me, because he's going to know—he is that kind of person who would be, like, 'Something happened.' I've got to get past the guard at the castle . . . and into my room without him seeing me, and that's basically going to be impossible. But I did it. I got in. He said, 'Did you have fun?' or whatever he usually said. 'Good night.' I didn't really look him in the eye. I went into my room and shut my door."

She told herself it was no big deal. "I was relieved, and I was like, I survived this thing. I was not raped. I didn't get raped and nothing happened, nothing happened."

The consequences manifested themselves in the future, Ford came to believe, with problems in college, lingering anxiety and occasional claustrophobia. Yet the statistician in her also resisted assigning clear cause and effect. "Without a randomized clinical trial where there's two of me and one is assigned to be attacked by Brett and one is assigned not to be and we follow longitudinally, which is an impossible design, I can't do it. You can't just say, 'That caused that,'" she said. "Everyone has risk factors that are biological and environmental, and then you have an acute event that is going to have sequelae."[7]

Statistics—specifically, probability—were at the forefront of Ford's mind as she grappled with what to do about her memory of Kavanaugh. She knew he had become a prominent federal judge; she knew his name was on Trump's Supreme Court list. But the idea of his being tapped for the spot seemed remote, especially after Trump chose Gorsuch, another Georgetown Prep graduate, to fill the Scalia vacancy. Surely Trump wouldn't go back to the same generation of the same small Catholic boys' school twice in a row.

Then came Kennedy's announcement and, in the following days, the growing chatter: Kavanaugh was on the short list. Kavanaugh was the leading contender. "I started panicking," Ford said. In Santa Cruz, she and her friends spend hours in the ocean: Ford paddles her surfboard, looking out for sharks, while her friends swim. One morning a few days after Kennedy's retirement, the sharks were in the water, which meant no swimming. Ford pulled aside a beach friend, Jim Gensheimer, a photojournalist, and poured out her story. She felt a responsibility—"civic duty" was the phrase Ford used repeatedly—to alert someone.

But Ford was not a person who craved the limelight—she hated it. Even standing up in front of her statistics students felt like an ordeal before she got to know them better over the course of a year. Flashes of the Thomas-Hill hearings went through her mind—Hill sitting alone at the witness table as the cameras whirred. Ford had been in that very hearing room for high school field trips; she had watched a bit of the hearings when she was a master's degree student in psychology, living in Malibu. "I'm not sitting in that huge room and have people interview me," Ford thought. "That's never going to happen."[8]

She and Gensheimer imagined alternative scenarios, remote possibilities that seemed fanciful even at the time and that look even more so in retrospect. One possibility: Ford would call Mark Judge, remind Judge of what had happened, tell him to call Kavanaugh, and advise him to spare his family the ordeal. She dug up Judge's Twitter handle but wasn't sure how to go about contacting him. Another possibility was to contact Kavanaugh directly, but he didn't seem to be on Facebook or Twitter, and she didn't know how else to reach him. Yet another idea, even more far-fetched, was to somehow call the White House and warn them off.

None of her options seemed particularly good, but still, Ford thought, she needed to do something. "It wasn't even a decision," she recalled. "It was just, 'I have to do this. I have to tell someone this.' I don't think that anyone, if that happened to them, would have not told someone. How could you not say something?" Ford was a Democrat, although not a particularly active one; she had given small amounts to Democratic committees and candidates, including Bernie Sanders. And, like so many others in Palo Alto shocked by Trump's election, she had protested against the new administration—in Ford's case, by donning a knitted gray brain hat for the March for Science, which criticized Trump's policies on climate change and anticipated cuts to scientific funding.

But Ford didn't feel any particular urgency about keeping someone with Kavanaugh's conservative ideology off the court.[9] Whoever Trump picked, she figured, was going to be conservative. She read about the other candidates on Trump's short list, some of whom looked even more extreme. "I was like, 'Well, what if I end up actually making the court worse?'" she said. "I can't take that on, because I only have information about one person, so I just have to make sure the people who are deciding get that information." Russell Ford, a medical device engineer—"one of those super nanofocused people," in Ford's description—was supportive but not involved in the day-to-day discussions. "He was thinking I was working on it," Ford said. "He was like, 'Whatever you want to do, go, baby, go.'"

Ford's Palo Alto friends urged her to get a lawyer; she waved them off. Why would she need an attorney if she hadn't done anything wrong? So on their own, Ford and her friends came up with two parallel tracks. Ford could call one of the newspaper tip lines, at the *New York Times* or *Washington Post*. Or she could contact her local congresswoman, Anna Eshoo. Surely the thirteen-term Democrat would know what to do.

Meanwhile, the clock was ticking. Trump had said two days after Kennedy's announcement that he would unveil his nominee on Monday, July 9. It was now Thursday, July 5.[10] Sitting in the beach parking lot, in her Honda Odyssey minivan, its dark gray exterior festooned with surfing stickers, Ford paddled out. She called Eshoo's district office in Palo Alto, gave her name, and told the receptionist her story of being assaulted by Kavanaugh.

"Poor thing was probably like, 'Wow, that's a lot,'" Ford recalled. Someone would get back to her shortly, the receptionist assured her—usually it took around twenty-four hours. But Ford was anxious. Trump seemed to be narrowing in on Kavanaugh. So she reached out to the anonymous tip line at the *Washington Post* as well. "Potential Supreme Court nominee with assistance from his friend assaulted me in mid 1980s in Maryland," Ford wrote at 10:26 a.m. on July 6. "Have therapy records talking about it. Feel like I shouldn't be quiet but not willing to put family in DC and CA through a lot of stress." Then, at 11:47, "Brett Kavanaugh with Mark Judge and a bystander named PJ." There was no immediate response.[11]

Maybe this would take too long to make a difference, Ford thought, but she needed to know she had tried. [12]

Events quickly outpaced any hopes Ford had of somehow heading off a Kavanaugh nomination before it was made. Eshoo's longtime district director, Karen Chapman, did not call Ford until after the nomination, asking her, "Is it the person who was picked?" Ford was unhappy that it had taken so long to hear back. "I wish you had called me before he was announced," she told Chapman. Even after that, logistics—Eshoo would not be back in California until the following week—created further delay. Ford met with Chapman to relate her account on Wednesday, July 18, and met with Eshoo Friday afternoon. Eshoo had instructed her staff to schedule Ford as her last appointment of the day; she didn't want to rush what promised to be a sensitive conversation. It ended up lasting more than an hour and a half as Ford described her life and her encounter with Kavanaugh, choking up when she related the event.

"I think people need to know about this," Ford told Eshoo. But Ford was also conflicted. She did not want anyone to know her identity. She thought, naively, that it could all be handled behind closed doors. "When I walked into her office, I was terrified, because I thought, 'I'm taking off on the wave now,'" Ford recalled. She thought that she had probably lost any ability to control whether her identity would be revealed. Then Eshoo introduced a concept— "constituent confidentiality"—that made Ford feel better. She had not realized she could make such a demand. "If this story comes out, it won't be because of my office," Eshoo assured her.

The congresswoman left Ford with a lecture, advice she would find difficult to heed: stop talking about this with your friends. Keep it to yourself. There was no rush in dealing with the issue, Eshoo told Ford. The hearings were still weeks away, and they had plenty of time to decide how to proceed. [13]

The day after meeting with Ford, Eshoo called Feinstein at

home in Washington.[14] The two have a cordial relationship but not a particularly close one. "Ah-na," Feinstein said when Eshoo called, mispronouncing the congresswoman's name, as was her habit. Eshoo explained her purpose. Ford was not only Feinstein's constituent—Feinstein was also, more important, the ranking Democrat on the committee that would be considering Kavanaugh's nomination. Eshoo related Ford's story, not sharing Ford's name but telling Feinstein that she believed the account.

"You know this is very serious," Feinstein told Eshoo. "Have her write a letter to me."[15]

A screenwriter who cast Feinstein as the recipient of this information would be accused of being overly dramatic. Feinstein frequently described the moment in October 1991 when she joined a huge crowd clustered around a television screen at Heathrow Airport, in London, watching as a young University of Oklahoma law professor named Anita Hill, in an electric blue suit, testified before the all-male Judiciary Committee. In an unsettling foreshadowing of Ford's emergence almost three decades later, Hill, who had worked for Clarence Thomas at the Education Department and later the Equal Employment Opportunity Commission, was reluctant to go public with her allegations. She had told friends that Thomas, her boss, had engaged in bizarrely inappropriate workplace conduct, making repeated and unwelcome references to pornography and other sexually suggestive remarks, including bragging about his own sexual abilities, commenting on her attractiveness, and insistently asking her out.

But, like Ford years later, Hill did not want to surface publicly, and Democratic committee chairman Joseph Biden was not eager to deal with the mess that public allegations would generate. Contacted by committee staffers who had heard rumors of her reported experiences with Thomas, Hill agreed to relate her story and ultimately submit to an FBI interview, but she did not want her identity to become known. When Hill's allegations leaked the weekend before the Senate was scheduled to hold its final vote on the Thomas nomination, however, the Judiciary Committee was forced to hold a second round of hearings.

The furor over the committee's dismissive treatment of Hill helped create the "year of the woman," sweeping an unprecedented number of female candidates into office, Feinstein included. "What I remember was an all-male table, and I watched her being somewhat berated and asked some demeaning questions," Feinstein recalled in an interview in August 2018. It was the month before the Ford allegations surfaced, but of course Feinstein knew they were simmering. "Every woman that watched that changed. I think change happened at that moment," Feinstein said. "What I am thinking to myself is, can I change this? . . . Did it move me to action? Yes. And the action was to run."[16]

Now Feinstein was the ranking member of the very committee she had watched mistreat Anita Hill. Three other Democrats on the panel were women. When Hill testified, the all-male panel made noises, they said the right things, about taking her claims seriously, but it was evident, as Hill testified, that many of the senators lacked any understanding of the realities of sexual harassment and its aftermath. They could not comprehend why Hill stayed silent about the treatment she alleged, or how, if her story were true, she could have followed Thomas to a different job.

In the #MeToo era, such complaints needed to be taken far more seriously. Yet it was also a fundamental tenet of the movement that those who claimed to have been abused should retain the right—the agency, in the wording of the day—to decide for themselves whether to go public with their stories. Amazingly, even in the aftermath of Hill-Thomas, there was no real rule book for how to handle such sensitive material and balance the competing interests of investigation and privacy. The tragedy of the Ford situation was that Feinstein faced the same conundrum that had confronted Biden twenty-seven years earlier—and ended up with the same botched result.

Ford had reached out to Eshoo's office on July 5. She met with Eshoo on July 20. Now it was the following week, and Ford was flying east with her family for their annual vacation at her parents' beach house—but she had heard nothing about how to proceed.

"I'm flipping out," she recalled. "I don't know what's going to happen . . . I don't know if anybody's doing anything."

On July 30, Karen Chapman, the Eshoo aide, finally called.[17] Eshoo and Feinstein had spoken, she said. The next step, if Ford wanted to proceed, would be getting her information to Feinstein and the committee chairman, Grassley, in writing. Ford had to decide: attach her name to the letter or not? Without a name, nothing much could be done, Ford understood. In the end, Ford was swayed by Eshoo's assurance of "constituent confidentiality" and worried about whether including Grassley would expose her identity. Feinstein was her senator, she figured; she would submit the letter to Feinstein alone, stating her expectation that her privacy would be protected.[18]

Ford e-mailed the letter to Chapman later that day. Eshoo was having surgery that day, but she made arrangements for the letter to be handled with the utmost secrecy. Chapman forwarded it to Eshoo chief of staff Matthew McMurray, who was stationed at the printer as the document came through to make certain that no one else would see it. McMurray sealed the letter in an envelope addressed to Feinstein and called Duck, her senior judiciary staffer. "I have something for you," he told Duck. "I can't tell you what it is, and I have to give it to you directly, and you have to give it directly to the senator." This was too incendiary to be left with a receptionist.

And that was, for six interminable weeks, the last that Eshoo heard of the matter from Feinstein's office. Chapman checked in with Ford from time to time, but Eshoo didn't think it was her place to go back to Feinstein. "Every time it got to, 'Maybe, Anna, you should call Dianne,' there was just something in me that—I just didn't think it was appropriate," she said. Still, she added, "It was with me every second that I was awake: What's going to happen? I wonder what's going to be done; will anything come out of this? It was with me constantly. And I would be somewhere and people would come by the house or whatever, and I would think, 'It's a good thing we don't have screens in our foreheads. They have no idea what I know.'"[19]

If Feinstein was concerned or alarmed by Eshoo's information, she did not show it. During the ten-day period between Eshoo's call and the delivery of Ford's letter, Feinstein appears to have done nothing to follow up on the matter. Indeed, she did not even mention the Eshoo call to her staff or reveal the existence of a potential allegation against Kavanaugh to them. The first Duck knew of Ford's complaint was when she received the call from Eshoo's chief of staff, McMurray. When Duck took the letter, unopened, to Feinstein, the senator gave no indication she had been expecting anything of the sort.

The details were alarming. "Brett Kavanaugh physically and sexually assaulted me during High School in the early 1980's," Ford wrote. She described how Kavanaugh, along with Judge, pushed her into a bedroom, locked the door, and played loud music. "Kavanaugh was on top of me while laughing with Judge, who periodically jumped onto Kavanaugh. They both laughed as Kavanaugh tried to disrobe me in their highly inebriated state. With Kavanaugh's hand over my mouth, I feared he may inadvertently kill me."

With the letter in hand, Feinstein responded quickly. She had her scheduler put in a call to Ford in Rehoboth Beach; they connected the next day. Feinstein and Duck, who had not even seen the letter by that point, were on the line for a conversation that lasted perhaps ten to fifteen minutes. Ford sounded credible but nervous; she mentioned confidentiality a few times and said she had not even told her family. Had Ford been raped? Feinstein wanted to know. Feinstein asked several more fact-based questions, Ford recalled, then said she would follow up to let Ford know next steps. Ford felt that Feinstein "took it very seriously," but she was still anxious that time was running out. "I started freaking out, started panicking,"

Ford recalled. "I figure I'm . . . never coming back again until next summer. Now's the time if people from D.C. want to talk to me. If she [Feinstein] wants to meet with me I'll go meet with her tomorrow. I can drive to D.C. from Rehoboth."[20]

If that sense of urgency did not seem matched on Feinstein's side, that may have been because the California senator's instructions to her staff were difficult to implement—impossible, as it turned out. Feinstein told Duck she wanted Ford's allegations looked into, but not by the minority staff. She didn't want any inquiry to be seen as partisan.

But it was not clear at all how such an investigation would proceed, if it even could. Duck consulted the Senate Rules Committee and the Senate Ethics Committee, asking vague questions about how to go about hiring and paying for an independent lawyer. She called around to women's groups seeking recommendations for an attorney who might be able to handle such a probe. One of the names that came up was Debra Katz, a lawyer with extensive experience in high-profile sexual harassment cases as well as in representing whistle-blowers.

Heather Sawyer, Feinstein's chief investigator, called Katz, asking guarded questions about how one would investigate a decades-old allegation of sexual assault. Might Katz be interested? But the staff was also stymied by the logistical barriers to implementing Feinstein's plan. There was no way to bring in an outside lawyer without informing Grassley, the committee chairman, about Ford's allegation, and Ford had made it clear that she did not want her information shared. And Feinstein was adamant with the staff: violate Ford's confidentiality, and you're fired.

Duck had watched the Hill hearings as a student at St. Olaf College, in Minnesota; she had worked on campus sexual assault issues there. "Her story, her choice" was a tenet of that work—the notion that the decision about whether to speak publicly was the prerogative of the woman involved. But the stakes here were so enormous. Every night, Duck went to sleep worrying about Ford's story, trying to play out in her head whether there was another approach. She kept coming back to the imperative of protecting the victim. And at that point, Duck believed that Ford, eventually, would decide to share her account.

Should Feinstein have handled the matter differently? If so, how? When the Ford story ultimately and perhaps inevitably leaked, Grassley and other Republicans protested that Feinstein should have quietly shared the information with them so it could have been investigated appropriately. Grassley, in this view, had a decades-long record of protecting whistle-blowers; he knew how to maintain confidentiality. And the Senate Judiciary Committee has a process for handling sensitive allegations involving judicial nominees, Republicans point out. Such background investigations happen all the time, without leaks. Why would Feinstein not go through the regular order?

This argument generates snorts of derision from Senate Democrats, who note that it ignores the poisonous reality of current relations between the two sides. Not that the Thomas hearings, or Bork's, for that matter, had been held in an age of kumbaya bipartisanship, but things were so much angrier now, and trust was at a nadir. Even if Grassley and his staff could be relied on, alerting them to Ford, Democrats believed, would inevitably mean bringing her allegation to the attention of McGahn and others in the White House. Their interest, at least as Democrats saw it, was not in determining the truth. It was in getting Kavanaugh across the finish line.

Was Feinstein correct to assure Ford anonymity? Without question, her instincts and intentions were admirable. The final decision about whether to come forward should be up to the alleged victim in any situation, even more in circumstances where the accusations are guaranteed to produce a life-altering uproar. But assuring Ford of confidentiality under these circumstances was arguably heedless of reality. The lesson of Anita Hill was that, in the high-stakes arena of a Supreme Court nomination, information this significant was almost certainly bound to leak. And even this early in the process, Ford had shared her account with too many people. History suggested that any hope of maintaining its secrecy was likely to be dashed.

Perhaps Biden should have understood that about Hill back in the day. But to make the same set of errors in 2018, in the aftermath of that experience, was unforgivable, in the estimation of some Democratic veterans of the Senate Judiciary Committee. Once Ford's information came to Feinstein, their argument goes, Feinstein's primary obligation was not to Ford but to the Senate and the country; she needed to find a way, whether through the FBI or the Senate itself, to investigate Ford's claims, even at the risk of exposure.

Feinstein should, in this assessment, have essentially told Ford that the matter was out of her hands—that she had waived her privacy in coming forward, that Feinstein would do the best she could to maintain Ford's confidentiality, but that she was duty bound to share the information with Grassley in order to investigate further. This is a brutal approach, one that leaves many people uncomfortable. But no one, certainly not Ford or Kavanaugh, was well served by the way the story ultimately emerged. There had to have been a better way.

Whether or not Feinstein's distrust of Grassley was justified, her decision to keep the existence of Ford's complaints from her Democratic colleagues, even the Senate leadership—indeed, to wave away inquiries as rumors began to surface—meant that she remained the sole arbiter of how to handle a matter with such potentially grave consequences. In addition, it is hard not to wonder what would have happened had Feinstein been gently persistent with Ford, if she had sketched out the already significant risks of exposure she faced, and emphasized to Ford, who was clearly torn about whether to go public, the stakes for the country. Years earlier, Hill had been gingerly coaxed, over weeks of conversation with Senate staff, to submit an affidavit and then to permit an FBI investigation, even before the allegations became public. Once Ford hired Katz, Feinstein's approach was to leave any further investigating to the private lawyers. Her behavior was so passive, so hands-off, that it left the impression that she would have been just as pleased to see the entire mess disappear.

As Feinstein's staff struggled with how to deal with Ford's letter, for Ford the logistics were complicated in different ways. Ford's family was around, and she wasn't about to tell her parents about Kavanaugh—certainly not with her one-hundred-year-old grandmother in hospice care. So she found herself making furtive phone calls from the beach-house porch and the parking lot at the Rehoboth Walgreens. Starting from not having any lawyers, Ford proceeded to assemble an ad hoc flotilla of them. She sought advice from a trusted relative and conducted Google searches for "judiciary committee lawyers."

Sitting in her car in the Walgreens lot on a sweltering August afternoon, she found herself telling her story to William Taylor, an experienced Washington criminal defense lawyer recommended by a family member who knew another lawyer in his firm. "I have someone who would do a good job on this, and he's not afraid of the devil," Taylor told Ford, then put her in touch with Larry Robbins, a Supreme Court advocate.

Then, in a follow-up phone call with Ford, Heather Sawyer mentioned Katz. Meanwhile, Sawyer let Katz know that Ford might be reaching out to her. By that time, Ford's grandmother had died: the funeral was the next day, and she was packing up to leave Rehoboth and head to New Hampshire from the airport in Baltimore. Ford called Katz. As it happened, the lawyer was flying into Baltimore the next day.

So Katz and Lisa Banks, her law partner, met Ford in a second-floor conference room at the BWI Hilton on Monday, August 6. Their immediate assessment: this is a credible witness. "No one who's going to make up a story puts another witness in the room," Katz said. "When somebody tells a story, and it's completely neat and tied up in a bow . . . it's not true." To Katz, the gaps in Ford's account—she didn't remember where the party was; she was fuzzy about how she made her way home—were themselves evidence of Ford's veracity. So was her reluctance to come forward. "What we found impressive about her was she didn't want a starring role in a story that was going to be a national spotlight. There really was a sense of, 'How can I live with myself?,' not a sense of 'I want to force myself into something.'"[21] Katz arranged for a polygraph examiner. He was able to come to Baltimore the next morning, before the Ford family flew to New Hampshire.

As Feinstein's staff saw it, Ford's decision to hire Katz and Banks meant their hands were tied. Ford had lawyers, who would determine whether—and how—she wanted to go forward. It was now August. The hearings were to start early the next month. The next step, if Ford wanted to proceed, would be a letter to both Feinstein and Grassley. Would that be forthcoming? Duck checked in occasionally with Katz. That was the plan, she was told, but the letter never arrived.

In turning to Katz, Ford found a lawyer with undoubted expertise in handling high-profile sexual harassment cases—"D.C.'s leading #MeToo lawyer," *Washingtonian* magazine had called her that June—as well as one whose unabashed Democratic party activism eventually generated criticism that Ford's claims were politically motivated and pushed by political activists.[22] "Women's rights and social justice activist," Katz's Twitter bio proudly declares.[23] When her role as Ford's lawyer became public, critics seized on video of Katz protesting Jeff Sessions's confirmation as attorney general. "We are going to fight back," Katz proclaimed in the video. "We are going to resist. We will not be silenced."[24] During the 2017–18 election cycle, Katz contributed almost $20,000 to Democratic candidates.

The growth of the #MeToo movement meant that Katz's practice was booming. She had represented a manager who accused celebrity chef Mike Isabella and his business partners of "extraordinary sex-based hostility and abuse," a Weinstein Company executive who tried to stand up against what he termed "mistreatment of women," and aides to two members of Congress—one Democrat (Eric Massa of New York) and one Republican (Pat Meehan of Pennsylvania)—who resigned after claims of sexual harassment.[25]

In Ford's case, as Katz knew from past experience, it was important to locate other women with similar complaints, if they existed. Emma Brown, the *Washington Post* reporter who had spoken with Ford after she called the tip line, was pursuing some leads; so were others. And if Ford were to go forward, she needed a public relations plan. In that case, there was one obvious person to call: Ricki Seidman, a Washington communications consultant. Chuck Schumer had described Kavanaugh as "the Zelig of young Republican lawyers" at his first confirmation hearing, in 2004. The same could be said of Seidman's role in judicial confirmations.

If there was one person in Washington who understood the power and ramifications of Ford's story, it was Seidman. With the soothing voice of a late-night radio host, she was a veteran of the judicial nominations wars. As a young lawyer at the liberal activist group People for the American Way, she had been present at the creation of the liberal effort to block Reagan's push to populate the judiciary with conservative judges.

Seidman had worked on them all, from Jeff Sessions (his nomination to a federal district judgeship was blocked in 1986 amid charges of racism) to Kozinski to Bork. In 1991, as an investigator for Senator Edward Kennedy, Seidman was among the first Senate staffers to reach out to Anita Hill and inquire about rumors that she had been sexually harassed by Clarence Thomas. Later, as an aide in the Clinton White House and a private consultant, Seidman helped shepherd the confirmations of Democratic nominees Ruth Bader Ginsburg, Stephen Breyer, and, during the Obama administration, Sonia Sotomayor. Kavanaugh ran across Seidman as he investigated Vincent Foster's death: Seidman, as deputy communications director, had been involved in some of the issues Foster had handled. But she was sitting out the Kava-naugh nomination. Her role, or so she thought, would be limited to kibitzing from the sidelines.

"My view on Kavanaugh was the fix was in," Seidman said. "I didn't really see a path to defeating him. I didn't think that the opposition had made a case for defeating him that would be com-pelling to the people they needed to reach."[26]

Then, on August 15, Seidman's phone rang. It was Katz. The two—surprisingly, in the clannish networks of liberal Washington—had not met, although their office buildings were next door to each other. Katz got to the point: she was helping someone who claimed to have been sexually assaulted by Kavanaugh and wanted Seid-man's help. The client had passed a lie detector test, Katz told Seid-man. Could they meet?

"My immediate thought was to be skeptical," Seidman recalled. "Not about the person or that anything had happened, but know-ing what had befallen Anita Hill, it was something that I was very skeptical about, about the value in coming forward." Not only had the hearing process failed Hill, as Seidman saw it, "but it was also so personally damaging to Anita Hill . . . The idea of coming under so much abuse when I didn't see it having an impact—I was just skeptical of the value of it."[27]

If some people thought—if they hoped—that Ford's allega-tions could bring down the nominee, Seidman says she was not among them, especially as she learned the precise details. What-ever had happened, no rape had occurred; Kavanaugh and Ford were teenagers at the time. If the story were to surface, Seidman figured, Kavanaugh and the White House wouldn't deny it entirely but rather diminish its significance, make it look like an episode of youthful roughhousing, misunderstood.

And Ford's belief—that if she were just to speak quietly and in private with a few key senators, Kavanaugh would quietly with-draw, all without her having to leave California, all without expos-ing herself and her family to public scrutiny—was naive, Seidman thought. At that point, in mid-August, the story seemed containable. Only Eshoo, Feinstein, Katz, and Ford herself had the letter explaining her allegation. Although Ford had spoken to the *Washington Post*'s Emma Brown, it was with the understanding that nothing would be printed without Ford's consent.

But pushing things further would, Seidman thought, inevitably lead to public exposure. If Grassley were told of the allegations, he would no doubt alert the White House, and the situation would snowball. Seidman was headed to California for a business trip in late August, so she set aside a day to meet with Ford in person. Over three hours at a coffee shop in Palo Alto on August 28, a week before the hearings were to start, Seidman heard Ford's story in full.

That only strengthened her conclusion that the cost-benefit analysis tipped against going public. For one thing, Ford seemed fragile. For another, there was, at that point, no indication of other women with similar complaints against Kavanaugh. As much as Seidman found Ford's account compelling, there was little corroboration.

Kavanaugh's confirmation hearings were to start September 4, the day after Labor Day. It was an inflection point—decision time for Ford. "I'm freaking out," Ford recalled. "Deb and Lisa and I are talking every single day about what to do, because the time really was ticking." On Wednesday, August 29, Ford called her father to alert him to the possibility that she might be in the news. She wanted to give him time to prepare, especially since he knew Ed Kavanaugh from Burning Tree, the all-male golf club in Bethesda to which both men belonged.[28]

Critics later made much of Ford's supposed estrangement from her family, but throughout the summer, as she debated whether to come forward, the impact on her parents and other relatives back East was one of her chief concerns. Her parents were immersed in a community—a tribe, as Ford saw it, the Republican country club establishment of suburban Maryland—that would no doubt close ranks around the nominee. She worried that her parents would be shunned and that her nieces and nephews, with the Blasey name, would be exposed to unwanted attention.

When his daughter called to tell him about her encounter with Kavanaugh, Ralph Blasey was alarmed. She tried to reassure him: with the speeded-up modern media cycle, "we're just going to have to tolerate one week at the most being in the news, and then we'll move on." That provided some temporary relief, even if it turned out to be wildly off base.[29]

But even with her parents alerted—Ford relied on her father to pass the news on to the rest of the family—the final decision had yet to be made. Before Seidman's trip to California, the plan had been set: Ford would come forward. Katz and Banks had drafted a letter to Feinstein and Grassley outlining Ford's allegations and asking that she be heard. It would be made public before the hearings began. Seidman's concerns caused a sudden shift in the strategy. "My honest assessment is if you come forward, it's not going to change the outcome," Seidman told Ford. The chance of any delay in the hearings was slim to none. And the attention on Ford would make the Anita Hill uproar seem mild.

"I did not want to see Kavanaugh confirmed. I thought he was a terrible choice," Seidman recalled. Nonetheless, she thought, if Ford came forward, her life would be forever upended. If she stayed silent, "she would be able to continue living her life, and she had a great career and a lovely family and that in some ways letting go of it could be freeing, ultimately, too, and that the alternative was to be pilloried and attacked, and I personally did not want to see her go through that. If I had believed it would make a difference in whether he would be confirmed or not, I think I would have been a little less sensitive to her as a person. But I didn't have to make that choice—I didn't think it was going to affect the outcome."[30]

Ford had spent weeks obsessing about one question: "How can I minimize the annihilation and still make sure that they [senators] know this is the case?" In the end, after debating various scenarios and drafts of letters to the committee, she concluded that the two goals were irreconcilable. Katz and Banks informed Duck. It was a no go.

On Friday, August 31, the lawyers received a curt letter from

Feinstein, memorializing her understanding of the situation: Ford was not willing to have her name used; therefore Feinstein would proceed no further with the allegation. "I am writing now to confirm that my office will continue to honor the request for confidentiality and will not be taking action unless we hear from you," Feinstein wrote. "Please convey my deep appreciation to your client for her courage in sharing this information with me and assure her that I understand and regret the deep impact that this incident has had on her life."

Ford, once again rethinking what she wanted, called Larry Robbins and Barry Coburn, the lawyers she had consulted before retaining Katz, to complain. Katz was shutting her down. What could they come up with? Coburn talked to Katz and called Ford back: "Deb Katz is a fine lawyer, and we do agree with them that you're not going to go forward."

It was, or so Ford thought at the time, the worst weekend of her life. "I was like, 'I suck. I'm horrible. I cannot believe I was such a wimp. I can't do this. I can't believe I'm not strong enough to do this,'" she said. "Basically, I'm just really mad at myself because I didn't do what I set out to do."

She sent her son to watch television with Russell in the master bedroom. Christine Ford spent the night curled up in his tiny Ikea bed, unable to sleep. She told her Palo Alto friends, the ones she had consulted with all summer about what to do; one of them, Deepa Lalla, was particularly disappointed in her choice, and Ford worried that her friend was angry with her.[31]

After all the work, all the worry, Christine Ford had done the very thing she hated. She ended up paddling in.

Except, of course, it was not the end, and, despite the tormented decision-making, the choice turned out not to be Ford's to make. Among those who played a role in that development was Anna Eshoo, Ford's own congresswoman, the very person who had introduced her to the notion of constituent confidentiality and who had promised Ford that if the story got out it would not be because of her.

Eshoo insisted repeatedly that she had not discussed Ford with anyone other than Feinstein and a few trusted members of her own staff. But early on, Eshoo had shared the vague details with House Speaker Nancy Pelosi, her closest ally in Congress. Pelosi recalled advising Eshoo to have her constituent contact Feinstein and perhaps Grassley.[32] Eventually, as time passed and nothing seemed to be happening, Pelosi reached out to Chuck Schumer. There was a woman who had written a letter to Feinstein complaining of Kavanaugh's behavior, he was told. Schumer dispatched his staff to find out about it. Duck was unforthcoming. If there were anything like that, she assured Schumer's staff, we would be handling it appropriately. In other words, back off.[33]

That was not all—not by a long shot. After Ford had told Feinstein she did not want to proceed, Chapman, the Eshoo aide to whom Ford had first told her story in July, called. "Wow, nothing's happening," she told Ford. "Do you want me to talk to Kamala?" referring to Feinstein's California colleague. "I don't know," Ford replied.[34] They should talk another time.

Eshoo then took other steps. A former aide in the George W. Bush White House, of all places, received a call on September 7 from someone he would only identify as a close ally of Eshoo's who told him about the letter and about Eshoo's unhappiness with what she viewed as Feinstein's weak performance at the hearings. The Eshoo ally said the congresswoman wanted to get the word out, and so the former Bush aide did, reaching out to, among others, MSNBC's Lawrence O'Donnell and Ryan Grim, Washington bureau chief for the *Intercept*, an online left-leaning news site dedicated to what it describes as "fearless, adversarial journalism."

Finally, on September 9, Eshoo herself called Harris, according to a source familiar with the conversation. She told Harris about the letter, that it was in Feinstein's possession, and that nothing seemed to have been done about the allegation, which involved sexual misconduct by Kavanaugh. As the other senator from California and a member of the Judiciary Committee herself, Eshoo said, Harris should know about it. Harris, furious, called Duck and then Feinstein, demanding answers about this secret letter. Now that Feinstein's colleagues knew, the letter was not going to remain secret for long.

Indeed, even without Eshoo's intervention, the story was leaking, through a separate set of Palo Alto connections. In retrospect, that was entirely predictable. If anything, it was surprising that the secret had held so long. For all the well-intentioned efforts to keep the circle of knowledge about Ford's allegations as tight as possible, for all Eshoo's belief that she was burdened with a terrible secret, the reality was that in the chatty confines of liberal Palo Alto, more and more people knew about Ford's story, and more and more were whispering about it.

Ford had told not only her husband and Gensheimer but also her friend Keith Koegler and some swim-club friends who were authorized to reach out to others for advice. In one example of the way the information circulated through the Palo Alto community, a friend of Ford's knew someone who knew the sister of Sheryl Sandberg. The Facebook executive, without being given Ford's name or the specifics of her allegations, suggested that she hire a lawyer, preferably one without partisan ties, and offered up a few names.

Early on, shortly after the Kavanaugh nomination was announced, the information about Ford, in sketchy form, reached none other than Schumer himself through a Palo Alto connection. A friend of a friend of Ford's reached out to Connie Schultz, the Pulitzer Prize–winning columnist who happened to be married to Ohio senator Sherrod Brown. Brown in turn confided in Schumer about the existence of a woman making claims about Kavanaugh. But the woman didn't want to give her name, which left little to go on. Schumer's office suggested reaching out to the *Washington Post*.

By the time the story broke, by the count of one Ford friend, a few dozen people knew—and who knew how many others they had told in turn? In the aftermath of the Anita Hill leak twenty-seven years earlier, the Senate hired a special counsel to investigate how the story leaked. His report would not identify a particular culprit but rather uncover how much Hill's existence was being gossiped about at Washington dinner parties.[35] Palo Alto turned out to be even smaller and Ford's story even more viral.

As the gossip swirled, Ford herself had misgivings about having decided to remain silent. On the first day of the hearings, Katz attended an anti-Kavanaugh protest. She sent a picture of herself to Ford, holding a sign that said KAVANOPE. As Katz had dinner with a friend that night, Ford called her repeatedly. She was still anguished about her choice.

Then the story, in dribs and drabs, began to leak. On September 5, even before Eshoo's phone call to Harris, Chapman warned Ford that reporters were turning up at the office and knew about the letter. Seidman passed the warning on to Feinstein's office. Meanwhile, a reporter from *BuzzFeed*, Lissandra Villa, started to reach out to Ford with calls and texts. On September 6, she went to Ford's house, leaving a package of articles she had written about the sexual harassment allegations against former Michigan representative John Conyers, and returned a second time; on the tenth, Villa turned up at Ford's first statistics class of the year, and Ford, mistaking her for a student, stopped to talk to her at the end of the three-and-a-half-hour lecture. As Ford realized who she was and hurried away, the reporter shouted, "I know about the letter!" Marc Bodnick, a Silicon Valley entrepreneur and Sheryl Sandberg's brother-in-law, who had heard about Ford from Palo Alto friends, was lobbying them to persuade Ford to talk to *BuzzFeed*.

Meanwhile, as reporters scrambled to get the story, they ended up spreading it. On September 7, Whitehouse's staff called Feinstein's office to ask, what is this letter we keep hearing about? In an earlier age, before the Internet and the explosion of alternative media sites, perhaps the story would not have seen the light of day. The reporters who knew about the letter didn't have the details of the complaint. Was that really enough to go on? In the hyper-competitive modern media environment, the answer was likely yes. Ford's team recognized this was like a pressure cooker, threatening to explode. It was just a matter of time.

Then, on Tuesday, September 11, the *Intercept* contacted Feinstein's office: It was planning to publish a story about the letter. By Wednesday, September 12, *The New Yorker*'s Ronan Farrow was walking up and down the street by Ford's house, trying to placate her barking dog and freaking out the neighbors, who knew something was amiss when a guy in a blue blazer and white pants turned up, looking out of the ordinary in casual Palo Alto.

The Ford team decided it was time to try to take control of the narrative, to let Ford tell her own story. They cleared Emma Brown, the *Post* reporter, who had been keeping Ford's secret since early July, to meet with her. Brown headed to California, spending Wednesday and Thursday interviewing Ford. They had dinner at the Ritz-Carlton at Half Moon Bay; Christine and Russell Ford had their wedding reception there, after a marriage ceremony among the redwoods, so it felt like a happy place for Ford to tell a difficult story.

The Feinstein staff was also making preparations. Too many senators now knew about the letter, they realized. It was time to let them and their colleagues know what was going on. Katz and Banks were alerted; they needed to be available to brief Democratic senators. Before that could happen, the lid came off. At 5:24 on Wednesday evening, September 12, all this frantic behind-the-scenes activity burst into public view. Grim posted an article headlined: DIANNE FEINSTEIN WITHHOLDING BRETT KAVANAUGH DOCUMENT FROM FELLOW JUDICIARY COMMITTEE DEMOCRATS.[36]

Grim's account had only the gauziest details of the story. A letter had been sent to Feinstein from "someone affiliated with Stanford University." Eshoo served as the intermediary. The missive "describes an incident involving a woman while they were in high school." The woman was now being represented by Katz. Democrats on the Senate Judiciary Committee "have privately requested to view" the letter, but Feinstein has refused, creating "tension on the committee." As Grim put it with what was, by then, distinct understatement, "Kept hidden the letter is beginning to take on a life of its own."

The story was incomplete, but enough to set off a chain of events that forever altered the lives of those involved and endangered a confirmation that had seemed assured.

CHAPTER THIRTEEN

Bathroom Summit

With the *Intercept* story, all hell broke loose. Actually, all hell was poised to break loose even before. That weekend, after the phone call from Eshoo and the brush-off from Feinstein and Duck, Harris had alerted Dick Durbin, a senior member of the committee and, as Democratic whip, Schumer's second in command, about the letter. Harris was alarmed, and now Durbin was, too. He went to Feinstein and told her it was essential to convene a meeting of committee Democrats. Her colleagues—the ones who didn't already know about the letter—needed to be briefed, the sooner the better. This information was not going to be contained, and Democrats needed to figure out how to handle it.

Staff members were alerted: their bosses were summoned to a senators-only meeting in the President's Room, off the Senate floor, at 6:30 that evening. Unusually, there was no word about the subject matter, just that the senators were urgently needed. There was, literally, a hurricane brewing: Florence was bearing down on the Carolinas, and the Senate was scrambling to get out of session early. When Durbin walked into the ornate chamber, with its Italian frescoes and crimson tufted upholstery, he didn't even realize that the *Intercept* story had posted an hour earlier. The problem he was trying to solve had just become that much more acute.

Speaking to her colleagues, Feinstein, one senator said, was "agitated and defensive." She seemed puzzled that her colleagues were so upset: she had done the right thing, she told them, honoring a repeated appeal for confidentiality, and she still felt duty bound to protect Ford's privacy.

Durbin was adamant. "Dianne," he said. "Stop, stop, listen to me. This is incredibly important. We have to get this right. You cannot keep this to yourself anymore." It had been a "huge mistake," he said, to have sat on this letter. "You must give this to the FBI," he repeated. "I respect your motives, but you cannot withhold this."

Harris was at least as unrelenting. She and her fellow Californian have had a frosty history that stretches back to 2004, just a few months into Harris's tenure as San Francisco district attorney. A police officer, Isaac Espinoza, had been shot in the line of duty, and Harris, an avowed opponent of capital punishment, faced intense criticism when she declared, just two days after the alleged killer's arrest, that she would not seek the death penalty. Feinstein, the former San Francisco mayor then in the midst of a fight to renew the assault-weapons ban, used the occasion of Espinoza's funeral to depart from her prepared remarks and express her disagreement. "This is not only the definition of tragedy, it's the special circumstance called for by the death penalty law," Feinstein said.[1] Harris sat in the front row, near the grieving family; the crowd of two thousand uniformed officers rose to their feet to applaud Feinstein's remarks.[2] Outside St. Mary's Cathedral, the senator was even more cutting. Feinstein would not have endorsed Harris, she said, had she known she opposed capital punishment.[3]

Now, fourteen years later, the two women found themselves again at odds. "There are going to be repercussions from this," Harris advised her senior senator. "You've got to figure this out."

The letter was eventually read aloud, with Ford's name redacted. Then a copy was passed around to the senators, which made them even more alarmed. This didn't look like adolescent horseplay—more like attempted rape. "I remember reading the letter two or three times and thinking, huh, okay, bad, bad, we need to hear from her," said one. Said another, "She shows us the letter and it just makes it worse. You read it and you go, 'Oooh.'"

Debra Katz had been speaking at a Women's Caucus panel on

workplace sexual harassment. When she left the hearing room in a House office building, she saw that her phone was exploding with texts—hurry over to the Capitol right away. As Katz and Banks tried to make their way there, they were trailed by a *BuzzFeed* reporter and repeatedly stopped by Capitol police because they didn't have the proper credentials to enter the building. When they finally made it, they weren't allowed inside the President's Room. They knocked on the door and were instructed to sit on chairs outside the entrance, feeling like schoolchildren sent to the principal's office. Senators hustled in and out of the room to vote, looking angry. Mazie Hirono rushed past, asking her staff, "What's *The Intercept*?" One senator likened the scene to a particularly dysfunctional family Thanksgiving dinner.

Katz and Banks had consulted with their client as they raced to the Capitol. She reaffirmed her position: she did not want the letter to be released. She was already being besieged by reporters. Going public would make things even worse—not just for her but also, more importantly, for her family.

By then, however, Ford's wishes were immaterial. The genie could not be put back in the bottle. The letter would have to be disclosed. Feinstein agreed, saying she would give the letter to the FBI the next day. No, her colleagues insisted. Turn it over tonight.

The letter went to the FBI that night.

In the White House war room, set up on the fourth floor of the Eisenhower Executive Office Building, staffers saw the *Intercept* report and were caught flat-footed. Raj Shah, the deputy press secretary who had been detailed to the Kavanaugh nomination, called McGahn. Was there anything in the FBI file? Did he know anything about this? McGahn said he had no clue, although he been alerted to the problem days before by someone who had heard the rumor from a reporter.

Around ten that night, Shah phoned his press counterparts in Grassley's office, George Hartmann and Taylor Foy. Did they have any idea what was going on? Garrett Ventry, another Grassley aide, called Zina Bash, a former White House aide and Kavanaugh clerk working on his confirmation team. Kavanaugh had no idea what this might be about, she assured him. The thinking was: this is a ridiculous article, nothing to really worry about at this point. Grassley keeps farmer's hours, in bed by 9:00 p.m. The staff decided not to wake him up. They would call and brief him at 6:30 the next morning.

That day, Thursday, September 13, the Senate Judiciary Committee was scheduled to take up the Kavanaugh nomination. The ritualistic fighting—Blumenthal demanded testimony from Manuel Miranda and others before being asked to vote; Republicans summarily defeated the motion—did not betray any of the drama simmering just beneath the surface. Grassley moved on his own to postpone the Kavanaugh vote until the following week, but this was committee procedure as usual, not a reflection of the unfolding Ford story.

At the end of the session, Dianne Feinstein was the first one into the anteroom that adjoins the hearing room. Some of the Senate's public spaces are grand and magisterial; not so, many of its private offices. The anteroom is a small, plain space with a dark wooden conference table and a bookshelf with a television and law books at one end. Grassley and his top judiciary staffer, Kolan Davis (no relation to Mike Davis, the nominations counsel), entered the room.

"Can I have a word with you?" Feinstein asked Grassley. "Can you step in here?" She motioned to the anteroom's small unisex bathroom, a utilitarian affair with all the charm of a faculty restroom at a public middle school. Feinstein held the door for Grassley, then asked his aide, "Kolan, can you get Jennifer?" Duck was still in the hearing room, speaking with senators. They waited a bit, several senators passing by the curious scene of the chairman and ranking member standing in a bathroom with the door ajar.

The four participants crowded into the space, no more than six feet by six feet, to discuss the fate of the president's Supreme Court nominee. It came to be known, by the Grassley staff, at least, as the Bathroom Summit.

It was the first Grassley had heard directly about the allegations against Kavanaugh, and he was less than pleased with Feinstein, with whom he had maintained a cordial relationship even through the contentious hearings. She had received a letter, Feinstein told Grassley; she planned to refer it to the FBI. (In fact, that had already happened.) She did not give him a copy of the letter or share Ford's name but merely described the substance.

"Thank you for sharing with me," Grassley replied. "You've got to do what you've got to do." Grassley later excoriated Feinstein for having sat on the "secret evidence," but that day he was businesslike and noncommittal.

Around noon, McGahn received a redacted copy of the letter from the FBI and immediately shared it with Grassley. "It was like a bomb dropped at the White House," one official said. Not long after, Feinstein, who had not responded to *The Intercept*'s earlier request for comment, released a statement in which she acknowledged the letter's existence but remained cryptic. "I have received information from an individual concerning the nomination of Brett Kavanaugh to the Supreme Court," the statement said. "That individual strongly requested confidentiality, declined to come forward or press the matter further, and I have honored that decision. I have, however, referred the matter to federal investigative authorities."[4] Within the hour, the *New York Times* reported that "the incident involved possible sexual misconduct between Judge Kavanaugh and a woman when they were both in high school."[5]

Late that afternoon, the phone rang at the home of Beth Wilkinson, a leading Washington trial lawyer. A former army lawyer and federal prosecutor, Wilkinson had sought—and won—the death penalty for Oklahoma City bomber Timothy McVeigh, under the direction, ironically, of Merrick Garland, then a senior Justice Department official.

Wilkinson's husband, television journalist David Gregory, picked up the phone. There was a slight pause, then, "David, it's

Brett Kavanaugh." The two men knew each other; their daughters played together on the middle-school basketball circuit, and they had had dinners at the home of their mutual friend Miguel Estrada.

"Hi, Brett," Gregory replied. "You must want to speak to my bride."

Kavanaugh got right to the point. "Something's come up," he told Wilkinson. "A story about a woman, and I understand if you don't want to but if you're interested, I would really like if you would represent me."

Wilkinson, as Kavanaugh well knew, was a Democrat who had represented a quartet of Hillary Clinton aides in the FBI's e-mail probe. But she was the kind of tenacious advocate who liked to think of herself as willing to take on anyone in need of legal help and who bristled at the notion that some clients were off-limits because of their politics. Still, she had partners to check with. Representing clients in #MeToo type situations was dicey. Wilkinson was also in the middle of a high-stakes trial, representing the NCAA in an antitrust lawsuit challenging its restrictions on paying student athletes. But Kavanaugh needed help, and she decided quickly: Wilkinson and her partner Alexandra Walsh, who had clerked for both Garland and Breyer, would represent him.

Wilkinson spoke with McGahn later that night. They were drafting a press release, and Wilkinson wanted to include an acknowledgment from Kavanaugh that sexual assault and harassment are grave problems, that he took them seriously as a husband and father. "We're not doing that," McGahn said. "I showed it to all the women on my staff, and nobody likes it." The eventual statement was more sparse but left no room for backtracking. "I categorically and unequivocally deny this allegation," Kavanaugh said. "I did not do this back in high school or at any time."[6]

In private, Kavanaugh was reeling. "I can't believe this is happening to me," he told one friend. "You know me. I don't do this with women."

•   •   •

More details leaked from there. On Friday morning, September 14, *The New Yorker*'s Ronan Farrow and Jane Mayer reported the unsettling details of the allegation, although without Ford's name—Kavanaugh's hand over her mouth, the music turned up to conceal the sound of her protests. Mark Judge, also not named, was quoted as saying he had "no recollection of that."[7] Judge spoke later that afternoon, on the record, with the *Weekly Standard*, offering a more vigorous refutation. "It's just absolutely nuts," he said. "I never saw Brett act that way."[8] The *New York Times* weighed in with an account that matched *The New Yorker*'s.

That day, Kavanaugh spent an hour on the phone with Susan Collins. The Maine senator, key to Kavanaugh's confirmation, had not yet tipped her hand, but she had been leaning all along toward voting for him and had told Republican colleagues that she planned to give a speech announcing her support for Kavanaugh at an event the next week. The Ford allegations put that plan on hold. The day before, Collins had seen the redacted letter from Ford, which had not been made public. Now, she and Kavanaugh went ahead with a follow-up call that had been planned since their truncated courtesy call. The substance—Collins had some questions about Kavanaugh's speech to AEI on Rehnquist—changed dramatically as a result of the news reports. "Is there any truth at all, in any way, to these allegations?" Collins asked. Did he have any idea who would be making these allegations, or why? Kavanaugh, she recalled, "said he had absolutely no idea who could be making the allegations nor the motivation, and he was emphatic in answering."[9]

For all the uproar, as the weekend began, Kavanaugh's confirmation appeared on track. NEW KAVANAUGH DISCLOSURE SHOWS LITTLE SIGN OF IMPEDING HIS NOMINATION, read the *New York Times* headline, posted Saturday afternoon, by Carl Hulse, the paper's well-regarded chief Washington correspondent.[10]

In Palo Alto, Ford was on again, off again about whether to let the *Post*'s Emma Brown use her name. By this point, Russell Ford thought his wife should come forward. Indeed, since the *Inter-*

cept story was posted, he had thought it was time to go public. "Your agony will end if you just go ahead and say it," he told his wife. "Let's call Emma; we'll end it."[11] At one point Saturday, Ford escaped to the Stanford football game, needing to get away from it all. Later that night, she made the decision: the *Post* could publish. "She seems calm and eager," Katz wrote in an e-mail to Brown. "She is going to sleep at home and then go to a hotel in Monterey for the next few nights." That was a dramatic underestimate. Ford would not be able to return to her home until Christmas Eve.

The story posted at 1:30 p.m. An unnamed allegation was one thing. But this was a flesh-and-blood human being, talking on the record about an incident she said had traumatized her for years. She had passed a polygraph test. She had told her husband about the attack years earlier and used Kavanaugh's name at the time.[12] The story had entered what was, for Kavanaugh, a dangerous new phase. It might not be survivable. "Everything changes," said a Republican aide.

Grassley's staff headed into the office, called the senator, and talked about next steps. Monday they would discuss further how to proceed, conducting basic due diligence, or trying to—for starters, holding routine background investigation calls with Kavanaugh and Ford. But there was a tougher tactical question: whether to reopen the hearings.

The immediate reaction suggested that it would be difficult for Republicans to avoid that step, as perilous as it might be. Mike Lee had been in regular touch with Jeff Flake of Arizona; both are Mormons and graduates of Brigham Young University, and both serve on the Judiciary Committee. Lee was keeping tabs on Flake, worried about whether the Arizonan, who was retiring from the Senate and had been a persistent Trump critic, would remain a solid vote for Kavanaugh. As the Ford story broke, both men were at different churches in Utah, where one of Flake's daughters lives. Lee called Flake from the church parking lot to get his take. If this is true, they agreed, Kavanaugh would have a big problem. The facts would reveal themselves, either corroborating Ford's story or not.

As he thought it over, Flake became increasingly convinced that the Senate couldn't simply wait for the facts to emerge—it needed to find them. "I've made it clear that I'm not comfortable moving ahead with the vote on Thursday if we have not heard her side of the story or explored this further," Flake told the *Washington Post* on Sunday. "For me, we can't vote until we hear more."[13] Another retiring Republican senator, Bob Corker of Tennessee, called for a delay, saying that it "would be best for all involved, including the nominee. If she does want to be heard, she should do so [speak up] promptly."[14]

Monday morning began with Katz, Ford's lawyer, making the rounds of morning shows—CBS, ABC, CNN. "Let's get to a question that is at the top of everybody's mind, which is, will your client, Christine Ford, be willing to testify in public to the Judiciary Committee?" asked CNN anchor Alisyn Camerota. "The answer is yes," Katz said flatly.[15] On CBS, Norah O'Donnell pressed the point. "Testifying in public under oath in front of the Senate Judiciary Committee with the American people watching, that's an enormous amount of pressure," she noted. "Is she willing to go that far?"

"She's willing to do what she needs to do," Katz replied.[16] In fact, no one had yet asked Ford to testify, but neither had she made any such commitment—far from it. This was more lawyerly bluff than metaphysical certitude.

At the same time, Kellyanne Conway, on *Fox & Friends*, was setting, or trying to set, the proper tone for dealing with Ford. "This woman should not be insulted and she should not be ignored," she decreed.[17] From an often bellicose White House, this response was uncharacteristically restrained, deliberately so. Attacking Ford's credibility, advisers knew, would be unhelpful, not only with the public but also with the very senators whose votes they needed, most prominently Collins and Murkowski. For a time, at least, that edict held.

Speaking to reporters a few hours later, Trump himself sounded distinctly un-Trumpian. Bob Woodward's newly published book, *Fear*, had quoted Trump's advice to a friend who had been accused of inappropriate behavior with women: "You've got to deny, deny, deny and push back on these women."[18] Now, the president managed to suppress his instinct to push back. Trump called Kavanaugh outstanding and observed, "This is something that should have been brought up long before this." But, he said, "At the same time, we want to go through a process. We want to make sure everything is perfect, everything is just right . . . If it takes a little delay it'll take a little delay."[19]

Achieving and maintaining that state of presidential Zen was no easy feat. In the coming days, Grassley's press staff was on the phone with Sanders and Shah, the White House press aides, imploring them: please don't let him tweet. "I'm trying, I'm trying," Sanders responded.

Trump's natural reaction to the allegation was to identify with Kavanaugh and disbelieve Ford; he had, after all, been in this situation himself. But other members of his family had different advice. "Jared and Ivanka both wanted to ditch him," one well-placed adviser said of Kavanaugh. "They both told the president, 'Get rid of Kavanaugh and start over' . . . They were like, 'cut your losses.'" By that point, of course, Jared and Ivanka were at odds with McGahn, so killing his candidate held additional appeal. To fend them off, McGahn eventually had McConnell reach out to stiffen Trump's spine. McConnell's message, the adviser said, was "you can ditch Kavanaugh if you really want," but "don't think you're gonna play a switcheroo here and I'm going to get it done before the election because I'm not." Trump decided to stay the course.

Now, the White House and the Kavanaugh confirmation team needed to figure out exactly what they were dealing with. Kavanaugh arrived at the White House around 10:00 a.m. and remained for the next nine hours, closeted with McGahn and making calls to senators. That morning, Kavanaugh issued a statement, once again unequivocally denying the allegations. "I have never done anything like what the accuser describes—to her or to anyone," he said.[20]

Now that Ford had gone public, now that Katz had asserted her client was willing to testify, the question facing the White House and Senate Republicans was what should happen next. Doing nothing was not an option. Flake and Corker had made that clear on Sunday. Now others weighed in—most important, Collins. At noon, Collins tweeted, "Professor Ford and Judge Kavanaugh should both testify under oath before the Judiciary Committee."[21] "I need to see them and listen to their answers to the questions in order to make an assessment," she told reporters.[22] Grassley issued a statement, saying that Ford "deserves to be heard . . . in an appropriate, precedented and respectful manner." He didn't specify exactly how.[23]

Figuring that out was the subject of intense discussions at the White House and the Capitol for the remainder of the day. Grassley, McConnell, and key staff recognized the need for some investigation, but they hoped to be able to avoid another hearing. Taking that step was like opening Pandora's box. Who knew what might fly out? Grassley had watched as the committee wrestled with the allegations against Clarence Thomas twenty-seven years earlier. "I hope we never have to go through an ordeal like this again," he said on the Senate floor as the nomination was debated.[24] Now he found himself presiding over another, eerily similar, situation.

At a meeting with Judiciary Republicans in McConnell's office late Monday afternoon, the leader and the chairman presented their plan: have the committee staff conduct a background investigation, interrogating the witnesses under oath. Maybe a hearing would make sense after evaluating that information, but not right away. Not every person who makes an allegation against a nominee gets a hearing, McConnell argued. That's just not done. This looked like a sandbagging—of the nominee, the committee, and the Senate.

That argument was a nonstarter with a surprising array of senators. The specter of the Hill-Thomas hearings hung in the air. So did the new reality of the #MeToo movement. Thomas had won confirmation, but the electoral backlash was felt the next year, with the election of four new women to the Senate. If the racial element was absent this time around—Thomas had famously called the hearings a "high-tech lynching"—the gender sensitivities were more fraught than they had been in 1991. As furious as Republicans were about what they viewed as yet another last-ditch effort to take down the nominee, they were exquisitely aware of the need to tread gingerly—far more than they had when the Hill allegations surfaced—where matters of gender and sexual misbehavior were concerned. Only two Republican veterans of the Thomas confirmation remained on the panel—Grassley and Hatch—but all of them understood that times had changed.

There needs to be a hearing, Flake said. Cruz agreed. So did Ben Sasse of Nebraska. So—somewhat surprisingly, given his later eruption at the hearing itself—did Graham. He was inclined to believe Kavanaugh, Graham observed, but Flake was right. In the age of #MeToo, not giving Ford the chance to tell her story herself, in public, wouldn't fly. With the committee divided 11–10, the views of a single Republican member were controlling. McConnell and Grassley were nothing if not pragmatic: they didn't have the votes on their side. That meant there would be a hearing after all.

But when? The court's new term would begin on the first Monday in October, not far away, and it was important to have a new justice in place. Flake scoffed at the notion that the court shouldn't have to operate shorthanded. "Sorry," he said. "That ship sailed with Garland." This was Monday. A hearing a week from now sounded reasonable.

Another issue came up at the meeting—if there was to be a hearing, how would it be conducted? It went without saying that what had been acceptable in 1991, when Republicans brutally interrogated Hill, was not going to work in 2018. Back then, Republicans had taken a prosecutorial, even inquisitorial, approach with Hill. Pennsylvania Republican Arlen Specter accused her of "flat-out perjury."[25] Wyoming Republican Alan Simpson had suggested she had passed a polygraph only because she suffered from a "delusional disorder."[26] Hatch had read aloud a passage from *The Exorcist* to insinuate that Hill had used the book as the basis for her account of Thomas asking about a pubic hair on his Coke can.[27] There would be no replay of that ugly performance. "I'm not cross-examining her," declared Cruz, who was in the midst of a hard-fought reelection campaign.

Who would? Here Republicans had a problem: there were no Republican women on the committee. The senators discussed hiring an outside lawyer, a woman to conduct the questioning. Finding the right "female assistant," the unfortunate term that McConnell later employed, ended up being easier said than done. A few dozen prominent women lawyers turned down the committee—their law firms were not eager to take on this kind of controversial task—before Republicans settled on Rachel Mitchell, an Arizona sex crimes prosecutor.

The senators agreed not to reveal the hearing plan right away, not before checking with Ford's lawyers. But reporters were gathered outside the majority leader's office, clamoring for information. As the meeting broke up that evening, Louisiana senator John Neely Kennedy spilled the beans. I'm not supposed to tell you guys this, he said, but we're having a hearing.

Grassley soon put out a statement. The committee would hold a hearing the following Monday, September 24. "She can do it privately if she prefers or publicly," McConnell said the next day. "Monday is her opportunity to have a meeting with the members on this topic."[28]

At six o'clock that night, Kavanaugh, joined by his lawyer Alexandra Walsh, had a thirty-minute telephone interview with the majority staff about Ford's allegations. Democrats declined to participate. "To clear my name," he said, "I want a hearing tomorrow."[29]

With the timing of the hearing in flux, the White House arranged a murder board on Tuesday to try to get Kavanaugh prepared as early as possible. The usually territorial McGahn was sensitive to the need to build support for Kavanaugh throughout the White

House now that the nomination was in peril, so he invited top communications staff including Sarah Sanders and Bill Shine. White House aides portraying Democratic senators grilled Kavanaugh not only on Ford's allegation, but also the details of his sexual history and drinking habits, aiming to make him as flustered and uncomfortable as possible. "I'm not going to answer that," he said at one point.[30] Attendees concluded the murder board had been a success. "We came at him probably more fiercely than Democratic senators," one recalled. "It hardened him."

The next several days were consumed by quarreling over whether and when a hearing would occur. Monday, "six short days from today," was too soon, Ford's lawyers told Grassley in a letter on Tuesday, September 18.[31] In any event, before any hearing, they wanted an FBI investigation, as there had been when Hill's allegations surfaced, and then White House counsel C. Boyden Gray directed the FBI to investigate. "The hearing should be as a result of the investigation," Ford lawyer Lisa Banks told CNN. "It shouldn't be a substitute for it."[32] Senate Democrats made the same argument, citing the Hill precedent. "In retrospect, this process has been heavily criticized as being rushed and incomplete, yet even then Republicans ensured the FBI performed an investigation and submitted a report before the Judiciary Committee moved forward with public hearings," committee Democrats wrote to McGahn and FBI director Christopher Wray.[33]

In private, some Republicans agreed. At the meeting in McConnell's office, Flake had pushed for an FBI investigation. And Lee had called McGahn as the story broke the weekend before, suggesting that the FBI conduct a supplemental background investigation. McGahn's answer was abrupt but unconvincing. The FBI has finished doing its job, the White House counsel insisted; there was nothing more for it to do. He was adamant. The FBI worked for him, not the Senate, and its work, in his view, was over.

Kavanaugh, too, pressed for an FBI investigation. He wasn't

going to publicly break with McGahn on this—after all, the White House counsel was his chief advocate, and certainly Kavanaugh needed McGahn in his corner now more than ever. But for Kavanaugh, this was increasingly a matter not merely of confirmation but also of survival. He wanted a way to clear his reputation. McGahn and McConnell had a different view. For them, the focus needed to be on one thing: securing fifty votes. Bringing in the FBI at this late point would only reward what they saw as a last-minute smear. It would slow things down. And, like a new hearing, an investigation could bring surprises: Who knew what other issues might pop up? Why risk all that if they had the votes to get Kavanaugh confirmed without it?

And so the jousting continued. As Republicans saw it, Ford's lawyers and the Democrats were just playing for delay, seeing whether other women would emerge. Katz and Banks had plenty of time to go on television to assert their client's demands, they argued, but they hadn't responded to the committee staff's efforts to interview Ford. Republican senators were becoming increasingly agitated. "All I can say is that we're bringing this to a close," Graham said on Tuesday. "This has been a drive-by shooting when it comes to Kavanaugh . . . I'll listen to the lady, but we're going to bring this to a close." Cornyn seemed to question Ford's account, the first evident cracks in the plan not to go on the attack. "The problem is, Dr. Ford can't remember when it was, where it was or how it came to be," he told reporters.[34]

By midweek, Kavanaugh's situation looked dire—so dire, in fact, that Mike Davis, once Kavanaugh's adversary and now his dogged defender, decided it was time to insist otherwise. "Unfazed and determined," Davis tweeted at 10:22 p.m. on Wednesday, September 19. "We will confirm Judge Kavanaugh. #ConfirmKavanaugh #SCOTUS."[35]

This provocation was, in the view of others in Grassley's office, a jab too far. It appeared to do exactly what Republicans had been trying to avoid—denigrating the seriousness of Ford's allegation. The alarm bells went off in Grassley's world. Take it down, Davis was told of the tweet. "Unfazed by rape allegations is not a thing I want appearing on fucking cable chyrons," said a Grassley aide. "It's not going to work. I don't know what he meant, and I didn't really care. This is one of those things—people are going to talk about this; it is going to appear everywhere, and you are reflecting on my boss."

The next morning, Thursday, September 20, the tweet was still there—and starting to garner the predictable media attention. Press aides Taylor Foy and George Hartmann went to Kolan Davis, Grassley's chief judiciary aide, and then, with his blessing, delivered an ultimatum to Mike Davis: if you don't fix this we're going to make Grassley fix this, and that's going to be bad. Davis deleted the tweet and posted an explanation. "To clear up any confusion, I was referring to Democrats' partisan political attacks and their refusal to take part in the committee's thorough and clear investigation," he tweeted. "I deleted the tweet to avoid any further misinterpretation by left wing media as so often happens on Twitter."[36]

That night came a flurry of two dozen tweets that made Davis's look mild and well advised by comparison. Ed Whelan, a prominent conservative lawyer, former Kavanaugh colleague in the Bush administration, and president of the Ethics and Public Policy Center, suggested that he had solved the mystery of Ford's assailant. Whelan had hinted at his supposed discovery earlier in the week. "By one week from today, I expect that Judge Kavanaugh will have been clearly vindicated on this matter," he tweeted on Tuesday. "Specifically, I expect that compelling evidence will show his categorical denial to be truthful. There will be no cloud over him." Other Republicans amplified Whelan's tantalizing suggestion. "Keep an eye on Ed's tweets the next few days," advised Matt Whitlock, deputy chief of staff for Senator Orrin Hatch, in a tweet that was later deleted.[37]

On Thursday night, September 20, Whelan unveiled his case. Ford had said the house where she was assaulted was "not far from" the Columbia Country Club, up Connecticut Avenue. None of those identified as attending the party—Kavanaugh, Judge, Kavanaugh's friend P. J. Smyth, or Ford's friend Leland Ingham Keyser—lived anywhere near there. But Whelan proposed another possibility, a house just a half mile from the country club, at 3714 Thornapple Street, in Chevy Chase. That house belonged to Chris Garrett, a close friend and Georgetown Prep classmate of Kavanaugh's. Posting side-by-side photos of the two, in their senior yearbook photos and as adults, Whelan suggested that Ford could have mistaken Garrett for Kavanaugh.

That wasn't all in Whelan's arsenal of supposed vindication. He posted a Zillow-derived floor plan of the Garrett house that, he said, "corresponds closely to Ford's description of the house where the gathering took place"—a small family room, a short stairwell running from the foyer next to the living room, a hallway bath with a bedroom nearby, all as if this rather common arrangement was somehow unique to 3714 Thornapple.

"To be clear, I have no idea what, if anything, did or did not happen in that bedroom at the top of the stairs, and I therefore do not state, imply or insinuate that Garrett or anyone else committed the sexual assault that Ford alleges," Whelan added. "Further, if Ford is now mistakenly remembering Garrett to be Kavanaugh, I offer no view whether that mistaken remembrance dates from the gathering or developed at some point in the intervening years."[38]

This was ridiculous and scurrilous. It was ridiculous because Ford knew Kavanaugh and the Georgetown Prep crew through Garrett, whom she had briefly dated. There was no way she would have mistaken one for the other, and Ford said as much in a statement that night. "I knew them both," Ford said. "There is zero chance that I would confuse them."[39] It was scurrilous because, notwithstanding Whelan's caveats, he was effectively accusing an innocent party of sexual assault, with no basis other than deducing from geographic proximity, floor plans, and supposed resemblance.

By the next morning, Whelan was profusely apologizing for publicly naming Garrett. "I made an appalling and inexcusable mistake of judgment in posting the tweet thread in a way that identified Kavanaugh's Georgetown Prep classmate," he tweeted. "I take full responsibility for that mistake, and I deeply apologize for it. I realize that does not undo the mistake."[40]

Leave aside the question of how a person at the head of a center on ethics—and a Harvard Law School graduate—could take it upon himself to slander another person in desperate pursuit of seeing Kavanaugh confirmed. The more important question is, who put Whelan up to this stunt—and provided him with the necessary information to execute it? Whelan was not acting alone. It would have taken serious sleuthing—most likely help from someone intimately familiar with Kavanaugh's cadre of Georgetown Prep friends (Garrett, later known as Squi, had not yet been publicly identified on Kavanaugh's high school calendars)—to come up with Garrett's name and to dredge up the Thornapple Street floor plans.

Whelan clearly was privy to inside information. As Ford would disclose, he had checked her LinkedIn profile on Sunday morning, September 16—*before* the *Post* story was published but within an hour and a half after the White House learned Ford's name. Whelan, who took a brief leave of absence from his Ethics and Public Policy Center post, later claimed he did not receive the name from anyone at the White House, which raises the question: from whom did he receive it, then?

In fact, Whelan was no rogue operator but a supremely well-connected inside player. As Steve Schmidt, the Republican political consultant who helped guide Supreme Court nominations during the Bush administration, noted in a tweet, "When I ran the Roberts and Alito confirmations Ed Whalen [*sic*] was the singularly most important and effective outside adviser involved in the confirmation effort. He knew every detail when it came to our strategy and everything he did was closely coordinated with the WH effort."[41]

In producing his Garrett-as-doppelgänger theory, Whelan was working hand in glove with Leonard Leo and the Federalist Society's public relations firm, CRC—in fact, CRC had assembled the material in a package it provided to Whelan. The company, which had received millions of dollars from the Federalist Society and relied on it for the largest chunk of its income, was best known for its work during the 2004 presidential campaign for a group known as Swift Boat Veterans for Truth. The organization claimed that Democratic nominee John Kerry was "unfit to serve" and had lied to obtain some of his combat medals. Arizona senator John McCain, who had spent five and a half years as a prisoner of war, denounced the claims as "dishonest and dishonorable."[42]

Now Swift Boat tactics were being imported to the nomination fight. CRC had tried, without success, to peddle the mistaken-identity theory to reporters. Even conservative writers and news organizations weren't willing to bite. Only then did the operatives resort to having Whelan unload the goods himself. As Eliana Johnson of *Politico* reported at the time, Whelan, after his suggestive tweets, "worked over the next 48 hours with CRC and its president, Greg Mueller, to stoke the anticipation."[43] As Whelan circulated his material among Kavanaugh backers, he was warned, as one friend put it, that "this is very dangerous stuff; you could be falsely accusing somebody." But rumors of a second accuser were swirling. *The New Yorker* and others were chasing the story. Meanwhile, the hearing had been postponed from Grassley's Monday target date, increasing the danger for Kavanaugh. In the heat of the moment, Whelan decided to go for it.

After the tweets and the uproar that ensued, Whelan denied that he had coordinated the attack with the White House or Kavanaugh. "I have not communicated at all with Donald McGahn or anyone at the White House, or Judge Kavanaugh, about the topic of the Twitter thread," he told the *Washington Post*.[44] But that statement omitted numerous other avenues of potential transmission. Whelan would later say privately that his information was drawn from details provided by Kavanaugh's Georgetown Prep friends. Before the tweets, Leo and Federalist Society vice president Jonathan Bunch had been assuring fellow Republicans that Whelan had the goods. "They were calling, saying, don't worry, we have the silver bullet," said one Republican source.

It was less silver bullet than self-inflicted wound. "Fucking face-palm moment," said one GOP aide. "All of us, in one breath, the Republican Senate, was like, 'What in God's name did you just do?'" said another. Yet even after the ugly caper blew up in Whelan's face, Leo defended the tweets, saying in private that Whelan had done the right thing and that there was a rationale behind them. At least they forced people to stop and consider the possibility of mistaken identity.

One reason for Whelan's lapse of judgment may have been the sensation that the Kavanaugh nomination was rapidly cratering. By Thursday, September 20, "I'm like, 'This guy's dead; we're gonna lose the Senate; Trump's gonna lose reelection; we're gonna lose the court; we're gonna lose the country,'" said Mike Davis, the Grassley aide. The Kavanaugh team was similarly demoralized.

Among other things fueling that assessment was the knowledge that another story might pop at any moment. It seemed only a matter of time before there would be more mess to deal with. As the rumors swirled, McConnell assured conservatives on Friday morning that they had no cause for alarm. "You've watched the fight. You've watched the tactics. But here's what I want to tell you. In the very near future, Judge Kavanaugh will be on the United States Supreme Court," McConnell vowed, to sustained applause, at the Values Voter Summit. "So, my friends, keep the faith, don't get rattled by all of this. We're going to plow right through it and do our job."[45] When Trump and McConnell talked on the phone later that day, Trump asked McConnell if he was determined to see Kavanaugh confirmed. "I'm stronger than mule piss," McConnell replied.[46]

By then, Trump could contain himself no longer. OFFICIALS IN OVERDRIVE TO KEEP TRUMP FROM ATTACKING KAVA-NAUGH ACCUSER, reported *Axios*'s Jonathan Swan on Friday morning. He quoted one White House source: "Hopefully he can keep it together until Monday. That's only, like, another 48 hours right?"[47] Actually, Trump couldn't keep it together more than a few more hours. "I have no doubt that, if the attack on Dr. Ford was as bad as she says, charges would have been immediately filed with local Law Enforcement Authorities by either her or her loving parents," Trump tweeted at 9:14 a.m. "I ask that she bring those filings forward so that we can learn date, time, and place!"[48] Then, 15 minutes later: "The radical left lawyers want the FBI to get involved NOW. Why didn't someone call the FBI 36 years ago?"[49]

This was ignorant. It was highly unlikely, back in the early 1980s, that a high school girl would have told her parents about such an event or that they would have taken the matter to the police. The fact that Ford didn't make such a complaint was no evidence at all. And, of course, the FBI tweet was ridiculous: this would have been a local matter, in any event. Worse than ignorant, however, the tweet was distinctly unhelpful. Collins declared herself "appalled by the president's tweet," noting that "allegations of sexual assault are one of the most unreported crimes that exist. So I thought that the president's tweet was completely inappropriate and wrong."[50] Flake termed the tweet "incredibly insensitive."[51] McConnell called Trump to urge him to stop.

Meantime, the negotiations over Ford's appearance continued. Grassley backed off from the Monday-or-nothing offer and held out the prospect of Wednesday instead. He set a deadline of 5:00 p.m. for Katz and Banks to respond, then extended it to 10:00 p.m. It was an indication that Republicans did not have the upper hand in the negotiations. As much as they wanted to plow right through it, to use McConnell's phrase, it was going to be difficult to get beyond this moment—to secure Kavanaugh the votes he needed in committee and on the Senate floor—without first hearing from Ford. Finally, on Saturday, Katz and Banks responded. "Dr. Ford accepts the Committee's request to provide her first-hand knowledge of Brett Kavanaugh's sexual misconduct next week," they wrote.[52]

By this point, with the Whelan gambit having failed, Leo was among those panicking. He called Davis, the Grassley aide, saying it was time to pull the plug on Kavanaugh. There were other nominees in the wings, Leo argued, and he could raise huge sums to make the Supreme Court an issue in the midterm elections and get a new nominee confirmed after that. Perhaps mirroring Leo's agitation, the Judicial Crisis Network's Carrie Severino was surprisingly noncommittal, the day before the hearing, when MSNBC's Craig Melvin asked whether Kavanaugh should still be confirmed. "I think we have to look into this further," Severino replied. "From what we know so far, we don't have corroboration yet. If the Senate votes on this soon, I think they would have to go on what they know so far. I know the Senate Judiciary Committee is going to look into this before they would move forward to a vote."[53]

Davis and others thought Leo had lost his mind. Pulling his nomination at this late stage would demoralize conservatives, which risked losing the Senate, which meant losing the ability to get a conservative nominee confirmed, which meant losing the White House in 2020.

Kavanaugh, in short, had become too big to fail.

CHAPTER FOURTEEN

Second Accuser

On Sunday night, September 23, the article that everyone knew was coming finally landed. SENATE DEMOCRATS INVESTIGATE A NEW ALLEGATION OF SEXUAL MIS-CONDUCT, FROM BRETT KAVANAUGH'S COLLEGE YEARS, reported Ronan Farrow and Jane Mayer.[1]

The rumors had been percolating all summer. Even as Ford agonized about how to proceed, another allegation about Kavanaugh and sexual misconduct was simmering—except this time, the talk was, strangely enough, unbeknownst to the woman involved.

Deborah Ramirez was a college classmate of Kavanaugh's, and, although they were both products of Catholic education, they could not otherwise have been more different. Ramirez had grown up in Shelton, just thirty minutes from New Haven but a world away from Yale. Her mother, a medical technician, was of French descent; her father, a telephone lineman, was from Puerto Rico. Although her light skin did not suggest her Puerto Rican heritage, Ramirez's last name marked her as different in overwhelmingly white Shelton, and it shaped her lifelong perception of herself as an outsider. Ramirez's mother pulled her out of the public schools after her first-grade teacher said she did not realize that the quiet little girl in her class spoke English. In fact, Ramirez did not know a word of Spanish. Later, in high school, some friends, intending to be nice, would tell Ramirez they didn't think of her as Puerto Rican.

Ramirez was, by her own account, a "pleaser." In the Catholic culture in which she was immersed, following the rules was prized above all. "I wanted to be the straight-A student and be the one the teacher called on—like that was my identity to just do everything right," she said. It didn't come that easily to her, but she worked hard and graduated at the top of the girls in her eighth-grade class (the boys also had a valedictorian), only to find, on the basis of standardized test scores, that she would not place in honors classes at St. Joseph High School in Trumbull, Connecticut. Ramirez pushed back. Her grades were good, she told her teachers after starting high school: she belonged in more challenging classes. To her, it felt like a pattern of "always being underestimated," with "assumptions about my upbringing, where I'm from, and who I am and my racial identity." She ended up getting into the honors classes and graduating with a grade point average above 4.0.[2]

Although her father had studied for an associate's degree, Ramirez would be the first in her family to go to college and knew nothing about how to apply. The University of Connecticut seemed like a solid choice. Then a guidance counselor suggested Yale, a place Ramirez hadn't really heard of. You should mark "Hispanic" on your application, the counselor suggested. To Ramirez, with her Catholic upbringing, this felt dishonest—she was Puerto Rican and French, and "this 'Hispanic' was not something I even understood what that was." When the Yale acceptance letter came, she said, "I didn't know anything about Yale, nothing about Yale. My counselor seemed to think it was a good school . . . And then what happened when people would hear that I got into Yale—you would have thought I just did the most unbelievably amazing thing." Ramirez's mother thought the University of Connecticut would be a better choice. Debbie was a shy, sensitive child, young for her age. Maybe she would fit in better at UConn. But Ramirez's father was determined. Yale it was.[3]

All this is to say that the eighteen-year-old Debbie Ramirez who arrived on the Yale campus was unprepared for the environment in which she found herself, surrounded by so many people who were so much more sophisticated, so much wealthier, so much more at ease in the world. It was overwhelming. She had never had a drink, never really kissed a boy. She had worn a uniform throughout school and didn't know what to wear to fit in. But Yale also offered Ramirez the opportunity to create a new identity for herself, to try to be the popular girl she hadn't been in high school. "So now I'm in this new school. Nobody knows me. Nobody knows anything about me. I can be whoever I want," she recalled. "That person who was quiet and shy before and got straight As, they don't know her. Now I'm just Debbie and whoever Debbie is."[4]

Cheerleaders were popular, she thought. Why not try out for cheerleading? This plan illustrated Ramirez's social cluelessness: in the sociology of Yale at the time, cheerleaders were the opposite of cool. But she tried out for the squad and got in. The night she was tapped to join was the first time she recalls ever having had a drink. "It was something that I wanted," she said. "To be part of this, I had to drink. So I drink." Friends would call her Debbie Cheerleader. And sometimes, also, Debbie Dining Hall, from Ramirez's work on the serving line at the Branford College dining hall, making the money that was required as part of her financial aid package.[5]

College friends recall Ramirez as sweet, naive, and to a certain extent victimized by the more sophisticated students around her. "She didn't even realize how much of a fish out of water she was," said Jamie Roche, a friend from freshman year.[6]

For some graduates, Kavanaugh included, Yale embodies their "bright college years," as its alma mater would have it, "the shortest, gladdest years of life." For Ramirez, Yale produced some close friends but was, by and large, an experience she preferred to forget. Her career path after graduation was steady but far from stellar— enough to help pay off the student loans but not particularly inspirational, selling accident and life insurance, then medical supplies in Houston, Chicago, and Connecticut. Eventually, Ramirez made her way to Colorado, where, by 2018, she was coordinating volunteers for the county's housing and human services department and serving on the board of a group that helped victims of domestic violence, the Safehouse Progressive Alliance for Nonviolence. She was, as one person described her, "vintage Boulder," the kind of person who signs her e-mail with an identification of her preferred pronouns (*she*, *her*, *hers*) and who, in 2014, wrote a letter to the local newspaper protesting what she considered to be the insensitive slogan on a T-shirt for the annual ten-kilometer Bolder Boulder race, "Sea level is for sissies."[7] Many Yale graduates return religiously for reunions and keep in close touch on social media. Ramirez was more alienated from the Yale environment. Like Christine Ford crafting a new life for herself in California, Ramirez had moved on.

But then came Kavanaugh's nomination and, with it, phone calls, e-mails, and texts among members of the class, sharing dim memories of something that had supposedly happened to Ramirez one night freshman year in Kavanaugh's Old Campus dorm, Lawrance Hall. Mark Krasberg, now an assistant professor of neurosurgery at the University of New Mexico, had a fuzzy impression of bad behavior involving Kavanaugh. He reached out to classmate Richard Oh, now an emergency room doctor in the Bay Area, who described an incident involving a woman—he couldn't pinpoint who it was—upset over a drunken party in which a penis had been waved in her face. And Oh recalled another potential witness: Ken Appold, who had lived in the Lawrance basement with Kavanaugh during their freshman year and was now a professor at Princeton Theological Seminary. Appold had been told, shortly after the fact, about a party in which Kavanaugh had exposed himself and thrust his penis in Ramirez's face. It was disturbing, Krasberg thought, but so long ago and so indistinct. He put it aside, but when the Ford story broke, he thought: perhaps I have some corroboration. He reached out to *The New Yorker*'s Jane Mayer, who, with Farrow, had been writing about the Ford incident.

Ramirez knew none of this. She had been following the Kavanaugh story only dimly since his name surfaced as a potential nominee. Ramirez and her husband, Vikram Shah, a software engineer, were listening to the radio on a drive to New Mexico when they heard that Kavanaugh was at the top of Trump's short list. "That guy drank a lot," Ramirez told her husband. His Yale days, Ramirez predicted, would come back to haunt him if he were chosen. She had no clue she would end up as the central figure in making that prediction a reality.

On Monday, September 17, the day after the *Washington Post* published its Christine Blasey Ford story, Ramirez noticed that the message light on her desk telephone in the Boulder County housing department was on. It was a reporter, Ronan Farrow of *The New Yorker*. Could she call him back, please? Farrow was already famous for his stories uncovering sexual harassment and misconduct, which had earned him a Pulitzer Prize. But Ramirez was unaware that she was being called by the man who had helped bring down the legendary Hollywood producer Harvey Weinstein. She assumed he wanted to ask about her agency's Family to Family program, which helped organize holiday gifts for those in need. Ramirez was used to dealing with reporters writing about the program, though an inquiry in late September seemed awfully early.[8]

When Ramirez returned Farrow's call, she learned that his subject was something far different: he was looking into reports of sexual misconduct by Brett Kavanaugh at Yale, he said. Did Ramirez know anything about that? No, she said. She remembered Kavanaugh was drunk a lot, but that was it. Farrow continued. There was a story about a party at which someone exposed himself. "Oh, that," Ramirez responded. "I knew exactly what he was talking about." It had suddenly clicked—that night freshman year when she was the target of a drinking game in Lawrance Hall, alone with a group of male students, Kavanaugh among them. She couldn't talk in the office. She would have to call him back, after work, and after her Safehouse meeting that night.

When she left work that afternoon, Ramirez called her husband to tell him about the puzzling call she had received from someone named Farrow. "Oh, my God, Ronan Farrow called you?" Shah said. The Safehouse group had much the same awestruck reaction. Farrow had done incredible work on behalf of the survivors they worked so hard to protect. When Ramirez returned Farrow's call that night, she told him a story she had spent years trying to forget. There had been a gathering in a suite in Lawrance Hall, and a drinking game—probably quarters, in which you try to flip a quarter into a cup of beer. If you succeed, you get to choose someone to drink the cup. Ramirez kept getting picked, so often that she was very drunk. Someone brandished a fake penis, parading around. Then there was another penis, close to her face. "That's not a real penis," she said drunkenly, touching it as she batted it away. She remembered the laughter, at her expense, and the overwhelming feeling of humiliation.

Back then, Ramirez, a good Catholic girl, had not expected to touch anyone's penis until she was married. She remembered two classmates, Kevin Genda and David Todd, laughing at her. But who had exposed himself? That she couldn't recall, not at that point. "I'm not going to be able to help you," she told Farrow. "I can't help you. All I can tell you is yes, this happened to me . . . but I can't tell you that was Brett's penis." Farrow was gentle. It was fine that Ramirez's memory was spotty. Others were filling in blanks. They should keep talking.[9]

The next morning, a Tuesday, Stan Garnett, a Denver lawyer and former Boulder County district attorney active in Democratic politics, was in the middle of a board meeting of the Legal Aid Foundation of Colorado when he received an urgent text: Michael Bennet, the state's Democratic senator, needs your cell number. When the meeting ended, Garnett received a call from Bennet's chief of staff, Jonathan Davidson. There's a woman in Boulder who was a classmate of Kavanaugh's at Yale, and we'd like you to talk to her, Davidson told Garnett. Davidson had been alerted to the Ramirez story by another Democratic Senate staffer who had heard about it. As it happens, Garnett, who lives in Boulder, knew Anne Tapp, executive director of Safehouse. He called Tapp, who had already heard the account from Ramirez herself. Could Tapp put him in touch with Ramirez?[10]

The next several days were a blur of meeting lawyers—Garnett brought in John Clune, a national expert in representing victims of sexual abuse, who happened to live in Boulder—and contacting friends and family members as Ramirez tried to figure out who might know something relevant. "I knew I had to be so careful because I didn't want anybody to say I put ideas in their head," Ramirez said months later, sitting on a brown sofa in her Boulder home. One friend who Ramirez thought had brought her to the party didn't have any recollection of being there. Then her mother reminded Ramirez of an incident freshman year when Debbie called her, crying uncontrollably. She wouldn't tell her mother what had happened or, despite her mother's urging, go to school authorities. "The episode, for me, it was something that I blamed myself for," Ramirez recalled.[11]

In thinking about whether to come forward, Ramirez was torn. One of those she remembered being in the room, Genda, had married one of her closest friends, Karen Yarasavage. Ramirez was godmother to their youngest daughter, although they had lost touch over the years. She didn't want to do anything to hurt Yarasavage. At the same time, Ramirez felt a responsibility to support Ford, to corroborate her story. "I have two bad choices," Ramirez recalled. "One, I come forward with what I know and join Dr. Ford in this scrutiny and criticism. Or two, I don't come forward and live with the fact that I did absolutely nothing to support her. I have two horrible choices."

On Saturday, Ramirez was once again on the phone with Farrow when he said something about the fact that she had mentioned Kavanaugh's laughter. At that point, Ramirez said, memories began flooding back, in distinct snapshots. Kavanaugh and the others were laughing—she doesn't know the difference between a real penis and a fake one. There was a penis in her face. Then Kavanaugh, pulling up his pants, hips thrust forward. "And so I followed the body up and that's when I saw that face"—Kavanaugh's face—"and that laughter, and the laughter coming out of his face," she said. Then, she said, David White, one of the students in the room, yelled down the hall, "Brett Kavanaugh just put his penis in Debbie's face."[12]

Kavanaugh and his team had been scrambling to deal with the Ramirez story even before it broke. In the week before it was published, Kavanaugh himself had reached out to David Todd, one of the students Ramirez recalled being in the room. According to Kathy Charlton, a Yale classmate who was working on a business project with Todd at the time, Todd mentioned to her that he had been contacted by *The New Yorker* and that he had told the reporter he had no memory of the episode. Todd then volunteered that "Brett called me and said, 'No bad, Dave, no bad.'" The next day, after a different reporter contacted Todd about the Ramirez incident, Todd, thinking Charlton had tipped the reporter off, angrily texted Charlton, "Don't F****** TELL PEOPLE BRETT GOT IN TOUCH WITH ME!!! I TOLD YOU AT THE TIME THAT WAS IN CONFIDENCE!!!" Charlton responded that she had not shared the information with the reporter.[13]

On Sunday morning, September 23, Kavanaugh, accompanied by the security detail that now traveled with him, arrived at Beth Wilkinson's home, in northwest Washington, D.C. He was wearing shorts and a baseball cap and seemed beaten down by the events. He was receiving threats; he and Ashley were having to explain the situation to their daughters. It had been eleven seemingly interminable days since the *Intercept* story broke, and now it looked like there was going to be another allegation to contend with. Was this ever going to end?

Alex Walsh, Wilkinson's partner, joined them. Wilkinson and Walsh got on the phone with Farrow and Mayer, then with *The New Yorker*'s general counsel. The account was thin, they argued. There wasn't enough corroboration; the magazine should consider the impact of publishing a story this shaky. Wilkinson needed to fly to California to resume her antitrust trial. Walsh went with Wilkinson to the airport, leaving Kavanaugh behind, then returned to join him. At that point, there wasn't much left to do; matters were out of their hands. The story posted a few hours later.

Kavanaugh's allies wouldn't be the only ones second-guessing *The New Yorker*'s decision to publish—there was some journalistic pushback as well—but to its credit, the magazine dealt head-on with the imperfections in Ramirez's account. Ramirez "was at first hesitant to speak publicly, partly because her memories contained gaps because she had been drinking at the time of the alleged incident," Farrow and Mayer wrote. "In her initial conversations with *The New Yorker*, she was reluctant to characterize Kavanaugh's role in the alleged incident with certainty. After six days of carefully assessing her memories and consulting with her attorney, Ramirez said that she felt confident enough of her recollections to say that she remembers Kavanaugh had exposed himself at a drunken dormitory party, thrust his penis in her face, and caused her to touch it without her consent as she pushed him away."[14]

As that summary makes clear, there were reasons to worry about the accuracy of Ramirez's account, however careful and precise she had tried to be. The *New York Times* reported that it "had interviewed several dozen people over the past week in an attempt to corroborate her story, and could find no one with firsthand knowledge."[15] The six days of recollecting would come in for particular derision from Kavanaugh's supporters. Two other students Ramirez remembered being present, David Todd and David White—although, at Ramirez's request, they were not named in the piece—said they recalled no such incident and that this behavior would have been completely out of character for Kavanaugh. "We can say with confidence that if the incident Debbie alleges ever occurred, we would have seen or heard about it—and we did not," those students and several other friends of Kavanaugh said in a statement. Yarasavage said Ramirez had never mentioned the incident. "This is a woman I was best friends with," she said, although she was not quoted by name. "We shared intimate details of our lives. And I was never told this story by her, or by anyone else. It never came up."[16]

But there were other witnesses who offered some corroboration, albeit imperfect. Appold, the Princeton professor, came forward—initially unnamed, then a week later on the record—with an account that matched Ramirez's recollection and, significantly, had been offered before he heard the account she had given to Farrow. In Appold's telling, he had heard of the incident that night or the day after from two classmates, one of whom had been in the room when it happened. Kavanaugh had exposed his penis and waved it in front of Ramirez, in this retelling. Appold recalled hearing something about the penis not being real—that made sense in hindsight, in light of Ramirez's memory of a fake penis. The story was so concerning to Appold that he had confided it to a graduate school roommate, Michael Wetstone, several years later. "It stood out in our minds because it was a shocking story of transgression," Wetstone told *The New Yorker*.[17]

Mike Davis, the Grassley aide, seized on the story's framing—"Senate Democrats are investigating a new allegation of sexual misconduct against Kavanaugh"—to paint Republicans and Kavanaugh as victims of yet another last-minute partisan smear. "Democratic staff should have made Republicans aware of these allegations to fully probe them rather than drop an eleventh-hour allegation at the tail-end of the confirmation process," he wrote in an e-mail that night to Garnett, Ramirez's lawyer, asking to be put in touch with Ramirez.[18] Five minutes later, Sawyer, Feinstein's chief investigator, shot back. "To be clear, Democratic staff also learned of these allegations from the New Yorker article this evening," she wrote to Garnett and Davis.[19] This was disingenuous; Democrats had clearly known of Ramirez, if not the details of her story.

The White House had responded with restraint and caution to Ford's account when it was printed in the *Washington Post*. Now, a week later, it took a far more aggressive, even ferocious, tack in response to *The New Yorker* story. "This 35-year-old, uncorroborated claim is the latest in a coordinated smear campaign by the Democrats designed to tear down a good man," spokeswoman Kerri Kupec said in a statement included in the article.[20] Driving back from seeing his mother in Connecticut, Raj Shah, the White House communications aide, was unruffled by the piece, even somewhat pleased. For the first time since the story began to emerge, it gave the White House a chance to go on offense, berating the magazine for shoddy journalism. By midnight, the White House had sent an e-mail memo to reporters—"What you need to know about the allegation made in the New Yorker article on Judge Brett Kavanaugh"—highlighting the gaps in Ramirez's story. "The New Yorker admits it has not confirmed through eyewitnesses Kavanaugh was even present at the party," the statement noted.[21]

On Monday, the attacks became even sharper, including those from the president himself. "This is starting to feel like a vast left-wing conspiracy," White House counselor Kellyanne Conway, who had urged caution and empathy in responding to Ford, told *CBS This Morning*. Trump, at the United Nations for the annual gathering of world leaders, weighed in with a new tone of belligerence, casting doubt not only on Ramirez but also on Ford. "For people to come out of the woodwork from 36 years ago and 30 years ago and never mention it, all of a sudden it happens," he said. "In my opinion, it's totally political."[22] By the next day, he let loose even more. "The second accuser has nothing," he said. Ramirez, he noted, "said she was totally inebriated and she was all messed up. And she doesn't know it was him, but it might have been him. 'Oh, gee, let's not make him a Supreme Court judge because of that.' This is a con game being played by the Democrats."[23]

Ramirez's story indeed had flaws and limitations—unsurprisingly, given the passage of time and the fact that those involved were inebriated. But another story, disturbingly similar and from a particularly credible source, was circulating in Washington. A Kavanaugh classmate who lived in his dorm freshman year recalled a second episode of Kavanaugh exposing himself, this time to a different woman. The man, now a prominent Washingtonian, was torn. He didn't want to put himself forward and risk his life's work, which depended on his reputation for bipartisanship, but he had evidence that would be relevant, if only he could get it before senators or if only the FBI would question him about it. The closing moments of the Kavanaugh confirmation would feature a desperate and ultimately unsuccessful effort to try to make that happen.

As if all this weren't enough, Michael Avenatti inserted himself. Minutes before *The New Yorker* story posted, the ubiquitous California attorney sent out an ominous tweet. "I represent a woman with credible information regarding Judge Kavanaugh and Mark Judge. We will be demanding the opportunity to present testimony to the committee and will likewise be demanding that Judge and others be subpoenaed to testify," he wrote. "The nomination must be withdrawn."[24] At the time, Avenatti was fresh off his celebrity turn as the lawyer for adult film star Stormy Daniels, who claimed she had an affair with Trump and had been paid $130,000 to keep quiet about it. He had become a cable-television phenomenon, was flirting with running for the Democratic presidential nomination, and, amazingly, was being taken somewhat seriously. It was not until the following spring that Avenatti was charged by federal prosecutors in New York with attempting to extort more than $20 million from sportswear manufacturer Nike and, on the opposite coast, with embezzlement, tax evasion, and fraud in connection with allegedly stealing tens of millions of dollars from clients. Now Avenatti followed the Whelan playbook, first dangling the prospect of another Kavanaugh accuser before delivering the goods, such as they were.

"If anyone has been paying attention over the last six to seven months, they know that I do not traffic in nonsense or rumor," Avenatti said on *The Rachel Maddow Show* on Monday, September 24.

"I utilize facts and evidence, and this woman will prove to be credible, and she is believable, and we are hopeful that the committee will launch an FBI investigation forthwith. We have also asked that she be permitted to take a polygraph examination, which she has agreed to do provided that Brett Kavanaugh does the same."[25] That might have been the first tell. Ford had taken—and passed—a polygraph, with no stipulations. Avenatti was making an offer that he knew Kavanaugh would refuse.

On Wednesday, September 26, the day before Ford's scheduled hearing, Avenatti unveiled his supposed evidence in the form of a three-page affidavit from Julie Swetnick, a former government contractor who claimed to have met Kavanaugh and Judge around the time she graduated from Gaithersburg High School, in suburban Maryland. Swetnick recalled attending "well over ten house parties" in the Washington area at which Judge and Kavanaugh were present. "On numerous occasions at these parties, I witnessed Mark Judge and Brett Kavanaugh drink excessively and engage in highly inappropriate conduct, including being overly aggressive with girls and not taking 'No' for an answer. This conduct included the fondling and grabbing of girls without their consent."[26]

In addition, Swetnick said, "I became aware of efforts by Mark Judge, Brett Kavanaugh and others to 'spike' the 'punch' at house parties I attended with drugs and/or grain alcohol so as to cause girls to lose their inhibitions and their ability to say 'No.'" Even worse, "I also witnessed efforts by Mark Judge, Brett Kavanaugh and others to cause girls to become inebriated and disoriented so they could then be 'gang raped' in a side room or bedroom by a 'train' of numerous boys." Kavanaugh and Judge, Swetnick added, were among the boys whom she had a "firm recollection" of seeing lined up outside these rooms. Finally, she said, "In approximately 1982, I became the victim of one of these 'gang' or 'train' rapes where Mark Judge and Brett Kavanaugh were present."[27]

These were incendiary charges for Avenatti to toss out there, with nothing in the way of corroboration provided and accusations so over-the-top as to strain credulity. No news organization would have printed such claims on its own without extensive vetting and corroboration. Where were these parties? How well did Swetnick know Kavanaugh and Judge? If she witnessed such events, why did she continue to attend these parties? If her own alleged assault took place in 1982, why did she say she attended parties through the following year? Who could back up her account? If these assaults took place, wouldn't someone else have heard about them? Did she report it to the police? Swetnick said she did, but the records would have taken weeks to access, the officer she said she spoke with had passed away, and she did not go to the hospital for a rape exam. Avenatti asked the Montgomery County police department about obtaining records but apparently dropped the matter after being informed that the cost would be around $3,700.[28]

Kavanaugh, through the White House, issued a statement describing the allegations as "ridiculous and from the Twilight Zone," adding, "I don't know who this is and this never happened."[29]

Avenatti insisted that "we have an extensive vetting process that we go through to make sure that people are legitimate."[30] But it did not take long for questions to arise over Swetnick's veracity. A lawsuit filed against Swetnick in 2000 by a former employer, Oregon-based software company Webtrends, ultimately dismissed with prejudice, alleged that Swetnick engaged in "unwelcome sexual innuendo" with coworkers and falsely stated on her job application that she had graduated from Johns Hopkins University with a degree in biology and chemistry. In a personal injury lawsuit that Swetnick filed in 1994 against the Washington Metropolitan Area Transit Authority, she claimed she lost more than $420,000 after hurting her nose in a fall on a train. To back her claim for lost income, Swetnick named "Konam Studios" as among those promising to employ her and identified Nam Ko, a representative of the company, as a possible witness. But Ko told the Associated Press that he was only a friend of Swetnick's, had never owned a company of that name, and had never agreed to hire her. The case was settled without any payment.[31] Swetnick also had a history of unpaid taxes, including a $63,000 lien placed against her by the state of Maryland and a $40,000 lien placed by the IRS. In a 1993 complaint filed with Maryland prosecutors, Swetnick accused a Maryland podiatrist and his wife of harassing her with repeated phone calls. In 2001, a former boyfriend, Richard Vinneccy, sought a restraining order against her. Both cases were dropped.[32]

Perhaps Swetnick was in the right in all these cases. The point is, a lawyer who had conducted due diligence and who had Swetnick's best interests at heart—and who was not interested in further boosting his own celebrity—would never have tossed her out there unprotected, with no explanation for the raft of legal problems she experienced and no corroboration for her allegations. Swetnick said later that she came forward only out of a sense of duty to help Ford, because she thought she had information that would back up Ford's claims. Her first outreach was to Ford's lawyers, who, coincidentally, had represented Swetnick in yet another lawsuit, this one in which she recovered some $600,000 in damages in a case involving another former employer, New York Life Insurance Company, over a sexual harassment complaint. Tellingly, in her September 19 e-mail to Lisa Banks, Swetnick did not mention any interactions with Kavanaugh or Judge, as she did in the later affidavit and interviews, only that she had attended house parties with unidentified "Georgetown Prep" boys.[33]

When Swetnick didn't hear back from Banks and began receiving calls from reporters, she decided she needed an advocate on her side, a fighter like Avenatti. A close friend had gone to George Washington University Law School with Avenatti. Swetnick reached out to the lawyer through the e-mail listed on his office website. He called her the next day—and started tweeting about his new client even before they had met in person. Swetnick had understood that her affidavit was to be submitted to the Judiciary Committee: Avenatti invited Showtime's *The Circus* to film him printing out the affidavit even before it was filed, and later sent Swetnick, demonstrably ill prepared, to an NBC interview at which she contradicted her written declaration. He seemed to be using Swetnick to help turbocharge his own celebrity, heedless of the consequences not only for Kavanaugh but also for his client.

It was possible, certainly, that Swetnick had been assaulted. Elizabeth Rasor, who had been Judge's girlfriend for three years in college, filed an affidavit saying that Judge had told her of losing his virginity in high school as part of a group of Georgetown Prep boys who "took turns having sex with a woman who was drunk."[34] Could this woman have been Swetnick? Judge disputed Rasor's account and denied knowing Swetnick. In any event, the linkage to Kavanaugh was tenuous, at best.

In the fevered atmosphere of the moment, the Swetnick story would raise some initial alarms, notwithstanding its evident weaknesses. Collins was rattled. "Obviously I take it seriously and believe that it should be investigated by the committee," she told reporters.[35] In a private meeting with fellow Republicans, brandishing a printout of Swetnick's declaration, she asked why Judge wasn't being subpoenaed. All ten Judiciary Democrats signed a letter to Grassley on Wednesday demanding that the hearings be postponed in order to probe the "shocking new allegations." Feinstein, at the opening of the second round of hearings the next day, cited Swetnick along with Ford and Ramirez, saying the FBI should investigate all three.[36]

The Swetnick story did not improve with age. The next week, Avenatti produced a sworn statement from another, this time unnamed, woman who described attending house parties with Kavanaugh and Judge at which, she said, "Brett and Mark would drink excessively and be overly aggressive and verbally abusive toward girls. This conduct included inappropriate physical contact with girls of a sexual nature." Even worse, the statement said, "During the years 1981–82, I witnessed firsthand Brett Kavanaugh, together with others, 'spike' the 'punch' at house parties I attended with Quaaludes and/or grain alcohol. I understood this was being done for the purpose of making girls more likely to engage in sexual acts and less likely to say 'No.'"[37]

Troubling, potentially, except that NBC would later report that the woman, in a phone interview arranged by Avenatti before the declaration was released, said she had never seen Kavanaugh act inappropriately toward girls. In an October 4 text to NBC after the declaration was published, the woman added, "It is incorrect that I saw Brett spike the punch. I didn't see anyone spike the punch . . . I was very clear with Michael Avenatti from day one." The next day she texted about Avenatti, "I do not like that he twisted my words."[38]

In the end, the flimsiness of Swetnick's case ended up eroding, not buttressing, the Ford and Ramirez allegations. This was trickle-down discrediting. Swetnick stepped on Ramirez's story—in the attention-deficit-disordered news cycle, her lurid account supplanted Ramirez's more complicated tale—and, by proximity, undercut Ramirez's credibility. If someone was willing to make these seemingly outlandish and unsupported assertions about a rape "train," why believe a more plausible, if imperfect, account of Kavanaugh's behavior at Yale? The effective undermining of Ramirez's allegations served in turn to do the opposite of what Ramirez had hoped: not to corroborate Ford's account but, in the view of many, to diminish it. It was the converse of the ordinary situation, in which an allegation standing alone is less credible than one backed up by accounts of similar misbehavior. In this case, as it developed, a single allegation might have proved more convincing.

Lindsey Graham called Trump and read him some of the Swetnick document. "I said, this is complete horseshit," Graham recalled.[39] "That was the turning point. Everybody dug in after that." Avenatti, said Davis, the Grassley aide, "was manna from heaven. He was the one who saved Kavanaugh."[40]

CHAPTER FIFTEEN

Eternity

The hearing was set for Thursday, September 27, but as Monday dawned, with the Ramirez story to deal with and Avenatti circling, that stretch felt like an eternity to Kavanaugh and his team. The situation was too volatile. They needed to do something to stabilize things in the interim. White House press adviser Raj Shah suggested it was time to do something that no Supreme Court nominee in history had done before—a televised interview. With allegations this explosive, merely putting surrogates on the air, even the nominee's wife, wasn't enough. Neither was a statement. Kavanaugh had to be heard from, at some length, or Thursday might be too late.

Kavanaugh's advisers—at this point, some of the alarmed Bush White House alumni were weighing in, including former political advisers Ed Gillespie and Dan Bartlett—were also pushing to let Kavanaugh speak. McGahn didn't like the idea. The senators are Kavanaugh's audience, he argued; they might be put out by such an appearance. But McGahn soon called Shah back, after hearing from McConnell and Trump. "We need to get him on TV," he said.

Around 10:30 Monday morning, the decision was made: Brett and Ashley Kavanaugh would do a joint interview with Martha MacCallum on Fox, a friendly venue. The White House thought MacCallum, a fifty-four-year-old mother of three, would be a good choice for the audience that the administration needed to hold, Republican-leaning women.

The interview took place at the Madison hotel, where Kavanaugh, his team of handlers, and the marshals threaded their way through a knot of astonished conventiongoers. There had been no time to prepare, yet Kavanaugh seemed programmed to the point of being robotic. "I am looking for a fair process, a process where I can defend my integrity and clear my name," he said as the interview opened. Then he said it again—and again. He used the phrase "fair process" seventeen times. "I've always treated women with dignity and respect," he said repeatedly.

In one of the most uncomfortable exchanges, Kavanaugh volunteered that "I did not have sexual intercourse or anything close to sexual intercourse in high school or for many years thereafter." It was not obvious what the state of his virginity had to do with his propensity to commit sexual assault, but in earlier conversations, including his murder board at the White House, Kavanaugh had raised the subject in his defense. How could he have done something like this when he was so inexperienced?

MacCallum followed up. "So you're saying that through all these years that are in question, you were a virgin?" she asked. "And through what years in college, since we're probing into your personal life here?"

"Many years after," Kavanaugh replied. "I'll leave it at that." It was an excruciating moment for a Supreme Court nominee.[1]

McConnell called Shah after the interview. We've got to get to Thursday, the majority leader said. We've got to get him out there every day between now and Thursday. Shah was incredulous: had McConnell watched the interview?

McGahn hated it. There were too many Bush people clustered around Kavanaugh, he thought, advising him to go soft, not to look too angry. Trump was also unhappy. He particularly disliked the discussion of Kavanaugh's virginity and thought that Kavanaugh had not seemed adequately indignant. Looking strong was what Trump valued, and all this mewling about fair process was weak. Just as important, Collins was similarly dismayed. She was troubled by the Ford allegations and, she let it be known to Kavanaugh, wasn't convinced by his statements. Kavanaugh was upset by Collins's response. How could she not believe me? he asked a friend. "Well," the friend replied, "you showed no emotion. Anybody that's been accused of horrible things would show more emotion."

Kavanaugh would not make that mistake again.

With the emergence of additional accusers, tensions were rising between McGahn on the one hand and Kavanaugh and his advisers on the other. McGahn remained adamantly against bringing in the FBI, which would only lead to delay. Kavanaugh wanted an FBI investigation to get the matter over with and help clear his name. McGahn countered that an FBI investigation was precisely not the way to end things. The hearing *was* the investigation, and Kavanaugh didn't need FBI exoneration—he needed fifty Senate votes.

As the investigation proceeded in advance of the hearing, the facts were developing in ways that were helpful to Kavanaugh. The others Ford had placed at the party did not provide corroboration. P. J. Smyth, one of the boys Ford had said was present, stated through his lawyer that he did not recall any such party and never saw Kavanaugh behave inappropriately with women. Ford's friend Leland Keyser said through her lawyer that she did not remember the party and did not know Kavanaugh. And Judge, the one whom Ford placed in the room along with Kavanaugh, continued to deny the incident. None of this was dispositive—besides Judge, the others at the party would not necessarily have remembered a random gathering years earlier at which, to their knowledge, nothing unusual occurred. And Judge had an obvious incentive not to admit to misconduct. Still, it was not good for Ford's case that no one remembered the event.

Other allegations were coming in, most if not all of dubious credibility. A Rhode Island man named Jeffrey Catalan contacted Sheldon Whitehouse's office on Monday, September 24, with what seemed on its face like an outlandish tale about a woman who had been sexually assaulted by two drunken men—one named Brett, the other Mark—in August 1985 on a boat in the Newport harbor.

Catalan claimed that he had beaten up the men and now recognized one as Kavanaugh from his high school yearbook photo. Whitehouse's staff immediately passed the information on to the majority and minority staff, alerted the FBI, and, at the caller's request, gave him the name of a Rhode Island reporter.[2]

Davis would weaponize these and other allegations, jujitsuing them to undermine the more serious accusers and, Democrats thought, intimidate any other potential witnesses, thus discouraging them from coming forward. On Tuesday, Davis told Whitehouse's Judiciary staffer Lara Quint that he had shared the Catalan complaint with Kavanaugh's lawyer and Justice Department officials and would be questioning Kavanaugh at midday about the allegations. A series of increasingly alarmed—and, ultimately, angry—e-mails ensued between Quint and Davis. Quint argued that it was premature to question Kavanaugh on the topic; she expressed concern about exposing Catalan's identity and the possibility that "this transcript release will be used for political ends."[3] Davis responded that the committee was just doing its job and went after Whitehouse in terms that were remarkably sharp for a staffer, even one from the opposing party. "Senator Whitehouse had no problem helping to peddle these absolutely garbage allegations to a reporter," he e-mailed Quint. "He politicized this, not us."[4]

For Democrats, this incident served as a cautionary tale. When they came forward to the appropriate authorities (in this case, Grassley) with a confidential allegation, rather than sitting on it—as Republicans complained they had in the case of Feinstein and Ford—it would be deployed against them. For Republicans, the Newport boat episode would come to be a symbol of what they saw as a smear campaign against Kavanaugh. Either way, the episode served to illustrate the deep distrust on both sides.

Even as Davis was leaping on the boat allegations, he found himself in a strange standoff with Ramirez's lawyers in a series of e-mails exchanged after *The New Yorker* story was published. Ramirez looked to be a potential problem. The day after the story broke, Collins said publicly that Ramirez should be questioned

under oath. Several days of back-and-forth ensued. Ramirez's lawyers wanted the FBI to investigate but said she might be willing
to speak to the committee as well. The lawyers, they suggested,
should get on the phone to discuss.

Davis was unwilling. He e-mailed Ramirez's lawyers on Tuesday morning: "Before we discuss a phone call or any other next
steps again, we need to have the following information: 1. Does
Ms. Ramirez have any other evidence, including other statements,
in addition to those that are contained in the New Yorker article?
2. Is Ms. Ramirez willing to provide her evidence, including her
testimony, to committee investigators? Again, we welcome the
receipt of Ms. Ramirez's (and anyone else's) evidence in the form
of a letter or email to the Chairman and Ranking Member, a letter
or email from counsel to the Chairman and Ranking Member, or a
statement to committee investigators."[5]

Sawyer, the Feinstein investigator, responded later that morning. "The committee does not usually refuse to talk with counsel
(or whistleblowers) and also does not usually place preconditions
on getting on the phone to discuss next steps, so I'm not sure why
that is happening here," she wrote in an e-mail to Davis and the
Ramirez lawyers.[6] Davis's position was that the Ramirez lawyers
were refusing to cooperate. "This is now my **6th request for evidence** from Ms. Ramirez that I have made **over the last 48 hours**,"
he wrote in an e-mail at 7:45 that evening.[7]

Sawyer fired back nine minutes later. "Mike, As you're aware,
Ms. Ramirez's counsel have repeatedly requested to speak with the
Committee, on a bipartisan basis, to determine how to proceed,"
she wrote. "You refused. I've never encountered an instance where
the Committee has refused even to speak with an individual or
counsel. I am perplexed as to why this is happening here except
that it seems designed to ensure that the Majority can falsely claim
that Ms. Ramirez and her lawyers refused to cooperate. That simply is not true."[8] At 8:05, it was Davis's turn: "Heather, I have not
refused to speak with anyone. I am simply requesting—for the **7th
time** now **over the last 48 hours**—that Ms. Ramirez' attorneys

provide the Senate Judiciary committee with any **evidence** that they have before we move to the next steps."[9]

Later that night, Ramirez lawyer John Clune appeared on Rachel Maddow's MSNBC show. "They won't talk to us," he said. "The demand that they keep making to us is, 'Give us every piece of information that you have now and then we can talk about scheduling a phone call.' And that's just not the kind of partisan game playing that our client deserves."[10]

It was a strange standoff, but one, perhaps, with a purpose. On Thursday, September 27, as the Ford testimony commenced, Grassley would emphasize that his staff had been trying to investigate other allegations only to be stymied by lack of cooperation. "My staff made eight requests—yes, eight requests—for evidence from attorneys for Ms. Ramirez," he said. "The committee can't do an investigation if attorneys are stonewalling." Feinstein, responding, lamented that the Ramirez and Swetnick allegations had not been investigated but failed to rebut Grassley's one-sided portrayal of the committee's efforts to question Ramirez.[11]

Meanwhile, the Grassley team was chasing after new mistaken-identity theories. Two men separately came forward to suggest that they, not Kavanaugh, were the individuals involved in the Ford encounter. One contacted the committee to say that in the summer of 1982, after graduating from high school, he visited D.C. several times and attended a house party where he made out with a woman he believed could have been Ford. He added that he thought he and Kavanaugh look similar. The second claimed that as a nineteen-year-old college student, he had visited D.C. during spring break and kissed a girl he thought might have been Ford; the encounter ended when a friend jumped on them as a joke.[12] The night before the hearing, committee Republicans released a "timeline" of the nomination that included the new dual doppelgänger theory.[13] The claim, especially problematic in the wake of the Whelan tweets, was weak on its face: as a matter of logic, the existence of two witnesses who claimed they were somehow responsible for Ford's accusations against Kavanaugh undercut the credibility of each.

But the move underscored the anger of the moment. When Democrats complained that they had not been informed about these new witnesses, Republicans were unsympathetic, given Feinstein's withholding of Ford's letter. "Some might find it exceedingly difficult to imagine Judiciary Committee Democrats expressing this concern with straight faces," Hatch tweeted Wednesday night.[14] Still, this supposed new evidence was a step too far, even for some Republicans. "One's crazy as a loon," Graham said the morning of the hearing about the new mistaken-identity witnesses. "I don't believe the other one. I'm not going to play this game."[15]

The stories of the two doppelgängers were quickly overtaken by events, although the search for such a person would continue. On Saturday, after the hearings had concluded, Davis circulated an e-mail from Joseph Smith, a Denver lawyer who was a year behind Kavanaugh at Yale. Smith identified by name another member of DKE, Kavanaugh's fraternity, as a student who had a reputation for exposing himself. Indeed, Smith said, he had witnessed that happen, at a party. "Yale College is a small school," he noted, "so I think it would have been widely known if, in addition to [the student], another student had also engaged in similar behavior."

Davis shared this e-mail, unverified and unredacted, not only with the Feinstein staff but also with journalists. "WARNING: The second attached photo contains nudity," he wrote, including the student's yearbook photo and a picture of him among his DKE fraternity brothers, bow tie on and briefs down at his knees.[16] This seemed less like evidence that was exculpatory to Kavanaugh than it was proof of Republicans' willingness to go to any length to get the nominee confirmed.

From the outside, a hearing Thursday may have looked like a certainty. From the inside, it was anything but. It was not clear that Ford would even board a plane to D.C. or that, if she did, she would be willing to appear in public. Astonishingly, until a break in the middle of her testimony, Ford did not really grasp that the whole event—like the Anita Hill hearings she had watched so long ago in Malibu—would be broadcast live on national television. As Ford kept texting that she couldn't promise to go to Washington, that she hadn't committed to doing anything, Katz nudged her along, reassuring her client that they were taking small and reversible steps.

Over the weekend, Avenatti—who had started his slow reveal of Swetnick's allegations—had weighed in with Ford's lawyers, much to their exasperation. You've got to get a new photo, he lectured them. Even more, he urged, you've got to put her out there, get her on TV. You don't know our client, they thought. This woman doesn't want the limelight. She is not going to be making the cable rounds, that's for sure.

The question of whether Ford suffered from fear of flying would become a contested issue in the hearings and afterward. Ford's biography listed her interest in "surf travel," and, as she would testify, she had flown frequently for work and pleasure. A former boyfriend, Brian Merrick, submitted an affidavit to the Judiciary Committee stating that Ford, during their lengthy relationship, had "never indicated a fear of flying."[17]

Did that undermine Ford's credibility? Republicans thought so. They suggested that she invented such a fear in order to avoid coming to Washington or to buttress her claim that the alleged attack by Kavanaugh had resulted in anxiety about being confined in enclosed spaces such as an airplane. As much attention as the issue received, the controversy seemed manufactured and overblown. It was clear from speaking with Ford's friends that two things were simultaneously true: she did have a fear of flying, and she could overcome it. When she flew, she took medication to calm her anxiety. Keith Koegler, her friend, would recall Ford's panic when, on a surfing trip to Hawaii, she forgot her antianxiety medication and had nothing to take to soothe her nerves on the return trip.

Katz strategized about how to get Ford to Washington. Ford's husband was planning to stay home with their sons. A former Obama administration official and Silicon Valley entrepreneur, DJ Patil, had reached out through intermediaries to a well-connected person in Washington: Did Ford need help with security? Transportation to Washington? Patil helped connect the Ford team to Reid Hoffman, the billionaire founder of LinkedIn, and Mark Pincus, the founder of the online social gaming company Zynga, who offered a private plane. Think about whom you want to bring with you, Katz asked Ford. She sent pictures of the plane, which made Ford even more nervous.

Every baby step got her closer to Washington, which got her closer to testifying. Ford assembled a group of friends—her team, she called them—to fly out to Washington with her. She wasn't yet committed to appearing in public, but the lawyers proceeded gingerly. On landing at Reagan National Airport, Ford glimpsed a familiar figure in the private-jet lounge. Kellyanne Conway strolled past Ford without recognizing her. That was not surprising: at that stage, the only photograph of Ford that the public had seen had her in sunglasses and surfing gear. Worried about being recognized, Ford was traveling wearing sunglasses and a baseball cap.

Kendra Barkoff, a former press secretary to Vice President Biden now with the Democratic political consulting firm SKD-Knickerbocker, had joined the team to help advise on media strategy. Barkoff arranged rooms—she wanted something off the beaten path, where the Ford team wouldn't run into reporters, and settled on the Watergate Hotel, away from downtown and Capitol Hill. Ford and her friends arrived and headed to the Watergate; as it happened, their rooms were on the same floor as the one rented by G. Gordon Liddy and E. Howard Hunt to orchestrate the Watergate break-in. Not much preparation was done on Tuesday. Ford was woozy from the medication and needed to rest.

The previous Friday, Michael Bromwich, a former inspector general at the Justice Department, had joined the legal team; he had extensive experience with congressional testimony. One critical issue Ford's lawyers negotiated with the Grassley staff: he and Katz would be sitting next to their client, not behind her. This was an unusual arrangement, but, Bromwich thought, it was essential.

If she managed to make it to the hearing room at all, Ford would be a witness who needed moral support close at hand.

Joseph Abboud, an associate at Katz's law firm, had drafted a proposed opening statement. Katz and Banks worked on it, then Bromwich. On Wednesday morning, they gave it to Ford. She edited it extensively, marking up her changes in a sea of red ink and stripping the verbiage to its essentials. "I am extremely terrified," Ford read in the draft, then excised "extremely." She fretted over dangling participles, over "yelled" versus "screamed." She asked for quiet in the room where they were gathered so she could concentrate on the text. So it went, past lunch, as the lawyers fended off anxious inquiries from Grassley aides seeking the opening statement, which is ordinarily due twenty-four hours in advance.

Witness preparation for a hearing this important can take days. Now time was running out. But it was important that the document be in Ford's voice and that she be comfortable with every single word. When the statement was finally finished, in early afternoon, the group turned its attention to the questions Ford might be asked. She balked at the notion of practicing any answers, not wanting to sound rehearsed. Still, they discussed some general lines of questioning. One was: how can you be so sure it was Kavanaugh? Ford launched into a discussion of the role of the hippocampus in encoding memory. The lawyers were aghast. That's not accessible, Katz told her. Just tell people how you knew him. "My reaction was, 'Really, we're going to get into that kind of stuff?'" Bromwich recalled.[18] Bromwich and Larry Robbins, the lawyer Katz had called over the summer and again in late August, offered basic pointers for testimony. Don't guess; don't speculate. Make sure you understand the question and that it is complete before you answer. Ask to have it repeated if you are confused.

Even at this late hour, even with the entire country poised to tune in for Ford's testimony the next morning, she had not committed to testifying in public. I'm scared of an open hearing, Ford told the group. I don't want cameras there. Her life had already been turned upside down. How much worse would it be if her face were plastered all over television and newspapers? The lawyers assured Ford that the final choice would be up to her, even though they were convinced, at this stage, that a closed session would be a disaster.

Ricki Seidman, with her calming demeanor and ever-present knitting, served as a kind of Ford whisperer. She was ensconced in a nearby office, dealing with hearing logistics and talking intermittently to Ford, describing what the hearing would be like. Seidman started to sketch the layout of the room for Ford, who stopped her. That will just freak me out, she said. Still, Seidman kept assuring the rest of the group, Katz, Banks, and Bromwich: don't worry about Christine. She'll do it. Seidman had a final conversation with Ford early that evening, before they left for the night. Ford thought the senators in the room were the ones who needed to hear her story. Seidman explained again, patiently: if the hearing isn't public, the other senators who have to vote won't be able to see you and assess your credibility. Finally, Ford agreed. The hearing would be open—unless, of course, Ford changed her mind again, which was entirely possible.

One question that needed to be addressed was what Ford was going to wear. Ford had sent her husband to the house to pick up some of the dresses that she wore for teaching—flowy pieces, with a California vibe—and sent photos of them to one of her communications advisers. Those weren't going to work. The consultant sent a friend to Saks to pick up some hearing-appropriate outfits. The friend arrived at the Watergate Tuesday evening with several possibilities, mostly black, a color that Ford did not tend to wear. But there was a navy jacket and sheath dress that looked good. In the midst of all the craziness, a seamstress came on Wednesday to make alterations. None of the shoes fit, so Ford just picked the cheapest, smallest ones. A hairdresser arrived to do Ford's hair, which confused her. What did it matter how she looked? she thought. It wasn't as if she was going to be on television.

The group broke up about 5:30 that evening. Ford, who seemed exhausted, practiced her opening statement for the first time that night, alone in her hotel room. She would pop awake shortly after midnight, unable to get back to sleep.

In Kavanaugh's chambers on the third floor of the federal courthouse, the mood was grim on Wednesday. The group around him felt besieged. That morning, Avenatti had released the Swetnick declaration, which required another emergency round of assembling Kavanaugh's high school friends to declare that they did not know this person and had never engaged, or heard of Kavanaugh engaging, in any of the activity that she described.

An opening statement had already been drafted—like Ford's, it was due to the committee twenty-four hours in advance—but Kavanaugh wanted to go back through it. This was his reputation, his fate, his life on the line. He felt as if everything he had worked for was being destroyed. Meanwhile, he was being stage-managed by some people who said he was being too strident, others who said he wasn't being tough enough. Kavanaugh was like a candidate the night before the debate; he had had enough coaching. Now it was time to make sure he put the statement in his own voice, conveying the anguish of the moment, the kind of person he had tried to be his whole life and his fury at having been accused of such conduct. For much of the afternoon, he closeted himself in his office, the door closed, joined by Chris Michel, a former Kavanaugh clerk and former Bush speechwriter. His lawyers, Beth Wilkinson and Alex Walsh, were there. So were a group of Kavanaugh's former clerks, including Travis Lenkner and Porter Wilkinson. Joel Kaplan, the Facebook executive and Kavanaugh's close friend, stopped in briefly.

Kavanaugh emerged early Wednesday evening. "I finished it," he told the group. "I feel good." He turned to his liberal-leaning lawyers. "I'm not sure you guys are going to like everything I'm going to say."

The day was not over, though. Shortly after 8:00 p.m., Kavanaugh had another phone interview with the Judiciary Committee lawyers, his third. Davis and other Grassley lawyers took Kavanaugh, at length and under oath, through the Swetnick allegations. No, he had never lined up outside a bedroom to await his turn raping a woman. No, he had never spiked a punch with grain alcohol or Quaaludes. No, he had never taken part in a gang rape of an inebriated woman. "It's a disgrace," Kavanaugh said. "It's a circus." Then the lawyers moved on, to a new allegation that had been passed along by Harris, from an unnamed California woman who claimed Kavanaugh and a friend had met her at a party, offered her a ride home, and sexually assaulted her. "The whole thing is just a crock, farce, wrong, didn't happen, not anything close," Kavanaugh said.[19]

Given that this allegation was anonymous, there was little need for Kavanaugh to be grilled about it so extensively: "Have you ever used fingers to penetrate a woman's vagina against her will?" "Have you ever slapped a woman and told her to be quiet while forcing her to perform oral sex on you?" "Have you ever told a woman you assaulted, 'No one will believe if you tell. Be a good girl'?"[20] There was a method to the questioning, however. Davis didn't just want Kavanaugh's denials on the record. He also wanted to goad Kavanaugh, to infuriate him, rev him up in advance of the hearings. The meek, give-me-due-process Kavanaugh of the Fox interview wasn't going to make it across the finish line. Republicans needed a fighter.

CHAPTER SIXTEEN

Indelible in the Hippocampus

Thursday morning, Michael Bromwich called Debra Katz on his way to the Watergate: Ford hadn't even practiced the statement before an audience, he said. What happens if she doesn't make it through the first paragraph? Bromwich could read it in her stead, he offered. Katz and Banks couldn't believe it— a man stepping in to take over for a woman, on this subject? That wasn't going to happen, as Bromwich quickly understood. If Ford couldn't get through the statement, so be it.

From the Watergate, the lawyers and their client headed to the Dirksen Senate Office Building, pulling into the underground garage and then heading up to the second floor. At that point, strange as it sounds, Ford still wasn't entirely clear that the testimony would be televised. "You know there can't be any recording or I'm going to freak out," she told her team.[1] They gently reminded her, once again, that if the hearing wasn't televised, other senators wouldn't be able to watch. In denial, Ford told herself it would just be on C-SPAN.

Her prepared statement was in a binder, each page encased in an individual plastic sleeve. Ford was still tinkering, taking out the pages one by one and making additional edits. Then, Ford, sitting on a couch in the holding room, read the statement out loud for the first time in public. "I remember thinking to myself, 'You're kidding me—right now you're going to read it?'" Bromwich recalled.[2]

Grassley came by to greet Ford and thank her for coming.
Then Feinstein arrived. It was the first time she and Ford had met
in person. I know how difficult this has been for you, she told
Ford. Feinstein grasped Ford's hand and held it for a while. Then
it was time for the hearing. Ford had the strange sensation that it
was like a wedding. Flanked by her lawyers, she headed down the
long corridor as staffers ventured out of their offices to greet her.
Grassley, she thought, was in the role of the minister, overseeing
the ceremony.

A wedding was an odd analogy to come to mind. If anything, Ford
looked stricken, not like a bride but like a prisoner about to face
sentencing. At 10:02, from behind the dais, where the senators
were still seating themselves, she emerged into the hearing room,
accompanied by Katz and Bromwich, and walked to the witness
table. Katz sat to her right, Bromwich to her left. Bromwich whispered to her, put his hand on hers.

Grassley began with a statement that excoriated Feinstein for
failing to share Ford's letter—what he called "the ranking member's secret evidence." He ticked through the multiple opportunities Feinstein had to raise the matter. Feinstein had sat on Ford's
letter. She did not raise Ford's allegation in her private meeting
with Kavanaugh, in the confirmation hearings, or in later written
questions. She didn't even bother to attend the closed session at the
end of the first round of hearings at which senators could raise sensitive matters.[3]

Feinstein was equally slashing about the majority's failure
to adequately investigate Ford's allegation—a process that, she
said, made the probe of Anita Hill's allegations against Clarence
Thomas twenty-seven years earlier look thorough by comparison.
"Despite repeated requests, President Trump and the Republicans
have refused to take this routine step," Feinstein said. Then, "the
Senate heard from twenty-two witnesses over three days. Today,
while rejecting an FBI investigation, Republicans are refusing to

hear testimony from any other witness." It was, she said, an "inex-cusable . . . rush to judgment."[4]

Grassley asked Ford to stand to be sworn in. She looked ques-tioningly at Bromwich; he had neglected to mention she would have to take an oath. A lock of blond hair hung in front of her face. She pushed it behind her ear, but it would keep falling as she testi-fied. Her voice, a voice the country had not heard previously, was high, almost girlish. "Thank you, Senator Grassley," she began. "After I read my opening statement, I anticipate needing some caf-feine, if that is available." The lack of practice and coaching turned out to be a benefit. Ford came off as she was, unscripted and un-Washington.

"I am here today not because I want to be," Ford said, her voice breaking. "I am terrified. I am here because I believe it is my civic duty to tell you what happened to me while Brett Kavanaugh and I were in high school."

What ensued was some of the most riveting testimony in con-gressional history. Ford went through her account of the evening, her torment over the summer about whether to speak out, the tor-rent of death threats that "have rocked me to my core" since her name became public. The precise details of her allegations were, by then, familiar. Yet hearing them directly from Ford was com-pelling, to use the word that would later become even the stan-dard Republican assessment of her testimony. She seemed eager to please and apologetic about her failure to remember key details.

Ford tackled some of the obvious questions. Why had she not told anyone at the time? Was there any later corroboration? "Brett's assault on me drastically altered my life," Ford said. "For a very long time, I was too afraid and ashamed to tell anyone these details. I did not want to tell my parents that I, at age fifteen, was in a house without any parents present, drinking beer with boys. I convinced myself that because Brett did not rape me, I should just move on and just pretend that it didn't happen."[5]

But, she said, the memory lingered. When she and her husband renovated their home, Ford said, she insisted on a strange accom-

modation: a second front door in what was then the master bedroom. She had told Russell Ford before they were married that she
had been the victim of a sexual assault, Ford said. But she did not
provide details until couples counseling in May 2012, when they
were discussing their argument over the renovation several years
earlier. "I recall saying that the boy who assaulted me could someday be on the U.S. Supreme Court and spoke a bit about his background at an elitist all-boys school in Bethesda, Maryland. My
husband recalls that I named my attacker as Brett Kavanaugh."

Ford took just under twenty minutes to finish reading her statement, her voice wavering as she said, "My motivation in coming
forward was to be helpful . . . It is not my responsibility to determine whether Mr. Kavanaugh deserves to sit on the Supreme Court.
My responsibility is to tell you the truth."

After Ford received her requested cup of coffee, the Republicans' appointed questioner, Rachel Mitchell, traded turns with
sympathetic panel Democrats. The arrangement was disjointed to
the point of being bizarre. Mitchell was matter-of-fact and low-
key, not aggressively prosecutorial. "I just wanted to tell you, the
first thing that struck me from your statement this morning was that
you are terrified, and I just wanted to let you know I'm very sorry,"
Mitchell began. "That's not right."

But the setup was inherently unwieldy and unproductive.
Mitchell's dutiful effort to take Ford through her account and to
prod, gently, for any inconsistencies might have worked in the
ordinary setting of a sustained deposition. But this was a congressional hearing, with rounds limited to five minutes. Mitchell could
barely get a line of inquiry launched before having to cede the
microphone.

At the Hill-Thomas hearings twenty-seven years before, Republicans had aggressively, even viciously, sought to undermine Hill's
veracity while Democrats had, for the most part, assumed the position of disinterested fact finders, not advocates for Hill. This time
was different. Republicans were—in public, at least—far less

inquisitorial toward the witness and Democrats far more supportive, lavishing praise on Ford for her bravery in coming forward.

Still, Mitchell clearly saw her role as laying the groundwork to
impeach Ford's credibility. She quizzed Ford about her asserted
fear of flying, insinuating that the phobia was bogus because Ford
had traveled frequently, particularly for surfing. Mitchell also
asked Ford if her attorneys had informed her that "the committee had asked to interview you and that they offered to come out to
California to do so." Bromwich objected on grounds of privilege,
and Ford asked to address Grassley directly. "I just appreciate that
you did offer that," she said. "If you were going to come out to see
me, I would have happily hosted you and . . . been happy to speak
with you out there. I just did not—it wasn't clear to me that that
was the case."[6]

Republicans seized on this answer as an illustration that Ford
was the unwitting pawn of partisan activists serving as her attorneys. They would return repeatedly to the exchange as evidence of
Democrats' bad faith. In fact, they were making way too much of
it. Ford had misunderstood the question to mean that senators, not
just staff, would have been willing to come interview her in California. She had always wanted senators to come to her, only to
be told that committee hearings don't work that way, and she had
always insisted that she wanted to tell her story to senators only,
not to staff members. The notion that the lawyers were keeping the
Republican offer a secret from their client in order to string matters
out or produce a public extravaganza was politically expedient, but
it was not accurate.

Leahy asked perhaps the most evocative question. What was
most memorable about the evening? What could she not forget?
"Indelible in the hippocampus is the laughter" of Kavanaugh and
Judge, Ford replied, "the uproarious laughter between the two,
and their having fun at my expense." The lawyers had urged her
to avoid this technical jargon, but as it turned out, Ford's scientific
language—she referred to "the sequelae of sexual assault" and "the

level of norepinephrine and epinephrine in the brain"; she noted
that "the etiology of anxiety and PTSD is multifactorial"—served
to reinforce her credibility.[7]

Republicans knew from the start that they had a problem. "She
looks credible, she sounds like your friend's mom, she looks like
your friend's mom, she doesn't look crazy," said one aide. As Ford
finished, Grassley's staff was in despair. "This is not good. RIP,
Brett. We're just thinking she killed it. Kavanaugh better match
that. There was just silence in the room," said one aide. Said
another, "We were one tick away from 'he's smoked.'"

As the rounds of questioning concluded and senators resumed
bickering among themselves, Bromwich asked if Ford could be
excused. She was exhausted. As they stood at the witness table to
gather their material, Ben Sasse of Nebraska came by to thank Ford
for her testimony. Then Mitchell, the prosecutor, walked over. "I'll
be praying for you," she told Ford. It was no doubt well inten-
tioned, but it had the effect, at the end of a grueling morning, of
unnerving Ford. Why did she need to be prayed for? What was
Mitchell trying to suggest? It felt creepy, and it bothered Ford, as
things tended to do, not just for hours but for days to come.

Back in the holding room, after the testimony, Flake stopped
by to thank Ford for her testimony. Seidman asked if she needed
something to eat. Hard-boiled eggs, Ford replied. That was the only
thing she thought she could keep down.

Kavanaugh waited at home, in Chevy Chase, with his wife, as Ford
testified. They might have been the only people in the Washington
metropolitan area not glued to the proceedings. Beth Wilkinson, his
lawyer, thought he should watch—it would look more respectful,
more sympathetic toward Ford—but Kavanaugh wanted to ready
himself for his own appearance. People could tell him if there was
something he needed to know. The Kavanaughs arrived at Dirksen
around noon, heading to a holding room down the hall from the
hearing room. Kavanaugh didn't want to see the testimony or be

distracted by the cable chatter, so the television was tuned to the Golf Channel, which was playing the opening ceremonies for the Ryder Cup. Kavanaugh, with his ever-present Sharpie, made one change in his prepared remarks, a moving story Ashley had told him about their younger daughter, Liza.

The Republican members of the committee gathered in the anteroom of the Senate Finance Committee, their temporary headquarters. "Almost all of us were saying, 'It's over,'" Jeff Flake recalled. "It was a pretty gloomy feeling for those of us who had been in support of him before and wanted to believe, obviously, that this hadn't happened."[8] Bob Corker had watched the entire hearing standing by the side of his desk, transfixed. "Had there been a vote right after her testimony, it would not have been good for Kavanaugh," he said.[9]

One isolated pocket of GOP optimism was within the McConnell office. His top aides—deputy chief of staff Don Stewart, counsel John Abegg, and press adviser Antonia Ferrier—argued that senators were the key audience, that they already had the necessary votes, and that Democrats had come up with no facts sufficient to dislodge them. The McConnell aides were "downright giddy," said one White House aide. "I was like, 'I don't think you guys are watching what I'm watching.'"

As McGahn waited for Kavanaugh to testify, his phone was buzzing. Trump called, not once, not twice, but several times, trying to reach his counsel. The most important man in the world could not get through to his own lawyer. More precisely, McGahn was deliberately not taking the call. He suspected that Trump, watching Ford's performance and seeing the reaction, was calling to instruct him to pull the nomination, to say that Kavanaugh needed to withdraw. On Fox News, Chris Wallace had called Ford's testimony "extremely emotional, extremely raw and extremely credible," adding, "This is a disaster for the Republicans."[10]

Trump was nothing if not responsive to such reviews. When the Ford story broke, Trump had been largely unfazed. The allegations against Kavanaugh felt familiar, like the attacks on Trump himself.

"He was just very dismissive of it, like, 'You know this happened to me—everybody gets accused of this stuff,'" said one adviser.

Ford's testimony, however, left Trump deeply worried. He started making the rounds of outside advisers, asking what they thought he should do. "He was concerned about the politics," said one person who spoke with Trump that day. "It was, 'Do we think this guy is too damaged to be confirmed? And if I pull him, can I salvage it and get another guy through?'" Much of the advice was along the same lines. You can probably get Kavanaugh across the finish line, Trump was told. Starting from scratch with a new nominee was a much dicier proposition. Republicans were favored to retain control of the Senate, but that wasn't guaranteed, and having to withdraw a nominee wasn't going to help matters electorally. As Steve Bannon would put it, "There's no walking this thing back. You get Kavanaugh, you're going to get turnout. You get turnout, you're going to get victory. This is march or die."[11]

McConnell saw it that way and tried to reassure the president when they spoke after Ford's testimony. "We're only at halftime," McConnell advised. McGahn agreed. He still saw a route to confirmation, and he didn't want Trump to tell him otherwise. White House officials said later that Trump had never wavered, that he was only trying to reach McGahn to tell Kavanaugh to buck up. McGahn wasn't taking any risks. "Don was worried about the president getting weak in the knees and pulling it," said one person close to McGahn. Donaldson, McGahn's deputy, contacted him with an urgent message: the president's trying to reach you; you've got to return his phone call. McGahn's response to Donaldson was curt, even insubordinate: "I don't talk to quitters."

The person McGahn wanted to talk to, at that moment, was Kavanaugh, alone. He had a message to deliver, in private, and asked the clerks and aides to clear the room; Ashley Kavanaugh could remain. Some of the advisers had broached the notion, in the aftermath of Ford's powerful testimony, of having Kavanaugh dial his remarks back. He should feel more of Ford's pain, they suggested, be soft and conciliatory. McGahn thought only a tougher approach would work. If Kavanaugh were to survive, he advised, he needed to go out and defend his reputation like his life was on the line—because it was.

Kavanaugh came out swinging. He had submitted prepared testimony the previous day, but, as he had signaled to his lawyers, that was a mild version of what he now unleashed. He had been seeking, indeed demanding, a way to clear his name since the Ford allegations first surfaced, he said. "In those ten long days, as was predictable, and as I predicted, my family and my name have been totally and permanently destroyed by vicious and false additional accusations," he said, almost shouting.[12]

This white-hot Kavanaugh was a different creature from the one who had appealed for procedural fairness on Fox News just three days earlier. "This confirmation process has become a national disgrace," he lectured the panel. "The Constitution gives the Senate an important role in the confirmation process, but you have replaced advice and consent with search and destroy." Kavanaugh's anger took an ominous tone. "You sowed the wind for decades to come," he told Democrats. "I fear that the whole country will reap the whirlwind."

That was just the start. "The behavior of several of the Democratic members of this committee at my hearing a few weeks ago was an embarrassment," Kavanaugh said. "But at least it was just a good old-fashioned attempt at Borking. Those efforts didn't work. When I did at least okay enough at the hearings that it looked like I might actually get confirmed, a new tactic was needed. Some of you were lying in wait and had it ready. This first allegation was held in secret for weeks by a Democratic member of this committee, and by staff. It would be needed only if you couldn't take me out on the merits. When it was needed, this allegation was unleashed and publicly deployed over Dr. Ford's wishes. And then—and then as no doubt was expected, if not planned—came a long series of false last-minute smears designed to scare me and drive me out of the process before any hearing occurred."

Kavanaugh continued for close to forty-five minutes. "This whole two-week effort has been a calculated and orchestrated political hit, fueled with apparent pent-up anger about President Trump and the 2016 election. Fear that has been unfairly stoked about my judicial record. Revenge on behalf of the Clintons. And millions of dollars in money from outside left-wing opposition groups. This is a circus . . . You may defeat me in the final vote, but you'll never get me to quit. Never."[13]

For anyone who had witnessed Clarence Thomas's testimony twenty-seven years earlier, it was an unsettling déjà vu moment. Then, Thomas had denounced the attack on him as a "high-tech lynching." The hearing was a "travesty," he said, "a circus," a "national disgrace." "No job is worth what I have been through, no job," Thomas said. "Confirm me if you want, don't confirm me if you are so led, but let this process end."[14] The racial element that had been so prominent in Thomas's remarks was absent. Otherwise the episodes felt identical, but with an amped-up dose of partisanship and personal attack in the Kavanaugh iteration. In both cases, the anger was volcanic, the sense of victimhood deep-seated, and the conflicting stories incapable of being reconciled. "He actually saw himself" in Kavanaugh's experience, Armstrong Williams, Thomas's close friend, said later of Thomas's reaction. "He said, 'Buddy, [the Kavanaughs'] lives are changed forever, no matter what the outcome is.'"[15]

Near tears, voice breaking, Kavanaugh invoked his daughter "little Liza, all of ten years old," who, he said, had told his wife the other night, "We should pray for the woman." Invoking his calendars as proof that the party could not have taken place as described—"all but definitively," Kavanaugh said, overreading the evidence—he told the committee that his practice of keeping a record of his activities was modeled on his father. "My dad started keeping detailed calendars of his life in 1978," Kavanaugh said. "He was a very organized guy, to put it mildly. Christmastime, we'd sit around, and he would regale us with old stories, old milestones, old weddings, old events from his calendars." Again, the nominee was close to tears. His tongue moved inside his cheek as he tried to keep himself from crying.[16]

The first few rounds of questioning featured the same strange combination of Rachel Mitchell's workmanlike queries and Democrats' protestations—this time of outrage over the failure to conduct a more thorough inquiry into the allegations against Kavanaugh. Although Kavanaugh had been telling advisers of that same frustration for days, his peculiar balance of duties—to himself and his reputation but also to the president who had nominated him and the White House counsel shepherding his confirmation—prevented him from acknowledging that. Durbin pressed Kavanaugh especially hard on this point. "Right now, turn to your left in the front row to Don McGahn, counsel to President Donald Trump," Durbin suggested. "Ask him to suspend this hearing and nomination process until the FBI completes its investigation of the charges made by Dr. Ford and others."

It was such a charged moment that Grassley stopped the clock to announce that the Senate was running the hearing, not Don McGahn or anyone else at the White House. Of course, this was a bit of senatorial theatrics: Durbin knew Kavanaugh was not about to call in the FBI on the spot, and, of course, Kavanaugh pushed back at what he knew was not kindly, disinterested advice. Still, Kavanaugh fumbled under the weight of contradictory impulses. He could not explain that he had already asked for an FBI investigation and been rebuffed. Instead he was reduced to repeating the preexisting Republican talking point on the matter: "The FBI doesn't reach conclusions."[17] That was true, but it had nothing to do with the central question of whether the FBI would do a better job of fact-finding than the judiciary panel, which did not seem open to dispute.

Into this maelstrom barreled Lindsey Graham. Mitchell disappeared from the scene, like an actor whose character suddenly dies and is written out of a television series. "I had a few more questions," Mitchell told Republican senators afterward. Those were never asked.

Graham said later that he had concluded it was time for a politician, not a prosecutor. "It was clear to me that Democrats were just going to go after him big-time, and that wasn't her thing," Graham said of Mitchell. "She's not a politician. This guy needed help. They were trying to destroy him." At the break, Graham asked Grassley to call on him. But Durbin's turn came first, and what Graham viewed as his bogus call for an FBI investigation further inflamed the South Carolina senator. "It just tripped a switch," Graham recalled.[18] It was the moment Republicans had been waiting for—and badly needed.

The South Carolina Republican had a maverick, sometimes bipartisan, streak, particularly when it came to judges. Back in 2005, when the notion of deploying the nuclear option to end the filibuster seemed unthinkable, Graham was a member of the Gang of 14, which defused the trigger. Joining that gang wasn't a heavy lift for some of the other Republican members of the group, such as Collins, her fellow Mainer Olympia Snowe, and Lincoln Chafee of Rhode Island, but it was a risky move for Graham, who was excoriated by conservatives in his home state unhappy with the compromise. During the Obama administration, Graham voted for both Supreme Court nominees, Sotomayor and Kagan, the lone Republican on the Judiciary Committee panel to do so. "How do we get our judges, and they don't get theirs?" Graham asked. The consequence was a primary challenge in 2014.[19]

So Graham's explosion over what he viewed as partisan mistreatment of Kavanaugh had been long in coming. Graham tends to make his case bit by bit, building to the climax, like the air force lawyer he once was. With Kavanaugh, he started hot and got hotter.

"If you wanted an FBI investigation, you could have come to us," Graham said, his voice raised as he looked at the Democrats' side of the dais. Graham gestured toward Kavanaugh. "What you want to do is destroy this guy's life, hold this seat open, and hope you win in 2020," he said. "You said that, not me," he continued, pointing now at Democrats.

Then, turning to Kavanaugh: "You've got nothing to apologize for. When you see Sotomayor and Kagan, tell them that Lindsey said hello because I voted for them." Again, Graham addressed

Democrats. "I would never do to them what you've done to this guy. This is the most unethical sham since I've been in politics."

He was just getting started. "Boy, you all want power. God, I hope you never get it. I hope the American people can see through this sham. That you knew about it and you held it. You had no intention of protecting Dr. Ford, none. She's as much of a victim as you are. God, I hate to say it, because these have been my friends, but let me tell you, when it comes to this, you're looking for a fair process? You came to the wrong town at the wrong time, my friend."

For Republicans on the committee, and perhaps even more important, for those watching, mesmerized, Graham's four-and-a-half-minute peroration served as a belated rallying cry. He summoned and galvanized the sense of injury and rage that Republicans had felt but not been able to express so passionately. It was the turning point, from Ford as victim to Kavanaugh as victim. "To my Republican colleagues," Graham concluded, "if you vote no, you're legitimizing the most despicable thing I have seen in my time in politics."[20]

Graham's outburst seemed only to wind Kavanaugh up even further. Rhode Island senator Sheldon Whitehouse was the next Democrat up. "Shall we let things settle a little bit after that?" he inquired. Whitehouse's assigned role was to question Kavanaugh about some of the yearbook references. Kavanaugh responded with a mixture of belligerence and off-topic aggrievement.

"If you're worried about my yearbook, have at it, Senator," Kavanaugh told him.

Whitehouse asked about a woman mentioned on Kavanaugh's page, Renate Dolphin, who had attended a Catholic all-girls' school nearby and had been one of sixty-five women to sign a letter attesting to Kavanaugh's respectful treatment of women. Kavanaugh's yearbook page identified him as a "Renate alumnius [sic]," one of at least fourteen references to her throughout the book. One student's entry featured a ditty that had been popular among the classmates: "You need a date / and it's getting late / so don't hesitate / to call Renate." Kavanaugh had said in his opening statement that the "alumnius" reference "was clumsily intended to show affection, and that she was one of us." The real disrespect, he insisted, was asking him about it. "To have her name dragged through this hearing is a joke. And, really, an embarrassment," he lectured. Dolphin herself had issued one public statement, a few days earlier, that suggested she put the blame elsewhere: "I can't begin to comprehend what goes through the minds of 17-year-old boys who write such things, but the insinuation is horrible, hurtful and simply untrue. I pray their daughters are never treated this way."[21]

Whitehouse turned next to the topic of beer, teeing up what would become one of the hearing's most viral lines.

Whitehouse: "Let's look at 'Beach Week Ralph Club—Biggest Contributor.' What does the word *ralph* mean in that?"

Kavanaugh: "That probably refers to throwing up. I'm known to have a weak stomach, and I always have . . . I got a weak stomach, whether it's with beer or with spicy food or anything."

Whitehouse: "So the vomiting that you reference in the Ralph Club reference [is] related to the consumption of alcohol?"

Kavanaugh deflected. "Senator, I was at the top of my class academically, busted my butt in school. Captain of the varsity basketball team. Got into Yale College. When I got into Yale College, got into Yale Law School. Worked my tail off."

So *ralph* related to alcohol, Whitehouse persisted.

Kavanaugh shot back. "I like beer. I like beer. I don't know if you do—do you like beer, Senator, or not? What do you like to drink?"

"Um, next," Whitehouse said, trying to move on.

Kavanaugh continued. "Senator, what do you like to drink?"[22]

It was uncomfortable, and the next encounter, with Democrat Amy Klobuchar, was even worse. Klobuchar's father, a famed Minneapolis sportswriter, is a recovering alcoholic. At ninety, he still attended Alcoholics Anonymous meetings, she told Kavanaugh as she began her round of questioning. She wanted to know:

he had said he sometimes had too many drinks. Had he ever drunk so much that he couldn't remember what had happened the night before?

"You're asking about, you know, blackout," Kavanaugh shot back. "I don't know. Have you?"

Klobuchar was taken aback. She needed to focus on getting Kavanaugh to answer her question, but she didn't want to leave his insinuation unrebutted and risk having her constituents think she drank to excess. "Could you answer the question, Judge?" she responded. "I just—so you—that's not happened. Is that your answer?"

> Kavanaugh: "Yeah, and I'm curious if you have."
>
> Klobuchar: "I have no drinking problem, Judge."[23]

This was more than a few steps over the line. Kavanaugh's team signaled Grassley to call a break. At the recess, Klobuchar predicted that Kavanaugh would apologize; she crafted the words she planned to say in response. Susan Collins, watching from her office, was alarmed at the exchange. Kavanaugh should tone it down, she told her chief nominations counsel, who urgently texted the White House war room. Collins's advice might not have reached the nominee, but he was receiving similar counsel from elsewhere as well. Dial it down a few notches, McGahn advised Kavanaugh. A senator texted: you need to go back to the Brett Kavanaugh we all know and love.

Kavanaugh got the message. "Sorry I did that," he told Klobuchar when the hearing resumed. "This is a tough process. I'm sorry about that."

"I appreciate that," Klobuchar responded. "I would like to add, when you have a parent that's an alcoholic, you're pretty careful about drinking."

The paradox of Kavanaugh's performance was that while it appalled and alienated many who watched the outburst and viewed it as intemperate, even disqualifying, it simultaneously served to energize precisely those demoralized supporters whose backing Kavanaugh needed. *Saturday Night Live* would lampoon Kavanaugh's performance two days later with a sniffing, finger-pointing, water-guzzling Matt Damon. "I'm going to start at an eleven," Damon shouted. "I'm going to take it to a fifteen real quick."[24] But the *SNL* audience was not Republicans' concern. "The goal was not to appeal to the left," said Davis. "The goal was to fire up the base, to keep the wavering Republicans strong and to keep pressure on Trump-state Democrats."

For those who looked at the allegations from Kavanaugh's vantage point—that he was being falsely vilified—the explosion of fury was understandable. At this stage, it was not only about winning confirmation—it was also, as Kavanaugh saw it, an existential battle to avoid complete destruction of his reputation and even livelihood. If he were to be defeated on the basis of Ford's allegations, it would be difficult for him to remain on the federal bench, difficult perhaps even to find another job.

Kavanaugh, though, did not limit himself to impassioned denials. Instead, he took it up an unsettling—and deliberately partisan—notch. Said one well-placed observer, "Brett made the calculation, which I think was shrewd politically," that unless he did something in the hearing to change the dynamic, "(a) he wasn't going to be confirmed, (b) they would have quickly moved on to another nominee, (c) his life and career would be over if any of those things happened . . . He was not only fighting for the nomination. He was fighting for his life, his career, legacy, his name. And the only way to do this was to turn it into a cause."

In that assessment, Kavanaugh's pivot to partisanship made sense, even with his bizarre invocation of the Clintons and complaint about left-wing dark money in a contest where the spending was lopsidedly in his favor.[25] What looked unhinged was in fact canny. "The 'Clintons' thing was the key," this observer said. "It turned this into tribalism: the Clintons are out to get me." It was, this person said, "like catnip" for the base.

Even in the view of some Republican senators who ended up voting for Kavanaugh, however, his behavior displayed a disturbing lack of judicial temperament. These senators included Jon Kyl, the Arizona Republican who had served as Kavanaugh's Senate sherpa for his courtesy calls and was now back in the Senate, filling the vacancy left by McCain's death until after the election. After the criticism that Kavanaugh had been too tepid in the Fox interview, said Kyl, "I could understand when he came out in a much more vociferous way . . . I thought, well, that's genuine emotion that wasn't contrived." At the same time, Kyl said, "it was a little bit over the top. If you're going to choreograph something like that, you don't do it the way he did it."[26]

Corker had a similar response. "I was talking to the television, saying somebody needs to call a break. I mean, what's going on here?" Still, Corker wondered, what would anyone do in a situation like that, if wrongly accused? And perhaps Kavanaugh's excessive behavior could be chalked up—like the testimony of so many cabinet secretaries he had witnessed—to trying to please the "audience of one" in the Oval Office, who might otherwise have been tempted to withdraw the nomination. As a result, Corker recalled, "I cut him some slack and focused more on what the content was."[27]

Flake, though he would, like Corker and Kyl, go on to vote for Kavanaugh, said even at the time that Kavanaugh's performance left him unsettled. "We can't have that on the court," he said, meaning that sort of behavior.[28] Still, he and others thought that Kavanaugh had finally shown the kind of righteous indignation that might be expected under such circumstances. "People thought, wow, that sounds like a man who was unjustly accused," Flake recalled.[29]

Kavanaugh's fury over the last-minute timing and its partisan impetus had some justification. The insinuation that committee Democrats—in particular Feinstein or members of her staff—had leaked the Ford allegations was not supported by the evidence. Yet it was also clear that the story emerged because Kavanaugh opponents decided to take matters into their own hands after Ford had decided she wanted to remain silent. There was some basis for Kavanaugh's description of "a frenzy on the left to come up with something, anything to block my confirmation."[30] Just because Kavanaugh sounded paranoid didn't mean there weren't people out to get him.

Those who saw Kavanaugh after the hearing described him as angry, exhausted, emotionally drained. Ashley Kavanaugh, who had held it together while the cameras were trained on her, was in tears. But the committee vote was set for the next morning. At least, Kavanaugh and his allies thought, it would all be over soon.

Ford's lawyers stayed behind to watch Kavanaugh's testimony from the hearing room. She returned to the Watergate, exhausted. The television was on, playing Kavanaugh's testimony with the sound muted, but Ford had no interest in watching. Her California friends were there as well as a crowd from her Holton days. "They were coming back and saying he was doing a bad job," Ford recalled. "I just didn't care." She felt only relief, as when an academic paper finally gets published after so much work.[31]

More important for Ford was that her parents had arrived from Delaware. The issue of her family—more precisely, the issue of the absence of her family—was a subject of chatter, especially among Kavanaugh allies. In 1991, Anita Hill's elderly parents had traveled from Oklahoma—it was her father's first time in the capital—to attend the hearings; five of her twelve siblings also came. Kavanaugh's wife and parents, looking stricken, had sat through his testimony and the painful questions. Where was Ford's family? Her husband's family had issued a supportive statement, but her brothers and parents were noticeably silent, which Kavanaugh supporters were happy to take as a tacit indication that her own family doubted her account.

Ford wasn't as much estranged from her family as uncomfortable with them: she had moved on, reinvented herself almost, as a Californian. "She didn't always get along with her parents because of differing political views," Russell Ford told the *Washington Post*. "It was a very male-dominated environment. Everyone was interested in what's going on with the men, and the women are sidelined, and she didn't get the attention or respect she felt she deserved. That's why she was in California, to get away from the D.C. scene."[32]

When she decided to come forward, Ford's parents had told her they were proud of her for speaking up, but no one in the family, in particular her brothers, was happy about being thrust into an uncomfortable public spotlight that put them at odds with their own community. CHRISTINE BLASEY FORD'S FAMILY HAS BEEN NEARLY SILENT AMID OUTPOURING OF SUPPORT, read a *Washington Post* headline the day of the hearing. "I think all of the Blasey family would support her. I think her record stands for itself. Her schooling, her jobs and so on," Ralph Blasey, Ford's father, told the *Post*. He hung up, then answered a second call. "I think any father would have love for his daughter," he said.[33]

Yes, but her family's reaction, especially her father's, had been a major worry while Ford was making her decision about whether to come forward. She had never considered that her parents might come to the hearing itself. Now she was thankful that they had driven in from the beach to see her at the Watergate. "That was a big deal," she recalled. "I flew out there [to D.C.], and I had not told them I was testifying, so they drove back from Rehoboth and came down with my sister-in-law to see me. It was nice to give them a hug. That's what stood out at that party, that they showed up."[34]

Later that evening, Republican senators gathered in the Strom Thurmond Room, an ornate space off the Capitol Rotunda that was once the home of the Law Library of Congress, to assess the day's events. Underneath ceiling murals depicting Justice, Prudence, Fortitude, and Peace, what had once promised to be a wake turned into an impromptu celebration by a relieved Republican caucus. Grassley entered the room, to a standing ovation. Then Graham, to another. Grassley received a second standing ovation when McConnell praised his handling of the situation. Mitchell briefed the senators on her assessment. There had been too many inconsistencies in Ford's story, she told the group. If this case had come to her as a prosecutor, there was no way she would pursue it, not based on facts like this.

But Collins wasn't fully satisfied. Neither was Flake. Judge had not been called to testify, and while his lawyer had submitted a statement asserting that Judge had no recollection of the incident that Ford described, they wanted to hear directly from Judge. Too late, McConnell said. Judge had lawyered up. "He had every excuse as to why it couldn't be done," Flake said.[35]

Collins, Murkowski, Flake, and Manchin met in Collins's hideaway on the third floor of the Capitol to discuss what to do. They didn't want to kill the nomination, but they were uncomfortable with where things stood. Within a few hours, McConnell's assertions notwithstanding, Judge's lawyer e-mailed a new statement—this time not from her but from Judge himself, denying any recollection of the assault Ford described.

As the four undecideds were huddling, Coons, Klobuchar, and their staffs had dinner in Coons's office to strategize over takeout Chinese: how could they obtain an FBI investigation, even at this late hour? Maybe Flake, they thought, could be induced to go along with a short delay. By this point, the situation had become dangerous. Collins arrived home to discover a man lurking outside her house, shining a flashlight in her face; she was terrified. Meanwhile, Murkowski had to retrieve her keys from her basement hideaway and found herself trapped by a media mob desperate for any morsels indicating her inclination. In a scene worthy of the Keystone Kops, Rob Portman and Wyoming senator John Barrasso had to rescue Murkowski by directing Portman's driver to the House side of the Capitol and diving with her into the car as reporters chased after them. Later that night, Coons spoke with Murkowski to see if she would be willing to support an investigation: if the nomination got to the Senate floor, Flake's support alone wouldn't be sufficient to stop it from proceeding. Murkowski said she was on board. More investigation was warranted.

Trump attended a Republican congressional fund-raiser at the Trump International Hotel in Washington that night. He was thrilled with Kavanaugh's testimony. "He listened to me," Trump proudly told one person in attendance. On Fox News, Conway praised Kavanaugh's performance. Kavanaugh, she said, "channeled his inner Clarence Thomas and his inner Donald Trump because he is not going to allow them to besmirch a good man's reputation."[36]

In Boulder, John Clune, Ramirez's lawyer, got hold of Flake's cell phone number. He called, around midnight Washington time, and was amazed when Flake answered a call from an unknown number. Clune offered to have the senator speak with Ramirez. Clune entreated him: "You don't need to hear from the lawyers, but you should talk to Debbie. Talk to her. I don't even need to be on the call. I'm going to text you her phone number—call her and decide for yourself what you think. This isn't right to just ignore this."[37]

To Clune's ear, Flake sounded exhausted, like the weight of the world was on him. There had been so much attention paid to Ford, Flake said; the committee hadn't even turned to Ramirez's claims. That was the problem, Clune replied. He sent Ramirez's information. Flake never called.

Flake, who was supposed to vote the next morning on whether to advance Kavanaugh's nomination, was in agony. Ford's allegation was old; the corroboration, as he saw it, lacking. But Kavanaugh's demeanor had been so troubling, so unjudicial. "That was the longest night I think I've had in the Senate, trying to decide," Flake recalled. "I was having a hard time." He went to bed that night "not knowing what I would do—not sure, anyway." He slept poorly. When he got out of bed, he had come, he thought, to a final decision.[38]

CHAPTER SEVENTEEN

By the Book

Just after 9:30 the next morning, Jeff Flake stepped inside a wood-paneled senators-only elevator in the Dirksen Senate Office Building. His finger was on the button, poised to push "close," when two women stepped in front of the bronze doors. Just a few minutes earlier, Flake had issued a statement that seemed to make Kavanaugh's confirmation a fait accompli: he would vote to support Kavanaugh, he said, moving the nomination out of committee and onto the Senate floor. Then Ana Maria Archila, a thirty-nine-year-old Colombian immigrant and community organizer from Queens, confronted Flake. "On Monday I stood in front of your office . . . I told the story of my sexual assault," she said. "I told it because I recognized from Dr. Ford's story that she is telling the truth." Flake nodded. "I need to go," he said. "I need to go to the hearing." Archila continued, pointing her finger at Flake, her voice rising. "What you are doing is allowing someone who actually violated a woman to sit on the Supreme Court . . . You have children in your family. Think about them."[1]

A second woman, Maria Gallagher, joined in. Gallagher, twenty-three, was crying as she spoke. "You're telling all women that they don't matter, that they should just stay quiet, because if they tell you what happened to them you're going to ignore them," she said. "That's what you're telling all of these women. That's what you're telling me right now." Flake looked down. "Look at me when I'm talking to you," Gallagher instructed. "You're telling me that my assault doesn't matter, that what happened to me doesn't matter, and that you're going to let people who do these things into power."

The encounter continued for four excruciating minutes, captured live on CNN. "I need to go to the hearing," Flake said. "I just issued a statement. I'll be saying more as well." The door closed.[2]

Chris Coons, the Delaware Democrat, was distraught when he learned of Flake's decision. The two senators were from opposite parties, but they were exactly the same age and had forged a close friendship, steeped in their shared commitment to faith (Flake was a devout Mormon, and Coons had earned a master's degree from Yale Divinity School along with his law degree). Coons, once a founding member of Amherst College Republicans, had studied in Kenya during his junior year and returned with more progressive politics.[3] Flake spent two years as a missionary in Zimbabwe and South Africa. Coons and Flake would return to Africa together as senators, fighting wildlife trafficking, holding a memorably awful meeting with Zimbabwean dictator Robert Mugabe, being chased by elephants on a safari outing in Mozambique.[4]

And by September 2018, the two senators were, in differing degrees, slightly out of step with their own parties. Coons was a moderate, temperamentally and politically, in a Democratic party whose restive base was tugging it to the left. Flake was a Barry Goldwater–inspired deficit hawk, a pro-immigration free trader in Donald Trump's Washington. A fifth-generation Arizonan from tiny Snowflake, named in part for his great-great-grandfather, a Mormon pioneer, Flake had served six terms in the House before being elected to the Senate in 2012.

His first term turned out to be his last, thanks in no small measure to Trump. Flake had taken on Trump during the campaign, calling on the candidate to withdraw in the aftermath of the *Access Hollywood* tape. Flake, unlike many of his colleagues, had persisted in his opposition to Trump even after the election, on issues such as trade and the travel ban. That stance took its toll, in hostile Trump tweets ("very weak and ineffective"; "Flake Jeff Flake"), falling poll numbers, and the prospect of an all-but-certain-to-succeed primary challenge. "The bottom line is if I were to run a campaign that I could be proud of and where I didn't have to cozy up to the president and his positions or his behavior, I could not win in a Republican primary," Flake acknowledged in explaining his decision not to seek reelection.[5] In the floor speech announcing his retirement, Flake lamented "the disrepair and destructiveness of our politics," the "indecency of our discourse," the "coarseness of our leadership," and "our complicity in this alarming and dangerous state of affairs." He never mentioned the president by name, but his words were aimed unmistakably at Trump.[6]

Yet his Democratic colleagues would note sourly that Flake's actions rarely matched his lofty rhetoric. Flake had declared himself "unchained from the necessities of politics for the next 14 months," only to vote for Trump's deficit-busting tax bill.[7] In doing so, Flake said he had received a "firm commitment from the Senate leadership" to find a way to protect Dreamers, the hundreds of thousands of undocumented immigrants who had been brought to the United States as children.[8] That promise turned out to be as evanescent as the tax cuts were long-lasting.

For weeks, since Anthony Kennedy's retirement, Coons had courted Flake. The Arizonan was a true conservative, Coons understood, and wanted to see a conservative Supreme Court. But Coons kept making arguments to Flake, in particular about what he viewed as Kavanaugh's dangerously deferential view of presidential power. He had watched Flake's face as Ford testified, and Coons thought the Arizonan looked troubled. "You've got a great big hammer in your hand, and it's got a letter K on the side," he had told Flake for weeks; you need to pick it up and start swinging. "Unless you do that, all your brave speeches are for naught."

So Coons retained a morsel of hope that Flake could be swayed—if not to vote against Kavanaugh, then at least to improve the process. Then a reporter showed him Flake's statement on her cell phone. "Oh, fuck," Coons said, cursing uncharacteristically. He was silent, fighting to keep his emotions in check. "I deeply respect—" he began, then paused. "We each make choices for our own reason. I'm struggling, sorry."9

In the hearing room, Grassley gaveled the proceedings to order. Richard Blumenthal made a motion to subpoena Mark Judge. "He has never been interviewed by the FBI. He has never been questioned by any member of our committee. He has never submitted a detailed account of what he knows," the Connecticut Democrat said. "We cannot in good conscience vote without hearing at least from Mark Judge."10

Grassley read from Judge's new letter, reiterating his denials. The motion was swiftly defeated. Then Grassley made his own motion, to vote on Kavanaugh at 1:30. "The ram job continues," Sheldon Whitehouse remarked. As the clerk called the roll, Cory Booker and Kamala Harris, the two most junior Democrats on the panel, refused even to respond. "They're not answering because this is so unfair, Mr. Chairman," Amy Klobuchar said.

As Grassley began to read his opening statement, Harris stood up and walked out, followed by Mazie Hirono, Whitehouse, and Blumenthal. The photographers in the well of the hearing room clustered around the empty chairs on the Democratic side. Grassley rapped his gavel. "Hey, you folks that are photographers know you're supposed to sit down," he said sharply. "Maybe you ought to leave the room if you don't know what the rules are." The tensions of the last three weeks were taking their toll.

As the discussion continued, Republicans lamented the mistreatment of Kavanaugh, invoked the presumption of innocence, and, none too subtly, threatened retribution. "We can't allow more time for new smears to damage Judge Kavanaugh, his family, his reputation, the reputation of the court, and of course, the reputation of the country," Orrin Hatch said. "We cannot allow more time for partisans on the left to try to beat Judge Kavanaugh into submission."

Republicans labored to reconcile their assertions of respect for Ford with their decision to disbelieve her identification of Kavanaugh. "I do believe that something very, very, very bad happened to Dr. Ford, and I am very sorry," said John Neely Kennedy of Louisiana. "But I do not believe that Judge Brett Kavanaugh was involved, and that's why I will support his nomination."

Graham noted ominously that he would be poised to chair the committee if Grassley, as expected, took the helm of the Senate Finance Committee after the election. "If I am chairman next year . . . I'm going to remember this," he warned. "There is the process before Kavanaugh and the process after Kavanaugh. If you want to vet the nominee, you can. If you want to delay things for the next election, you will not. If you try to destroy somebody, you will not get away with it."

For their part, Democrats contrasted Kavanaugh's outburst with Ford's demeanor and, seemingly fruitlessly, questioned how the vote could possibly proceed without further investigation. "This was not someone who reflected an impartial temperament or the fairness and evenhandedness one would see in a judge," Feinstein said of Kavanaugh. "This was someone who was aggressive and belligerent. I have never seen someone who wants to be elevated to the highest court in our country behave in that manner." The Republican response to the allegations against Kavanaugh, she said, "was not about ensuring a fair process. This was about doing the bare minimum."

Democrat after Democrat described what that bare minimum should entail: an FBI investigation. Durbin read into the record a new letter from the president of the American Bar Association. "The basic principles that underscore the Senate's constitutional duty of advice and consent on federal judicial nominees require nothing less than a careful examination of the accusations and the facts by the FBI," wrote ABA president Robert Carlson. Going forward without such an investigation, he wrote, "would not only have a lasting impact on the Senate's reputation but it will also negatively affect the great trust necessary for the American people to have in the Supreme Court."

Coons had decided, at the last minute, to rewrite his prepared remarks. The original version seemed more designed to be used as an "I told you so" when Kavanaugh disappointed once he was on the court than as an appeal to convince anyone (read: Flake) to act in real time. So Coons and his counsel, Erica Songer, hurriedly revised, trying to tone down the partisanship. Coons wanted to acknowledge Republicans' legitimate sense of grievance about the late-breaking nature of the allegations before seeking support for a delay. "To my colleagues across the aisle: you know me. You know I try to be fair to nominees that come before us, and I respect this process and the humanity of those—even those with whom I passionately disagree," Coons said. "If I were convinced this were nothing more than a partisan hit job designed to take down a good man and hold a position vacant past the election, I would not stand for it."

Coons delivered his remarks looking directly at Flake, even though he thought by then that the whole thing was a lost cause. Flake seemed troubled, but then again, that was just Flake's way, concern that was not always backed up with action. Still, Coons gave it a try. He outlined a compromise: a one-week pause to investigate, for the good of the nominee, the Senate, the court, and the country. "We're left with the reality that if his nomination goes forward this morning after testimony full of rage and partisanship and vitriol but without even a brief pause for nonpartisan investigation into the serious allegations presented," Coons said, "his service may well have an asterisk. Litigants coming to the court will have reason to question the fairness of the institution, and in my view that is too great a cost to impose on our system of justice in exchange for any one man."[11]

Coons finished speaking, and Idaho Republican Mike Crapo began his remarks. A few seconds later, Flake got up from his seat at the other end of the dais, walked to Coons's side, and tapped him on the shoulder. "Let's talk," Flake told his friend. Coons expected an explanation, an expression of regret from Flake that they did not see things the same way. Instead, Flake said he was receptive to Coons's proposal. "This is tearing our country apart. We have to do something," Flake said. "Can you deliver on what you just said?"

In the anteroom, the two friends talked, not only about how the investigation would proceed—Flake was insistent that it be limited in "time and scope"; Coons wanted to make sure it was thorough and credible—but also about their shared faith. Jesus Christ had been both hailed and pilloried. He had returned in triumph to Jerusalem on Palm Sunday, and later set upon by a jeering mob. Either could happen in this case, too. If an investigation brought down the nominee, Flake would be blamed, Coons acknowledged. But why was Flake's party so determined to jam this through? Why was Kavanaugh seemingly so resistant to calling for an investigation?

Flake was moved. "If it was anybody else, I wouldn't have taken it as seriously," he said later that day. "But I know Chris . . . We trust each other. And I thought if we could actually get something like what he was asking for . . . we could maybe bring a little unity."[12]

Other senators began to recognize that something was up. Klobuchar, who knew from dinner the previous night that Coons still harbored hopes of striking a deal with Flake, quickly followed them. Other senators began to leave the dais and huddle in the anteroom's narrow hallway. Meanwhile, committee staffers filled the main space. Flake was practically pinned against the wall as senators from both parties lobbied him. Thom Tillis, Ted Cruz, and John Cornyn beseeched Flake not to hold up the vote. It was just a delaying tactic, they argued with increasing vehemence, and it would create the space for even more frivolous allegations. It wasn't fair to the judge or his family. Flake had insisted he wouldn't support moving the nomination out of committee until he heard from Ford. That had happened. Why wasn't that enough? Graham joined the throng trying to talk Flake out of pursuing an investigation. We're not going to be in a better place afterward, Flake recalled Graham telling him.

By this point, nearly the entire committee was squeezed into the hallway. Flake raised his hand. "Enough. Okay. Everybody stop. I only want to talk to him," he said, gesturing to Coons. The two senators squeezed into the old-fashioned phone booth on one side of the hallway. Coons called Murkowski, to fill her in on the plan for a one-week investigation and make certain of her support. Flake did the same with Collins. "What do you think of reopening the background investigation?" he asked her. Good idea, she replied. Now Coons and Flake needed to figure out how to make that happen. Flake tried to reach FBI director Christopher Wray, and then, when he was unavailable, deputy attorney general Rod Rosenstein, who was visiting his daughter at college.

A lawyer on the Grassley staff frantically texted an administration colleague: Flake is peeling off. This would be a good time to get George W. Bush on the phone. A few minutes later, as the senators congregated in the narrow hallway, someone walked through holding a phone. Bush was on the line for Flake, who said he was too busy to speak to the former president right then. It was beginning to look like the crowded stateroom scene in the Marx Brothers film *A Night at the Opera* as senators crammed into the corridor, until Feinstein intervened and ordered the staff out. They didn't leave, but they did cede the larger space to the senators.

Nebraska Republican Ben Sasse strode angrily into the room, looking for the senator from Rhode Island. "Where's Sheldon?" he asked. "I want to fight that guy." Sasse, a first-term senator with a doctorate in history from Yale and a Flake-like penchant for criticizing Trump but pulling back at the brink of taking action, was upset about the Newport boat story, the Rhode Island man who claimed a friend was sexually assaulted by two men named Brett and Mark in the summer of 1985. From Whitehouse's point of view, he had done what he was supposed to—immediately forward the allegation to Grassley and the FBI; it was the Grassley staff that had fanned the flames of the story. They had not only questioned Kavanaugh about it, they had also read him anti-Trump tweets from the witness—a move that could not possibly have elicited useful information from Kavanaugh but that let reporters quickly identify the individual. Sasse was unhappy that Whitehouse had steered the witness to a reporter. That felt like an underhanded move. Whitehouse asked Sasse to join him back at the dais, where Whitehouse offered his side of the story. He thought Sasse understood, but months later, both senators remained unhappy over the incident.

At 1:50, twenty minutes after the committee was to have voted on the nomination and more than ninety minutes after he first got up from his chair, Flake reentered the hearing room. He stopped by Grassley's seat and put his hand on the chairman's shoulder. "Can I ask for UC to speak for a minute?" he asked Grassley, using the Senate shorthand for "unanimous consent."[13]

Flake laid out the contours of the arrangement. He would vote to advance the Kavanaugh nomination out of the judiciary committee but on the understanding that the vote on the Senate floor would be delayed, for no longer than a week. During that time, the FBI would conduct an investigation, "limited in time and scope to the current allegations."

Flake repeated in public what he had said to Coons. "This country is being ripped apart here, and we have got to make sure that we do due diligence."[14]

What diligence was due, exactly? That would be the subject of furious negotiations over the next hours and days, beginning in McConnell's office when he summoned the troublemaking Republicans to a tense meeting. The answer boiled down to: whatever was needed to satisfy Collins, Flake, and Murkowski. But not a phone call more.

Graham asked Flake to have dinner that night at Cafe Berlin, near the Capitol. The group grew to include Collins, Murkowski, and Flake's son Austin, who was working for the Senate sergeant at arms. Occasionally interrupted by diners who had watched the previous day's hearing, they discussed the contours of the investigation ahead. Graham, who had first pressed for a hearing and then been the loudest voice in the room denouncing the proceedings, was now gung ho for an FBI investigation. Graham, Flake recalled, said, "That's great, that's great, we should have done this a long time ago."[15] The South Carolina senator always liked to be on the winning team.

•　　•　　•

Even as the FBI investigation got under way, Mitchell, the Republican questioner, submitted a five-page account of her conclusions about the strength—or lack of it, in Mitchell's assessment—of the case against Kavanaugh. "While I am a registered Republican," she wrote in the account, submitted Sunday, September 30, "I am not a political or partisan person."[16]

Her bottom line was stark: "A 'he said, she said' case is incredibly difficult to prove. But this case is even weaker than that. Dr. Ford identified other witnesses to the event, and those witnesses either refuted her allegations or failed to corroborate them." Consequently, Mitchell said, "I do not think that a reasonable prosecutor would bring this case based on the evidence before the Committee. Nor do I believe that this evidence is sufficient to satisfy the preponderance-of-the-evidence standard."

Mitchell picked apart the details of Ford's admittedly hazy recollections. Ford, she noted, had given differing accounts of when the alleged assault occurred—the "mid-1980's" (text to *Washington Post*); "early 80's" (letter to Feinstein); "summer of 1982" (*Washington Post* article). "While it is common for victims to be uncertain about dates, Dr. Ford failed to explain how she was suddenly able to narrow the timeframe to a particular season and particular year."

Mitchell presented herself as a prosecutor plunged into an unfamiliar political world. Yet her report appeared to be less a dispassionate legal analysis than a defense lawyer's diligent effort to pick apart the supposed flaws in the prosecution's case, with loaded language and a thumb on the scale in the direction of weighing the evidence in the light most favorable to the nominee. It was clear which side had hired her.

For example, Mitchell wrote, "Dr. Ford has struggled to identify Judge Kavanaugh as the assailant by name." The evidence of this supposed struggle was that the two sets of therapy notes did not mention the identity of Ford's alleged attacker. Although Russell Ford "claims to recall" that his wife identified Kavanaugh by name in 2012, Mitchell wrote, "at that point, Judge Kavanaugh's name

was widely reported in the press as a potential Supreme Court nominee if Governor Romney won the presidential election." Mitchell
may have been suggesting that Kavanaugh's emergence in news
reports somehow triggered a false memory on Ford's part. But it
would appear just as likely that mentioning Kavanaugh's name
made sense then precisely because of his new prominence.

"In any event, it took Dr. Ford over thirty years to name her
assailant," Mitchell wrote. "Delayed disclosure of abuse is common so this is not dispositive." Omitted by Mitchell were sworn
statements by three of Ford's friends, saying that Ford had told
them in 2013, 2016, and 2017 that she had been sexually assaulted
by a man who was now a federal judge.

Likewise, Mitchell argued that Ford had "changed her description of the incident to become less specific" in conversations with
her husband. Ford testified that she told her husband about a "sexual
assault" before they were married. But, Mitchell noted, the *Washington Post* story described Ford telling her husband at the beginning of their marriage about being the victim of "physical abuse."[17]
Given that Ford's description of the event had always included both
a sexual and physical component—"Brett Kavanaugh physically
and sexually assaulted me during High School in the early 1980's,"
she wrote in her letter to Feinstein—that seemed a rather slender
reed on which to hang a claim of shifting stories.

The next day, Feinstein's staff issued its own rebuttal. As to the
timing of the event, Ford had tried to narrow it down, the Feinstein
memo noted. The best way to do that would be, as Ford suggested,
to try to find the records of Mark Judge's employment at Safe-
way, where she recalled seeing him later that summer. Ford hadn't
"struggled" to identify Kavanaugh, the Feinstein memo said: she
had testified she was "100 percent certain" of his identity, a statement that Mitchell neglected to include. More broadly, the memo
said, Ford's spotty memories of that evening were "entirely consistent with traumatic memory," in which victims often "form dura-
ble memories of their attack but have incomplete memories of the
events before and after the attack took place."[18]

None of this mattered much except as fodder in the ensuing partisan back-and-forth. The exchange of competing memos would make little dent on the public discussion or in senators' assessments. The FBI investigation, such as it was, was under way. That would be the whole ball game.

Christine Ford was flying back to California—"maybe the only flight I've ever looked forward to," she recalled—when word started to filter through the plane's WiFi: the Kavanaugh vote would not go forward.[19] The FBI investigation that her lawyers had been seeking for eleven days would finally take place. Ford's lawyers began to make plans to head out to California so they could be by her side for the inevitable FBI interview. Surely speaking with the two chief protagonists—Ford and Kavanaugh—would be part of any FBI probe. Neither had been subjected to sustained professional questioning. Rachel Mitchell's five-minute increments were no substitute for the real thing.

At eleven o'clock on Friday night, Michael Bromwich was frantically trying to reach Wray, the FBI director, to make contact with the relevant agents and arrange the interview. They could meet as early as the next morning, Bromwich offered. Finally, Dana Boente, the FBI general counsel, returned his call. Boente declined even to give Bromwich the name of the lead agent. Bromwich had been inspector general at the Justice Department; he knew how the FBI would set up and execute a top-priority investigation. It would bring in an up-and-coming star agent to oversee the investigation. It would set up command posts in every relevant part of the country. It would follow leads 24-7. That wasn't happening.

The next several days were an exercise in frustration. It was becoming increasingly clear that Ford was not going to be interviewed; neither was Kavanaugh. That was inexcusable, Bromwich felt. He e-mailed Boente at 11:49 on Saturday morning. "Dana, any word on this? Thanks," Bromwich wrote.[20] Then again, at 2:05, attaching a letter with the names of more than a dozen potential interviewees.[21] Boente responded less than an hour later. "Michael, I have forwarded your letter to the Security Division."[22] The next afternoon, when Ford's lawyers still hadn't heard anything, Bromwich e-mailed again. "Who is running the investigation?" he asked.[23] "Michael, the Security Division is coordinating investigative steps with various field offices," came the reply.[24]

Just as disturbing, the FBI was not reaching out to others who had relevant information. The list of witnesses Bromwich and Katz had sent Wray on Saturday included Ford's husband, Russell Ford; the friends to whom she had confided her account of being assaulted; and the polygraph examiner. None was ever contacted. The next day, Sunday, the lawyers followed up, with more suggested names—and another request that their client be interviewed. "We have read press accounts that Dr. Christine Blasey Ford is not on the list of witnesses the White House has authorized the FBI to interview," they wrote. "We hope that this is not the case as it is inconceivable that a credible investigation could be conducted without interviewing Dr. Ford."[25]

On Saturday evening, speaking to reporters before a rally in West Virginia, Trump had announced that the FBI would have "free rein" to investigate and predicted that "having the FBI go out and do a thorough investigation . . . will be a blessing in disguise."[26] That was, as it turned out, half true. The FBI did not have free rein, far from it. McGahn set the narrow parameters of the investigation. He would authorize the FBI to do only what the Republican senators asked for and no more. But the fact that Kavanaugh supporters would have an FBI investigation to cite, however flawed and limited it was, would turn out to be the blessing Trump had predicted.

In Boulder, the Ramirez lawyers ended up having a similarly difficult experience, although it began, at least, on a more positive note. On Sunday, a trio of FBI agents arrived at Clune's law office to interview Ramirez. The questioning lasted two hours, and as the agents were leaving, Clune recalled, they were supportive. "They said, 'Look, it's not our job to determine credibility . . . but we find you credible,'" he said. The agents left the number for the

Denver field office; any witnesses who wanted to reach out should call there, they advised. "We felt pretty encouraged," Clune said. "I had this image of somebody sitting at a desk somewhere in Denver being ready to take down information."[27]

That did not turn out to be the case. Ken Appold, the Kavanaugh classmate who recalled hearing about the incident just after it occurred and was "100 percent certain" that he was told Kavanaugh had exposed himself to Ramirez, tried to contact the FBI but did not hear back. Appold eventually submitted a statement online but heard nothing further.[28] Yale classmate Richard Oh, the emergency room doctor who recalled a female student "emotionally reporting" an account of a woman who had tried to push away an exposed penis and ended up touching it, also found himself stymied in getting that information to authorities. He tried to contact the FBI on Saturday and Sunday to inform them he was willing to be interviewed. There was no response.[29] Nor did the FBI respond to Alan Abramson, the lawyer for a friend of Ramirez in whom she had confided about the exposure incident a few years after graduating, although without using Kavanaugh's name.[30] Kathy Charlton, the Yale classmate, submitted a statement to the FBI, with copies to Grassley and Feinstein, that, among other things, described Kavanaugh's outreach to David Todd in advance of the Ramirez story: "Dave shared the surprising news that Brett had called him," Charlton wrote. "He said that Brett was giving him a heads-up that press would likely make contact and wanted to make sure Dave would share 'no bad.' It seemed Dave understood this to mean he was not to speak ill of Brett's history."[31] Whatever Todd's understanding was—he declined requests for comment—the reality may have been less nefarious than the interpretation placed on it. Kavanaugh had e-mailed Todd, not called him, to say that Lenkner, his former clerk, would be reaching out to deal with anticipated press reports but assuring him that the Lenkner inquiry was "nothing bad."

One person who was, at least initially, frustrated by the scope of the FBI investigation—or, perhaps more accurately, frustrated by criticism of the scope of the FBI investigation—was the president himself. Seething over an NBC News report that the White House had imposed a "significant constraint" on the probe, Trump tweeted on Saturday evening that "I want them to interview whoever they deem appropriate at their discretion."[32] He called McGahn the next day, instructing the White House counsel: tell the FBI it can investigate whatever it wants. McGahn advised caution. An unbounded inquiry could be a dangerous thing.

Coons called McGahn later Sunday. What was going on? McGahn repeatedly assured the senator that the FBI investigation was being done "by the book." What book? Coons wanted to know. Where can I read what is in this book? What were the rules the agents were following? With the list of people the FBI was interviewing seemingly limited to four—Mark Judge, P. J. Smyth, Leland Keyser, and Deborah Ramirez—this looked less like a searching inquiry than a con job. Coons called Flake, asking if he had agreed that only four witnesses would be interviewed. No, Flake said: it would be done "by the book"—that phrase again.

In the aftermath of the initial criticism, the universe was expanded, somewhat. The FBI ended up reaching out to eleven people, of whom ten cooperated. (When it comes to background investigations, the FBI doesn't have subpoena authority, and people aren't under an obligation to speak with agents.) On the Ford part of the investigation, the expanded group included two others who appeared on Kavanaugh's July 1 calendar entry, Timothy Gaudette and Chris Garrett, and a lawyer for another, unnamed, witness. On the Ramirez side, those interviewed, besides Ramirez herself, included Kevin Genda, who was supposedly in the room, and his wife, Karen Yarasavage, Ramirez's close friend.[33]

Coons had worried that the problem with the investigation would be that other incidents would emerge and that, under the parameters he himself had agreed to, those would be off-limits for probing. Instead, he said, "the dynamic I had anticipated unfolded, but in a different way. It's not that four, five, six, seven people came forward with different accusations. It was that a group of corroborative witnesses around two core credible accusations were simply shut out."[34]

If the FBI had been serious, if agents had been free to pursue credible leads, they would have quickly found a story that was also making its way to senators and Senate staff. Buried inside the letter that Ford's lawyers sent to Wray detailing possible witnesses was a potential time bomb. It concerned a woman named Tracy Harmon, a close friend of Ramirez from their days at Yale. (She was identified in the letter by her married name, Joyce.) "We have been advised that while at Yale, Mr. Kavanaugh exposed himself to Ms. Harmon Joyce and forced her to touch his penis," the lawyers wrote. "Witnesses were present and we have been advised that they will be contacting the FBI with their first-hand accounts."[35]

In his September 30 letter to the FBI, Clune, the Ramirez lawyer, identified one of those potential witnesses, although without linking the name to Harmon's account. Rather, without additional explanation, he listed as a possible witness a Washington lawyer named Max Stier. "We understand," he wrote, "that Mr. Stier has information regarding your background investigation of Judge Kavanaugh."[36] The Ford and Ramirez lawyers didn't have the information nailed down, but in the chaos of the moment, rumors were circulating about Harmon and Stier. Reporters were chasing the allegations, and the lawyers were desperate to have the FBI look into the matter.

Stier was no household name, but among a certain group in Washington he was a well-respected figure. He had been a college classmate of Kavanaugh's and, most relevant, had lived in an entryway near Kavanaugh's freshman-year suite in Lawrance Hall, the dorm where the exposure incident allegedly took place. He had gone on to Stanford Law School and, the year after Kavanaugh spent with Kennedy, a clerkship for David Souter. Coincidentally, Stier not only practiced law for a stretch at Williams & Connolly, the firm that Kavanaugh was poised to join before the Kozinski clerkship opened up, but also litigated against Kavanaugh when Williams & Connolly was representing the Clintons and Kavanaugh was working for Starr.

In 2001, Stier created a nonprofit organization called the Partnership for Public Service, dedicated to improving the effectiveness of the federal government. It was an impressive organization that provided valuable advice for new presidents on navigating the transition process and better managing the federal government. Every year, it awarded the Samuel J. Heyman Service to America Medals—better known as the Sammies—to federal workers who had performed exemplary service. The Sammies were the Oscars for good government geeks, and, in a jaded city, Stier's group served as a useful reminder that government was often a force for good and that much-derided bureaucrats could be dedicated public servants.

Michael Lewis would write about Stier in his book *The Fifth Risk* as he described Trump's disorderly transition planning. "At that moment in American history, if you could somehow organize the entire population into a single line, all 350 million people, ordered not by height or weight or age but by each citizen's interest in the federal government, and Donald Trump loitered somewhere near one end of it, Max Stier would occupy the other," Lewis wrote. "By the fall of 2016 Max Stier might have been the American with the greatest understanding of how the U.S. government actually worked. Oddly, for an American of his age and status, he'd romanticized public service since he was a child . . . He thought the U.S. government was the single most important and most interesting institution in the history of the planet and couldn't imagine doing anything but working to improve it."[37]

That was the dilemma facing Stier. He was a registered Democrat, but the very effectiveness of his organization hinged on its ability to rise above partisanship and maintain its reputation as an honest broker in the all-important, too-often-neglected process of fixing the federal government. For Stier to be publicly swept up in the Kavanaugh mess would be to threaten his life's work.

Yet Stier also had information of immense relevance—information that, had it emerged at the time, could have been devastating to Kavanaugh. He had not been at the gathering at which Ramirez recalled Kavanaugh exposing himself. But he had witnessed something similar: as Stier related the incident to others, he was passing by a suite in Lawrance Hall freshman year when he saw Kavanaugh with his pants pulled down and his penis exposed. Kavanaugh was leaning up against a wall, and Tracy Harmon, seemingly drunk, was being led over to him by two classmates, her hand placed on his penis. This was, potentially, the corroboration that had been lacking, although one significant problem was that Harmon herself had told friends she didn't recall any such incident and she refused to speak with reporters chasing the story. That didn't necessarily mean it didn't happen, however: Harmon, in Stier's recollection, appeared heavily inebriated at the time. And if Stier's memory was accurate, that would buttress Ramirez, which would, in turn, add force to Ford's account. It was the mirror image of the Avenatti-Swetnick effect—or would have been, had it become public.

This was exactly the kind of tip a credible FBI investigation would pursue. It had been given a road map that led directly to Stier. It simply chose not to follow the trail. Stier, clearly ambivalent about going public, had enlisted lawyers—veterans of the U.S. attorneys' office in Manhattan, with close ties to law enforcement—to try to get his account to the FBI. It didn't work. The Bureau would speak only to those with whom it had been instructed to speak. Stier was not among them.

The FBI's failure, or refusal, to pursue the Stier allegations was a subject of mounting frustration in the frenzied final days of the Kavanaugh vote. Stier contacted Coons, with whom he had worked on good government initiatives, and shared his recollection of the incident: that Kavanaugh had "exposed himself to someone in an inebriated state at a party. It was something that to him corroborated what Debbie Ramirez was saying," Coons recalled. "Boy, that's disturbing," Coons thought. Stier had not yet contacted the FBI; he "was looking for advice on whether or not that was a good idea and if so how to do it in a way that would guarantee that it would be heard and yet not risk his confidentiality."

Stier came back to Coons again on the night of October 1, concerned that the investigation was almost over and that his information was being ignored. "It was in the spirit of 'I have really tried,'" Coons recalled. Stier said his information had been shared with the Ramirez lawyers; he had tried to reach Collins and hadn't been able to get through, and he hadn't been able to speak to anyone at the FBI. "I would really like the chance to talk to Senators Flake and Murkowski and Collins, and I know that Susan Collins knows me and I think my sharing this with her would be important," Stier told Coons.[38]

Coons, trying to help, sent a letter the next day to FBI director Wray, with copies to Grassley and Feinstein, providing Stier's contact information. "There is one individual whom I would like to specifically refer for prompt and appropriate follow-up," Coons wrote.[39] His account was deliberately vague in order to protect Stier's privacy, but Coons thought he had been insistent enough for his entreaty to receive some attention.

It didn't. The FBI acknowledged receipt of the Coons letter, but that was it. Wray did not respond to this serious letter from a serious senator—not just any senator, either, but one who had been his Yale Law School classmate.

Grassley, who issued a report boasting of "a serious and thorough investigation that left no stone unturned in our pursuit of the facts," would later point out that Stier had not brought his complaint to the committee. But Grassley was copied on Coons's letter to Wray and his staff who, in contrast to their energetic leap to interview any witness that might lend support to Kavanaugh's story, exhibited no interest in what Stier might have to say.

The FBI "did everything we asked them to," Grassley said later, after Robin Pogrebin and Kate Kelly of the *New York Times* pub-

lished *The Education of Brett Kavanaugh*, recounting the Stier allegations. "The problem is, there was just a name given . . . So I
think it's just a case of somebody saying you ought to talk to somebody. That doesn't give you much to go on."[40] Following up on the
Coons letter, a Grassley aide added, "would require that we dedi-
cate resources to cold-calling somebody versus continuing to pursue allegations or claims that we had in front of us that we could
assess. Given that Coons had it and sent it to the FBI, that was
where we left it."

Feinstein was similarly, and perhaps even more infuriatingly,
passive. Coons had made clear he wanted the matter looked into by
the FBI, Feinstein's staff said later, and the committee acceded to his
wishes. Feinstein said later that she "had no other information at that
time," pointing the finger at the FBI. "The FBI did not do the investigations that we hoped they would do," she said.[41] That raises the
question: Where was Feinstein in pressing the FBI to look at Stier?

By this point in the investigation, Coons was barely sleeping.
He repeatedly asked for guidance about where to direct significant potential witnesses and was rebuffed, despite promising to
keep that contact information confidential. Just have them call
the general tip line number, Coons was told. Asking for a more
senior contact seemed like a reasonable request coming from a sitting senator, but it didn't work. Having been shut out by the FBI,
Coons was increasingly desperate to get Stier's information the
attention he thought it deserved, while at the same time preserving
Stier's confidences. He reached out to the colleagues who were
effectively determining the scope of the FBI investigation, having one-on-one conversations with Flake and Murkowski. Coons
wasn't explicit about what Stier had witnessed, but he said he
had a potential corroborating witness, not to that exact incident
but to an almost identical episode. "I have one person you have
to talk to," Coons told Flake. The Arizonan begged off. "I spent
the whole morning dealing with people who are trying to kill my
family," he replied. "I'm sorry, Chris, but that has to be [my] first
priority."[42]

On October 4, the evening before the cloture vote, Coons e-mailed Collins. It was late in the process, he understood, but he had information from Stier that he thought she should know. As Stier had mentioned in his earlier conversation with Coons, Collins had worked closely with him on issues of government reform; she had even served on the advisory board of Stier's group. That was why Stier had tried to reach out to her and was puzzled when he received no response. Now the senator seemed to ignore Coons's note as well.

There was, it turned out, an explanation for her silence in response to Coons's e-mail: Collins's personal e-mail address had been released and she was being deluged with e-mails. She had changed it, and circulated an update to her colleagues, but Coons used the old address. Collins said she did not discover the Coons e-mail until asked about it for this book. She also said she had no recollection and no record of Stier having reached out to her, directly or indirectly, and thought she would have remembered, since he was someone she knew. But it was't entirely clear that the message would have made a difference if it had been received. The cloture vote was the next morning; Collins was working on her speech. "The fact is that the alleged victim has said she has no memories of it at all," Collins said. "If the person who allegedly is harmed has no memory of the incident, then I don't know how you can evaluate the memory of a bystander."[43] Of course the only way to accurately evaluate is to thoroughly investigate, which is precisely what did not happen here.

The FBI's failure to interview Stier, and the Senate's collective failure to insist that he be interviewed, was an inexcusable lapse. Kavanaugh had forcefully denied engaging in any such behavior—not just with Ramirez but with anyone. Perhaps Stier's memory was faulty. Perhaps others could be found to corroborate the incident; Stier's account had other students involved. Who were they? There was no way to be certain, not without a credible investigation. That this did not happen was nothing short of dereliction of duty. FBI officials insisted that they were simply executing the wishes of their client, the White House, and that under a preexisting memorandum of understanding with the White House, the Bureau's ability to interview people was dictated by the instructions it received. Wray, in testimony after Kavanaugh's confirmation, would describe the FBI's conduct as "consistent with the standard process for such investigations going back quite a long ways."[44]

If so, the FBI has a bigger problem than one botched background check. The Bureau is supposed to be the nation's premier investigative agency. Where was its pushback at being so unduly constrained? The FBI's compliant attitude demonstrates a disturbingly narrow vision of its professional responsibilities. The Bureau allowed itself to be used not as a conscientious fact-finder but as a cover to legitimize an investigation that was demonstrably inadequate.

CHAPTER EIGHTEEN

The Vote

I f Trump over the weekend was chafing over the limits on the FBI investigation, by early in the week he had transferred his ire to the Democrats and, more ominously from Republicans' point of view, to Ford herself. Trump had directed criticism at Ford in assorted tweets, but he had been, for the most part, on what passed for good behavior. She had been treated, as Kellyanne Conway later put it, "like a Faberge egg by all of us, beginning with me and the president."[1]

That was about to end.

On Tuesday evening, October 2, Trump flew to Mississippi for a rally, accompanied by the state's two Republican senators. Don't attack her, they implored him. But Trump can only be contained for so long, and at this point the political and communications teams had decided it was time to engage more sharply. They had been holding the president back on the biggest issue of the day. Trump took his prepared remarks and launched into a riff in which he mocked Ford's spotty memory. "'How did you get home?' 'I don't remember.' 'How did you get there?' 'I don't remember.' 'Where is the place?' 'I don't remember.' 'How many years ago was it?' 'I don't know. I don't know. I don't know. I don't know.'" The audience went wild. Trump kept going. "'What neighborhood was it in?' 'I don't know.' 'Where's the house?' 'I don't know.' 'Upstairs, downstairs, where was it?' 'I don't know. But I had one beer, that's the only thing I remember.'"

Trump pivoted from the unfairness to Kavanaugh to the risk

such attacks pose to ordinary Americans. "This is an important time for our country. This is a time when your father, when your husband, when your brother, when your son could do great. 'Mom, I did great in school. I've worked so hard. Mom, I'm so pleased to tell you, I just got a fantastic job with IBM. I just got a fantastic job with General Motors. I just got—I'm so proud.' 'Mom, a terrible thing just happened. A person who I've never met said that I did things that were horrible and they're firing me from my job, Mom. I don't know what to do. Mom, what do I do? What do I do, Mom? What do I do, Mom?'"[2]

Trump's remarks would help frame the midterm debate, turning Kavanaugh into every mother's falsely accused son and amplifying Graham's message of aggrieved outrage. But in the short term, his outburst posed a problem for the audience whose votes he needed more immediately: wavering senators. Flake, Collins, Murkowski, and Manchin all noted their displeasure. Graham called the president and told him, "Don't do this, not helpful." Trump argued back. "They wanted it down there," Trump said. "Well," Graham replied, "they don't get to vote."[3]

Flake's last-minute anxieties were what forced a pause in the process. Yet in the last stage of the confirmation battle, as at the start, Kavanaugh's fate was largely in the hands of just two senators, Collins and Murkowski. With their pro-choice views, they had always been the most likely Republicans to defect and vote against Kavanaugh. Now that volatile issues of gender and sexual assault had entered the debate, the pressure on them was even more intense. The two are best friends in the Senate—Collins's future husband, Tom Daffron, served as Murkowski's chief of staff early in her Senate career—and they tend to vote as a unit. The motto in presidential politics has long been "As Maine goes, so goes the nation." In the Kavanaugh fight, the governing assumption was that where Collins went, so would Murkowski. As a result, McGahn remained focused on Collins throughout. "The only way ever to convince

Don of anything: Does Susan Collins need you to do that?" said one person who worked on the nomination.

Davis, the Grassley aide who had once tried to sink Kavanaugh's nomination but was now working around the clock to get him confirmed, made repeated entreaties to Collins and Murkowski. "Kavanaugh is your guy," he told them—he's not some culture-warrior or right-wing ideologue but an establishment Republican. "He's too big to fail at this point," Davis argued. "If he fails we lose the Senate, Trump loses reelection, we lose the Supreme Court, we lose the country." Then came the warning. "If Kavanaugh fails," Davis said, "you're going to get Amy Coney Barrett next."

At sixty-five, Collins, who grew up in remote Caribou, in the northern corner of the state, was part of a vanishing breed—New England Republican. (There was only one other remaining, a House member from Maine, Bruce Poliquin, and he would lose to a Democrat in November 2018.) The fate of her fellow moderate Republicans was not lost on Collins, who was up for reelection in 2020 in a state that was trending increasingly Democratic. The odds on Collins, however, were always stacked in Kavanaugh's favor. She had never opposed a Supreme Court nominee from a president of either party.

But neither could Collins be taken for granted, as Kavanaugh and his advisers well knew. She had her limits, too. She had written an op-ed for the *Washington Post* in August 2016 announcing that she would not be voting for Trump. "This is not a decision I make lightly, for I am a lifelong Republican," Collins wrote. "But Donald Trump does not reflect historical Republican values nor the inclusive approach to governing that is critical to healing the divisions in our country."[4] She cast a write-in vote for then House speaker Paul Ryan.

Once Trump was elected, Collins was more careful: like every Republican lawmaker in the age of Trump, she had to protect herself from a primary challenge by Trump supporters intolerant of any deviations. She had witnessed Flake's fate up close. Still, Collins on occasion—and on more occasions than most of her colleagues—

had demonstrated her willingness to cross Trump. She voted against repealing the Affordable Care Act, against confirming Scott Pruitt to be administrator of the Environmental Protection Agency, and against confirming Betsy DeVos to be secretary of education.

Collins's father operated the family's lumber mill in tiny Caribou (population 8,189 in 2010), but politics was the family business as well. Both parents served as mayor; her father, grandfather, and great-grandfather were elected to the state legislature. But the experience that defines Collins and best explains her approach to a decision as momentous as a Supreme Court confirmation is her dozen years as a staffer for another moderate Maine Republican, William Cohen.

Collins, then a government student at St. Lawrence University, applied for an internship with Cohen, a family friend and then a freshman congressman, during the fateful summer of 1974. Cohen sat on the House Judiciary Committee, which that July voted to approve articles of impeachment against Richard M. Nixon. Cohen was one of seven Republicans who joined the Democratic majority. In a precursor to the thousands of coat hangers that would be sent to her office by Kavanaugh opponents, Cohen's office, where one of Collins's tasks was to open the mail, was deluged with letters containing tiny stones wrapped in paper: "Let him who is without sin cast the first stone."[5]

A quarter century later, after following Cohen to the Senate and then being elected to his seat herself, Collins, then just a freshman senator, voted against convicting Bill Clinton in his Senate impeachment trial, one of only five Republican senators to take that position. "In voting to acquit the President, I do so with grave misgivings for I do not mean in any way to exonerate this man," Collins said. "He lied under oath; he sought to interfere with the evidence; he tried to influence the testimony of key witnesses."

The speech was classic Collins. The former staffer had immersed herself in the facts against Clinton, painstakingly parsing the evidence against him. Then she pivoted to a nuanced assessment of the Senate's constitutional role. Were she a juror in a criminal obstruction of justice case against Clinton, Collins noted, she might well vote to convict him. But, she said, "as much as it troubles me to acquit this president, I cannot do otherwise and remain true to my role as a Senator. To remove a popularly elected president for the first time in our nation's history is an extraordinary action that should be undertaken only when the President's misconduct so injures the fabric of democracy that the Senate is left with no option but to oust the offender from the office the people have entrusted to him."[6]

Looking back at Clinton's impeachment was not a bad way of understanding Collins's approach to complex issues: painstaking, methodical, and conflicted. The best way to handle the sometimes prickly Mainer, Republicans knew, was to let Collins be Collins—not to lean on her, definitely not to threaten, but instead to ply her with briefings, with access to the nominee and his supporters, as much as she wanted. She had a stubborn side, which would emerge in the course of the confirmation battle. Pushing her was bound to backfire, as McConnell understood. Better to kill her with kindness—or, better yet, information.

If Kavanaugh's close Bush connections had once been a nearly fatal liability, they were now a lifeline, perfectly calibrated to help him win the support of the one senator he needed most. Collins had long-standing ties to the Bush family and often visited them at their Maine retreat, in Kennebunkport. Alumni of the George W. Bush administration, establishment Republicans like Collins, were not shy about sharing with her their impressions of Kavanaugh, from the time he was nominated right up to the frantic close. Her close friend in the Senate, Rob Portman, who had worked with Kavanaugh in the White House, told her how impressively he had performed as staff secretary. She spoke with Karl Rove before she met with the nominee. And, perhaps most significant was that George W. Bush vouched enthusiastically for Kavanaugh.

Collins assembled a phalanx of advisers—including three lawyers who had worked for her, one of whom was Michael Bopp, a Washington attorney who had been her legislative director and general counsel, and a platoon of lawyers from the Congressional Research Service, to assess Kavanaugh's legal record and brief her on it. By Collins's count, the roster of attorneys totaled nineteen. There were six study sessions with the CRS attorneys, plus seven meetings with the current and former staffers prepping her.

A nonlawyer, Collins nonetheless approached her meeting with the nominee as would an advocate preparing for oral argument, reading cases and law review articles. She immersed herself in issues such as severability (whether an entire law should fall if a particular provision is ruled unconstitutional, a critical question when it comes to the Affordable Care Act) and the constitutional dimensions of *stare decisis*. There was no courtesy call for which Kavanaugh prepared more intensively and none that lasted longer. The August 21 session, attended by Collins's legal brain trust, would stretch more than two hours, truncated only because Collins had to leave for a vote. "There were times when I think she felt that he was being a little too cautious and noncommittal, and I think she pressed as hard as she felt was responsible," said Stephen Diamond, a Maine lawyer and former Collins staffer who attended the meeting.[7] As the session broke up, Kavanaugh offered to wait around until Collins returned from the vote. His handlers "just looked at him with utter frustration on their faces, and said, 'You've already spent twice as long with Senator Collins as any other senator,'" Collins recalled.[8]

The investment of time paid off. Collins emerged from the meeting calling it "excellent" and touting Kavanaugh's statement to her that *Roe v. Wade* was "settled law."[9] That, it seemed, would settle it for Collins.

From the point of view of Kavanaugh's opponents, convincing Collins to vote against him presented a paradox. Pushing too hard could boomerang, yet there was no way to persuade her to vote no without a significant public outcry, as much as she insisted she was immune to such tactics. For too long, some progressive activists in Maine thought, Collins had been treated with kid gloves, lavished with praise on the rare occasions when she did the right thing from the liberal point of view and never held to account when she marched in lockstep with the conservative majority.

This time would be different. Protesters dressed in *Handmaid's Tale* costumes demonstrated outside her Bangor home. Even before Collins's meeting with Kavanaugh, two progressive groups, Mainers for Accountable Leadership and Maine People's Alliance, along with Ady Barkan, a health care activist with amyotrophic lateral sclerosis, announced plans for a crowdfunding effort to raise money for a to-be-named Collins opponent—*if* the senator voted for Kavanaugh. (The money would be returned to donors if Collins voted against the nominee.) The donations poured in, most in amounts of $20.20; by September 12, just as the Ford story was beginning to break, the effort had raised more than $1 million. Collins was furious, calling the campaign "the equivalent of an attempt to bribe me."[10]

Meantime, the calls and letters flooding her Senate office at times crossed the line from angry to abusive, further alienating Collins. Her office was happy to supply details. There was the caller who left a voice mail saying, "If you care at all about women's choice, vote no on Kavanaugh. Don't be a dumb bitch. Fuck you also." There was the letter writer who warned, "EVERY waitress who serves you is going to spit in your food, and that's if you're lucky, you fucking cunt! Think of that every meal." In one episode that particularly upset Collins, a caller told a young female staffer that he hoped she would be raped and impregnated.[11]

For all her public posture that she was immune to pressure tactics, the assault was beginning to take its toll. At one of the weekly Republican Senate lunches, the ads running against Collins were played on the screens in the room so that her colleagues had a sense of what she was up against. They were mostly in safe red states; this was not a hard vote for them. For Collins, the politics were far more precarious. "For all of you here, it's pretty easy, but in Maine they're running commercials on me," Collins told her colleagues. "You need to see what they're doing."

But if Collins was paying attention to the onslaught of ads, they were not having the effect that advocates had hoped. As the first round of hearings concluded, Collins made the decision that seemed fated all along. She would vote for Kavanaugh. The announcement was written, and she was prepared to deliver it just as the first hints of the Ford story began to emerge.

The pressure only heightened once the Ford story broke. Collins's staff was fielding threats; one aide in Maine quit because she was so upset about the abuse. Collins struggled. She reached out to friends of Kavanaugh, including Lisa Blatt, a liberal Supreme Court advocate who had introduced Kavanaugh at the hearing, asking if they could imagine him doing anything like this. No, they assured her. Bush had called two days after the nomination; now he reached out again, two days after the *Post* story on Ford. Condoleezza Rice, Bush's national security adviser, spoke with Collins the day after Ford's testimony. And visiting the ailing elder Bush at Kennebunkport, Collins saw Portman and longtime George W. Bush aide Joe Hagin, who had just left his position as deputy chief of staff at the Trump White House. As a Bush staffer, Hagin had spent weeks sharing a double-wide trailer with Kavanaugh at the ranch in Crawford. Could the person he knew so well have done such a thing? Inconceivable, he assured Collins.

From the opposite end of the country, Lisa Murkowski faced a set of political considerations in weighing the Kavanaugh nomination that made her political situation more similar to Collins's than would be apparent at first glance, comparing purplish Maine to bright-red Alaska. Murkowski, sixty-one, had been named by her father, Frank Murkowski, to fill his unexpired term when he became Alaska governor, in 2002. She won a close race for a full term in 2004, beating former Democratic governor Tony Knowles by just three points. Alaska was Republican territory: the only Democratic presidential candidate to win the state in the fifteen elections held since it entered the union, in 1959, was Lyndon Johnson,

in his 1964 landslide. While Trump lost Maine by three percentage points, his margin over Hillary Clinton in Alaska was fifteen
points. But the redness of the state did not dictate the contours of
Murkowski's politics when it came to Kavanaugh.

In the formative experience of her political career, Murkowski
found herself blindsided in 2010 by a Sarah Palin–backed Tea Party
challenger, Joe Miller. When Miller, a little-known Fairbanks lawyer, unexpectedly beat Murkowski in the GOP primary by 2,006
votes, she pondered her options for three weeks, then mounted a
write-in campaign against Miller. It was an uphill, and ugly, battle.
National Republican leaders closed ranks behind Miller; Republican consultants and pollsters in the Lower 48 recoiled from working for Murkowski for fear of being blackballed.[12] Murkowski was
asked to resign from the Senate Republican leadership. "I informed
her that by choosing to run a campaign against the Republican
nominee, she no longer has my support for serving in any leadership roles," McConnell said at the time.[13] No senator had won
election as a write-in candidate since South Carolina's Strom Thurmond in 1954, and Murkowski had the extra challenge of teaching
voters to spell her name correctly.

Two groups propelled Murkowski to her improbable victory—
Alaskan natives and women. They played a central role, eight years
later, in the Kavanaugh battle. The Alaska Federation of Natives
announced its opposition to Kavanaugh on September 12, just
before the Ford story broke, criticizing what it saw as Kavanaugh's
hostility toward federal protection of tribes.[14] Hawaii senator Mazie
Hirono had deliberately laid the groundwork for this opposition in
her questioning of Kavanaugh. The subject matter was arcane—
the contours of the Indian Commerce Clause and the legal status of
Alaskan natives—but Hirono's questioning was microtargeted at
an audience of one. She never lobbied Murkowski directly, but she
knew her colleague would be listening closely.

Women's groups in Alaska—in particular, abortion rights
activists—were geared up from the start to battle Kavanaugh. With
the emergence of the Ford allegations, that opposition kicked into

higher, and more emotional, gear with last-minute meetings that would, in the end, help Murkowski come to a final decision on what she described as perhaps the closest call of her Senate career.

An arcane bit of Senate procedure set the stage for the conclusion of the fight. On Wednesday evening, October 3, McConnell filed a motion to invoke cloture on the Kavanaugh nomination. That meant the first hurdle would be a vote Friday morning to end debate on the nomination—the critical test of whether Kavanaugh would have the fifty votes he needed. The second, final vote could then take place once thirty hours had elapsed, on Saturday afternoon.

Early the next morning, around 2:30, the FBI submitted its report on Kavanaugh and delivered the material to the Senate. The interview summaries totaled forty-five pages, and there were another 1,600 pages of information from the FBI tip line. Only 109 people would have access to the documents—the senators, four staffers each from the majority and minority, and a committee clerk.[15]

As senators spent Thursday reviewing the report in a secure facility known as a SCIF (secure compartmented information facility), set up in the bowels of the Capitol Visitor Center, Ramirez's and Ford's legal teams sent Wray final letters expressing their disappointment with an investigation that Katz, Banks, and Bromwich called "a stain on the process, on the FBI and on our American ideal of justice." They again listed possible interviewees and noted, rather forlornly, "They remain available to talk with law enforcement."[16] Despite repeated requests, Bromwich had never even been told the name of the lead agent on the investigation. The Ramirez lawyers directed the FBI to some two dozen interviewees. Only a few were called. Those who tried to reach out found that calling the Denver field-office number—as the agents who interviewed Ramirez had said they should do—yielded only an endless phone tree with no human being available. Now that the investigation was over, Ramirez's lawyers sent Wray the sworn declarations of Richard Oh, the Yale classmate who recalled hearing a woman tearfully describe an incident like the one Ramirez recalled, and the unnamed friend whom Ramirez had told about the incident several years later. Both had been unable to reach the FBI.[17] Senators might never read their accounts, but at least they would be part of the record.

Republicans and Democrats took turns reading the documents, with control of the room rotating every hour. There was only a single copy of the material, divided among a dozen folders, which made digesting it all the more difficult. During Republicans' early hours in the room, the judiciary staff read out loud from the materials. Democrats divided up the material among themselves, passing around the sections and discussing the most relevant parts.

Republicans had developed something of a buddy system, with Kavanaugh proponents shadowing the wavering members. Flake and Lee spent much of the day together in the SCIF, studying the report. "So I'm a yes," Lee told his friend. He didn't see any corroborating evidence for the allegations. Flake agreed: he said he, too, would vote to confirm. Portman spent much of his time in the SCIF with Collins, who attended a staff briefing in the morning and returned later to read through the material herself. In another piece of good news for Kavanaugh, Manchin indicated privately that he planned to vote yes, though it would be another twenty-four hours before that became public.[18] Collins and Murkowski were the wild cards, although with Manchin seemingly in favor, and Collins predisposed to Kavanaugh, things were looking good. "It appears," she observed, "to be a very thorough investigation." Said Flake, "Thus far, we've seen no new credible corroboration. No new corroboration at all."[19]

Democrats had a dramatically different interpretation. "The most notable part of this report is what's not in it," Feinstein said.[20] Durbin was in the SCIF with more than a dozen fellow Democrats that afternoon, sitting next to Maryland senator Ben Cardin as they read through the reports. "Obvious questions and lines of inquiry were not followed," Durbin said later. "Witnesses would say they had a spotty recollection but suggest someone else to speak with, but it just seemed like they were determined to do the requisite number, end the interviews, be finished. It was a real disappointment."[21]

For Democrats, the perceived shoddiness of the investigation would not affect their vote; most had long before come out against Kavanaugh. Heidi Heitkamp was in a different posture. She was facing a difficult election in a ruby-red state and was unlikely to win in any event. But voting against Kavanaugh was not going to help her case with North Dakota voters. As a matter of sheer politics it was the wrong move. As she sat in the SCIF with her colleagues, Heitkamp looked up from the documents. "I believe her, and I don't believe him, and I'm voting against him," she announced. "There was silence in the room because we realized she was going to lose her election," Durbin said. "There were tears shed, and embraces."[22]

In hindsight, there are two ways to think about the FBI investigation. The rosier, more charitable one is that, for all its manifest limitations, at least the insistence on a pause and an investigation signaled to women across the country that their allegations would be taken seriously, that their complaints would no longer be brushed aside. Some progress, in this view, was better than none at all. Indeed, Democratic senators still say that constituents approach them and offer quiet thanks for ensuring that Ford's voice was heard and for giving them courage to tell their own stories of harassment and assault. The more negative, and perhaps more accurate, assessment is that the FBI investigation was, as Trump had predicted, "a blessing in disguise" for Republicans. As much as they had resisted the probe, it served to give Kavanaugh's confirmation an aura of legitimacy that it would not otherwise have had.

One unexpected voice that day belonged to retired Justice John Paul Stevens. Speaking at an event for retirees in Boca Raton, Stevens said Kavanaugh's remarks "suggest that he has demonstrated a potential bias involving enough potential litigants before the court that he would not be able to perform his full responsibilities. And I think there is merit in that criticism and that the senators should really pay attention to it."

The ninety-eight-year-old Stevens, a Gerald Ford appointee who had ended up being a liberal leader on the court before retiring in 2010, said he had thought of Kavanaugh as "a fine federal judge, and he should have been confirmed when he was nominated." But, he said, "Kavanaugh's performance during the hearings caused me to change my mind," and he went so far as to contrast Kavanaugh, unfavorably, with Clarence Thomas. "There's nothing that Clarence did in the hearings that disqualified him from sitting in cases after he came on the court," Stevens said. "You cannot help but like Clarence Thomas, which I don't think necessarily would be true of this particular nominee."[23] Even from a retired justice, it was an amazing public rebuke.

As Republicans and Democrats shuttled in and out of the SCIF to review the FBI materials, Murkowski met in her office with Alaskan women who had flown to the capital, a journey underwritten by the American Civil Liberties Union, for a last-ditch lobbying campaign. The ACLU did not routinely wade into the judicial nominations wars, but it had departed from that policy in several past circumstances, opposing Rehnquist, Bork, and Alito. This, the group decided in the wake of the Ford allegations, was another of those "extraordinary circumstances."[24] Casey Reynolds of the Alaska ACLU received a call from the national organization: we can give you $100,000 to get Alaskans to Washington. Then, as dozens of Alaskan women clamored to be included, it came up with another $100,000.[25]

There was some reason to think that Murkowski might be receptive to their arguments. In the week before Ford's testimony, Liz Ruskin, a reporter for Alaska Public Media, had asked Murkowski if she had experienced her own #MeToo moment. "She answered with an immediate and emphatic 'yes,'" Ruskin reported. "And that's about all she wanted to say about that."[26] The Kavanaugh confirmation, Murkowski said then, had transcended the question of his qualifications. "We are now in a place where it's . . . about whether or not a woman who has been a victim at some point in her life is to be believed."[27]

Around 120 women came from Alaska to the capital to make the case against confirming Kavanaugh. Murkowski met with two groups of them on Thursday afternoon, around eighteen each. The first were women lawyers organized by an Anchorage attorney, Michelle Nesbett. They crowded into a room in Murkowski's fifth-floor office in the Hart Senate Office Building. As the women gathered around the table and perched on the arms of a couch, protesters thronging the building's atrium could be heard shouting about Kavanaugh. The lawyers' argument was not about Kavanaugh's ideology or even his alleged assault of Ford. It was that Kavanaugh's conduct in his testimony demonstrated an alarming absence of judicial temperament. Nesbett handed Murkowski a copy of the American Bar Association's Code of Judicial Conduct, Rule 1.2, which provides that "a judge should act at all times in a manner that promotes public confidence in the integrity and impartiality of the judiciary." How could anyone who watched Kavanaugh believe he had done that? Murkowski seemed relieved that the lawyers were not haranguing her about Kavanaugh's position on *Roe v. Wade* or native rights.

One of those present was Moira Smith, an Anchorage lawyer who had, after the release of Trump's *Access Hollywood* tape, accused Clarence Thomas of groping her at a 1999 dinner party.[28] "We already have one person who has the cloud of sexual harassment allegations on the court," Smith said. "I don't think we as a country would be well-served to have another." Another woman, Carolyn Heyman, became teary-eyed as she told Murkowski that one of her daughters asked why women were believed less than men after Ford came forward. Nesbett was forceful. "You cannot vote to confirm this guy," she told Murkowski. "If you do so it will be a betrayal to the women of Alaska."

The next meeting, with women who had been victims of sexual assault, was even more powerful—it stretched to well over an hour as woman after woman described her experience and talked about the terrible message that confirming Kavanaugh would send. One, a native Alaskan, described how she and nearly every other woman in her family—her mother, her aunt, her sisters—had been the victim of rape. Another brought photos of her baby daughter, saying that she had been sexually assaulted and did not want her daughter raised in a society where such actions have no consequences. Still another described having been the victim of a date rape in high school, how she had not filed a complaint because it would have been his word against hers, and how believable she found Ford. Murkowski mentioned her own #MeToo moment, without elaborating. She seemed burdened, almost devastated. "I feel six inches shorter than when I walked in here," Murkowski told the women as the meeting broke up. "I'm so humbled by all of your stories."

At 10:30 that night, she headed back to the SCIF to take one last look at the FBI report.

By the time a nomination makes it to the Senate floor, the outcome is almost always a foregone conclusion. Bork had pressed for a floor vote even though his nomination was by then a lost cause. Everyone knew Thomas had the votes to win once the Hill testimony had concluded. With Kavanaugh, the situation was more precarious. It wasn't exactly a cliff-hanger—even if Murkowski turned out to be a no, all signals were that Flake, and probably Collins, had been mollified by the FBI investigation—but no one knew for certain. If two Republicans peeled off, would Manchin follow? He had quietly let the White House know the day before that he would be a yes, but no one was sure what might happen if his turned out to be the deciding vote. There was a risk that Republicans could be in for a repeat of the health care vote, when McCain's surprise thumbs-down doomed the bill. "This was one of the rare instances where I didn't know," Cornyn, the Republican whip, said.[29] The cloture vote set for that morning would almost certainly signal the final outcome.

As Grassley spoke on the Senate floor, the angry tenor of his remarks reflected the intensity of the battle. "What left-wing groups and their Democratic allies have done to Judge Kavanaugh is nothing short of monstrous," Grassley said. "I saw what they did to Robert Bork. I saw what they did to Clarence Thomas. That was nothing compared to what we have witnessed in the last three months. The conduct of left-wing, dark money groups and their allies in this body has shamed us all. The fix was in from the very beginning." He flayed Feinstein for having "shamefully sat on" the Ford allegations and declared, "It would be a travesty if the Senate did not confirm the most qualified nominee in our nation's history."[30]

Grassley's anger over the delay in informing him about Ford's allegations was understandable. What is not understandable, in hindsight—or is at least not forgivable—is that Grassley, having been informed by Coons about a potentially critical witness, pressed forward with a vote and never apparently paused to consider whether this avenue of inquiry should be pursued.

Instead Grassley proclaimed, "There is nothing in the supplemental FBI background investigation report that we didn't already know. These uncorroborated accusations have been unequivocally and repeatedly rejected by Judge Kavanaugh, and neither the Judiciary Committee nor the FBI could locate any third parties who can attest to any of the allegations."[31] That was false. The Judiciary Committee and the FBI had been made aware of a third party, Stier. They simply chose not to pursue the information he was eager to provide. As a consequence, senators who trooped to the secure facility to make their way through the FBI's findings, only to conclude there was nothing there, had no way of knowing what might have been there had those responsible behaved appropriately.

Feinstein, who bears her own share of the blame for not following up on Coons's letter, rose to respond to Grassley's assault. This was her ninth Supreme Court nomination, she said, and "never before have we had a Supreme Court nominee where over 90 percent of his record has been hidden from the public and the Senate. Never before have we had a nominee display such flagrant partisanship and open hostility at a hearing, and never before have we had a nominee facing allegations of sexual assault."[32] Schumer, following her, was even more biting. Kavanaugh's nomination, he said, "will go down as one of the saddest, most sordid in the long history of the federal judiciary."[33]

Collins had been up until two a.m. working on her floor speech. Five hours later, the protestors who had been gathering outside her Capitol Hill town house for days now began their chanting. Collins checked in with Murkowski, to tell her she planned to vote for Kavanaugh. Murkowski responded that she was still undecided. The Alaskan would later tell colleagues that she hadn't known for sure until she walked onto the Senate floor how she would vote. With the roll call set for 10:30, the chamber was filling up. Murkowski arrived slightly before Collins. The pair sat in their usual seats, side by side, third row from the front, just across the aisle from the Democrats. Murkowski reached over and touched Collins on the arm. "I just want you to know that I can't vote for him," she said. The Maine senator broke into a huge smile. "That's great," Collins said. "I have to admit, I'm relieved." "No, you misheard me," Murkowski corrected her. "I said I'm not voting for him."[34]

The clerk called the roll, in alphabetical order. Yes, Collins said. When it came to Murkowski, she stood and paused. Her voice was barely above a whisper as she voted: "No." Murkowski sat down, expressionless. She and Collins sat side by side, hands clasped in their laps, stone-faced. Toward the end of the vote, Collins leaned toward Murkowski, putting her hand on the Alaskan's chair as the two spoke.

Collins's vote on cloture was a major signal but not an ironclad guarantee. There had been times in the past when Collins would support getting a controversial nominee or piece of legislation to the floor only to oppose it on final passage. She would explain herself, and outline her final position, in a floor speech at 3:00 p.m.

Collins headed to the Senate Dining Room for what she thought would be a solo lunch, holding a copy of the speech she had stayed up writing until early that morning. McConnell and Cornyn waved her over; did she want to join them? "I think they were all exercising great control," not asking her what she would do, Collins recalled. "And so I told them that I had decided to vote for Judge Kavanaugh and that I felt that it was the right thing to do."[35] Collins's counsel, Katie Brown, went up to Davis as Collins headed into the chamber. "You're going to like this," she told the Grassley aide.

For anyone who was still in suspense about how Collins would come down, the setting was a tell. Sitting behind her as she spoke were three female colleagues. Shelley Moore Capito of West Virginia, Cindy Hyde-Smith of Mississippi, and Joni Ernst of Iowa shifted from their ordinary seats in order to present an all-woman tableau. As she began to speak, protesters began to scream. "Vote no! Show up for Maine women!" Collins looked down at her notes until they were led out of the chamber.

Her opening words sealed the deal. "Today," Collins said, "we have come to the conclusion of a confirmation process that has become so dysfunctional, it looks more like a caricature of a gutter-level political campaign than a solemn occasion." She inveighed against a process that had become so partisan that interest groups decried the nominee even before his identity became known. She ticked through the substantive questions about Kavanaugh—whether he would overturn protections for people with preexisting conditions, whether he would rule reflexively for Trump, whether he would jettison *Roe v. Wade*—and dismissed each in turn.[36]

Kavanaugh had not only assured her of his respect for precedent and reluctance to overturn it, Collins emphasized, he had also located the command of such reluctance, *stare decisis*, within the Constitution itself—an approach that, Collins asserted, provided additional assurance that Kavanaugh would not be overturning cases on a whim. Those who disagreed had been proved wrong in the past, Collins said, citing the buttons that the National Organization for Women circulated in 1990—STOP SOUTER OR WOMEN WILL DIE.

As to the Ford allegations, Collins said, "the Senate confirmation process is not a trial. But certain fundamental legal principles about due process, the presumption of innocence, and fairness do bear on my thinking, and I cannot abandon them. In evaluating any given claim of misconduct we will be ill served in the long run if we abandon the presumption of innocence and fairness, tempting though it may be."

Collins turned opponents' argument that confirming Kavanaugh would undermine confidence in the judiciary on its head. "The presumption of innocence is relevant to the advice and consent function when an accusation departs from a nominee's otherwise exemplary record," Collins said. "I worry that departing from this presumption could lead to a lack of public faith in the judiciary and would be hugely damaging to the confirmation process moving forward."

As to Ford, Collins acknowledged, her testimony was "sincere, painful, and compelling," adding, "I believe that she is a survivor of a sexual assault and that this trauma has upended her life." But she said she was disturbed by the fact that none of the others Ford identified as having been present could corroborate her account. If Ford had left the party distraught, Collins wondered, why did no one, including her close friend Leland Keyser, check back with her the next day?

"The facts presented do not mean that Professor Ford was not sexually assaulted that night—or at some other time—but they do lead me to conclude that the allegations fail to meet the 'more likely than not' standard," Collins said. "Therefore, I do not believe that these charges can fairly prevent Judge Kavanaugh from serving on the Court."

She ended with a plea that seemed disengaged from the reality of the moment. "Despite the turbulent, bitter fight surrounding his nomination," Collins concluded, "my fervent hope is that Brett Kavanaugh will work to lessen the divisions in the Supreme Court so that we have far fewer 5–4 decisions and so that public confidence in our Judiciary and our highest court is restored."[37]

As Collins spoke, Kavanaugh and several clerks had gathered in his chambers, which had no television and balky WiFi. So rather than watching her live, they were reduced to following what she was saying—and learning the final verdict—via text messages from another clerk, who was relating Collins's comments in real time.

Republican praise for Collins poured in, many comparing her to Margaret Chase Smith, the moderate Maine Republican senator renowned for being among the first to stand up to Joseph McCarthy. There were many things to admire about Collins's handling of the nomination. She had devoted more time to assessing Kavanaugh's record and spoken to more people about the nominee than any senator not on the Judiciary Committee and perhaps more than some who served on the panel. But it was difficult, listening to Collins, to escape the notion that the entire enterprise had been geared to an inevitable conclusion. She consistently assessed every piece of evidence in the light most favorable to Kavanaugh.

After Collins finished, McConnell led Republicans in a standing ovation. Grassley gave her a bear hug, then, in tears, retreated to the Republican cloakroom. As Grassley collected himself, South Carolina senator Tim Scott came to his side, asking, "Chuck, can I pray for you?"

Four minutes after Collins concluded her remarks, Manchin tweeted: "I will vote to support Supreme Court nominee Judge Brett Kavanaugh."[38] Manchin retained "reservations about this vote given the serious accusations against Judge Kavanaugh and the temperament he displayed in the hearing," he said in a longer statement. However, he said, he had been persuaded that Kavanaugh was "a qualified jurist who will follow the Constitution" and who had assured him that, in weighing the future of coverage for people with preexisting conditions, "he would consider the human impacts and approach any decision with surgical precision to avoid unintended consequences."[39]

Manchin, who often hosted Chuck Schumer for drinks aboard

the houseboat the West Virginian lived in when in the capital, had once promised the minority leader that, if it came to that point, he would not provide the fiftieth vote for Kavanaugh. As the prospect of defeating Kavanaugh came closer to reality with the emergence of Ford, the two would disagree about the nature of that promise and how binding it was. But all that was immaterial. Now Manchin's position did not matter, at least not to the question of whether Kavanaugh would be confirmed. Kavanaugh had the votes with or without Manchin.

Manchin, who also had a harrowing meeting with women sharing their stories of sexual assault, had read the FBI report the day before. With two statements ready to go—one for Kavanaugh, one against—he returned to the SCIF right before the vote and concluded that there was not enough information to oppose Kavanaugh. "I can't not give the guy a job with no evidence," he told his staff.

For his yes vote, Manchin was rewarded with a nasty tweet from Donald Trump Jr. "A real profile in courage from Lyin' liberal @JoeManchinWV," the president's elder son tweeted. "Waited until Kavanaugh had enough votes secured before he announced his support. I bet he had another press release ready to go if Collins went the other way."[40]

George H.W. Bush also weighed in, not long after Collins had finished her remarks. "@SenatorCollins—political courage and class," he tweeted. "I salute my wonderful friend and her principled leadership."[41] It was the 41st president's final tweet.

Murkowski returned Friday evening to the Senate chamber, now nearly empty, to explain her vote in what she described as the "gut-wrenching" process of the Kavanaugh nomination. In a somber voice, she said that, in the end, she was not opposing Kavanaugh because she feared he would vote to overturn *Roe v. Wade*, strip protections for people with preexisting conditions, or pose a threat to the rights of Alaska natives. Kavanaugh was a "learned judge," she said, and a "good man." But his appearance before the committee had rattled her and made her doubt that he had met the standard in the code of judicial conduct, which stipulates that a judge should "act at all times in a manner that promotes public confidence." Public confidence, Murkowski repeated, in a soft, pained voice. "Where's the public confidence?"[42]

Murkowski said she had been "deliberating, agonizing about what is fair. Is this too unfair a burden to place on somebody that is dealing with the worst, the most horrific allegations that go to your integrity, that go to everything that you are? And I think we all struggle with how we would respond."

But, she said, "I am reminded there are only nine seats on the bench of the highest court in the land . . . With my conscience, I could not conclude that he is the right person for the court at this time. And this has been agonizing for me with this decision. It is as hard a choice, probably as close a call as any that I can ever remember."

When Kavanaugh's nomination came up for final passage the next day, Murkowski said, she would be voting present, not against the nomination. It was not a statement on the merits but a token of friendship—pairing her vote against that of a colleague who disagreed so that they would cancel each other out—to accommodate Montana Republican Steve Daines, whose daughter was being married that day. "At just about the same hour that we're going to be voting, he's going to be walking his daughter down the aisle, and he won't be present to vote, and so I have extended this as a courtesy to my friend," Murkowski said. "It will not change the outcome of the vote, but I do hope that it reminds us that we can take very small, very small steps to be gracious with one another, and maybe those small, gracious steps can lead to more."[43] It was a brief moment of decency in an otherwise ugly process.

As Murkowski concluded her remarks, there was no applause.

The debate stretched on through Saturday morning and into the afternoon as the Senate slogged through the allotted time toward an outcome that was no longer in doubt. Among the pathetic few powers that Democrats retained was the ability to insist on running out the full thirty hours. And so at 4:02 a.m. on Saturday, Oregon Democrat Jeff Merkley took to the floor for more than two hours, reading from the letters of thirty-eight women who described being victims of sexual assault and harassment. "There are so many more letters pouring into my office, reading, 'Take our experiences seriously. Take seriously the voices of Dr. Ford and Debbie Ramirez,'" Merkley said. "This institution has failed them."[44]

Ramirez, who had not been heard from publicly since *The New Yorker* story ran, issued a statement. "Thirty-five years ago, the other students in the room chose to laugh and look the other way as sexual violence was perpetrated on me by Brett Kavanaugh," she wrote. "As I watch many of the Senators speak and vote on the floor of the Senate I feel like I'm right back at Yale where half the room is laughing and looking the other way. Only this time, instead of drunk college kids, it is U.S. Senators who are deliberately ignoring his behavior. This is how victims are isolated and silenced."[45]

As the time for the vote drew near, Vice President Pence sat in the chair, presiding. In the front row of the gallery was McGahn, the White House counsel who had fought so hard to get Kavanaugh confirmed. Leonard Leo and Jonathan Bunch of the Federalist Society were in the chamber; so were the bevy of Kavanaugh clerks who had worked on the nomination, including Travis Lenkner, Porter Wilkinson, and Claire Murray. Katz and Banks, the Ford lawyers, had space in Schumer's box. At 3:44, the clerk began to call the roll. It was an emotional scene as demonstrators, many wearing black T-shirts, began yelling and were escorted—dragged, in some cases—out of the chamber, their voices echoing down the marble hallways as they were removed. "Shame, shame, shame!" one woman cried. "This is a stain on American history. Do you understand that?" screamed another. Five times, Pence had to halt the vote, rapping his gavel to restore order. "The sergeant at arms will restore order in the gallery," he instructed time after time, seemingly unperturbed by the spectacle.

The clerk called the roll in alphabetical order: "Mr. Gardner, aye. Mrs. Gillibrand, nay. Mr. Graham, aye." Grassley, anxious to have it all over, rose to his feet at "Gillibrand," even before his name was called. He cast his vote, and, before the roll call was done, walked out of the chamber, not even letting his aides know he was leaving. They had wanted him to take a victory lap on the Sunday shows, but Grassley wasn't interested. He wanted to get home to Iowa.

The outcome was as expected: 50–48. It was the closest margin for a successful nominee since the little-known Stanley Matthews was confirmed in 1881 by a vote of 24–23, the closest in history. "I always thought landslides were kind of boring anyway," McConnell said later.[46]

Colleagues gathered around Collins after she cast her vote. "Well, they're going to come after me with everything they can get," she said. "You don't worry," Graham replied. "We've got Sheldon Adelson as chairman of your campaign finance committee," referring to the Las Vegas casino billionaire who was the GOP's most generous donor. Collins was all but certain to have a tough race on her hands in 2020, tougher now with the Kavanaugh vote. She sometimes exasperated her colleagues and sometimes disappointed them. On Kavanaugh, however, she had delivered. The party—and its financiers—would not forget.

Senators and staff gathered underneath the crystal chandeliers in the majority leader's office suite to celebrate with champagne and sweets that evening. McConnell gave a toast, thanking his chief lawyer John Abegg, and Mike Davis, then talking about the importance of the broader mission they had all embarked on, to confirm conservative judges. In addition to the champagne, a special drink was served, concocted for the occasion. They called it "mule piss."

The security detail brought Kavanaugh and his family from his home in Chevy Chase to the Supreme Court. As throngs of demonstrators surrounded the building, the cars drove into the basement and Kavanaugh was escorted to his new chambers. They had been Alito's before he moved into Kennedy's old space and William Brennan's before that. Now they were empty, awaiting the arrival of the newest justice, computer terminals sitting on bare desks.

The private swearing-in occurred just a few hours after the vote, in the justices' private conference room, beneath a portrait of the fourth chief justice, John Marshall. Roberts and Kennedy administered the oaths; Thomas, Alito, Ginsburg, and Kagan made it to the hastily arranged ceremony. Sunday morning, as Kavanaugh and his clerks prepared in the new chambers for his first oral arguments on Tuesday, an unexpected message appeared in Ed Kavanaugh's e-mail. Ralph Blasey, Ford's father, reached out to his golf club friend to say that both families had gone through a hard time and that he was glad Kavanaugh had been confirmed. Throughout the ordeal, Ralph Blasey and his family had remained silent in public; they were a private family and wanted to preserve as much dignity as possible under the difficult circumstances. But Ralph and Paula Blasey had been quietly supportive of their daughter; she had always been one to speak up, and they were proud of her, they told her. Ralph Blasey passed along supportive messages to Christine from his friends. Did this e-mail, saying flatly that he was glad Brett had been confirmed, suggest that he did not believe his daughter or was discounting the significance of what had happened to her? It was tempting, if you were a Kavanaugh partisan, to interpret it that way.[47]

The public swearing-in took place Monday night in the White House East Room, a legally unnecessary but hard-to-resist victory dance, complete with cocktails and a band. By this point, Trump had abandoned any pretense of a respectful approach toward Kavanaugh's accusers. Leaving the White House on his way to speak to police chiefs in Florida on Monday morning, Trump called Kavanaugh "a man that did nothing wrong, a man that was caught up in a hoax that was set up by the Democrats, using the Democrats' lawyers."[48]

On his way back, Trump fiddled with the text of his speech, marking it up with a Sharpie. McGahn won't like it, Trump told aides, but there was a particular point he wanted to make. And so, in the East Room that night, before the assembled justices of the Supreme Court, Trump let it rip. "On behalf of our nation, I want to apologize to Brett and the entire Kavanaugh family for the terrible pain and suffering you have been forced to endure," Trump said, adding, "I must state that you, sir, under historic scrutiny, were proven innocent."[49] The move was vintage Trump—inflaming and overstating where another president might have attempted to soothe, turning what might have been liability into electoral advantage.

Kavanaugh alluded to the "contentious and emotional" confirmation but said that was behind him. "I take this office with gratitude and no bitterness," he said. "I was not appointed to serve one party or one interest, but to serve one nation."[50]

At ten the next morning, Kavanaugh took the bench for the first time, wearing the same robes he used on the appeals court. Protesters had arrived before sunrise, hoisting signs that read WE THE PEOPLE DO NOT CONSENT and WE WILL NOT FORGET as black SUVs with tinted windows whisked the justices into the garage. Inside the marble chamber, all was business as usual, save for the rearranged seating assignments to accommodate the newest member, who took his spot at the end of the bench.

"Justice Kavanaugh," Roberts said in the traditional greeting, "we wish you a long and happy career in our common calling."

The Aftermath

I t had taken 101 days from Anthony Kennedy's retirement to Brett Kavanaugh's confirmation, but the aftereffects of the vote would reverberate long after—for the political parties, for the individuals involved, and for the court itself.

In an interview with the *Washington Post* hours before Kavanaugh's near-certain confirmation, McConnell was jubilant—not only because Kavanaugh had made it through but also because the politics of the nomination battle were looking like a welcome electoral plus for Republicans. "It's been a great political gift for us," McConnell said. "I want to thank the mob, because they've done the one thing we were having trouble doing, which was energizing our base."[1]

McConnell had even more reason to celebrate on Election Day, when voters ousted four incumbent Democrats who voted against Kavanaugh—McCaskill, Heitkamp, and Donnelly, along with Florida's Bill Nelson. (Manchin, the sole Democrat to back Kavanaugh, survived.) What was less clear was the degree to which the Kavanaugh vote determined those outcomes or whether those senators were already destined to lose, their opposition to Kavanaugh simply hammering another nail in an already closed coffin.

McCaskill, Heitkamp, and Donnelly were convinced that Kavanaugh had helped propel them to defeat and bitter about the fact that the letter had come out at the last minute. "The process was fatally flawed," Heitkamp said. "If there's one wish I have it's that Senator Feinstein would have shared this letter with Senator Grassley."[2]

From the moment of Kennedy's retirement, McCaskill said, "I knew it was trouble, and it turned out to be even more trouble because of the spectacle that it turned into." While "I think I could have survived a no vote," McCaskill said, "it was the late-breaking letter and the kind of hearing that it devolved into that did it for most voters, especially most voters in my state that don't see elections through a party prism."[3]

Collins was not up for reelection that November, but there was every indication that she was taking the 2020 race seriously—and that Graham's promise that the party would take care of her was bearing fruit. A group of Kavanaugh supporters held an emotional fund-raiser for Collins the month after the confirmation vote. Collins told the group that the police in Maine had stationed a dummy car outside her home for protection; McConnell stopped by to express his support. By the end of June 2019, Collins had collected an impressive $6.45 million—as much as she had raised in her entire previous campaign, with sixteen months to go.[4] An astonishing 96 percent of the money came from out of state, compared to 69 percent during her last race.[5] Sheldon Adelson and his wife, Miriam, contributed the maximum amount, $11,200 combined.[6] And Leonard Leo hosted a fund-raiser for Collins in August 2019 at his summer home in Maine.[7]

But Collins's Kavanaugh vote had taken a toll on her popularity. A few days after the Leo event, the *Cook Political Report* changed its assessment of the Maine Senate race from "lean Republican" to "toss-up."[8]

Because of continuing security threats, Ford and her family were not able to return to their home until Christmas Eve, which meant that they had been living in hotels and, toward the end, a borrowed home for more than three months. The emotional toll was often more difficult than the physical displacement. Ford had become an unintentional celebrity, and there were some good aspects of that. She texted with Anita Hill and had the chance to go backstage at a benefit concert by Metallica—she is a huge fan—whose lead guitarist, Kirk Hammett, told her she didn't need to bid on the chance to surf with him; they'd just go out on the water together. In December, her first emergence into public view since the testimony, she appeared in a video for the *Sports Illustrated* Inspiration of the Year award, given to Rachael Denhollander, praising the gymnast for finding "the courage to talk publicly to stop the abuse of others."[9] For months after the hearings, people would approach her on the Stanford campus to express their thanks.

More often, though, Ford stewed over the impact on her life, her family, her friendships. A month after the confirmation, Grassley issued a lengthy report on the investigation to detail his case that "there was no credible evidence to support the allegations against the nominee."[10] The report received almost no media attention, but Ford worried for months about a skewed version of her story sitting on the Senate Judiciary Committee website for anyone to see. She was hurt and angry that committee Democrats did not produce a supportive rebuttal. Ford was named to the *Time* 100, a list of the most influential people of the year—complete with a blurb by Kamala Harris—but Kavanaugh was also among the honorees, with a testimonial from McConnell, and his inclusion grated on Ford. A Kavanaugh-sympathetic book published in July 2019 by Federalist writer Mollie Hemingway and Carrie Severino of the Judicial Crisis Network asserted, without providing supporting evidence, that "many high school acquaintances of Ford's revealed unflattering details about her behavior in high school—some of them truly salacious," and that depiction, too, upset Ford.[11]

Ever the pleaser, she has more than 200,000 letters and e-mails, many of them from women from across the country sharing their own stories of abuse and assault—"much, much worse things . . . than what happened to me"—that she feels duty bound to answer. Ever the statistician, she plans to code it by allegation and state and zip code, to see what patterns might emerge.[12]

•   •   •

Just as Ford could not venture out in public without being recognized, just as she had security concerns that persisted months after the hearings, so, too, did Kavanaugh—although, like other justices, he had Supreme Court police assigned to protect him. Security measures for all the justices have been increased in recent years, but Kavanaugh's ability to appear in public was additionally circumscribed. He resumed his coaching duties; he attended Nats games; he turned up at events such as Republican power couple Matt and Mercedes Schlapp's Christmas party, looking slightly uncomfortable, as everyone in the room craned their necks to see whether he had a beer in hand. Teaching at Harvard was out, but Kavanaugh was hired by George Mason University's Antonin Scalia Law School—over protests from some students who said it reflected a dismissive attitude toward sexual assault survivors— to teach a summer course in England on the "origins and creation of the U.S. Constitution."[13] The Chevy Chase Club offered a more sheltered environment, as did the court itself, where Kavanaugh would invite friends to visit. One day, he hosted his D.C. Circuit and district court colleagues for lunch at the court; another time he invited the female friends who had rallied to support him.

After Kavanaugh's searing confirmation, one question was how that experience would affect his performance on the bench— whether it would push him more firmly into the arms of the conservatives who rallied around his nomination at the point of most peril. The obvious, and alarming, precedent was Clarence Thomas, who had gone through a similar ordeal. Thomas was always likely to be a conservative justice, but the confirmation process seemed to embitter him and further entrench him even more on the far-right end of the spectrum. On the current court, Thomas is by far the most conservative, and Kavanaugh's first year was also Thomas's most conservative ever, so much so that there was speculation in the court that Thomas was preparing to leave and wanted to issue some final, furious doctrinal blasts.

But Thomas and Kavanaugh are very different individuals. Thomas disliked his experience at Yale Law School—he wrote in his memoir that he "peeled a 15-cent price sticker off a package of cigars and stuck it on the frame of my law degree to remind myself of the mistake I'd made by going to Yale"—and resented the establishment.[14] Kavanaugh craved being part of it—he always had and wanted someday to be welcomed back. "Brett cares what they think of him at Harvard and Yale, and he wants to be able to go back and teach there and talk there, and he knows he can't now," said one friend. Although there were moments when he privately seethed over the accusations against him, Kavanaugh told friends that he was committed to being the same justice he would have been if none of that had happened.

If the impact of Thomas's experience had been to push him rightward, some who knew Kavanaugh well suggested that the effect on the new justice might be the opposite, at least in the short term: to find opportunities to ingratiate himself with liberals, to prove he is a good guy after all. Perhaps that would take place in the cases that didn't much matter, not the front-page blockbusters, but it was something for otherwise despairing liberals to hold on to. And, at the very least, it might induce Kavanaugh to go slow out of the box. A Kavanaugh champing at the bit to overturn precedent would not be the Kavanaugh of Collins's depiction—or his own, for that matter.

The greatest impact of Kavanaugh's confirmation, of course, was on the court itself. Some justices had been quietly appalled by the hearings and by Kavanaugh's intemperate outburst. But the court is a body that is adept at healing itself after traumas like this, not only for the benefit of the new justice but also for the good of the institution.

This healing has an internal dimension and an outward-facing aspect. Oliver Wendell Holmes famously described the Supreme Court as "nine scorpions in a bottle," and, often even more pointedly in their written opinions than in their personal dealings, the current occupants of the bottle are more than capable of vehement disagreement. But the justices are stuck with one another for life. When situations like the fractious Kavanaugh confirmation arise, they have a tendency to blame other actors—the Senate, with a confirmation process at once hapless and partisan; the media, with its instinct for the sensational over the substantive—rather than their new colleague.

This is human nature, but it is also smart politics. A new justice means a colleague to be wooed, a vote that is up for grabs—perhaps not in most cases, but in some, and in some that matter enormously. The court is, in this sense, an undeniably political institution, and the most effective, most influential justices are not the purists who issue sole dissents but the pragmatists who understand how to craft coalitions and bring along reluctant votes to assemble and maintain a majority. William Brennan, the court's liberal leader for decades, was fond of instructing his clerks of the most important maxim in Supreme Court jurisprudence: the rule of five. "Five votes," Brennan would say, wiggling his fingers. "Five votes can do anything around here."[15]

Thus, for reasons both personal and strategic, some of the court's most liberal members went out of their way to be privately cordial to and publicly supportive of Kavanaugh. Kagan, who sits next to him on the bench, joked with Kavanaugh and shook his hand at the end of their first oral argument together; she later hosted a dinner for him and other leading lawyers and judges. Sotomayor, in a comment that particularly pained Ford, used a gentler metaphor to describe the court than Holmes's scorpions. "The nine of us are now a family and we're a family with each of our own burdens and our own obligations to others, but this is our work family, and it's just as important as our personal family," she said.[16] Toward the end of his first term, she had Kavanaugh and his family over to her place for dinner. "We are all human beings, we all have pasts," Sotomayor told a judicial conference in September 2019. "Now, whether things occurred or didn't occur, all of that is irrelevant. It is yesterday, today is today, and moving forward, I have to work with him."[17]

Ginsburg, for her part, took pains to praise Kavanaugh for

"a very important first," having a chambers consisting of all women law clerks, a development that also meant the court had a majority-female class of law clerks for the first time. When Duke Law School professor Neil Siegel, a former Ginsburg clerk, lamented in a question-and-answer session with her that "nominees for the Supreme Court are not chosen primarily anymore for independence, legal ability, personal decency," Ginsburg quickly shot him down. "My two newest colleagues are very decent, very smart individuals," she retorted.[18]

This judicial wagon circling has an internal dimension: to protect the court itself. The Kavanaugh confirmation had, once again, put an unwelcome spotlight on the institution and called into question Roberts's famous formulation—repeated by Kavanaugh at his confirmation hearings—of judges as impartial umpires merely calling balls and strikes. This reputational risk had been on the justices' minds even before Kennedy's departure, in part thanks to Trump's continuing attacks on the federal judiciary. In November 2018, Trump condemned a ruling against the administration's asylum policy as having been issued by an "Obama judge." That prompted the normally restrained chief justice to issue a pointed retort. "We do not have Obama judges or Trump judges, Bush judges or Clinton judges," Roberts said in a statement. "What we have is an extraordinary group of dedicated judges doing their level best to do equal right to those appearing before them. That independent judiciary is something we should all be thankful for."[19]

Roberts was not alone in his concern about the court's standing and its politicization in the eyes of the public. As the Senate prepared to confirm Kavanaugh, Kagan expressed her worry about public perceptions of the court. "Part of the court's strength and part of the court's legitimacy depends on people not seeing the court in the way that people see the rest of the governing structures of this country now," Kagan said. "It's an incredibly important thing for the court to guard—this reputation of being fair, of being neutral, and of not being some extension of the terribly polarized political process and environment that we live in."

The court in years past had a justice at the center—O'Connor and, later, Kennedy—whose positions weren't entirely predictable, Kagan noted. "That's enabled the court to look as though it was not owned by one side or another and was indeed impartial and neutral and fair . . . It's not so clear, I think, going forward, that that sort of middle position—it's not so clear whether we'll have it."[20]

Not so clear was an optimistic understatement. The legacy of the Kavanaugh hearings was hardly a court that looked impartial or neutral, not after the partisan outburst by the newest justice. Conservatives owned this court, and the chief justice only occupied the middle by default.

So what can be gleaned from Kavanaugh's first term on the court? Seeking to deduce a justice's future course from his or her first year can be a futile endeavor. Kennedy offers one striking example. His first full term on the bench was that of a remarkably conservative jurist. The longtime Supreme Court correspondent for the *Los Angeles Times*, David Savage, observed that civil rights groups who had rejoiced over Bork's defeat may have "won a skirmish, but lost the battle." Kennedy "has proven to be quiet, steady and consistently conservative—perhaps more even so than Bork," Savage wrote. "Thanks to Kennedy, former President Ronald Reagan and his attorney general, Edwin Meese III, gained what they wanted all along: a five-member conservative majority that can roll back the liberal high court rulings of the 1960s and 1970s."[21] Over the following decades, that supposedly solid majority turned out to be fleeting and, to the extent it persisted, unstable.

David Souter offers another cautionary tale about reading too much into a justice's first-year performance. ENERGIZED CONSERVATISM RULES HIGH COURT, the author reported for the *Washington Post* at the end of his first term, in 1991. With Souter replacing liberal William Brennan, the *Post* concluded, "there was a solid and energized conservative majority in place on the high court—poised to reverse three decades of liberal precedents, and already starting to do so . . . With conservatives in control, the question before the court becomes not so much the outcome of cases, but what to change, how fast and how dramatically."[22] Again, reports of conservative dominance turned out to be greatly exaggerated.

That said, Souter—as George H. W. Bush's prescient worry over whether he would be Earl Warren had suggested—was more of a judicial wild card than the conservative justices who came later. Republicans, thanks in part to extensive Federalist Society vetting, learned well from their past mistakes. Souter's successors—Clarence Thomas, John Roberts, Samuel Alito, and Neil Gorsuch—all turned out to be reliable, consistent conservative votes. Kavanaugh's dozen years on the appeals court offered every reason to believe that he would join them. Still, the court's conservative wing is not a monolith: it is a continuum, from establishment conservative (Roberts) to ultraconservative (Thomas). The real question, as Kavanaugh began his first term and Roberts found himself at the helm of a new court, was precisely where along that spectrum he would settle and, once again, how far and how fast the fortified conservative majority would move.

If John Roberts had his way—and as it turned out, he largely did—the answer would be: we'll see how far, but definitely not so fast. The chief justice's unstated but evident goal for October Term 2018 was to make it as boring as possible, and the newest justice, for the most part, was an eager ally in the chief's quest for dullness.

One way to understand Kavanaugh is as someone who wants to be liked, and his first-term record seemed to bear that out: he was in the majority 91 percent of the time, more than any other justice. Kavanaugh situated himself far more closely with Roberts than with the more conservative of the conservative justices. Kavanaugh and Roberts voted together 94 percent of the time, more than any other pair.[23]

Roberts's agenda for the term was to keep controversial cases off the docket, and Kavanaugh was his eager wingman. In December

2018, for example, he joined with Roberts in declining to provide the fourth vote necessary to hear a case involving state efforts to cut off public funding for Planned Parenthood—a move that triggered an angry dissent from the three most conservative justices, Thomas, Alito, and Gorsuch.[24] Behind the scenes, Kavanaugh maneuvered to help keep other controversial cases off the court's docket without provoking similar outbursts. The court sidestepped cases involving an Oregon baker fined for refusing to create a wedding cake for a same-sex couple and abortion restrictions in Alabama and Indiana.

Still, it was clear, Kavanaugh was no liberal. On the highest-profile cases of the term, in the ones where it mattered, Kavanaugh did not disappoint his conservative backers. The impact of switching Kavanaugh for Kennedy manifested itself on the last day of the term, when the justices, voting 5–4, determined that federal courts could not hear challenges to partisan gerrymandering, the practice of drawing voting-district lines for political advantage. Kennedy had toyed for years with the notion that the Constitution might prohibit the most extreme forms of this practice, but he ducked the issue in his final term. When the issue arose again in gerrymandering cases from Maryland and North Carolina, Kavanaugh shut the door that Kennedy had left ajar. With the other conservative justices, he joined a Roberts opinion that firmly renounced any role for the federal judiciary in such cases.[25]

And in several significant instances where Roberts sided with the court's liberals, Kavanaugh broke in the other direction. On the other big decision of the term's final day, rejecting the Trump administration's effort to add a question about citizenship to the census, Roberts provided a surprise fifth vote on the side of the liberal justices. He agreed to block the citizenship question because of what he described as its "contrived" justification. Kavanaugh sided with the dissenters in saying the administration should have been allowed to proceed. Yet before agreeing to sign on, he asked that Thomas, who wrote the main dissenting opinion, excise an attack on the chief justice, who, it was later reported, had defected after initially voting with the conservatives.[26]

The census case wasn't Kavanaugh's only notable—and, for liberals, troubling—deviation from Roberts. The chief justice gave the liberals another fifth vote in declining to overrule a case involving deference to administrative agencies. Kavanaugh, like Thomas, Alito, and Gorsuch, would have jettisoned the precedent. Kavanaugh wrote separately to note that the court's position on this form of deference (to agencies' interpretations of their own ambiguous regulations) did not foreclose a different outcome on the more important question of *Chevron* deference (to agencies' interpretations of ambiguous laws).[27] The decision, Gorsuch noted, "is more a stay of execution than a pardon."[28]

Likewise, when the court was called on to consider whether to let a Louisiana abortion law take effect, Roberts voted with the liberals to block the statute while a challenge to its constitutionality made its way through the courts. The move was additional evidence of Roberts's desire to deflect hot-button issues and avoid disruptive rulings. He had dissented three years earlier when the court struck down a Texas law that was effectively identical to the Louisiana statute.

Kavanaugh broke with the chief justice to side with the three other conservatives, who would have let the law take effect. In doing so, he wrote a solo dissent that was reminiscent of his wait-and-see approach in the appeals court to the pregnant seventeen-year-old migrant. Then, Kavanaugh wanted to give the government time to find the teen a sponsor and perhaps solve the problem. Now, he said, he would let the law take effect and see if it posed such a problem in practice that it would have to be enjoined.[29] One of his guiding judicial instincts was conflict avoidance.

As friends had predicted, Kavanaugh had his more liberal moments. He provided the liberal justices the fifth vote in an antitrust case, siding with plaintiffs who were suing Apple. Ginsburg, who as the senior justice in the majority had the power to decide who would write the opinion, rewarded Kavanaugh by assigning the case to him. And in a fitting coda to his law-student note about racial discrimination in jury selection, Kavanaugh wrote for a seven-justice majority (Thomas and Gorsuch dissented) in the case of Curtis Flowers, a Mississippi man accused of a quadruple murder in 1996. By the time the case arrived at the Supreme Court, Flowers had been tried six separate times by the same prosecutor, who consistently used his peremptory challenges to remove African Americans. "Equal justice under law requires a criminal trial free of racial discrimination in the jury selection process," Kavanaugh wrote. "By taking steps to eradicate racial discrimination from the jury selection process, *Batson* sought to protect the rights of defendants and jurors, and to enhance public confidence in the fairness of the criminal justice system."[30]

Kavanaugh's split with Gorsuch in the case was emblematic of the difference between the two newest justices. They were in agreement only 70 percent of the time; Kavanaugh sided with Kagan and Breyer, two liberal justices, just as often.[31] In addition to the peremptory challenge case, Kavanaugh and Gorsuch disagreed on two criminal justice cases in which the libertarian-leaning Gorsuch gave the liberals a majority while Kavanaugh took a more traditionally conservative, law-and-order approach. The divisions were striking: in their first terms together on the bench, Roberts and Alito had agreed 90 percent of the time, Kagan and Sotomayor 96 percent of the time.[32]

Remarkably, the court's liberal justices had more success in October Term 2018, Kavanaugh's first, than they had the previous year, with Kennedy still on the court. In the 2017 term, the conservative justices formed the majority in fourteen of nineteen cases in which the court divided 5–4.[33] In the 2018 term, the ordinary alliances scrambled into an unusual number of configurations. The supposedly strengthened conservative bloc voted together in just seven of the twenty-one 5–4 decisions.[34] Still, this seeming success may have been more of an anomalous pause than a harbinger of squishiness to come.

One signal, ominous for liberals, was the willingness of the five conservative justices, Kavanaugh included, to overturn two prior cases. They were reasonably obscure—one involved states' immunity to being sued, the other how quickly plaintiffs can turn to federal court to claim that a state or local government took their property without paying just compensation. But the court's willingness to throw precedents overboard—one from 1979, the other from 1985—alarmed the liberal justices. "Today's decision can only cause one to wonder which cases the Court will overrule next," Breyer wrote in the state immunity case.[35] "Well that didn't take long," Kagan observed in the takings case just five weeks later. "Now one may wonder yet again."[36]

The October 2019 term promises to be far more tumultuous and far more revealing about Kavanaugh's willingness to shift the court to the right. The justices will take up the legality of Trump's decision to cancel the Obama-era DACA (Deferred Action for Childhood Arrivals) policy, providing special protection for so-called Dreamers who arrived in the United States as children. They will consider whether the federal law prohibiting job discrimination on the basis of sex protects gay, lesbian, and transgender employees.

And the Louisiana abortion law that the court prevented from taking effect in February 2019, over Kavanaugh's dissent, will be back before the justices for a ruling on its constitutionality. The law requires doctors who perform abortions to have admitting privileges at nearby hospitals, a rule that challengers said would force most Louisiana abortion clinics to close and leave just one physician in the state permitted to perform abortions. It is all but identical to a Texas statute that the court struck down in 2016, concluding that the admitting privilege requirement imposed an undue burden on women's access to abortion. The vote in that case was five to three, with Kennedy in the majority. Now, with two new conservative justices, Gorsuch and Kavanaugh, the court has the opportunity at the very least to relax the undue burden standard in a way that could allow new restrictions on abortion. Meanwhile, in the wake of Kavanaugh's confirmation, a number of states enacted near-total bans on abortion; those, too, are making their way to the high court and would, if the court agreed to hear them, pose a direct challenge to *Roe v. Wade*. The country is poised to learn, soon enough, what Kavanaugh means by "settled law."

This is a court on the verge of a constitutional revolution of as yet undetermined dimensions. All eyes will be on the hottest buttons—abortion rights, gay rights, and how those should be balanced against religious freedom; the continuing constitutional viability of affirmative-action programs; the scope of permissible gun regulation. Yet the changes could also come in ways that are more esoteric but equally fundamental. The court will weigh in on whether the Consumer Financial Protection Bureau—with a single agency head who can be removed by the president only "for cause"—violates the constitutional separation of powers by intruding on executive authority. The case provides a potential opening for the conservative assault on independent regulatory agencies—and another chance for Kavanaugh to reiterate, and this time perhaps help write into law, his strongly held views on the matter. Kavanaugh issued a fiery dissent as an appeals court judge about "the serious threat to individual liberty" posed by the agency's "unaccountable, unchecked" sole director when the D.C. Circuit rejected a separate constitutional challenge to the CFPB in 2018. If not in this case, in coming years the court could upend the post–New Deal architecture of independent regulatory agencies whose decisions cannot be countermanded by the executive branch and are, thanks to *Chevron*, shielded, if not immune, from judicial second-guessing.

One worrisome sign for liberals came in a seemingly obscure case argued in early October 2018, before Kavanaugh's arrival. As a technical matter, *Gundy v. United States* involved how a 2006 federal law requiring the registration of sex offenders applied to individuals convicted of such crimes before the law's passage. The law mostly left that decision up to the attorney general, and the plaintiff, a sex offender, argued that it was unconstitutional for Congress to cede that power. That raised the more fundamental question in the case: whether the conservative justices would use the opportunity to revive the nondelegation doctrine, a long-dormant principle that Congress cannot transfer too much of its own power to executive departments or regulatory agencies. The court has only employed the nondelegation doctrine twice in its history to strike down statutes, in cases dating to the New Deal.[37]

But in *Gundy*, three justices—Gorsuch, in an opinion joined by Roberts and Thomas—expressed willingness to do so again. Alito provided a reluctant vote to join with liberals to uphold the law— but with a warning that the nondelegation doctrine might be ripe for a revival. "If a majority of this court were willing to reconsider the approach we have taken for the past 84 years, I would support that effort," he said.[38] This technical-sounding move could pose a major challenge to the modern administrative state, as Kagan explained in her opinion for the court's four liberals. "If [the sex offender law's] delegation is unconstitutional," she wrote, "then most of government is unconstitutional."[39] Maybe she was overstating things, but it is a scary prospect that four justices seem prepared to restore the law to its pre–New Deal state. Alito sent an open invitation to raise the question in other cases, and Kavanaugh, the judge who told his clerks that every case is a separation of powers case, seems a reasonable bet to join with his fellow conservatives.

With Kavanaugh's confirmation, the three-decades-long conservative quest for control of the court is complete but not necessarily concluded. Even before the end of Trump's first term, a conservative justice could choose to retire, a liberal justice could be forced to leave, or both. Substituting one conservative justice with a younger one would fortify the current majority for years to come. Replacing a liberal justice with a conservative would be even more significant. Conservatives would enjoy the luxury of a spare vote in cases where a colleague defects. And having a six-justice majority, rather than a scant five, might further embolden the conservative justices, especially the more cautious among them, to overturn precedents or otherwise move the court to the right. The current configuration could change—a conservative justice could be forced to leave during a future Democratic presidency—but for the foreseeable future, the shape of the court is set. Control rests with the right. The middle is episodic and evanescent, if it has not vanished completely.

The arc of Kavanaugh's career has mirrored the evolution of the conservative legal movement from quirky outlier to establishment power broker. The individual and the institution grew up together; their ambitions flourished in tandem. Conservatives have been seeking this elusive moment as long as Kavanaugh has been questing after it. His confirmation represents the twin realization of his lifelong ambition and that of the movement that fueled his success. Leonard Leo and other Federalist Society stalwarts may have worried about Kavanaugh; they may have believed another candidate would be even more energetic, less restrained, in enacting the conservative legal project, and their doubts may have been justified. Kavanaugh may well turn out to be more like Roberts, incremental and institutional, than he is like Thomas or Scalia, itching for a jurisprudential fight. Still, if Kavanaugh is not leading the charge by the new conservative court, there is little doubt he will serve as its loyal soldier. As Kavanaugh has realized his lifelong ambition, so, too, after three decades of disappointment and frustration, have conservatives fulfilled theirs.

Zeal to Win

In plowing through thousands of pages of Kavanaugh e-mails released by the Bush library, I ran across one that was of particular personal interest: "Ruth Marcus of the Washington Post called and left me a voice mail inviting me to the White House Correspondents Dinner," Kavanaugh wrote on March 5, 2001. "I have NOT talked to her (or any other reporter) since taking this job, but I had been assigned to deal with her quite a bit and got to know her in Whitewater/Lewinsky. In any event, can we go? . . . Feel free to say no; I obviously am under no illusions about her intent (buttering me up)."[1] Kavanaugh must have gotten the go-ahead, because he ended up attending.

As this e-mail suggests, I have known Kavanaugh for a quarter century, although not well. I have tried to keep myself and my personal views largely out of the pages of this book because I wanted to let readers draw their own conclusions from the reporting itself. But I concluded in the end that it is fair for readers, having come this far, to know what I think, having watched the events closely in real time and spent the better part of a year reporting about Kavanaugh and his confirmation.

I have always liked Brett Kavanaugh. In conversations with him as a reporter, I found him to be smart, helpful, and friendly. He provided useful analyses of the legal issues involved in the Starr investigation without violating grand jury secrecy or ethical rules. He did not display the edgy hostility of some conservatives in dealing with reporters; rather, he was open and gracious. I was surprised and somewhat disappointed not to see him on Trump's original Supreme Court list, and when he was the eventual nominee, I was relieved that it was not someone far more conservative. Kavanaugh would not have been my pick if I were president, and I don't expect to like what he does as a justice. But Trump won the election, and Kavanaugh would have been a reasonable, even logical, choice for any Republican president. He was, as I wrote at the time of his selection, more likely to be a justice in the mold of Scalia or Rehnquist than of Kennedy, but that was to be expected, again, from any Republican.

And, as much as I sympathize with Democrats' continuing fury over the theft of the Scalia seat and worry over the rightward tilt of the court, I did not, at the time of Kavanaugh's nomination, see a substantive basis for opposing him. This may be a naive and outmoded approach in an era of near automatic party-line votes; it is an easier position to adopt for an opinion columnist than for a senator, who has to answer to voters. But I think Lindsey Graham had it right when he voted for Sotomayor and Kagan, and I do not perceive Kavanaugh as out of the judicial mainstream in the way that Bork was. As his nomination progressed, my continuing concerns centered largely on process, in particular Republicans' withholding of documents.

Then came Ford. "There is no middle ground today," Yale law professor Stephen Carter observed about the Thomas-Hill hearings three years after they took place, "and for true believers of our era, there will be no middle ground thirty or forty years from now."[2] That assessment seems destined to be even truer in the case of Kavanaugh and Ford. Anyone who professes absolute certainty about what took place, in high school or college, is not grappling fairly with the imperfect state of the evidence. Here is my take:

It is true that the allegations emerged only at the last minute, and in a partisan environment. That is a matter of legitimate grievance for Kavanaugh and his allies, but the unfortunate timing and political motivation of some of the players (Ford and Ramirez not among them, in my view) do not go to the merits of the charges. It is also true that Kavanaugh has a lengthy and admirable track record of working with and promoting women, including as his law clerks, most of whom went on to clerk at the Supreme Court. The array of female friends and colleagues who rallied on his behalf counts as a mark in his favor. That Kavanaugh's friends, across the political spectrum, insist they cannot imagine him having behaved in this manner also has to be taken into account. If the evidence pointed in the other direction, indicating a history of dismissive or disrespectful treatment of women, it would have reasonably been held against him. At the same time, treating some or many women well does not disprove having behaved inappropriately or worse with other women, especially when he was far younger.

And so the case comes down to the specifics of the allegations. Ford did not complain about Kavanaugh's behavior when she says it happened, even privately to her closest friends, but that does not seem surprising in the context of the time and in the particular context of her family. But neither did she suddenly summon this memory at the very moment of Kavanaugh's selection. She mentioned it, in vague form, to her husband around the time of their marriage, and with more details—in Russell Ford's recollection, with Kavanaugh's name attached—in therapy sessions in 2012 and 2013. More recently, as issues relating to sexual assault entered the headlines, she confided to several friends about having been assaulted in high school by someone who was then a federal judge. As Katz noted when they first met, if Ford was making something up she would have invented a better, more detailed, story. No one puts a purported eyewitness in the room when that witness could refute what happened.

Could she be mistaken in her recollection? The assessment of Flake and Collins, among others, was that something terrible happened to Ford but that Kavanaugh was not the perpetrator. This was a comforting way to try to square the circle. It also made no sense. Ford clearly knew who Kavanaugh was. Long before his calendars were made public, she identified two friends he spent time with that summer—Mark Judge and P. J. Smyth—as having been at the party. How could Ford get that right and Kavanaugh's identity wrong?

At the same time, there were obvious gaps in Ford's account, including where the party took place and how she got home. As Kavanaugh and his allies emphasized, no one else at the gathering that Ford recalls—not Judge, Smyth, or Leland Keyser—remembers the event or anything untoward. Yet two of those witnesses, Smyth and Keyser, would have no reason to recall something that was, as they experienced it, uneventful. Keyser's growing conviction that she had never met Kavanaugh and that, as she looked back on that summer, she had not attended such a party is a factor to weigh in Kavanaugh's favor.[3] Keyser, a Democrat, would not have any incentive to protect him and every reason to support Ford, her friend. At the same time, her history of substance abuse might call into question the accuracy of her memory. In the end, her lack of recollection is not dispositive.

Likewise, Judge's declaration, untested by cross-examination, is either self-serving or unconvincing. For him to corroborate Ford's account would be not only to go up against a group of his peers but also to confess to participation in an assault. At the same time, you do not have to condemn Judge as a knowing liar to discount his lack of recollection. By Judge's own account he drank excessively at the time. It is entirely possible that the assault occurred and that he has no recollection of it.

What of Kavanaugh himself? What is the best way to understand his vociferous, indignant denial of any wrongdoing? One possibility, of course, is that he is telling the truth and that Ford, Ramirez, and now Max Stier are all mistaken. Another is that he lied outright in pursuit of a position that he had sought for decades and, perhaps even more motivating, to protect his reputation and his family. Certainly between Kavanaugh and Ford, the nominee was the one with the greater motivation to give false testimony. My assessment is that Kavanaugh is telling the truth as he believes it. I have found no hint in reporting on his conversations with friends and advisers that he thought the episodes occurred but had been exaggerated or mis-interpreted. To the contrary, Kavanaugh vehemently resisted any suggestion that he account for the disconnect in this way.

Some Kavanaugh critics may dismiss this as naive. Perhaps; Clarence Thomas was similarly forceful in his denials of any mis-conduct toward Anita Hill. But the difference between Thomas and Kavanaugh is that it is implausible that Thomas would have forgot-ten his behavior toward Hill. It occurred when he was an adult, less than a decade earlier, and he was not inebriated. To me, the more likely explanation for the Ford-Kavanaugh disconnect is not that Kavanaugh was lying but that what was so searing to Ford was a passing frolic for Kavanaugh—that he was, as Ford recalled, heav-ily intoxicated and that he simply does not remember the incident. Notwithstanding Kavanaugh's angry denials about drinking to the point of blacking out, there is ample evidence that he drank to excess in high school and college and that he became more aggres-sive and belligerent under the influence of alcohol.

Then there is the matter of Kavanaugh's behavior in college. It seems fairly clear that something disturbing happened to Deborah Ramirez during her freshman year—that there was some incident in which a male student exposed himself to her. Was that Kava-naugh? Her memory is hazy and the corroborating evidence incom-plete. A more thorough FBI investigation might have produced a more conclusive result.

That is what makes Stier's account so important. I was aston-ished when I first heard early in the reporting for this book, the month after Kavanaugh's confirmation, that Stier had surfaced as a supposed eyewitness to a second exposure incident. I have known Stier for years—I have served as a judge for his organi-zation's Sammy awards—and consider him a highly credible wit-ness, restrained and sober-minded. Stier's involvement emerged into public view in September 2019, with the publication of *The Education of Brett Kavanaugh.*

In the aftermath of the book, conservatives leaped to disparage Stier, a registered Democrat, as biased. Davis, who left Grassley's

staff after the confirmation and launched a new nonprofit organization, the Article III Project, to "fight for the confirmation of President Trump's judicial nominees," offered an illustrative comment.
"Max Stier is a political hack masquerading as nonpartisan," he
said.[4] Davis and others cited Stier's work on the Clintons' legal
team during the Starr investigation—although, coincidentally,
another attorney for the defense was Emmet Flood, who ended up
working as Trump's White House lawyer during the Mueller probe.
They also pointed to Stier's political donations ($1,000 to Obama
in 2007 and $250 to the Democratic National Committee in 2000),
and his service as a political appointee in the Department of Housing and Urban Development in the Clinton administration.[5] They
noted that his wife, a career prosecutor who had clerked for conservative judges Michael Mukasey and Ralph Winter and was a judge
in the local Washington, D.C. court system, had been tapped by
Obama for a federal district court judgeship, only to see the nomination lapse as a result of Republican inaction.[6]

It is understandable that conservatives would raise these concerns, and they are important to include in any report. In my experience, however, Stier is the opposite of a partisan operative. He
had little to gain, and a lifetime's work to lose, by trying to get his
information to the FBI and the Senate. If his sole goal was a partisan takedown of Kavanaugh, why not go public? If his story were
untrue, why would he take the enormous risk of reaching out to the
FBI and putting himself in legal jeopardy—under "penalty of fel-
ony," in the phrase Republicans had begun to use? If anything, the
harder questions for Stier would seem to come from the other side:
given the stakes involved, why didn't he have the courage to just
speak out on the record? In any event, for Stier to remember seeing Kavanaugh expose himself to another woman strongly bolsters
Ramirez's recollection. And that in turn suggests that Kavanaugh,
whatever kind of man he turned out to be, was a teenager capable
of the sort of behavior that Ford alleges.

Would this be disqualifying so many years later? That would
have been a hard question, but it is not the one that senators and the

country confronted. If Kavanaugh had presented a different, more benign version of the encounter than the one that Ford related—he was just horsing around, he never would have gone further—that might have triggered a difficult discussion about whether there is some kind of statute of limitations for teenage misbehavior. But Kavanaugh's absolute, adamant denials meant that was not the question before the Senate and the nation. The issue was whose testimony was more credible.

Honesty requires acknowledging that the evidence against Kavanaugh is far from slam-dunk, beyond-a-reasonable-doubt proof. As a consequence, there was a risk of extraordinary injustice either way, whether Kavanaugh was rejected or confirmed. If Kavanaugh was innocent of the allegations, defeating his nomination would have meant that his reputation and his life would be forever ruined. If Kavanaugh was guilty, confirming him would leave a permanent stain on the court itself and send a terrible signal to women—another one—about whether allegations of sexual misconduct are taken seriously.

In assessing how to navigate those competing risks of injustice, the analogies used by partisans on both sides were unhelpful and misleading. This was not, as Kavanaugh opponents claimed, akin to a mere job interview, with the nominee possessing no advance claim on the post. Job interviews aren't ordinarily played out in public, on live television, with the consequence of permanent harm to reputation and livelihood. Republican claims that rejecting Kavanaugh would violate the presumption of innocence that is a bedrock principle of the rule of law were similarly off base. The presumption of innocence is essential in the setting of a criminal trial; it is a bedrock principle of the rule of law. In assessing a nominee, however, that guidance gets the priorities backwards. The institution is more important than the individual. In the case of a justice, the confirmation is to a lifetime position, not an elective office for which voters can rectify their mistakes in a few years. So the correct standards are not those of the criminal justice system. In the language of law, it is not that the nominee enjoys the presumption of innocence; rather, he shoulders the burden of persuasion. Kavanaugh did not meet this test.

If that was not an easy decision to make, for me, Kavanaugh's performance on the afternoon of September 27 offered another, and perhaps most compelling, argument against confirming him. Yes, a man falsely accused might lash out at his accusers, especially as the charges became increasingly implausible and outrageous. But raw emotion is one thing, partisan intemperance another. It was telling that Kavanaugh's attack on the Clintons was crafted in advance, not something that tumbled out of his mouth in the heat of the moment. Here Murkowski's citation of the ethical canon that a judge "act at all times in a manner that promotes public confidence in the integrity and impartiality of the judiciary" is on point, and her anguished question is the most important of all: "Where's the public confidence?"[7]

Robert Byrd, the veteran West Virginia Democrat, grappled eloquently with these issues in his Senate floor speech on the Thomas nomination. He had been planning to vote for Thomas, Byrd said; he even entered into the record the statement he had prepared in support of confirmation. But Byrd said he had changed his mind after hearing the testimony of both Thomas and Hill and being convinced that the latter was telling the truth. "I realize that it is possible in the process a man could have been wronged," Byrd said. "If it were a criminal trial, it would be different. That is what it is not."

No individual has the right to a Supreme Court seat, Byrd emphasized when speaking of Thomas. "Why give him the benefit of the doubt?" he asked. "If we are going to give the benefit of the doubt let us give it to the court. Let us give it to the country."[8] That is what failed to happen in the case of Brett Kavanaugh. The investigation that should have been pursued vigorously was instead short-circuited by a partisan zeal to win. That is unfortunate, but what is done is done. There is no prospect that Kavanaugh could be charged with perjury, which would require proof beyond a reasonable doubt not only that his testimony was false but that it was knowingly so. That would be almost impossible to prove. Likewise, the notion of Kavanaugh being impeached, as some Democrats have demanded, is both unlikely and unwise. Congress has a legitimate role to play in unearthing what went wrong in the FBI process and how that can be prevented in the future, but revisiting the disputed facts of the confirmation hearings themselves is not the right approach. Further fact-finding is unlikely to be conclusive; even if it were, the question of Kavanaugh's honesty would remain at issue, for the reasons explained earlier. The country has lived with the results of badly run or tainted elections. For the same reasons, it has to endure the consequences of a flawed confirmation process.

But it does not have to excuse what happened. The Kavanaugh confirmation discredited the White House and the Senate, which is supposed to play an independent advise-and-consent role. In the end, it disserved both Kavanaugh and the country. As a result, his tenure will forever have an asterisk attached—a blot on Kavanaugh and the court that is, to use Christine Blasey Ford's phrase, indelible.

AUTHOR'S NOTE

This book is based on thousands of pages of documents released during the Kavanaugh hearings, Justice Kavanaugh's lengthy judicial record, and nearly three hundred interviews. Some were on the record, and in such cases that fact is reflected in endnotes. However, many sources spoke only on the understanding that they would not be quoted by name, or, in even more cases, that they would not be quoted at all but that their information could be used without attribution to any source. Where I describe meetings and conversations, I have done my best to double-check the participants' recollection and the accuracy of their quotes against one another. Every writer would prefer that sources speak on the record, but where it was not possible to obtain such approval, I believe that the resulting insights and detail have been worth the trade-off in transparency, and I hope that my decades of experience writing about these issues has earned me readers' trust.

ACKNOWLEDGMENTS

Hundreds of people from across the political spectrum, in every branch of government and in private life, trusted me enough to share their perspectives on the individuals and events described in this book. Some spoke for extensive hours over the course of repeated interviews; many were kind enough to read excerpts of particular passages that applied to them to ensure accuracy. I appreciate every bit of that guidance, and while no one is likely to agree with everything contained in these pages, I hope that those who were kind enough to help will come away believing that I conveyed their perspectives and involvement accurately and fairly. Although I have known many of the players in the Kavanaugh drama for years—in some cases, decades—my relationship with one in particular merits special acknowledgment. Ricki Seidman, who provided communications advice to Christine Ford, has been my close friend of more than thirty years, a friendship that has survived numerous professional intersections and differences. This is no secret to anyone involved in the Kavanaugh nomination, and I mention it here not to single out Ricki for her help but to make certain that it is equally transparent to readers who may find it relevant.

Several books that focus or touch on Justice Kennedy's retirement or the Kavanaugh nomination were published as I worked on this one, including *The Most Dangerous Branch*, by David Kaplan; *The Hill to Die On*, by Jake Sherman and Anna Palmer; *Confirmation Bias*, by Carl Hulse; *She Said*, by Jodi Kantor and Megan Twohey; *The Education of Brett Kavanaugh*, by Robin Pogrebin and Kate Kelly; and, on the conservative side, *Justice on Trial*, by

Mollie Hemingway and Carrie Severino, and *Search and Destroy*, by Ryan Lovelace. I benefited from reading each of them, but the reporting in this book is entirely my own, except where noted. My friend Jackie Calmes of the *Los Angeles Times* became my friendly competitor, and I am very much looking forward to reading her book. In understanding the history of the Supreme Court and the confirmation process, I relied on, among other books, *Battle for Justice*, by Ethan Bronner; *Supreme Conflict*, by Jan Crawford Greenburg; *Strange Justice*, by Jane Mayer and Jill Abramson; and *Confirmation Wars*, by Benjamin Wittes. Special thanks to Kathy Arberg and the staff of the Supreme Court public affairs office for their cheerful and professional assistance.

This book took a year to report and write, but it came into being very quickly, just days after Brett Kavanaugh was confirmed, thanks largely to the enthusiasm and confidence of two people: my agent, Rafe Sagalyn, and my editor at Simon & Schuster, Priscilla Painton. Both have been the best of companions along the way to its completion. Rafe waited patiently, enduring years of lunches, for me to figure out the book I wanted to write. Once I landed on the right topic, he was a steady and wise counselor from start to finish. Priscilla is a writer's dream, a conceptualizer, hand-holder, and, when needed, ass-kicker. I have never had a smarter reader or more dedicated advocate. She and Rafe, in cahoots, helped make this book so much better than it would have been without them. Many thanks, as well, to the larger team at Simon & Schuster, including Jonathan Karp, Megan Hogan, Emily Simonson, Julia Prosser, Elise Ringo, Elizabeth Gray, and Hana Park, along with Jackie Seow for her arresting cover design, Eric Rayman for careful lawyering, Kayley Hoffman, Barbara Clark, and Jon Evans for smart, meticulous, and amazingly fast copyediting. I could not have gotten this project launched, much less completed, without the help of Isabelle Taft, my smart, energetic, resourceful, and endlessly cheerful researcher, who kept me on track, provided consistently intelligent advice, and saved me from more mistakes than I care to admit. Any remaining errors are, of course, my own responsibility.

Because this is a book that I've been preparing to write my entire career, I want to especially thank everyone associated with the *Washington Post*, where I have been privileged to spend my career. Thanks to the Graham family, especially Don Graham, for creating such a special institution and having the wisdom to entrust it to Jeff Bezos, who has empowered and inspired us to new heights. My gratitude to publisher Fred Ryan and my boss and dear friend, editorial page editor Fred Hiatt, for giving me the generous leave I needed to complete this project; to all my colleagues on the opinion staff, most especially deputy editorial page editor Jackson Diehl, op-ed editor Michael Larabee, and Michael Duffy, who materialized to step seamlessly into my shoes during my absence. My newsroom colleagues, past and present, were unfailingly generous with their time, knowledge, and support. Rick Atkinson, Leonard Downie, David Hoffman, Robert Kaiser, Al Kamen, Steve Luxenberg, David Maraniss, and Bob Woodward provided wise counsel along the way. Dan Balz, Robert Barnes, Emma Brown, Robert Costa, Josh Dawsey, Marc Fisher, Amy Gardner, Tom Hamburger, Rosalind Helderman, Paul Kane, Seung Min Kim, Michael Kranish, Carol Leonnig, Ann Marimow, and Philip Rucker did remarkable reporting during the confirmation process and were immensely helpful in providing advice as I trotted in their footsteps. My fellow authors Barbara Demick, Karen Tumulty, and Susan Page, along with Robin Sproul, were great hand-holders and gal pals. Colleagues from other news organizations, including Eliana Johnson and Daniel Lippman of *Politico*, Jane Mayer of *The New Yorker*, and Maureen Dowd of the *New York Times* were similarly giving of their expertise, as were David Kaplan and Evan Thomas, author of the excellent O'Connor biography *First*.

The Brookings Institution was generous in providing me with office space and companionship: thanks especially to Darrell West, director of Governance Studies, and my hall mate, Elaine Kamarck. American University president Sylvia Burwell was kind enough to invite me to apply to become part of the first year of fellows at the Sine Institute of Policy & Politics, and the ensuing seminar on the judicial confirmation process was valuable in helping me refine my thinking about the development of the judicial confirmation process. Suzy Cohen, Carolyn Lerner, and Al Kamen plowed their way through messy drafts to offer insightful comments.

They and other cherished friends, including the Wintergreen Group (Suzy and David Cohen, Beth Heifetz, Susan Kaplan and Matthew Gerson, Jennifer Klein and Todd Stern, Monica Medina and Ron Klain, Sarah Walzer and John Barrett); the Saturday morning Brunch Squad (Amanda Bennett, M. T. Connelly, Beth Donovan, Carolyn Lerner, Tricia Neuman, and Ricki Seidman); Bonnie Goldstein and Jim Grady, Janice Kaplan, Rachel Kronowitz, and Emily Yoffe and John Mintz indulged my disappearance for the better part of a year and limited their eye-rolling as I turned up on spa dates toting laptop and iPad. Two of my closest friends, Marjorie Williams and Marilyn Keefe, are no longer here but I felt their presence with me. By my side throughout, and managing to get me out of the house for walks, was our dog, Tank, whom I am assured would be hurt were he not included in this roster.

No one could have been a more supportive partner than my beloved and patient husband, Jon Leibowitz; our marriage is a happy by-product of the Clarence Thomas hearings, where we met so many years ago. Jon advised me months ago that he deserved an especially enormous acknowledgment, and he was right. Every spouse of a book author suffers, but Jon put up with more than most, including a twenty-fifth anniversary dinner that was entirely devoted to talk about Brett Kavanaugh. I promise the fiftieth will be better. Our daughters, Emma and Julia, were equally long-suffering and supportive; they are the best advisers and cheerleaders a writer, or mother, could have, and I am proud of them beyond measure. They and my extended family, including my brother and sister-in-law Joel and Sharon Marcus-Kurn and Bill and Janice Marcus, stepped up to handle holiday dinners when I begged off. My parents, Arnold and Judith Marcus, did not end up with the practicing lawyer they expected when they sent me off to law school, but their support provided me with the education that has proved so important in my chosen career and in the writing of this book. I only wish my father were alive to see it.

NOTES

PROLOGUE: THE BENEFICIARY

1 Donald Trump, "Remarks by President Trump and Justice Gorsuch at Swearing-in of Justice Gorsuch to the Supreme Court," White House release, April 10, 2017, https://www.whitehouse.gov/briefings-statements/remarks -president-trump-justice-gorsuch-swearing-justice-gorsuch-supreme-court/.

2 Philip Bump, "A quarter of Republicans voted for Trump to get Supreme Court picks—and it paid off," *Washington Post*, June 26, 2018, https://www .washingtonpost.com/news/politics/wp/2018/06/26/a-quarter-of-republicans -voted-for-trump-to-get-supreme-court-picks-and-it-paid-off/; Jon Huang, Samuel Jacoby, Michael Strickland, and K. K. Rebecca Lai, "Election 2016: Exit Polls," *New York Times*, November 8, 2016, https://www.nytimes.com /interactive/2016/11/08/us/politics/election-exit-polls.html.

3 David Jay, "Rand Paul supports Matt Rosendale in U.S. Senate race," KTVQ.com, October 28, 2018, https://ktvq.com/news/2018/10/28/rand -paul-supports-matt-rosendale-in-u-s-senate-race/. At a campaign event for Montana Republican senate candidate Matt Rosendale, Paul recounted a conversation he had had with President Trump: "I said, 'Well, Mr. President, I think you could possibly,' this is after he's only gotten one, I said, 'You could possibly get three Supreme Court Justices.' And this is vintage Trump, he said, 'I think I'm going to get five.'"

4 Gregory Kennedy denied that he ever spoke with Conway about his "father's views about the election or any other subject." Gregory Kennedy, e-mail to author, August 5, 2019.

5 Mark Hensch, "Trump hits Cruz on John Roberts—a court 'disaster,'" *The Hill*, February 25, 2016, https://thehill.com/blogs/ballot-box/presidential -races/270856-trump-cruz-very-very-strongly-pushed-justice-roberts.

6 Trump, "Remarks by President Trump and Justice Gorsuch at Swearing-in of Justice Gorsuch to the Supreme Court."

CHAPTER ONE: THE MISSING MAN

1 Discussion between Mitch McConnell and Don McGahn, the Federalist Society's 2018 National Lawyers Convention, Washington, D.C., November 15, 2018.

2 Donald J. Trump, remarks in CBS News Republican presidential debate, February 13, 2016, transcript published by the *Washington Post*, https://www.washingtonpost.com/news/the-fix/wp/2016/02/13/the-cbs-republican-debate-transcript-annotated/.

3 *Korte v. Sebelius*, 735 F.3d 654 (7th Circ. 2013).

4 Discussion between McConnell and McGahn, 2018 National Lawyers Convention. Referring to her opinion in the 2014 case *Wisconsin Right to Life, Inc., v. Barland*, McGahn said, "You'll appreciate this—Judge Sykes had written a very strong First Amendment opinion on campaign finance. So Judge Sykes, good job."

5 Bill Rankin, "Judge William Pryor in his own words," *Atlanta Journal-Constitution*, January 27, 2017, https://www.ajc.com/news/local/judge-william-pryor-his-own-words/64D3lGRd7oqmXDGXrD0RmJ/#; Kelly Green, "Bill Pryor Hopes to Ride Court Crusade to the Top," *Wall Street Journal,* May 21, 1997.

6 Discussion between McConnell and McGahn, 2018 National Lawyers Convention.

7 Donald J. Trump on *This Week with George Stephanopoulos*, ABC News, February 14, 2016, https://abcnews.go.com/Politics/week-transcript-ted-cruz-john-kasich-marco-rubio/story?id=36918872.

8 Jenna Johnson, "Donald Trump says his older sister isn't interested in becoming a Supreme Court judge," *Washington Post*, October 11, 2015, https://www.washingtonpost.com/news/post-politics/wp/2015/10/11/donald-trump-says-his-older-sister-isnt-interested-in-becoming-a-supreme-court-judge/.

9 *Planned Parenthood, C. New Jersey v. Farmer*, 220 F.3d 127 (3rd Cir. 2000).

10 Carrie Severino, "Don't Trump the Supreme Court," *USA Today*, October 12, 2015, https://www.usatoday.com/story/opinion/2015/10/12/trumps-suspect-judicial-credentials-supreme-court-nominations-column/73470706/. In her book on the Kavanaugh nomination with Mollie Hemingway, Severino would assert that Trump's remark had been "misinterpreted" and that his "carefree comment was obviously not serious."

11 David Weigel, "Jeb Bush's campaign shames Donald Trump for praising pro-choice sister," *Washington Post*, August 28, 2015, https://www.washingtonpost.com/news/post-politics/wp/2015/08/28/jeb-bushs-campaign-shames-donald-trump-for-praising-pro-choice-sister/.

12 Katie Zezima, "Cruz calls Trump's sister a 'radical pro-abortion extremist'

judge," *Washington Post*, February 15, 2016, https://www.washingtonpost
.com/news/post-politics/wp/2016/02/15/cruz-calls-trumps-sister-a-radical
-pro-abortion-extremist-judge/.

13 Elizabeth Williamson, "Political Substance Abuse: Donald Trump's
Washington Press Conference," *New York Times*, March 22, 2016, https://
takingnote.blogs.nytimes.com/2016/03/22/political-substance-abuse-donald
-trumps-washington-press-conference/.

14 John Santucci, "Trump Says He Stands with Israel, Daughter Having
'Beautiful Jewish Baby,'" ABC News, March 21, 2016, https://abcnews.go
.com/Politics/trump-stands-israel-daughter-beautiful-jewish-baby/story?id
=37825989.

15 Newt Gingrich, interview with author, February 25, 2019.

16 Rudy Giuliani, interview with author, June 19, 2019.

17 Williamson, "Political Substance Abuse."

18 Jason Zengerle, "How the Trump Administration Is Remaking the Courts,"
New York Times Magazine, August 22, 2018, https://www.nytimes.com/2018
/08/22/magazine/trump-remaking-courts-judiciary.html.

19 Michael Kruse, "The Weekend at Yale That Changed American Politics,"
Politico Magazine, September/October 2018, https://www.politico.com/maga
zine/story/2018/08/27/federalist-society-yale-history-conservative-law-court
-219608.

20 Steven M. Teles, *The Rise of the Conservative Legal Movement: The Battle
for Control of the Law* (Princeton, NJ: Princeton University Press, 2008),
137–38.

21 Kruse, "The Weekend at Yale That Changed American Politics."

22 Leonard Leo, "Leonard Leo on the Trump Administration and the future of
the federal judiciary," remarks delivered at the Acton Institute, May 11, 2017,
https://acton.org/video/leonard-leo-trump-administration-and-future-federal
-judiciary.

23 Leonard Leo, "Leonard Leo's Acceptance Speech at the 2017 Canterbury
Medal Gala," May 4, 2017, https://www.becketlaw.org/leonard-leo-speech
-2017-canterbury-medal-gala/.

24 Sam Nunberg, interview with author, December 18, 2018.

25 Donald McGahn, Barbara K. Olson Memorial Lecture at the Federalist
Society's National Lawyers Convention in Washington, D.C., November
17, 2017, https://www.c-span.org/video/?437462-8/2017-national-lawyers
-convention-white-house-counsel-mcgahn&start=1663.

26 Jeffrey Toobin, "The Conservative Pipeline to the Supreme Court," *New
Yorker*, April 10, 2017, https://www.newyorker.com/magazine/2017/04/17
/the-conservative-pipeline-to-the-supreme-court.

27 Zengerle, "How the Trump Administration Is Remaking the Courts."

28 David G. Savage, "Leonard Leo of the Federalist Society is the man to see if you aspire to the Supreme Court," *Los Angeles Times*, July 6, 2018, https://www.latimes.com/politics/la-na-pol-leo-court-search-20180706-story.html.

29 Ed Whelan, "Mistaken Attack by Andy Schlafly on Leonard Leo," *National Review*, December 9, 2016, https://www.nationalreview.com/bench-memos/schlafly-attack-leonard-leo/.

30 Robert O'Harrow Jr. and Shawn Boburg, "A conservative activist's behind-the-scenes campaign to remake the nation's courts," *Washington Post*, May 21, 2019, https://www.washingtonpost.com/graphics/2019/investigations/leonard-leo-federalists-society-courts/.

31 Ibid.

32 Release of Mortgage from Bank of America to Leonard A. Leo and Sally A. Leo, July 1, 2019, Hancock County, Maine Registry Office, document 2019009859. The document is accessible by searching here: http://remote.co.hancock.me.us/MEHancock/AvaWeb/#!/search.

33 Dalton Bennett, Jesse Mesner-Hage, and Jorge Ribas, *Pathways to power: The conservative movement transforming America's courts*, documentary by the *Washington Post*, May 21, 2019, https://www.washingtonpost.com/video/national/pathways-to-power-the-conservative-movement-transforming-americas-courts/2019/05/21/e1465572-549f-466d-9c09-9bafc1665a71_video.html.

34 McGahn, Barbara K. Olson Memorial Lecture.

35 David Wright, Tal Kopan, and Julia Manchester, "Cruz unloads with epic takedown of 'pathological liar,' 'narcissist' Donald Trump," CNN, May 3, 2016, https://www.cnn.com/2016/05/03/politics/donald-trump-rafael-cruz-indiana/index.html.

36 Josh Holmes, interview with author, February 21, 2019.

37 Peter Schroeder, "No Trump endorsement from Cruz: 'Vote your conscience,'" *The Hill*, July 20, 2016, https://thehill.com/blogs/ballot-box/presidential-races/288607-no-trump-endorsement-from-cruz-who-tells-gop-vote-your.

38 Alan Rappeport and Charlie Savage, "Donald Trump Releases List of Possible Supreme Court Picks," *New York Times*, May 18, 2016, https://www.nytimes.com/2016/05/19/us/politics/donald-trump-supreme-court-nominees.html.

39 Cristian Farias, "Donald Trump Expands His Supreme Court Wish List, Because Nothing Matters," *Huffington Post*, September 23, 2016, https://www.huffpost.com/entry/trump-second-supreme-court-wishlist_n_57e52004e4b08d73b830ad81.

40 Ted Cruz, Facebook post, September 23, 2016, https://www.facebook.com/tedcruzpage/posts/this-election-is-unlike-any-other-in-our-nations-history-like-many-other-voters-/10154476728267464/.

41 John Corrales, "Donald Trump Asks for Evangelicals' Support and Questions Hillary Clinton's Faith," *New York Times*, June 21, 2016, https://www.nytimes.com/2016/06/22/us/politics/donald-trump-asks-for-evangelicals-support-and-questions-hillary-clintons-faith.html.

42 Todd J. Gillman, "Trump vows to lead spiritual rejuvenation," *Dallas Morning News*, June 22, 2016.

43 Jesse Byrnes, "Trump: Republicans 'have no choice' but to vote for me," *The Hill*, July 28, 2016, https://thehill.com/blogs/blog-briefing-room/news/289716-trump-republicans-have-to-vote-for-me-because-of-supreme-court.

44 Politico staff, "Full transcript: Third 2016 presidential debate," *Politico*, October 20, 2016, https://www.politico.com/story/2016/10/full-transcript-third-2016-presidential-debate-230063.

45 Donald Trump, remarks at the Family Research Council's 11th Annual Values Voter Summit, September 9, 2016, transcript published by *Politico*, https://www.politico.com/story/2016/09/full-text-trump-values-voter-summit-remarks-227977.

46 Donald Trump, remarks in Waukesha, Wisconsin, September 28, 2016, https://factba.se/transcript/donald-trump-speech-waukesha-wi-september-28-2016.

47 Among other places, Kavanaugh publicly discussed his decision to stop voting when he became a judge in his answers to questions for the record submitted by senators after his first round of Supreme Court confirmation hearings. In response to a question from Jeff Flake ("Should a president be able to use his authority to pressure executive or independent agencies to carry out his directives for purely political purposes?"), Kavanaugh wrote in part: "I cannot comment on issues likely to come before me or on current political controversies, in keeping with the nominee precedent from all eight sitting Supreme Court Justices. Indeed, this is why, as a judge, I no longer vote in elections." See: "Kavanaugh Responses to Questions for the Record," Senate Judiciary Committee, released September 12, 2018, https://www.judiciary.senate.gov/imo/media/doc/Kavanaugh%20Responses%20to%20Questions%20for%20the%20Record.pdf, p. 4.

CHAPTER TWO: MAKING THE LIST

1 U.S. Congress, Senate Committee on the Judiciary, *Hearing on the Nomination of Brett Kavanaugh to be an Associate Justice on the Supreme Court*, 115th Cong., 2nd sess., Day 2, September 5, 2018.

2 Judge Brett Kavanaugh, Nominee, Associate Justice of the Supreme Court

of the United States, Responses to Questions for the Record, published by the Senate Judiciary Committee September 12, 2018, p. 220, https://www .judiciary.senate.gov/imo/media/doc/Kavanaugh%20Responses%20to%20 Questions%20for%20the%20Record.pdf.

3 Oral arguments in *Seven-Sky v. Holder* at the United States Court of Appeals for the District of Columbia Circuit, September 23, 2011, http:// joshblackman.com/blog/wp-content/uploads/2018/07/HC-CTA-Transcript -Oral-Argument-9-23-11-1.pdf.

4 Josh Blackman, interview with author, April 1, 2019.

5 *Priests for Life v. US Department of Health and Human Services*, 772 F.3d 229, 249 (D.C. Cir. 2014), https://www.leagle.com/decision/infco20141114147.

6 *Priests for Life v. US Department of Health and Human Services*, 808 F.3d 1, Kavanaugh, J., dissenting, 22-23 (D.C. Cir. 2015), https://www.cadc .uscourts.gov/internet/opinions.nsf/425C0AE29F10AFD785257E4B00767 BF5/$file/13-5368.pdf.

7 *Priests for Life v. US Department of Health and Human Services*, Kavanaugh, J., dissenting, 18–19.

8 Brett M. Kavanaugh, "Two challenges for the judge as umpire: statutory ambiguity and constitutional exceptions," keynote address delivered at Notre Dame Law School as part of Federal Courts, Practice & Procedure Symposium: Justice Scalia and the Federal Courts, February 3, 2017, https:// scholarship.law.nd.edu/cgi/viewcontent.cgi?article=4733&context=ndlr.

9 Ibid.

10 Remarks by Brett M. Kavanaugh, "From the Bench: The Constitutional Statesmanship of Chief Justice William Rehnquist," at the American Enterprise Institute in Washington, D.C., September 18, 2017, http://www.aei.org /wp-content/uploads/2017/12/From-the-Bench.pdf.

11 Ibid.

12 Nancy Cook, "He's Going to Be an Enabler," *Politico Magazine*, February 21, 2017, https://www.politico.com/magazine/story/2017/02/trump-mcgahn -white-house-lawyer-214801.

13 Shane D'Aprile, "Movers and Shakers: Don McGahn," *Campaigns & Elections*, December 17, 2013, https://www.campaignsandelections.com /campaign-insider/movers-shakers-don-mcgahn.

14 Donald McGahn, remarks at the Federalist Society's National Lawyers Convention in Washington, D.C., November 15, 2018.

15 *Garza v. Hargan*, 874 F.3d 735, 736–737 (D.C. Cir. 2017) https://www.cadc .uscourts.gov/internet/opinions.nsf/C81A5EDEADAE82F2852581C30068 AF6E/$file/17-5236-1701167.pdf.

16 *Garza v. Hargan*, LeCraft Henderson, J., dissenting, 743.

17 *Garza v. Hargan*, Kavanaugh, J., dissenting, 752–56.

18 U.S. Congress, Senate Committee on the Judiciary, Hearing on the Nomination of Brett Kavanaugh.

19 The White House, "President Donald J. Trump Announces Five Additions to Supreme Court List," November 17, 2017, https://www.whitehouse.gov /briefings-statements/president-donald-j-trump-announces-five-additions -supreme-court-list/.

20 McGahn, Barbara K. Olson Memorial Lecture at the Federalist Society's National Lawyers Convention, November 17, 2017.

CHAPTER THREE: THE SWING JUSTICE DEPARTS

1 Donald Trump, Twitter post, February 4, 2017, 8:12 a.m., https://twitter.com /realdonaldtrump/status/827867311054974976?lang=en.

2 David A. Kaplan, *The Most Dangerous Branch: Inside the Supreme Court's Assault on the Constitution* (New York: Crown, 2018), 161.

3 David Lat, "No, Justice Anthony M. Kennedy Is Not Retiring Tomorrow," *Above the Law*, June 25, 2017, https://abovethelaw.com/2017/06/no-justice -anthony-m-kennedy-is-not-retiring-tomorrow/.

4 *New York Times* editorial board, "Please Stay, Justice Kennedy. America Needs You," *New York Times*, April 28, 2018, https://www.nytimes.com/2018 /04/28/opinion/sunday/justice-kennedy-supreme-court-open-letter.html.

5 Rebecca Morin, "Grassley tries to nudge Supreme Court justices into early retirement," *Politico*, May 10, 2018, https://www.politico.com/story/2018 /05/10/chuck-grassley-supreme-court-retirement-579901.

6 Marc Short, interview with author, January 3, 2019.

7 David Rubenstein, "The David Rubenstein Show: Anthony Kennedy," Bloomberg TV, released November 28, 2018, interview filmed November 16, 2018, https://www.bloomberg.com/news/videos/2018-11-28/the-david-ruben stein-show-anthony-kennedy-video. Rubenstein asked Kennedy how he had managed to keep his retirement plans a secret. "In part it was a secret even from Mary and the family," Kennedy said. "I'm trying to make up my mind to balance these various things. I think it was a Wednesday, which was our last conference day, and I made up my mind Tuesday night, that this was what we should do, and told Mary then."

8 Carl Hulse, *Confirmation Bias: Inside Washington's War Over the Supreme Court, from Scalia's Death to Justice Kavanaugh* (New York: Harper/Harper-Collins, 2019), 243.

9 *Trump v. Hawaii*, 585 U.S. _____ (2018), Kennedy, J., concurring, June 26, 2018, https://www.supremecourt.gov/opinions/17pdf/17-965_h315.pdf.

10 When Justice Harry Blackmun retired from the court in April 1994, he went

to the White House and stood by President Bill Clinton's side for a press conference.

11 Donald Trump, "Remarks by President Trump and President Rebelo de Sousa of the Portuguese Republic Before Bilateral Meeting," June 27, 2018, https://www.whitehouse.gov/briefings-statements/remarks-president-trump -president-rebelo-de-sousa-portuguese-republic-bilateral-meeting/.

12 Sources familiar with the Kennedy-Trump meeting offer conflicting accounts of whether Kavanaugh was the only name that Kennedy mentioned or whether he also recommended Kethledge, another former clerk.

13 Al Kamen, "Justice Powell Resigns, Was Supreme Court's Pivotal Vote," *Washington Post*, June 27, 1987, p. A1, https://www.washingtonpost.com/wp -srv/national/longterm/supcourt/stories/powell062787.htm.

14 Edwin Meese, remarks to the American Bar Association, July 9, 1985, https:// www.justice.gov/sites/default/files/ag/legacy/2011/08/23/07-09-1985.pdf.

15 Justice William J. Brennan, Jr., remarks at the Text and Teaching Symposium at Georgetown University, October 12, 1985, published online by the Federalist Society, https://fedsoc.org/commentary/publications/the-great-debate -justice-william-j-brennan-jr-october-12-1985.

16 David Jackson, "New issue in Trump-Cruz battle: John Roberts," *USA Today*, January 17, 2016, https://www.usatoday.com/story/news/politics/onpolitics /2016/01/17/donald-trump-ted-cruz-john-roberts-supreme-court-obamacare /78931780/.

17 Linda Greenhouse, "High Court, 5-4, Affirms Right to Abortion but Allows Most of Pennsylvania's Limits," *New York Times*, June 30, 1992, https:// www.nytimes.com/1992/06/30/us/supreme-court-high-court-5-4-affirms -right-abortion-but-allows-most-pennsylvania.html.

18 Adam Liptak, "Supreme Court Strikes Down Texas Abortion Restrictions," *New York Times*, June 27, 2016, https://www.nytimes.com/2016/06/28/us /supreme-court-texas-abortion.html.

19 Robert Barnes, "Supreme Court upholds University of Texas affirmative-action admissions," *Washington Post*, June 23, 2016, https://www .washingtonpost.com/politics/courts_law/supreme-court-upholds-university -of-texas-affirmative-action-admissions/2016/06/23/513bcc10-394d-11e6 -8f7c-d4c723a2becb_story.html.

20 *Lawrence v. Texas*, 539 U.S. 558 (2003), 579, https://supreme.justia.com/ cases/federal/us/539/558/case.pdf.

21 *Obergefell v. Hodges*, 576 U.S. ___ (2015), 17–18, https://www.supreme-court.gov/opinions/14pdf/14-556_3204.pdf.

22 *Obergefell v. Hodges*, Roberts, C. J., dissenting, 2.

23 Amelia Thomson-Deveaux, "Justice Kennedy Wasn't a Moderate," *Five-

ThirtyEight, July 3, 2018, https://fivethirtyeight.com/features/justice -kennedy-wasnt-a-moderate/.

24 Erwin Chemerinsky, "A New Era for the Supreme Court," *American Prospect*, July 2, 2018; Adam Liptak, "Supreme Court Upholds Ohio's Purge of Voting Rolls," *New York Times*, June 11, 2018, https://www.nytimes.com /2018/06/11/us/politics/supreme-court-upholds-ohios-purge-of-voting-rolls .html.

25 Robert Barnes, "Justice Kennedy, the pivotal swing vote on the Supreme Court, announces his retirement," *Washington Post*, June 27, 2018, https:// www.washingtonpost.com/politics/courts_law/justice-kennedy-the-pivotal -swing-vote-on-the-supreme-court-announces-retirement/2018/06/27/a40 a8c64-5932-11e7-a204-ad706461fa4f_story.html.

26 Jason Zengerle, "How the Trump Administration Is Remaking the Courts," *New York Times Magazine*, August 22, 2018, https://www.nytimes.com/2018 /08/22/magazine/trump-remaking-courts-judiciary.html.

27 Charles Homans, "Mitch McConnell Got Everything He Wanted. But at What Cost?" *New York Times Magazine*, January 22, 2019, https://www.nytimes .com/2019/01/22/magazine/mcconnell-senate-trump.html?module=inline.

28 Tessa Berenson, "'We'd Like to See America Right of Center.' Mitch McConnell Explains His Strategy on Judges," *Time*, February 8, 2018, https://time.com/5138247/mitch-mcconnell-judicial-strategy/.

29 Mitch McConnell, *The Long Game: A Memoir* (New York: Sentinel, 2016), 7–8, 134.

30 Eric Bradner, "McConnell 'committed to supporting' Trump," CNN, May 4, 2016, https://www.cnn.com/2016/05/04/politics/mitch-mcconnell-donald -trump-republican-nominee/index.html.

31 Donald J. Trump, Twitter post, August 10, 2017, 12:40 p.m., https://twitter .com/realdonaldtrump/status/895686351529672704?lang=en.

CHAPTER FOUR: THE NOT-SO-INVISIBLE PRIMARY

1 Stephanie Ebbs, "Trump to announce his pick to replace Kennedy on Supreme Court after July 4," ABC News, June 29, 2018, https://abcnews .go.com/Politics/trumps-announce-pick-supreme-court-justice/story?id =56261772.

2 Aaron Blake, "Brett Kavanaugh's first claim as a Supreme Court nominee was bizarre," *Washington Post*, July 10, 2018, https://www.washington post.com/news/the-fix/wp/2018/07/10/brett-kavanaughs-first-claim-as-a -supreme-court-nominee-was-bizarre/.

3 Andrew P. Napolitano, "Judge Andrew Napolitano: Did President Trump obstruct justice?," Fox News, April 25, 2019, https://www.foxnews.com /opinion/judge-andrew-napolitano-did-president-trump-obstruct-justice.

4 Donald J. Trump, Twitter post, April 27, 2019, 10:57 p.m., https://twitter.com /realdonaldtrump/status/1122334000519868416?lang=en.

5 Andrew Napolitano interview, "Trump slams Judge Napolitano on obstruction of justice claims," *Mornings with Maria*, Fox Business Network, April 29, 2019, https://video.foxbusiness.com/v/6031037418001/#sp=show-clips.

6 Kimberly Kindy, "Pryor: Perhaps the most polarizing Supreme Court justice possibility," *Washington Post*, January 28, 2017, https://www.washington post.com/national/pryor-perhaps-the-most-polarizing-supreme-court-justice -possibility/2017/01/28/f25bb7e2-e4ae-11e6-ba11-63c4b4fb5a63_story .html?utm_term=.3fe726b3373c.

7 David Skinner, "A Souter They Should've Spurned," *Weekly Standard*, July 25, 2005, https://www.weeklystandard.com/david-skinner/a-souter-they -shouldve-spurned.

8 George H. W. Bush's handwritten notes on Supreme Court candidate David Souter, July 23, 1990, Daily Files series, Office of the President, Bush Presidential Records, George H. W. Bush Presidential Library & Museum, College Station, Texas.

9 Handwritten notes of President Bush re: his thoughts on the Supreme Court candidates, July 23, 1990, Daily Files series, Office of the President, Bush Presidential Records, George H. W. Bush Presidential Library & Museum, College Station, Texas.

10 Donald McGahn, remarks at the Federalist Society's National Lawyers Convention, November 17, 2017, https://www.c-span.org/video/?437462-8 /2017-national-lawyers-convention-white-house-counsel-mcgahn.

11 *Gutierrez-Brizuela v. Lynch*, No. 14-9585 (10th Cir. 2016), August 23, 2016, Gorsuch, J., concurring, 15, https://www.ca10.uscourts.gov/opinions/14/14 -9585.pdf.

12 Julie Hirschfeld Davis, "Supreme Court Nominee Calls Trump's Attacks on Judiciary 'Demoralizing,'" *New York Times*, February 8, 2017, https://www .nytimes.com/2017/02/08/us/politics/donald-trump-immigration-ban.html.

13 Ashley Parker, Josh Dawsey, and Robert Barnes, "Trump talked about rescinding Gorsuch's nomination," *Washington Post*, December 19, 2017, https://www.washingtonpost.com/politics/trump-reportedly-considered -rescinding-gorsuchs-nomination/2017/12/18/ad2b3b68-e1c7-11e7-9eb6 -e3c7ecfb4638_story.html.

14 Donald Trump, Twitter post, February 9, 2017, 7:57 a.m., https://twitter.com /realDonaldTrump/status/829660612452036608?ref_src=twsrc%5Etfw%7C twcamp%5Etweetembed%7Ctwterm%5E829660612452036608&ref_url=

https%3A%2F%2Fwww.npr.org%2F2017%2F02%2F08%2F514195859%2F gorsuch-calls-trump-tweets-about-judges-demoralizing-and-disheartening. Blumenthal served in the Marine Reserve but not in Vietnam. Trump received a medical exemption from the draft, based on a letter citing bone spurs.

15 Parker, Dawsey, and Barnes, "Trump talked about rescinding Gorsuch's nomination."

16 Hope Yen and Ken Thomas, "Collins would oppose court pick with *Roe v. Wade* 'hostility,'" Associated Press, July 1, 2018, https://www.apnews.com /b0c5cb5c48c143d69fbf12b8b7440639.

17 Susan Collins on *This Week with George Stephanopoulos*, ABC News, July 1, 2018, https://abcnews.go.com/Politics/week-transcript-18/story?id=56292891.

18 Susan Collins, interview with author, September 27, 2019.

19 Helmut Schmidt, "Trump gets rock-star treatment from red-state crowd in Fargo," *Jamestown Sun*, June 27, 2018, https://www.jamestownsun.com /news/government-and-politics/4466043-trump-gets-rock-star-treatment -red-state-crowd-fargo.

20 Heidi Heitkamp, interview with author, December 5, 2018.

21 Hugh Hewitt, "Here's who Trump should pick for the Supreme Court," *Washington Post*, July 2, 2018, https://www.washingtonpost.com/opinions /why-trump-should-nominate-raymond-kethledge/2018/07/02/e13e0540 -7e37-11e8-b660-4d0f9f0351f1_story.html.

22 Michelle Boorstein and Julie Zauzmer, "The story behind potential Supreme Court nominee Amy Coney Barrett's little-known Catholic group, People of Praise," *Washington Post*, July 7, 2018, https://www.washingtonpost.com /news/acts-of-faith/wp/2018/07/06/the-story-behind-potential-supreme-court -nominee-amy-coney-barretts-little-known-catholic-group-people-of-praise/.

23 Ibid.

24 Amy C. Barrett, "Precedent and Jurisprudential Disagreement," *Texas Law Review* 91:1711 (2012–2013): 1728, https://scholarship.law.nd.edu/cgi/view content.cgi?article=1274&context=law_faculty_scholarship.

25 Ramesh Ponnuru, interview with author, January 11, 2019.

26 Matt Schlapp, "With Brett Kavanaugh, America will have a bold, brilliant Supreme Court justice," *The Hill*, July 5, 2018, https://thehill.com/opinion/ judiciary/395524-with-brett-kavanaugh-america-will-have-a-bold-brilliant -supreme-court.

27 Donald J. Trump, Twitter post, March 9, 2019, 5:04 p.m., https://twitter.com /realdonaldtrump/status/1104503216111321089?lang=en.

28 Ann Coulter, Twitter post, July 4, 2018, 1:09 p.m.,https://twitter.com/ann coulter/status/1014556729823186944?lang=en.

29 Ann Coulter, Twitter post, July 4, 2018, 1:14 p.m, https://twitter.com/ann coulter/status/1014558022033723397?lang=en.

30 Ann Coulter, Twitter post, July 4, 2018, 1:56 p.m, https://twitter.com/ann coulter/status/1014568715097198592?lang=en.

31 Ann Coulter, Twitter post, July 7, 2018, 11:32 a.m, https://twitter.com/ann coulter/status/1015619532117901312.

32 Sarah E. Pitlyk, "Judge Brett Kavanaugh's Impeccable Record of Constitutional Conservatism," *National Review*, July 3, 2018, https://www .nationalreview.com/2018/07/judge-brett-kavanaughs-impeccable-record-of -constitutional-conservatism/.

33 Ibid.

34 Christopher Jacobs, "How Potential SCOTUS Pick Brett Kavanaugh Wrote a Roadmap for Saving Obamacare," *The Federalist*, July 2, 2018, https:// thefederalist.com/2018/07/02/potential-scotus-pick-brett-kavanaugh-wrote -roadmap-saving-obamacare/.

35 Justin Walker, "Brett Kavanaugh Said Obamacare Was Unprecedented and Unlawful," *The Federalist*, July 3, 2018, https://thefederalist.com/2018/07/03 /brett-kavanaugh-said-obamacare-unprecedented-unlawful/.

36 *Seven-Sky v. Holder*, 661 F. 3d 1 (D.C. Cir. 2011), Kavanaugh, J., dissenting, 51–53, https://scholar.google.com/scholar_case?case=122831400684626475 56&hl=en&as_sdt=6&as_vis=1&oi=scholarr.

CHAPTER FIVE: A THORN IN THE FLESH

1 Special Counsel Robert Mueller, "Report on the Investigation into Russian Interference in the 2016 Presidential Election," U.S. Department of Justice, March 2019, vol. I, pp. 113–17, https://www.justice.gov/storage/report.pdf.

2 Phillip L. Jauregui to conservative group leaders, "Re: Brief Comparison of Two Leading Supreme Court Prospects: Judge Brett Kavanaugh (D.C. Cir.) and Judge Amy Coney Barrett (Seventh Cir.)," June 27, 2018.

3 Judicial Action Group Inc. form 990 for fiscal year ending December 2017, published by *ProPublica*'s Nonprofit Explorer, https://projects.propublica .org/nonprofits/organizations/202603039/201841799349300249/IRS990.

4 Peter Montgomery, "JAG's Phillip Jauregui: Barrett Is God's Anointed, Kavanaugh a 'Usurper' Out to Steal God's SCOTUS Seat," *Right Wing Watch*, July 6, 2018, https://www.rightwingwatch.org/post/jags-phillip-jauregui-barrett -is-gods-anointed-kavanaugh-a-usurper-out-to-steal-gods-scotus-seat/.

5 Tim Wildmon, Terry Schilling, Mat Staver, Phillip L. Jauregui, and Debbie Wuthnow to Donald Trump, "Re: The Nomination of the Next Justice to the Supreme Court of the United States," June 28, 2018, https://www.afa.net /media/231721/letters-to-trump-on-nominating-judge-barrett.pdf.

6 "Marjorie Dannenfelser," biography page, SBAList.org, https://www.sba-list .org/marjorie-dannenfelser, accessed September 24, 2019.

7 The Judicial Crisis Network gave Susan B. Anthony List $700,000 in the 2016–2017 fiscal year and $75,000 the following year. Judicial Crisis Network form 990 2016, p. 23, https://www.documentcloud.org/documents/4463990 -Judicial-Crisis-Network-990-2016-2017.html; Judicial Crisis Network form 990 2017, p. 29, https://www.documentcloud.org/documents/6007244-JCN -2017-990.html.

8 Tara Palmeri, "Anti-abortion rights groups quietly lobbying against Supreme Court finalist," ABCNews.com, July 2, 2018, https://abcnews.go.com/Politics /anti-abortion-rights-groups-quietly-lobbying-supreme-court/story?id=563 30232.

9 Benny Johnson, "Movement Conservatives Fume at Trump SCOTUS Favorite: 'This Is the Low-Energy Jeb Bush Pick,'" *Daily Caller*, July 3, 2018, https://dailycaller.com/2018/07/03/conservatives-trump-supreme-court -brett-kavanaugh/.

10 Glenn Beck, Twitter post, July 3, 2018, 10:04 a.m., https://twitter.com/glennbeck /status/1014147989319880704.

11 Ryan Lovelace, "Conservative Lawyer Bopp Urges Trump to Pass on Kavanaugh for SCOTUS," *National Law Journal*, July 3, 2018, https://www .law.com/nationallawjournal/2018/07/03/conservative-lawyer-bopp-urges -trump-to-pass-on-kavanaugh-for-scotus/.

12 Johnson referenced the document in a story about the broader conservative opposition effort against Kavanaugh. Eliana Johnson, "Trump's Supreme Court search unleashes fierce politicking," *Politico*, July 4, 2018, https://www .politico.com/story/2018/07/04/trump-supreme-court-pick-brett-kavanaugh -694787.

13 Jim DeMint, "DO NOT Waste a Once-in-a-Generation Opportunity to Cement a Conservative Supreme Court Majority," *Daily Caller*, July 2, 2018, https://dailycaller.com/2018/07/02/mike-lee-for-supreme-court/.

14 John Bowden, "Who top conservatives want Trump to pick for Supreme Court," *The Hill*, July 7, 2018, https://thehill.com/homenews/administration /395960-who-top-conservatives-want-trump-to-pick-for-supreme-court.

15 Peter Vicenzi, "FreedomWorks President Adam Brandon Signs Letter with Conservative Leaders Supporting Senator Mike Lee as a Nominee for Supreme Court Justice," FreedomWorks press release, July 6, 2018, https:// www.freedomworks.org/content/freedomworks-president-adam-brandon -signs-letter-conservative-leaders-supporting-senator.

16 *Klayman v. Obama*, 805 F.3d 1148 (D.C. Cir. 2015), Kavanaugh, J. concurring, 1149, https://scholar.google.com/scholar_case?case=18099556907815522361

&q=Klayman+v.+Obama&hl=en&as_sdt=2006https://scholar.google.com
/scholar_case?case=18099556907815522361&q=Klayman+v.+Obama&hl
=en&as_sdt=2006.

17 Maggie Haberman and Jonathan Martin, "McConnell Tries to Nudge Trump
Toward Two Supreme Court Options," *New York Times*, July 7, 2018, https://
www.nytimes.com/2018/07/07/us/politics/trump-mcconnell-supreme-court
.html.

18 Lindsey Graham, interview with author, August 24, 2019.

19 Josh Gerstein, "'Ranting and raving': The time Kavanaugh knocked Chris
Ruddy," *Politico*, July 11, 2018, https://www.politico.com/story/2018/07/11
/kavanaugh-ruddy-trump-ranting-raving-starr-712865.

20 United States Conference of Catholic Bishops, reading 2, July 8, 2018: 2 Corinthians 12:7–10, http://www.usccb.org/bible/readings/070818.cfm.

21 Media reports in the days after Kavanaugh's nomination claimed that Ashley
Kavanaugh joined her husband, President Trump, and the First Lady for
dinner at the residence, based on information from the White House, but
Kavanaugh actually attended on his own.

22 "George Bush Sr. calls Trump a 'blowhard' and voted for Clinton," BBC News,
November 4, 2017, https://www.bbc.com/news/world-us-canada-41871958.

23 Max Greenwood, "Trump hits Bush: Invading Iraq 'the single worst decision
ever made,'" *The Hill*, March 3, 2018, https://thehill.com/homenews/adminis
tration/376605-trump-hits-bush-invading-iraq-the-single-worst-decision
-ever-made.

CHAPTER SIX: NO REBEL, NO CAUSE

1 Transcript of Investiture of Brett M. Kavanaugh, United States Court of
Appeals for the District of Columbia Circuit, September 27, 2006, pp. 31–32,
held by the library at the District Court of Appeals for the D.C. Circuit.

2 U.S. Congress, Senate, Committee on the Judiciary, *Confirmation Hearing
on the Nomination of Brett M. Kavanaugh to be Circuit Judge for the District
of Columbia Circuit*, 108th Cong., 2nd sess., April 27, 2004, 1, https://www
.govinfo.gov/content/pkg/CHRG-108shrg24853/pdf/CHRG-108shrg24853
EveryoneCanBake_1p_SC1009_single.pdf.

3 Lorraine Woellert, "Trump asks business groups for help pushing Kavanaugh
confirmation," *Politico*, July 9, 2018, https://www.politico.com/story/2018
/07/09/brett-kavanaugh-business-groups-trump-705800.

4 Douglas C. McGill, "Cosmetics Companies Quietly Ending Animal Tests,"
New York Times, August 2, 1989, https://www.nytimes.com/1989/08/02
/business/cosmetics-companies-quietly-ending-animal-tests.html.

5 Sam Donaldson, "Business as Usual," segment on *Primetime Live*, ABC News, October 25, 1990.

6 Brett Kavanaugh, "Full text: Brett Kavanaugh confirmation hearing opening statement," *Politico*, September 4, 2018, https://www.politico.com/story /2018/09/04/full-text-brett-kavanaugh-confirmation-hearing-opening-state ments-806420.

7 Cynthia Grant Bowman, "Women in the Legal Profession from the 1920s to the 1970s: What Can We Learn from Their Experience about Law and Social Change?" *Cornell Law Faculty Publications*, 2009, p. 15, https://scholarship .law.cornell.edu/cgi/viewcontent.cgi?article=1011&context=facpub.

8 Elizabeth M. Hengeveld and Stuart M. Wise, "Justice is Blonde," *National Law Journal*, October 31, 1983, vol. 6, p. 22.

9 Brett Kavanaugh, remarks following his announcement as Supreme Court nominee, released by the White House, July 9, 2018, https://www.white house.gov/briefings-statements/remarks-president-trump-announcing-judge -brett-m-kavanaugh-nominee-associate-justice-supreme-court-united-states/.

10 Maryland Manual On-Line, "Montgomery County Circuit Court Former Judges: Martha Gamble Kavanaugh," https://msa.maryland.gov/msa/md manual/31cc/former/html/msa12367.html.

11 Mark Gauvreau Judge, *God and Man at Georgetown Prep: How I Became a Catholic Despite 20 Years of Catholic Schooling* (New York: Crossroad Publishing Company, 2005), 93.

12 Kate Kelly and David Enrich, "Kavanaugh's 1983 Letter Offers Inside Look at High School Clique," *New York Times*, October 2, 2018, https://www .nytimes.com/2018/10/02/us/brett-kavanaugh-georgetown-prep.html.

13 Martha MacCallum interview with Brett Kavanaugh, *The Story with Martha MacCallum*, Fox News, September 24, 2018.

14 Transcript of Investiture of Brett M. Kavanaugh, 29–30.

15 Neil Bermel, "College masters abolish annual Tang competition," *Yale Daily News* 106, no. 1 (September 8, 1983): 1.

16 *Yale Daily News* stories published in September and October 1983, archived at https://web.library.yale.edu/digital-collections/yale-daily-news-historical -archive.

17 Hailey Fuchs and Britton O'Daly, "A flag of underwear: Photo from Kavanaugh's time shows DKE hijinks," *Yale Daily News*, September 20, 2018, https://yaledailynews.com/blog/2018/09/20/a-flag-of-underwear-photo -from-kavanaughs-time-shows-dke-hijinks/.

18 Aaron C. Davis, Emma Brown, and Joe Heim, "Kavanaugh's 'choir boy' image on Fox interview rankles former Yale classmates," *Washington Post*, September 25, 2018, https://www.washingtonpost.com/investigations/2018 /09/25/ea5e50d4-c0eb-11e8-9005-5104e9616c21_story.html.

19 Lynne Brookes, interview with author, December 7, 2018.

20 Sams, interview with author, January 29, 2019.

21 Chad Ludington, interview with author, January 29, 2019.

22 Sams interview.

23 Emily Bazelon and Ben Protess, "Kavanaugh Was Questioned by Police After Bar Fight in 1985," *New York Times*, October 1, 2018, https://www.nytimes.com/2018/10/01/us/politics/kavanaugh-bar-fight.html.

24 The *Wall Street Journal*'s Jess Bravin reported this account on October 5, 2018, the day of the cloture vote. The author independently reviewed the full FBI affidavit. Jess Bravin, "Among the Thousands of FBI Tips, a Statement From an Aggrieved Truck Owner," *Wall Street Journal*, October 5, 2018, https://www.wsj.com/livecoverage/Kavanaugh/card/1538782969.

25 Pema Levy, "Brett Kavanaugh Gave a Speech about Binge Drinking in Law School," *Mother Jones*, September 17, 2018, https://www.motherjones.com/politics/2018/09/brett-kavanaugh-gave-a-speech-about-binge-drinking-in-law-school/.

26 Dan Levy, interview with author, February 14, 2019.

27 Jonathan Franklin, interview with author, January 11, 2019.

28 Brett M. Kavanaugh, "Defense Presence and Participation: A Procedural Minimum for *Batson v. Kentucky* Hearings," *Yale Law Journal* 99 (1989): 199, https://digitalcommons.law.yale.edu/cgi/viewcontent.cgi?article=7241&context=ylj.

29 *Webster v. Reproductive Health Services*, 492 U.S. 490 (1989), Blackmun, J., dissenting, 560, https://supreme.justia.com/cases/federal/us/492/490/#tab-opinion-1958093.

30 Walter Stapleton, interview with author, December 11, 2018.

31 *Planned Parenthood v. Casey*, 947 F.2d 682; 707 (3rd Cir. 1991), https://www.npr.org/documents/2006/jan/alitodocuments/casey1991.pdf.

32 Ibid., 711–12.

33 Ibid., Alito, J., dissenting, 726.

34 Michael Decourcy Hinds, "Appeals Court Upholds Limits for Abortions," *New York Times*, October 22, 1991, https://www.nytimes.com/1991/10/22/us/appeals-court-upholds-limits-for-abortions.html.

35 *Federal and State Judicial Clerkship Directory*, National Association for Law Placement, 1990.

36 George Priest, interview with author, December 5, 2018.

37 Ibid.

38 Alanna Durkin Richer and Jennifer Peltz, "At Yale, Kavanaugh stayed out of debates at a time of many," AP News, August 28, 2018, https://apnews.com/ce93f04d0594441ebe14f7cfb2442f11.

39 Linda Greenhouse, "Fierce Combat on Fewer Battlefields," *New York Times*, July 3, 1994, https://www.nytimes.com/1994/07/03/weekinreview/the-nation -fierce-combat-on-fewer-battlefields.html.

40 Stephen Smith, interview with author, June 21, 2019.

41 Gary Feinerman, interview with author, December 12, 2018.

42 Sandra Day O'Connor, "Memorandum to the Conference re: 92-854 *Central Bank of Denver v. First Interstate Bank of Denver*," May 28, 1993, Harry A. Blackmun papers, Box 634, Folder 4, Library of Congress, Washington, D.C.

43 Harry Blackmun, notes from the justices' conference, December 3, 1993, Blackmun papers, Box 634, Folder 4. The notes indicate that Justice Kennedy's initial vote sided with the court's liberals, but caveated: "for now."

44 Anthony M. Kennedy to Harry Blackmun, February 17, 1994, Blackmun papers, Box 634, Folder 3. Kennedy wrote, "After working through the cases, particularly *Blue Chip Stamps*, *Ernst & Ernst*, *Pinter*, and *Musick*, I came to the conclusion that our precedents require us to confine the 10b-5 cause of action to primary violators, without extension to aiders and abettors. Though that still brings me out to reverse, it seems appropriate to circulate this in memorandum form to highlight the change from the conference position."

45 *Central Bank of Denver, N.A. v. First Interstate Bank of Denver, N.A.*, 511 U.S. 164, 177 (1994).

46 Ibid., Stevens, J., dissenting, 192, 195, 198.

47 Correspondence between justices, October 20, 1993, through June 29, 1994, Blackmun papers, Box 631, Folder 9.

48 William Rehnquist, memorandum to the conference re: No. 91-2012 *Holder v. Hall*, June 21, 1994, Blackmun papers, Box 631, Folder 9.

49 *Holder v. Hall*, 512 U.S. 874, 881 (1994).

50 Ibid., Blackmun, J., dissenting, 955 (1994).

CHAPTER SEVEN: RIGHT TURN

1 Ken Gormley, *The Death of American Virtue: Clinton vs. Starr* (New York: Crown Publishing, 2010), 146.

2 Jan Crawford Greenburg, *Supreme Conflict: The Inside Story of the Struggle for Control of the United States Supreme Court* (New York: Penguin, 2007), e-book edition, location 1337–60.

3 Ken Starr, *Contempt: A Memoir of the Clinton Investigation* (New York: Sentinel, 2018), 40.

4 Brett Kavanaugh memorandum to OIC attorneys, "Overall Plan," December 24, 1998 [digitized record]; URTS 16315, Document ID 70105246, Brett

Kavanaugh Attorney Work Files, Records of Independent Counsel Kenneth W. Starr, National Archives, https://www.archives.gov/files/research/kavanaugh /releases/docid-70105246.pdf.

5 Neil A. Lewis, "Federal Jury Acquits McDougal on One Charge and Is Split on Two," *New York Times*, April 13, 1999, https://archive.nytimes.com/www .nytimes.com/library/politics/041399mcdougal-trial.html.

6 "Final report of the independent counsel (in re: Madison Guaranty Savings & Loan Association)," United States Court of Appeals (District of Columbia Circuit) Division for the Purpose of Appointing Independent Counsels, March 16, 2000, vol. III, "Part E: The Discovery and Removal of Items from Vincent W. Foster's Office," pp. 315–16, https://www.govinfo.gov/content /pkg/GPO-ICREPORT-MADISON/pdf/GPO-ICREPORT-MADISON-3 -3.pdf.

7 Colleen Covell, interview with author, January 8, 2019.

8 United States Congress, Senate, Committee on the Judiciary, *Hearing on the Nomination of Brett Kavanaugh to be an Associate Justice on the Supreme Court, Day 5, Focusing on Allegations of Sexual Assault*, 115th Cong., 2nd sess., September 27, 2018.

9 R. W. Apple, Jr., "Note Left by White House Aide: Accusation, Anger and Despair," *New York Times*, August 11, 1993, https://www.nytimes.com/1993 /08/11/us/note-left-by-white-house-aide-accusation-anger-and-despair.html.

10 Jose A. DelReal and Robert Costa, "Trump escalates attack on Bill Clinton," *Washington Post*, May 23, 2016, https://www.washingtonpost.com/politics /trump-escalates-attack-on-bill-clinton/2016/05/23/ed109acc-2100-11e6 -8690-f14ca9de2972_story.html.

11 Ronald J. Ostrow and John Broder, "Bitter Lament by Foster Revealed Depth of Despair," *Los Angeles Times*, August 11, 1993, https://www.latimes.com /archives/la-xpm-1993-08-11-mn-22695-story.html.

12 Robert B. Fiske, Jr., "Report of the Independent Counsel: In re Vincent W. Foster, Jr.," June 30, 1994, pp. 6–7, 58.

13 Starr, *Contempt*, 85–86.

14 Brett Kavanaugh to Judge Starr, Mark Tuohey, Bill Duffey, Hickman Ewing, John Bates, Professor Dash, and Alex Azar, Memorandum re: Foster Death Investigation, March 24, 1995.

15 Kavanaugh to Starr, Tuohey, Duffey, Ewing, and Bates re: Foster Investigations, March 4, 1995 [digitized record], URTS 16305, Document ID 70105100, pp. 391–392, Brett Kavanaugh Attorney Work Files, Records of Independent Counsel Kenneth W. Starr, National Archives, https://www .archives.gov/files/research/kavanaugh/releases/docid-70105100.pdf.

16 Brett Kavanaugh to Judge Starr, Mark Tuohey, Hickman Ewing, John Bates, Ed Lueckenhoff, and Chuck Regini re: Summary of Foster Meeting on 6-15-95,

June 16, 1995 [digitized record], URTS 16305, Document ID 70105100, link
ibid, pp. 394–95, Brett Kavanaugh Attorney Work Files.

17 S.A. C.L Regini to Associate I.C. Brett Kavanaugh, Subject: Death Investigation Status, July 18, 1995 [digitized record], URTS 16305, Document ID
70105100, link ibid, pp. 16–17.

18 Brett Kavanaugh, draft of letter to Jim Hamilton prepared for John Bates,
December 4, 1995 [digitized record], URTS 16304, Document ID 70105002, pp.
168–70, archives.gov/files/research/Kavanaugh/releases/docid-70105002.pdf.

19 Brett Kavanaugh to File, Memorandum re: Meeting with Hamilton, October
21, 1995 [digitized record], URTS 16304, Document ID 70105002, pp.
173–74, link ibid.

20 Kavanaugh to Starr, Tuohey, Ewing, Bates, Lueckenhoff, and Regini re:
Summary of Foster Meeting, June 16, 1995 [digitized record], URTS 16305,
Document ID 70105100, pp. 394–95, Brett Kavanaugh Attorney Work
Files, https://www.archives.gov/files/research/kavanaugh/releases/docid
-70105100.pdf.

21 Report on the Death of Vincent W. Foster, Jr., by the Office of Independent
Counsel In Re: Madison Guaranty and Savings & Loan Association, United
States Court of Appeals (District of Columbia Circuit), Division for the
Purpose of Appointing Independent Counsels, October 10, 1997, p. 114.

22 Ruth Marcus, "Legal Battle Mired in Tangle of Privilege," *Washington Post*,
February 26, 1998, https://www.washingtonpost.com/wp-srv/politics/special
/clinton/stories/legal022698.htm.

23 *Swidler & Berlin v. United States*, 524 U.S. 399 (1998), 410.

24 Brett M. Kavanaugh to Judge Starr and All Attorneys, Memorandum Subject:
"Slack for the President?" August 15, 1998, Brett Kavanaugh Attorney Work
Files, published online by the *Washington Post*, https://www.washingtonpost
.com/apps/g/page/politics/read-the-memo-from-brett-kavanaugh-to-judge
-starr/2322/?tid=a_inl_manual.

25 Kavanaugh memo, "Slack for the President?"

26 Ibid.

27 Bob Bittman, interview with author, January 31, 2019.

28 Gormley, *The Death of American Virtue*, 551–52.

29 Susan Schmidt and Michael Weisskopf, *Truth at Any Cost: Ken Starr and the
Unmaking of Bill Clinton* (New York: HarperCollins, 2000), 252–54.

30 Ibid., 259.

31 Brett Kavanaugh to All Present and Former Attorneys and Consultants
Involved in Lewinsky Investigation, Memorandum re: Public Statements
re: Referral, February 5, 1999 [digitized record], URTS 16315, Document
ID 70105246, pp. 6–7, https://www.archives.gov/files/research/kavanaugh
/releases/docid-70105246.pdf.

32 Ibid.

33 Brett Kavanaugh to All Attorneys, Memorandum Subject: Status, October 16, 1998 [digitized record], URTS 16315, Document ID 70105246, link ibid, pp. 2–3.

34 Brett Kavanaugh to All Attorneys, Memorandum re: Overall Plan, December 24, 1998 [digitized record], URTS 16315, Document ID 70105246, link ibid, pp. 4–5.

35 David Stout, "Clinton Reaches Deal to Avoid Indictment and to Give Up Law License," *New York Times*, January 19, 2001, https://www.nytimes.com /2001/01/19/politics/clinton-reaches-deal-to-avoid-indictment-and-to-give -up-law-license.html.

36 Michael Isikoff, *Uncovering Clinton: A Reporter's Story* (New York: Three Rivers Press, 1999), e-book edition, location 6139.

CHAPTER EIGHT: WHITE HOUSE YEARS

1 Alberto Gonzales, interview with author, December 17, 2018.

2 Ibid.

3 Andrew Card, interview with author, February 27, 2019.

4 George W. Bush White House, "President Attends Swearing-In Ceremony for Brett Kavanaugh to the U.S. Court of Appeals for the District of Columbia Circuit," press release and transcript, June 1, 2006, https://georgewbush -whitehouse.archives.gov/news/releases/2006/06/text/20060601-4.html.

5 Card interview.

6 Barton Gellman and Jo Becker, "Pushing the Envelope on Presidential Power," *Washington Post*, June 25, 2007, http://voices.washingtonpost.com /cheney/chapters/pushing_the_envelope_on_presi/.

7 David A. Graham, "How Kavanaugh's Last Confirmation Hearing Could Haunt Him," July 17, 2018, *Atlantic*, https://www.theatlantic.com/politics/archive/2018 /07/how-kavanaughs-last-confirmation-hearing-could-haunt-him/565304/.

8 Brett Kavanaugh e-mail exchange with Courtney Elwood, "Subject: Figel," March 9, 2001 [digital record], White House Counsel's Office (hereafter cited as "WHCO") emails from Brett Kavanaugh, Bush Presidential Library, https:// www.georgewbushlibrary.smu.edu/Research/Digital-Library/~/link.aspx?_id =BA9DAD98902F497495C43455B95115FA&_z=z.

9 Brett Kavanaugh to Timothy Flanigan, "Subject: Adarand," August 8, 2001 [digital record], WHCO emails from Brett Kavanaugh, Bush Presidential Library.

10 Alberto R. Gonzales, *True Faith and Allegiance: A Story of Service and Sacrifice in War and Peace* (Nashville: Nelson Books, 2016), 208–9.

11 Ibid., 217.

12 Ibid., 222.

13 Robert H. Bork, Brett M. Kavanaugh, and Roger Clegg, brief as amici curiae in support of petitioner, *Rice v. Cayetano*, 528 U.S. 495 (2000), filed May 27, 1999, https://www.findlawimages.com/efile/supreme/briefs/98-818/98 -818fo3/98-818fo3.pdf; Brett M. Kavanaugh, "Are Hawaiians Indians? The Justice Department Thinks So," *Wall Street Journal*, September 27, 1999.

14 Brett Kavanaugh to White House Counsel's Office attorneys, "Subject: New time for counsel staff meeting," September 25, 2001, WHCO emails from Brett Kavanaugh, Bush Presidential Library.

15 Brett Kavanaugh to WHCO attorneys, "Subject: National Journal," May 30, 2001, WHCO emails from Brett Kavanaugh, Bush Presidential Library.

16 Brett Kavanaugh to WHCO attorneys, "Subject: The rest of the story," June 12, 2001, WHCO emails from Brett Kavanaugh, Bush Presidential Library.

17 Brett Kavanaugh and Brad Berenson exchange, "Subject: Kavanaugh," August 13, 2002, WHCO emails from Brett Kavanaugh, Bush Presidential Library.

18 Brett Kavanaugh and Courtney Elwood exchange, "Subject: Yale LS dinner Monday," June 21–22, 2001, WHCO emails from Brett Kavanaugh, Bush Presidential Library.

19 Brett Kavanaugh to Alberto Gonzales and Timothy Flanigan, no subject, November 2, 2001, WHCO emails from Brett Kavanaugh, Bush Presidential Library.

20 Brett Kavanaugh to WHCO attorneys, "Subject: Way to go Justice Kennedy," March 30, 2001, WHCO emails from Brett Kavanaugh, Bush Presidential Library.

21 Charles Lane, "2 Justices Defend Court's Intervention in Fla. Dispute," *Washington Post*, March 30, 2001, https://www.washingtonpost.com/archive /politics/2001/03/30/2-justices-defend-courts-intervention-in-fla-dispute /2cb7eb2b-442c-4dfe-b21f-845f57237dd4/.

22 Brett Kavanaugh email to White House Counsel's Office and Brad Berenson response, no subject, February 21, 2001 [digital record], WHCO emails from Brett Kavanaugh, Bush Presidential Library.

23 *Ashcroft v. Free Speech Coalition*, 535 U.S. 234 (2002), 253, https://supreme .justia.com/cases/federal/us/535/234/case.pdf.

24 Brett Kavanaugh and Stuart Bowen email exchange, "Subject: ?" April 19, 2002, WHCO emails from Brett Kavanaugh, Bush Presidential Library.

25 *Harvey v. Horan*, 285 F.3d 298 (4th Cir. 2002), 299.

26 Brett Kavanaugh to Courtney Elwood, "Subject: Luttig/Wilkinson on DNA testing," March 29, 2002, WHCO emails from Brett Kavanaugh, Bush Presidential Library.

27　Brett Kavanaugh exchange with Brad Berenson and other WHCO lawyers, "Subject: Press," March 18, 2001, WHCO emails from Brett Kavanaugh, Bush Presidential Library.

28　Brett Kavanaugh to Matthew Smith, "Subject: Federalist Society event Wednesday at 5:00," November 11, 2002, WHCO emails from Brett Kavanaugh, Bush Presidential Library.

29　Brett Kavanaugh to Matthew Smith, "Subject: Seating," May 8, 2003, WHCO emails from Brett Kavanaugh, Bush Presidential Library.

30　Brett Kavanaugh to Leonard Leo, "Subject: Fed Soc invitations," May 8, 2003, WHCO emails from Brett Kavanaugh, Bush Presidential Library.

31　Brett Kavanaugh to Tim Goeglein, no subject, June 30, 2003, WHCO emails from Brett Kavanaugh, Bush Presidential Library.

32　Brett Kavanaugh and Alberto Gonzales e-mail exchange, "Subject: Planning session for meeting with president," March 5, 2001, WHCO emails from Brett Kavanaugh, Bush Presidential Library.

33　Brett Kavanaugh and Miguel Estrada e-mail exchange, no subject, May 7–8, 2003, WHCO emails from Brett Kavanaugh, Bush Presidential Library.

34　Brett Kavanaugh, responses to written questions from the Senate Judiciary Committee, November 19, 2004, p. 145, https://www.govinfo.gov/content/pkg /CHRG-108shrg24853/pdf/CHRG-108shrg24853.pdf.

35　Condoleezza Rice, interview with author, April 23, 2019.

36　Brett Kavanaugh, "One Government, Three Branches, Five Controversies: Separation of Powers under Presidents Bush and Obama," *Marquette Lawyer*, Fall 2016, pp. 9–13, 10, https://issuu.com/marquetteu/docs/marquette-lawyer -fall-2016.

37　George W. Bush, *Decision Points* (New York: Crown Publishers, 2010), e-book edition, location 1744–49.

38　For a discussion of O'Connor's disappointment when Bush did not name a woman to succeed her, see: Jan Crawford Greenburg, *Supreme Conflict: The Inside Story of Control for the Supreme Court*, e-book edition, chapter nine: "Except He's Not a Woman."

39　NPR, "Harriet Miers: A 'Pit Bull in Size 6 Shoes,'" NPR, October 3, 2005, https://www.npr.org/templates/story/story.php?storyId=4933735.

CHAPTER NINE: AUDITIONING

1　"Judging Brett Kavanaugh and the Supreme Court with John Yoo," *Uncommon Knowledge with Peter Robinson* (Hoover Institution), released September 5, 2018, recorded August 28, 2018, https://www.hoover.org/research/judging -brett-kavanaugh-and-supreme-court-john-yoo. Yoo was making the point that Kavanaugh had been angling for the nomination for so long that there was unlikely to be any damaging information in his background.

2 James Gordon Meek and Joel Siegel, "Mull Bill Prober for Fed Bench," *New York Daily News*, June 6, 2003.

3 Brett Kavanaugh to Ashley Snee, "Subject: You," June 6, 2003, WHCO emails from Brett Kavanaugh.

4 Brett Kavanaugh to Joel Kaplan, "Subject: Web blogs are already going crazy," June 18, 2003, WHCO emails from Brett Kavanaugh, Bush Presidential Library.

5 Neil Gorsuch to Brett Kavanaugh, "Subject: Your Nomination!," June 19, 2003, WHCO emails, Bush Presidential Library.

6 Rod Rosenstein to Brett Kavanaugh, "Subject: Good luck!," June 19, 2003, WHCO emails, Bush Presidential Library.

7 Jay Apperson to Brett Kavanaugh, "Subject: Congratulations," June 19, 2003, WHCO emails, Bush Presidential Library.

8 Ted Cruz to Brett Kavanaugh, "Subject: Congratulations!," June 20, 2003, WHCO emails, Bush Presidential Library.

9 Senate Judiciary Committee hearing on the nomination of Brett Kavanaugh to the D.C. Circuit, April 27, 2004.

10 Ronald Weich, interview with author, April 7, 2019.

11 Patrick Leahy, statement, "Leahy on Judicial Nominations," May 1, 2006. Leahy criticized Kavanaugh and Terrence Boyle before urging a new hearing for Kavanaugh. "As Associate White House Counsel and staff secretary, Mr. Kavanaugh has served in the inner circle of the White House at a time when many controversial policies and decisions were being considered. Senators have not had a chance to question him about his role in connection with those matters. For example, what was Mr. Kavanaugh's role in connection with the warrantless spying on Americans? What was his involvement in the policies affecting detainee treatment and interrogation? . . . It is important to know whether Mr. Kavanaugh has had a role in connection with the actions of Jack Abramoff, Michael Scanlon, David Safavian, the matters being investigated in connection with the Plame matter, and many other matters."

12 Senate Minority Leader Harry Reid threatened to filibuster Kavanaugh. Laurie Kellman, "Reid says he's considering filibuster of two Bush judicial nominees," Associated Press, May 2, 2006.

13 Laurie Kellman, "Kavanaugh to get new Judiciary Committee hearing," Associated Press, May 4, 2006.

14 Editorial Board, "A Tale of Two Judges: New skirmishes in the judicial nomination wars are brewing. But their merits aren't the same," *Washington Post*, May 9, 2006.

15 Editorial Board, "An Unqualified Judicial Nominee," *New York Times*, May 3, 2006.

16 "Statement of Stephen L. Tober on behalf of the Standing Committee on Federal Judiciary of the American Bar Association Concerning the Nomination of Brett Michael Kavanaugh to be Judge of the United States Court of Appeals for the District of Columbia Court before the Committee on the Judiciary, United States Senate, May 8, 2006," p. 9, https://www.americanbar.org/content/dam/aba/migrated/scfedjud/statements/kavanaugh.authcheckdam.pdf.

17 U.S. Congress, Senate, Committee on the Judiciary, *Confirmation Hearing on the Nomination of Brett Kavanaugh to be Circuit Judge for the District of Columbia Circuit*, May 9, 2006, 109th Cong., 2nd sess., https://www.congress.gov/109/chrg/shrg27916/CHRG-109shrg27916.htm.

18 United States Senate, roll call vote on the nomination (Confirmation Brett M. Kavanaugh of Maryland to be U.S. Circuit Judge for the D.C. Circuit), May 26, 2006, https://www.senate.gov/legislative/LIS/roll_call_lists/roll_call_vote_cfm.cfm?congress=109&session=2&vote=00159#position. The four Democrats who voted to confirm Kavanaugh were Robert Byrd of West Virginia, Tom Carper of Delaware, Mary Landrieu of Louisiana, and Ben Nelson of Nebraska.

19 White House press release, "President Attends Swearing-In Ceremony for Brett Kavanaugh to the U.S. Court of Appeals for the District of Columbia Circuit," June 1, 2006, https://georgewbush-whitehouse.archives.gov/news/releases/2006/06/20060601-4.html.

20 Reproduced in the photographs section of Mollie Hemingway and Carrie Severino, *Justice on Trial: The Kavanaugh Confirmation and the Future of the Supreme Court* (Washington, D.C.: Regnery Publishing, 2019).

21 Andrew Nolan, "Judge Brett Kavanaugh: His Jurisprudence and Potential Impact on the Supreme Court," Appendix, Table A-1: "Dissents and Concurrences Authored on the D.C. Circuit," Congressional Research Service, August 21, 2018, p. 177, https://www.everycrsreport.com/files/20180821_R45293_82b60213576bb5fccb8367209ab2f3ceaa9ccc56.pdf.

22 "The Dissents of Judge Brett Kavanaugh: A Narrow-Minded Elitist Who Is Out of the Mainstream," People for the American Way, July 12, 2018, p. 1, http://files.pfaw.org/uploads/2018/07/Kavanaugh-Dissent-Report.pdf.

23 Fred Lucas, "What Kavanaugh Is Like behind the Scenes: Former Clerks Share Stories," *Daily Signal*, August 9, 2018, https://www.dailysignal.com/2018/08/09/what-Kavanaugh-is-like-behind-the-scenes-former-clerks-share-stories/.

24 *Bais Yaakov of Spring Valley v. FCC*, 852 F.3d 1078 (D.C. Cir. 2017), 1079, https://scholar.google.com/scholar_case?case=9545735107531796005&q=Bais+Yaakov+of+Spring+Valley+v.+FCC&hl=en&as_sdt=2006.

25 *Belize Social Development Limited v. Government of Belize*, 668 F.3d 724 (D.C. Cir. 2012), Kavanaugh, J., dissenting, 734, https://scholar.google .com/scholar_case?case=7398265651551773962&q=BELIZE+SOCIAL +DEVELOPMENT+LIMITED+v.+GOVERNMENT+OF+BELIZE&hl=en &as_sdt=2006.

26 *Lorenzo v. SEC*, 872 F.3d 578 (D.C. Cir. 2017) Kavanaugh, J., dissenting, https://cases.justia.com/federal/appellate-courts/cadc/15-1202/15-1202 -2017-09-29.pdf?ts=1506695506.

27 Brett Kavanaugh, "The Joseph Story Distinguished Lecture," October 25, 2017, Heritage Foundation, Washington, D.C., https://www.heritage.org/ josephstory2017.

28 *US Telecom Association v. FCC*, 855 F. 3d 381 (D.C. Cir. 2017), Kavanaugh, J., dissenting, 417–18, https://scholar.google.com/scholar_case?case=60835 7842885836722&q=U.S.+Telecom+Association+v.+FCC&hl=en&as_sdt =4,130#[3].

29 *US Telecom Association v. FCC*, Srinivasan, J., and Tatel, J., concurring, 382–88.

30 *PHH Corporation v. Consumer Financial Protection Bureau*, 881 F.3d 75 (D.C. Cir. 2018), 77, https://scholar.google.com/scholar_case?case=1373 5252432428480002&hl=en&as_sdt=6&as_vis=1&oi=scholarr.

31 *PHH Corp. v. CFPB*, 80.

32 Ibid., 164.

33 Ibid., 165.

34 Ibid., 166.

35 Ibid., 194, footnote 18.

36 *Ayissi-Etoh v. Fannie Mae*, 712 F.3d 572 (D.C. Cir. 2013), Kavanaugh, J., concurring, 580, https://scholar.google.com/scholar_case?case=156518695 38398594284&q=Ayissi-Etoh+v.+Fannie+Mae,+et+al&hl=en&as_sdt=2006.

37 Brett Kavanaugh Senate Judiciary Questionnaire, released July 21, 2018, 43, https://www.judiciary.senate.gov/imo/media/doc/Brett%20M.%20Kava naugh%20SJQ%20(PUBLIC).pdf.

38 Senate Judiciary Committee, Brett Kavanaugh Supreme Court confirmation hearing, Day 2, September 5, 2018.

39 *Heller v. District of Columbia*, 670 F.3d 1244 (D.C. Cir. 2011), Appendix, 1264–69, https://scholar.google.com/scholar_case?case=835494993957 6611637&q=heller+v.+district+of+columbia+2011+dc+circuit&hl=en&as _sdt=2006.

40 *Heller v. District of Columbia*, Kavanaugh, J., dissenting, 1271, 1287.

41 *Heller v. District of Columbia*, Appendix, 1265.

42 *Garza v. Hargan*, Order, 874 F.3d 736 (D.C. Cir. 2017) Kavanaugh, J., dissenting, 752, https://scholar.google.com/scholar_case?case=70329533

63014972270&q=Rochelle+Garza+v.+Eric+Hargan+%5BORDER+IN
+SLIP+OPINION+FORMAT%5D&hl=en&as_sdt=2006.

43 *Garza v. Hargan*, Order, Millett, J., concurring, 742.

CHAPTER TEN: AN IMPENDING SENSE OF DOOM

1 Rebecca Shabad, "Schumer: I'm going to fight the Kavanaugh nomination
   'with everything I've got,'" NBC News, July 10, 2018, https://www.nbcnews
   .com/politics/congress/schumer-Kavanaugh-i-m-going-fight-nomination
   -everything-i-ve-n890246.

2 Ronald Klain, interview with author, February 12, 2019.

3 Michael Bennet on *Meet the Press with Chuck Todd*, NBC News, May 5,
   2019, https://www.nbcnews.com/meet-the-press/meet-press-may-5-2018
   -n1002141.

4 Josh Holmes, interview with author, February 21, 2019.

5 Edward Kennedy, remarks on Robert Bork's Supreme Court nomination on
   the Senate floor, July 1, 1987, C-SPAN, https://www.c-span.org/video/?45973
   -1/robert-borks-america.

6 Ethan Bronner, *Battle for Justice: How the Bork Nomination Shook America*
   (New York: Sterling, 1989), 52–54, 78. In 1981, Bork told Congress that he
   believed *Roe* was "an unconstitutional decision, a serious and wholly unjus-
   tifiable judicial usurpation of state legislative authority." Bork famously
   criticized the public accommodations section of the Civil Rights Act in a
   1963 article in *The New Republic*, arguing that it constituted a state effort to
   "coerce you into more righteous paths. That is itself a principle of unsurpassed
   ugliness." The following year, he wrote a brief for the Goldwater campaign
   outlining a constitutional critique of the Public Accommodations Act.

7 The *Washington Post* editorial board, "Brett Kavanaugh could drastically shift
   the court to the right. The Senate should take care," July 9, 2018, https://www
   .washingtonpost.com/opinions/what-the-senate-must-demand-of-brett-kava
   naugh/2018/07/09/38a813ca-83bf-11e8-8553-a3ce89036c78_story.html.

8 Claire McCaskill, interview with author, March 14, 2019.

9 Rachel Gordon, "Feinstein recalls S.F.'s 'Day of Infamy,'" *San Francisco
   Chronicle*, November 26, 2008, https://www.sfgate.com/bayarea/article/Fein
   stein-recalls-S-F-s-day-of-infamy-3260395.php.

10 Carolyn Lochhead, "Feinstein assault-weapons ban defeated," *San Francisco
   Chronicle*, April 18, 2013, https://www.sfgate.com/politics/article/Feinstein
   -assault-weapons-ban-defeated-4443319.php.

11 Carl Hulse, "For Dianne Feinstein, Torture Report's Release Is a Signal
   Moment," *New York Times*, December 9, 2014, https://www.nytimes.com

/2014/12/10/us/politics/for-dianne-feinstein-cia-torture-reports-release-is-a
-signal-moment.html.

12 Nicholas Fandos, "Dianne Feinstein Rode One Court Fight to the Senate. Another Has Left Her under Siege." *New York Times*, September 21, 2018, https://www.nytimes.com/2018/09/21/us/politics/dianne-feinstein-brett -kavanaugh-sexual-misconduct.html.

13 Carolyn Lochhead, "Dianne Feinstein: 4 decades of influence," *San Francisco Chronicle*, October 22, 2012, https://www.sfgate.com/politics/article /Dianne-Feinstein-4-decades-of-influence-3968314.php.

14 *San Francisco Chronicle* Editorial Board, "Moderation is not obsolete: Chronicle recommends Dianne Feinstein for U.S. Senate," *San Francisco Chronicle*, April 16, 2018.

15 Senate Judiciary Committee, "Supreme Court Nominee Brett Kavanaugh Sexual Assault Hearing, Judge Kavanaugh Testimony," C-Span recording, September 27, 2018, https://www.c-span.org/video/?451895-2/supreme -court-nominee-brett-kavanaugh-sexual-assault-hearing-judge-kavanaugh -testimony. Feinstein's exchange with John Cornyn, including her interaction with Jennifer Duck, begins at 2:44:19.

16 Patrick Leahy, "Statement on the Nomination of Judge Sonia Sotomayor to the Supreme Court," June 23, 2009, https://www.leahy.senate.gov/press/statement -on-the-nomination-of-judge-sonia-sotomayor-to-the-supreme-court.

17 Alexander Bolton and Lydia Wheeler, "Gorsuch rewrites playbook for confirmation hearings," *The Hill*, March 22, 2017, https://thehill.com/homenews /news/325343-gorsuch-rewrites-playbook-for-confirmation-hearings.

18 "SCOTUSblog Briefing Paper: Elena Kagan—Privilege and Release of Kagan Documents," *SCOTUSblog*, June 30, 2010, https://www.scotusblog .com/wp-content/uploads/2010/06/kagan-issues_privilege-June-30.pdf.

19 Senator John Cornyn, remarks at Senate Judiciary Committee Executive Business Meeting, July 19, 2019, https://www.judiciary.senate.gov/meetings /07/19/2018/executive-business-meeting.

20 Seung Min Kim, "White House counsel huddles with Senate Republicans on dispute over documents from Supreme Court nominee," *Washington Post*, July 24, 2018, https://www.washingtonpost.com/powerpost/white-house -counsel-huddles-with-senate-republicans-on-dispute-over-documents-from -supreme-court-nominee/2018/07/24/f7e7ea0a-8f57-11e8-bcd5-9d911 c784c38_story.html.

21 Chuck Grassley to Patrick X. Mordente, director of the George W. Bush Presidential Library and Museum, July 27, 2018, https://www.archives.gov /files/foia/07.27.2018-grassley-to-bush-library-re-Kavanaugh.pdf.

22 Gary Stern to Chuck Grassley, August 2, 2018, https://www.archives.gov/files /foia/stern-letter-to-grassley-8-2-2018.pdf.

23 National Archives News Staff, "National Archives Works to Release Records Related to Judge Kavanaugh," *National Archives News*, August 15, 2018, https://www.archives.gov/news/articles/archives-staff-release-records-related-to-judge-kavanaugh.

24 William A. Burck to Charles Grassley, September 12, 2018, https://www.judiciary.senate.gov/imo/media/doc/2018-09-12%20Burck,%20Cannon,%20Young%20to%20Grassley%20-%20Kavanaugh%20Records.pdf.

25 William A. Burck to Charles Grassley, August 31, 2018, https://www.judiciary.senate.gov/imo/media/doc/2018-08-31%20Burck%20to%20Grassley%20-%20Accounting%20of%20Kavanaugh%20WHCO%20Records.pdf.

26 Charles Grassley, Senate floor remarks "On the Most Transparent Supreme Court Confirmation Process in History," July 31, 2018, https://www.judiciary.senate.gov/scotus_the-most-transparent-confirmation-process-in-history.

27 Ibid.

28 Sarah D. Wire, "Why Democrats are talking more about missing Kavanaugh documents than abortion in the Supreme Court battle," *Los Angeles Times*, August 24, 2018, https://www.latimes.com/politics/la-na-pol-democrats-documents-kavanaugh-20180824-story.html.

29 Brian Fallon, interview with author, November 20, 2018.

30 Ibid.

31 Alex Rogers, "Wednesday Q+A with Brian Fallon," *National Journal*, May 22, 2018, https://www.nationaljournal.com/s/668297/wednesday-q-amp-with-brian-fallon.

32 "Ditch the List—Brett Kavanaugh," uploaded June 12, 2018, https://vimeo.com/274711431.

33 Chuck Schumer, "Schumer Floor Remarks on the Supreme Court Vacancy," June 27, 2018, https://www.democrats.senate.gov/newsroom/speeches/schumer-floor-remarks-on-the-supreme-court-vacancy.

34 Dianne Feinstein, "Feinstein Statement on Kennedy Retirement," June 27, 2018, https://www.feinstein.senate.gov/public/index.cfm/press-releases?ID=F02BA515-7E19-4AF8-846D-4CC1D16188AF.

35 Leigh Ann Caldwell and Frank Thorp V, "Progressive group launches ad campaign urging Democrats to oppose Kavanaugh," NBCNews.com, July 13, 2018, https://www.nbcnews.com/politics/congress/progressive-group-launches-ad-campaign-urging-democrats-oppose-kavanaugh-n891021.

36 Brian Fallon, Twitter post, July 9, 2018, 10:39 p.m., https://twitter.com/brianefallon/status/1016512104810123264?lang=en.

37 Brian Fallon, Twitter post, September 13, 2018, 10:21 a.m., https://twitter.com/brianefallon/status/1040244121947000832?lang=en.

38 Letter from CREDO, Democracy for America, Indivisible, UltraViolet, 350

.org, Color of Change, DailyKos, Demand Progress, Friends of the Earth, Justice Democrats, Social Security Works, #VOTEPROCHOICE, and Women's March to Chuck Schumer, September 5, 2018, https://d2omw6a1 nm6pnh.cloudfront.net/images/Schumer_sign-on_letter.pdf.

39 Jeffrey M. Jones, "Views of Kavanaugh Confirmation Remain Closely Divided," Gallup, September 4, 2018, https://news.gallup.com/poll/241883 /views-Kavanaugh-confirmation-remain-closely-divided.aspx.

40 Ibid.

41 Gallup found that in July, just after Kavanaugh's nomination, 22 percent of respondents said they had "no opinion" as to whether the Senate should vote to confirm him. In August, that figure had risen to 24 percent. A poll by the AP-NORC Center for Public Affairs Research found that 46 percent of Americans had no strong opinion on Kavanaugh by late August: Kevin Freking and Emily Swanson, "AP-NORC Poll: Many indifferent to Kavanaugh nomination," Associated Press, August 29, 2018, https://apnews .com/96ec11854a77474c8e89710bafff4e39.

42 Jones, "Views of Kavanaugh Confirmation Remain Closely Divided."

43 Sheldon Whitehouse to Charles Grassley, August 20, 2018, https://www .whitehouse.senate.gov/imo/media/doc/Letter%20to%20Grassley%20 on%20Committee%20Confidential%20Documents.pdf.

44 Charles Grassley to Sheldon Whitehouse, August 22, 2018, https://www .judiciary.senate.gov/imo/media/doc/2018-08-22%20CEG%20to%20 Whitehouse%20(Kavanaugh%20Records%20Related%20to%20the%20 Federalist%20Society).pdf.

45 Fred Barbash and Seung-Min Kim, "Hours before Kavanaugh nomination hearings, Bush lawyer releases 42,000 pages of documents to Judiciary Committee," *Washington Post*, September 3, 2018, https://beta.washington post.com/news/morning-mix/wp/2018/09/03/hours-before-Kavanaugh -nomination-hearings-bush-lawyer-releases-42000-pages-of-documents-to -judiciary-committee/.

CHAPTER ELEVEN: NOTHING ABOUT THIS IS NORMAL

1 U.S. Congress, Senate, Committee on the Judiciary, *Hearing on the Nomination of Brett Kavanaugh to be an Associate Justice on the Supreme Court*, 115th Cong., 2nd sess., Day 1, September 4, 2018 (hereafter cited as "Senate Judiciary Committee, Brett Kavanaugh Supreme Court confirmation hearing").

2 Ibid.

3 Ibid.

4 Neil A. Lewis, "The Supreme Court: Ginsburg Promises Judicial Restraint if She Joins Court," *New York Times*, July 21, 1993, https://www.nytimes.com/1993/07/21/us/the-supreme-court-ginsburg-promises-judicial-restraint-if-she-joins-court.html.

5 Elena Kagan, "Confirmation Messes, Old and New," review of *The Confirmation Mess* by Stephen L. Carter (Basic Books, 1994), *The University of Chicago Law Review* 62, no. 2 (Spring 1995): 919–42, https://cdn.theatlantic.com/static/mt/assets/politics/Kagan%20review%20of%20Confirmation%20Messes.pdf.

6 Senate Judiciary Committee, Brett Kavanaugh Supreme Court confirmation hearing, Day 1, September 4, 2018.

7 James R. Dickenson, "Breaking Rules, Flying High: Iowa's Grassley Seems to Cross Reagan With Impunity," *Washington Post*, March 25, 1985, https://www.washingtonpost.com/archive/politics/1985/03/25/breaking-rules-flying-high/748fae03-986b-411e-b633-73dde127feb6/.

8 Senate Judiciary Committee, Brett Kavanaugh Supreme Court confirmation hearing, Day 2, September 5, 2018.

9 David G. Savage and Evan Halper, "Gorsuch promises he would be independent on Supreme Court, including from President Trump," *Los Angeles Times*, March 21, 2017, https://www.latimes.com/politics/la-na-pol-gorsuch-senate-democrats-20170321-story.html.

10 *Janus v. American Federation of State, County, and Municipal Employees*, 585 U.S. __, June 27, 2018, J. Kagan, dissenting, 2, https://www.supremecourt.gov/opinions/17pdf/16-1466_2b3j.pdf.

11 Senate Judiciary Committee, Brett Kavanaugh Supreme Court confirmation hearing, Day 2, September 5, 2018.

12 Robert Barnes and Michael Kranish, "Kavanaugh advised against calling *Roe v. Wade* 'settled law' while a White House lawyer," *Washington Post*, September 6, 2018, https://www.washingtonpost.com/politics/courts_law/Kavanaugh-advised-against-calling-roe-v-wade-settled-law-while-a-white-house-lawyer/2018/09/06/f30216dc-b1df-11e8-a20b-5f4f84429666_story.html.

13 Senate Judiciary Committee, Brett Kavanaugh Supreme Court confirmation hearing, Day 3, September 6, 2018.

14 Brett M. Kavanaugh, "Separation of Powers During the Forty-Fourth Presidency and Beyond," *Minnesota Law Review* 93 (2009): 1454–86, http://www.minnesotalawreview.org/wp-content/uploads/2012/01/Kavanaugh_MLR.pdf.

15 Josh Gerstein, "Kavanaugh signaled sitting president couldn't be indicted," *Politico*, July 11, 2018, https://www.politico.com/blogs/under-the-radar/2018/07/11/brett-kavanaugh-president-indicted-709641.

16 Mark Sherman, "Kavanaugh: Watergate tapes decision may have been

wrong," Associated Press, July 21, 2018, https://apnews.com/3ea406469d3
44dd8b2527aed92da6365.

17 Brett Kavanaugh, interviewed by Paul Gigot on "Federal Courts and Public
Policy" at the American Enterprise Institute, Washington, D.C., March 31,
2016. Video published by C-SPAN: https://www.c-span.org/video/?407491
-1/discussion-politics-supreme-court.

18 Senate Judiciary Committee, Brett Kavanaugh Supreme Court confirmation
hearing, Day 3, September 6, 2018.

19 "Justice Kagan and Judges Srinivasan and Kethledge Offer Views from the
Bench," *Stanford Lawyer*, no. 92, Spring 2015, https://law.stanford.edu/stanford
-lawyer/articles/justice-kagan-and-judges-srinivasan-and-kethledge-offer
-views-from-the-bench/.

20 Elena Kagan, "Presidential Administration," *Harvard Law Review* 114:8
(2001): 2245–384, https://harvardlawreview.org/wp-content/uploads/pdfs
/vol114_kagan.pdf.

21 Senate Judiciary Committee, Brett Kavanaugh Supreme Court confirmation
hearing, Day 2, September 5, 2018.

22 Ibid.

23 Senate Judiciary Committee, Brett Kavanaugh Supreme Court confirmation
hearing, Day 3, September 6, 2018.

24 Ibid.

25 Ibid.

26 Ibid.

27 Ibid.

28 Kathleen Parker, "Cory Booker's 'Spartacus' moment," *Washington Post*,
September 7, 2018, https://www.washingtonpost.com/opinions/cory-bookers
-spartacus-moment/2018/09/07/8c97eaee-b2f6-11e8-aed9-001309990777
_story.html.

29 U.S. Congress, Senate, Committee on the Judiciary, *Hearing on the
Nomination of Brett M. Kavanaugh to be Circuit Judge for the District of
Columbia Circuit*, 108th Cong., 2nd sess., April 27, 2004, https://www
.congress.gov/108/chrg/shrg24853/CHRG-108shrg24853.htm (hereafter
cited as "Senate Judiciary Committee, Brett Kavanaugh circuit court confirmation hearing, 2004").

30 Brett M. Kavanaugh, responses to questions for the record from members of the
Senate Judiciary Committee, November 19, 2004, p. 94, https://www.govinfo
.gov/content/pkg/CHRG-108shrg24853/pdf/CHRG-108shrg24853.pdf.

31 Brett Kavanaugh to David Leitch, Alberto Gonzales, and Benjamin Powell,
"Subject: Hatch's staffer just told DOJ there would be a hearing on Pryor next
week," June 4, 2003 [digital record], WHCO emails from Brett Kavanaugh,
ARMS emails, June 1, 2003–July 7, 2003.

32 Emails between William Hall, Brett Kavanaugh, and Benjamin Powell, "Subject: Pryor paper," June 6, 2003 [digital record], ibid.

33 Brett Kavanaugh to Ben Wittes, email, no subject, June 12, 2003 [digital record], ibid; Brett Kavanaugh to David Leitch and Alberto Gonzales, "Subject: Pryor Prejudice" [digital record], ibid.

34 Brett Kavanaugh to Benjamin Powell, "Subject: I would tell Pryor . . . ," July 7, 2003 [digital record], ibid.

35 Senate Judiciary Committee, Brett Kavanaugh circuit court confirmation hearing, 2004.

36 U.S. Congress, Senate, Committee on the Judiciary, *Confirmation Hearing on the Nomination of Brett Kavanaugh to be Circuit Judge for the District of Columbia.* 109th Cong., 2nd sess., May 9, 2006, https://www.congress.gov /109/chrg/shrg27916/CHRG-109shrg27916.htm.

37 Manuel Miranda to Brett Kavanaugh, Viet Dinh, and Don Willett, "Subject: Highly confidentail," [*sic*] July 18, 2002 [digital record], George W. Bush Library document production, released by the Senate Judiciary Committee September 6, 2018, p. 9, https://www.judiciary.senate.gov/imo/media/doc /08-21-18%20GWB%20Document%20Production%20-%20Leahy,%20 Coons,%20Blumenthal,%20Booker%20(Released%2009-06-18).pdf.

38 Emails between Manuel Miranda, Don Willett, Nathan Sales, Steve Koebele, and Brett Kavanaugh, "Subject: Owen," July 19–21, 2002, George W. Bush Library document production, released by the Senate Judiciary Committee August 2, 2018, p. 3825, https://www.judiciary.senate.gov/imo/media/doc/08 -02-18%20GWB%20Document%20Production%20-%20Pages%201%20 -%205,735.pdf.

39 Manuel Miranda to Brett Kavanaugh, Nathan Sales, Steve Koebele, and Don Willett, "Subject: Help requested," July 28, 2002, released by the Senate Judiciary Committee September 6, 2018, p. 24, https://www.judiciary.senate .gov/imo/media/doc/08-21-18%20GWB%20Document%20Production%20 -%20Leahy,%20Coons,%20Blumenthal,%20Booker%20(Released%2009 -06-18).pdf.

40 Manuel Miranda to Brett Kavanaugh, Don Willett, Viet Dinh, and Heather Wingate, "Subject: NEWS," July 30, 2002, released by the Senate Judiciary Committee September 6, 2018, p. 27.

41 Manuel Miranda to Brett Kavanaugh, "Subject: For use and not distribution," March 18, 2003, released by the Senate Judiciary Committee September 6, 2018, p. 35.

42 Lisa Graves, "I Wrote Some of the Stolen Memos That Brett Kavanaugh Lied to the Senate About," *Slate*, September 7, 2018, https://slate.com/news -and-politics/2018/09/judge-brett-kavanaugh-should-be-impeached-for -lying-during-his-confirmation-hearings.html.

43 Salvador Rizzo, "Brett Kavanaugh's unlikely story about Democrats' stolen documents," *Washington Post*, September 20, 2018, https://www.washington post.com/politics/2018/09/20/brett-kavanaughs-unlikely-story-about -democrats-stolen-documents/.

44 Senate Judiciary Committee, Brett Kavanaugh Supreme Court confirmation hearing, Day 2, September 5, 2018.

45 Senate Judiciary Committee, Brett Kavanaugh Supreme Court confirmation hearing, Day 3, September 6, 2018.

46 Rizzo, "Brett Kavanaugh's unlikely story about Democrats' stolen documents."

47 Patrick Leahy, "Brett Kavanaugh misled the Senate under oath. I cannot support his nomination," *Washington Post*, September 13, 2018, https://www .washingtonpost.com/opinions/brett-kavanaugh-misled-the-senate-under -oath-i-cannot-support-his-nomination/2018/09/13/ea75c740-b77d-11e8 -b79f-f6e31e555258_story.html.

CHAPTER TWELVE: PADDLING IN

1 Christine Blasey Ford, interview with author, February 6–7, 2019.

2 Ibid.

3 Samantha Guerry, interview with author, April 24, 2019.

4 Ford interview.

5 Ibid.

6 Ibid.

7 Ibid.

8 Ibid.

9 The question of Ford's motivation would come up again with the publication of a book by conservative writer Ryan Lovelace: *Search and Destroy: Inside the Campaign against Brett Kavanaugh* (Washington, D.C., Regnery Publishing, 2019). Lovelace quoted Ford's lawyer, Debra Katz, speaking to a feminist conference in April 2019 at the University of Baltimore School of Law. Lovelace quoted Katz as saying of Kavanaugh, "He will always have an asterisk next to his name. And when he takes a scalpel to *Roe v. Wade*, we will know who he is, we know his character, and we know what motivates him, and that is important. It is important that we know, and that is part of what motivated Christine." The quotation was used as evidence of Ford's true, ideological intent. "Before the confirmation, Ford had maintained that she came forward out of a sense of civic duty," Lovelace wrote (e-book location 2020). "Among friends . . . however, Katz admitted that Ford came forward, in part, to taint any Supreme Court decision altering *Roe v. Wade*

by undermining Kavanaugh's authority." The difficulty with this interpretation was that the video on which Lovelace based his quotation included audio with an infuriating tendency to fade in and out, including at the critical moment following the final quotation, "and that is part of what motivated Christine." Katz later said that Lovelace's depiction wasn't what she had intended to convey, and a separate audiotape of the session has Katz saying something that is not audible on the video: "It is important that we know, and that was part of what motivated Christine *in discharging her civic duty* [italics added]." Katz's meaning appears less conclusive in proving Ford's suggestion than Lovelace asserted. In any event, I found no indication, in extensive interviewing, that Ford was motivated by a desire to protect *Roe* or to undermine Kavanaugh's credibility in a future ruling on the case.

10 Eshoo's office has the date of the call as July 6. But Ford texted her friend Deepa Lalla on July 6 and told her, "I called Eshoo yesterday."

11 Exhibit 3, Christine Blasey Ford messages to *Washington Post* tipline, included in memorandum from Chuck Grassley to Senate Republicans re: "Senate Judiciary Committee Investigation of Numerous Allegations against Justice Brett Kavanaugh during the Senate Confirmation Proceedings," November 2, 2018, p. 46, https://www.judiciary.senate.gov/imo/media/doc /2018-11-02%20Kavanaugh%20Report.pdf.

12 Ford interview.

13 Ibid.

14 Eshoo and Ford differ about whether Eshoo specifically mentioned contacting Feinstein. Eshoo says she only contacted Feinstein because Ford explicitly authorized that contact. Ford does not recall Eshoo mentioning Feinstein's name, only that she would speak to someone whom she trusted about how to proceed.

15 Anna Eshoo, interview with author, December 12, 2018.

16 Michael Barbaro, Annie Brown, and Jessica Cheung, "Special Episode: The Last 'Year of the Woman,'" *Daily*, August 25, 2018, https://www.nytimes .com/2018/08/25/podcasts/the-daily/women-midterm-elections.html?module =inline.

17 Eshoo said that Chapman contacted Ford "immediately" after Eshoo's conversation with Feinstein. Eshoo email to author, September 16, 2019: "It took her ten days to write the letter." Ford distinctly recalled receiving the telephone call from Chapman only after she arrived in Rehoboth, which was July 29, 2018.

18 Ford interview.

19 Eshoo interview.

20 Ford interview.

21 Debra Katz, interview with author, March 14, 2019.

22 Luke Mullins, "Meet DC's Leading #MeToo Lawyer," *Washingtonian*, June 14, 2018, https://www.washingtonian.com/2018/06/14/meet-debra-katz-dc-leading-metoo-lawyer/.

23 Debra Katz Twitter page, https://twitter.com/debrakatzkmb.

24 Isaac Stanley-Becker, "Christine Blasey Ford's lawyer Debra Katz: The feared attorney of the #MeToo moment," *Washington Post*, September 24, 2018, https://www.washingtonpost.com/news/morning-mix/wp/2018/09/24/meet-christine-blasey-fords-lawyer-debra-katz-nerves-of-steel-and-proud-to-be-among-the-top-10-plantiffs-attorneys-to-fear-most/.

25 Danielle Paquette, "Lawsuit accuses celebrity chef Mike Isabella of 'extraordinary' sexual harassment," *Washington Post*, March 19, 2018, https://beta.washingtonpost.com/business/economy/celebrity-chef-mike-isabella-is-sued-for-extraordinary-sexual-harassment/2018/03/19/4cc47bf4-27a4-11e8-b79d-f3d931db7f68_story.html; Ronan Farrow, "From Aggressive Overtures to Sexual Assault: Harvey Weinstein's Accusers Tell Their Stories," *New Yorker*, October 10, 2017, https://www.newyorker.com/news/news-desk/from-aggressive-overtures-to-sexual-assault-harvey-weinsteins-accusers-tell-their-stories; Carol Leonnig, "Staffers' accounts paint more detailed, troubling picture of Massa's office," *Washington Post*, April 13, 2010, http://www.washingtonpost.com/wp-dyn/content/article/2010/04/13/AR2010041302257.html; Jonathan Tamari, "Rep. Pat Meehan resigns, will pay back $39,000 used for harassment settlement," *Philadelphia Inquirer*, April 27, 2018, https://www.inquirer.com/philly/news/politics/pat-meehan-pa-resigns-will-pay-back-sexual-harassment-settlement-20180427.html.

26 Ricki Seidman, interview with author, January 29, 2019.

27 Ibid.

28 Ford interview.

29 Ibid.

30 Seidman interview.

31 Ford interview.

32 Author conversation with Nancy Pelosi, September 11, 2019.

33 Pelosi said through an aide that she did not recall speaking with Schumer.

34 Ford interview.

35 William J. Eaton, "Probe Fails to Trace Thomas Case Leaks: Supreme Court: Senate investigator unable to determine who gave data to press about Anita Hill harassment allegations," *Los Angeles Times*, May 6, 1992, https://www.latimes.com/archives/la-xpm-1992-05-06-mn-1283-story.html.

36 Ryan Grim, "Dianne Feinstein Withholding Brett Kavanaugh Document from Fellow Judiciary Committee Democrats," *Intercept*, September 12, 2018,

https://theintercept.com/2018/09/12/brett-kavanaugh-confirmation-dianne
-feinstein/.

CHAPTER THIRTEEN: BATHROOM SUMMIT

1 Phillip Matier and Andrew Ross, "Feinstein's surprise call for death penalty puts D.A. on spot," *San Francisco Chronicle*, April 21, 2004.

2 Mary Anne Ostrom, "New S.F. Prosecutor's Trial by Fire; Stance against Death Penalty in Cop Killing Draws Criticism," *San Jose Mercury News*, April 22, 2004.

3 Matier and Ross, "Feinstein's surprise call for death penalty puts D.A. on spot."

4 "Feinstein Statement on Kavanaugh," September 13, 2018, https://www .feinstein.senate.gov/public/index.cfm/press-releases?id=FB52FCD4-29C8 -4856-A679-B5C6CC553DC4.

5 Nicholas Fandos and Catie Edmondson, "Dianne Feinstein Refers a Kavanaugh Matter to Federal Investigators," *New York Times*, September 13, 2018, https://www.nytimes.com/2018/09/13/us/politics/brett-kavanaugh -dianne-feinstein.html.

6 Seung Min Kim, "Kavanaugh denies decades-old allegation of potential sexual misconduct," *Washington Post*, September 14, 2018, https://beta.washington post.com/politics/Kavanaugh-denies-decades-old-allegation-of-potential -sexual-misconduct/2018/09/14/60ee3ae8-b831-11e8-94eb-3bd52dfe917b _story.html.

7 Ronan Farrow and Jane Mayer, "A Sexual Misconduct Allegation against the Supreme Court Nominee Brett Kavanaugh Stirs Tension among Democrats in Congress," *New Yorker*, September 14, 2018, https://www.newyorker.com /news/news-desk/a-sexual-misconduct-allegation-against-the-supreme-court -nominee-brett-kavanaugh-stirs-tension-among-democrats-in-congress.

8 John McCormack, "Kavanaugh Classmate Named in Letter Strongly Denies Allegations of Misconduct," *Weekly Standard*, September 14, 2018, https:// www.washingtonexaminer.com/weekly-standard/kavanaugh-classmate -named-in-letter-strongly-denies-allegations-of-misconduct.

9 Susan Collins, interview with author, September 27, 2019.

10 Carl Hulse, "New Kavanaugh Disclosure Shows Little Sign of Impeding His Nomination," *New York Times*, September 15, 2018, https://www.nytimes .com/2018/09/15/us/politics/brett-kavanaugh-confirmation.html.

11 Ford interview.

12 Emma Brown, "California professor, writer of confidential Brett Kavanaugh letter, speaks out about her allegation of sexual assault," *Washington Post*,

September 16, 2018, https://beta.washingtonpost.com/investigations/cali
fornia-professor-writer-of-confidential-brett-kavanaugh-letter-speaks-out
-about-her-allegation-of-sexual-assault/2018/09/16/46982194-b846-11e8
-94eb-3bd52dfe917b_story.html.

13 Sean Sullivan, Seung Min Kim, and Felicia Sonmez, "GOP senator: Hold off
on Kavanaugh vote until accuser is heard," *Washington Post*, September 16,
2018, https://beta.washingtonpost.com/powerpost/senators-say-kavanaugh
-letter-wont-hold-up-confirmation-process/2018/09/16/cbee4b4c-b9b9-11e8
-9812-a389be6690af_story.html.

14 Burgess Everett, "Flake opposes quick vote on Kavanaugh, putting confirmation in doubt," *Politico*, September 16, 2018, https://www.politico.com
/story/2018/09/16/kavanaugh-allegation-anonymous-republicans-825855.

15 Alisyn Camerota, John Berman, David Sanger, and Sanjay Gupta, "Lawyer
Says Kavanaugh Accuser Willing to Testify before Congress," *CNN New
Day*, CNN, September 17, 2018.

16 Norah O'Donnell, John Dickerson, and Bianna Golodryga, "Interview with
Debra Katz, the attorney representing Christine Blasey Ford," *CBS This
Morning*, CBS News, September 17, 2018.

17 Emily Birnbaum, "Conway: Kavanaugh accuser 'should not be ignored,'"
The Hill, September 17, 2018, https://thehill.com/homenews/administration
/406966-conway-on-kavanaugh-accuser-this-woman-should-not-be-insulted
-and-she.

18 Bob Woodward, *Fear: Trump in the White House* (New York: Simon &
Schuster, 2018), 174–75.

19 Aaron Blake, "The storm brewing in Trump's muted response to Brett Kavanaugh's accuser," *Washington Post*, September 17, 2018, https://beta.wash
ingtonpost.com/politics/2018/09/17/storm-brewing-behind-trumps-muted
-response-brett-kavanaughs-accuser/.

20 White House press pool report #1, Kavanaugh statement, September 17,
2018, https://publicpool.kinja.com/subject-pool-report-1-9-17-18-kavanaugh
-statement-1829106888.

21 Susan Collins, Twitter post, September 17, 2018, 12:03 p.m., https://twitter
.com/senatorcollins/status/1041719261142679553?lang=en.

22 Sheryl Gay Stolberg and Julie Hirschfeld Davis, "Hearing Set for Monday
to Hear Kavanaugh and His Accuser," *New York Times*, September 17, 2018,
https://www.nytimes.com/2018/09/17/us/politics/kavanaugh-allegations
-ford-palo-alto.html.

23 Senate Judiciary Committee, "Grassley Statement on the Supreme Court
Nomination," September 17, 2018, https://www.judiciary.senate.gov/press
/rep/releases/grassley-statement-on-the-supreme-court-nomination.

24 Chuck Grassley, remarks on Senate floor, *Congressional Record-Senate*, October 15, 1991, 26277, https://www.govinfo.gov/content/pkg/GPO-CRECB -1991-pt18/pdf/GPO-CRECB-1991-pt18-8-2.pdf.

25 U.S. Congress, Senate, Committee on the Judiciary, *Nomination of Judge Clarence Thomas to be Associate Justice of the Supreme Court*, 102nd Cong., 1st sess., Part 4 of 4, October 12, 1991, 230 (hereafter cited as "Clarence Thomas Supreme Court confirmation hearing, Part 4"), https://www.loc.gov /law/find/nominations/thomas/hearing-pt4.pdf.

26 Clarence Thomas confirmation hearing, Part 4, October 13, 1991, 373.

27 Ibid., October 12, 1991, 206.

28 CNN, September 18, 2018, transcript: http://transcripts.cnn.com/TRAN SCRIPTS/1809/18/cnr.05.html.

29 Senate Judiciary Committee interview with Brett Kavanaugh, September 17, 2018, p. 16, https://www.judiciary.senate.gov/imo/media/doc/09.17.18%20 BMK%20Interview%20Transcript%20(Redacted).pdf.

30 Seung Min Kim and Josh Dawsey, "'Incredibly frustrated': Inside the GOP effort to save Kavanaugh amid assault allegation," *Washington Post*, September 22, 2018, https://www.washingtonpost.com/politics/incredibly -frustrated-inside-the-gop-effort-to-save-kavanaugh-amid-assault-allegation /2018/09/22/6808baf6-bde0-11e8-b7d2-0773aa1e33da_story.html.

31 Debra Katz and Lisa Banks to Charles Grassley, September 18, 2018, https:// www.judiciary.senate.gov/imo/media/doc/2018-09-18%20Blasey%20 Ford%20to%20Grassley%20(Kavanaugh%20Allegations).pdf.

32 Anderson Cooper, "CNN Exclusive: Judge Kavanaugh's Accuser Wants FBI Investigation before Testifying on Capitol Hill," CNN, September 18, 2018.

33 Senate Judiciary Committee Democrats to Don McGahn and Chris Wray, September 18, 2018, https://www.feinstein.senate.gov/public/_cache/files /c/d/cd4c7ce9-ccc4-44cc-923e-de004c99dccc/579C490B3C739B3426FF9 841E3588AE0.2018.09.18-jud-dems-to-white-house-and-fbi-re-kavanaugh -investigation.pdf.

34 Seung Min Kim, Robert Costa, and John Wagner, "Woman who accused Brett Kavanaugh of sexual assault wants FBI to investigate incident before she testifies to Senate," *Washington Post*, September 18, 2018, https:// beta.washingtonpost.com/politics/grassley-says-mondays-hearing-will -be-limited-to-two-witnesses-kavanaugh-and-his-accuser/2018/09/18 /301da074-bb48-11e8-a8aa-860695e7f3fc_story.html.

35 William Cummings, "'Unfazed and determined': Top Grassley aide vows to confirm Kavanaugh despite allegations," *USA Today*, September 20, 2018, https://www.usatoday.com/story/news/politics/onpolitics/2018/09/20/brett -kavanaugh-confirmation-furor-over-mike-davis-tweets/1366391002/.

36 Mike Davis, Twitter post, September 20, 2018, 10:12 a.m., https://twitter
    .com/mrddmia/status/1042778511906430977?lang=en.

37 Avi Selk, "Conservatives hyped a pundit who promised to prove Kavanaugh
    innocent. Then they saw his theory," *Washington Post*, September 21, 2018,
    https://beta.washingtonpost.com/politics/2018/09/21/ed-whelans-kavanaugh
    -tweets-conservatives-hyped-pundit-who-promised-prove-judge-innocent/.

38 Joe Patrice, "Kavanaugh Truther Outlines Pet Conspiracy Theory for Ford's
    Attempted Rape," *Above The Law*, September 21, 2018, https://abovethelaw
    .com/2018/09/kavanaugh-truther-outlines-pet-conspiracy-theory-for-fords
    -attempted-rape/.

39 Seung Min Kim, Josh Dawsey, and Emma Brown, "Kavanaugh accuser
    won't testify Monday but open to doing so later next week," *Washington
    Post*, September 21, 2018, https://beta.washingtonpost.com/politics/gop
    -vows-to-move-ahead-with-kavanaugh-vote-if-his-accuser-doesnt-testify
    -monday/2018/09/20/a7132ee8-bcf5-11e8-8792-78719177250f_story.html.

40 Ed Whelan, Twitter post, September 21, 2018, 8:38 a.m. https://twitter.com
    /edwhelaneppc/status/1043117304152817664?lang=en.

41 Steve Schmidt, Twitter post, September 21, 2018, 12:34 a.m., https://twitter
    .com/steveschmidtses/status/1042995741453500417?lang=en.

42 "McCain deplores anti-Kerry ad," Associated Press, August 5, 2004 (repub-
    lished by NBC News), http://www.nbcnews.com/id/5612836/ns/politics/t
    /mccain-deplores-anti-kerry-ad/#.XXmMppNKgdU.

43 Eliana Johnson, "PR firm helped Whelan stoke half-baked Kavanaugh alibi,"
    Politico, September 21, 2018, https://www.politico.com/story/2018/09/21/ed
    -whelan-kavanaugh-tweets-pr-firm-836405/.

44 Elise Viebeck, Emma Brown, and Robert Costa, "Kavanaugh ally says he did
    not communicate with White House or Supreme Court nominee about theory
    of another attacker," *Washington Post*, September 21, 2018, https://beta.wash
    ingtonpost.com/politics/kavanaugh-ally-says-he-did-not-communicate-with
    -white-house-or-supreme-court-nominee-about-theory-of-another-attacker
    /2018/09/21/88335f1a-bdaa-11e8-b7d2-0773aa1e33da_story.html.

45 Eliza Collins, "McConnell: We're going to 'plow right through' and get
    Kavanaugh confirmed despite assault allegation," *USA Today*, September
    21, 2018, https://www.usatoday.com/story/news/politics/2018/09/21/mitch
    -mcconnell-were-going-plow-right-through-ford-allegation/1380905002/.

46 Carl Hulse, *Confirmation Bias: Inside Washington's War over the Supreme
    Court, from Scalia's Death to Justice Kavanaugh* (New York: Harper/Harper
    Collins, 2019), 288–99.

47 Jonathan Swan, "Officials in overdrive to keep Trump from attacking
    Kavanaugh accuser," *Axios*, September 21, 2018, https://www.axios.com

/trump-brett-kavanaugh-accuser-christine-blasey-ford-d94ab8e3-1416-4d92
-97c9-a78cdad99482.html.

48 Donald J. Trump, Twitter post, September 21, 2018, 9:14, https://twitter.com
/realdonaldtrump/status/1043126336473055235?lang=en.

49 Donald J. Trump, Twitter post, September 21, 2018, 9:29, https://twitter.com
/realdonaldtrump/status/1043130170612244481?lang=en.

50 Eli Stokols, Noah Bierman, and Jennifer Haberkorn, "Trump raises doubts
about Kavanaugh's accuser, suggests assault allegations made up by 'radical
left,'" *Los Angeles Times*, September 21, 2018, https://www.latimes.com
/politics/la-na-pol-trump-kavanaugh-tweets-20180921-story.html.

51 Natalie Andrews and Kristina Peterson, "Kavanaugh Accuser Asks for More
Time to Negotiate on Hearings," *Wall Street Journal*, September 22, 2018,
https://www.wsj.com/articles/trump-questions-kavanaugh-accusers-account
-as-senators-continue-negotiations-1537537419.

52 Seung Min Kim, Sean Sullivan, and Emma Brown, "Christine Blasey Ford
moves closer to deal with Senate Republicans to testify against Kavanaugh,"
Washington Post, September 23, 2018, https://beta.washingtonpost.com
/politics/lawyers-for-christine-blasey-ford-say-she-has-accepted-senate
-judiciary-committees-request-to-testify-against-kavanaugh/2018/09/22/e81
99c6a-be8f-11e8-8792-78719177250f_story.html.

53 Paige Lavender and Paul Blumenthal, "Judicial Crisis Network on Kavanaugh
Allegations: 'We Have to Look into This Further,'" *Huffington Post*,
September 26, 2018, https://www.huffpost.com/entry/judicial-crisis-network
-brett-kavanaugh-allegations_n_5babbc29e4b091df72ecbbcd.

CHAPTER FOURTEEN: SECOND ACCUSER

1 Ronan Farrow and Jane Mayer, "Senate Democrats Investigate a New
Allegation of Sexual Misconduct, from Brett Kavanaugh's College Years,"
New Yorker, September 23, 2018, https://www.newyorker.com/news/news
-desk/senate-democrats-investigate-a-new-allegation-of-sexual-misconduct
-from-the-supreme-court-nominee-brett-kavanaughs-college-years-deborah
-ramirez.

2 Debbie Ramirez, interview with author, February 22 and 23, 2019.

3 Ibid.

4 Ibid.

5 Ibid.

6 Jamie Roche, interview with author, February 12, 2019.

7 Debbie Ramirez, letter to the editor: "Bolder Boulder T-shirt is highly

offensive," *Boulder Daily Camera*, April 18, 2014, https://www.dailycamera .com/2014/04/18/debbie-ramirez-bolder-boulder-t-shirt-is-highly-offensive/.

8 Ramirez interview.

9 Ibid.

10 Stan Garnett, interview with author, November 2, 2018.

11 Ibid.

12 Ramirez interview.

13 Charlton's statement to the FBI, sent on October 3, 2018, was reported by NBC, among other outlets: Heidi Przybyla, "The battle over accusations goes on as Kavanaugh nomination advances," NBC News, October 5, 2018, https://www.nbcnews.com/politics/supreme-court/battle-over-accusations -goes-kavanaugh-nomination-advances-n917136.

14 Farrow and Mayer, "Senate Democrats Investigate New Allegation of Sexual Misconduct."

15 Sheryl Gay Stolberg and Nicholas Fandos, "Christine Blasey Ford Reaches Deal to Testify at Kavanaugh Hearing," *New York Times*, September 23, 2018, https://www.nytimes.com/2018/09/23/us/politics/brett-kavanaugh-christine -blasey-ford-testify.html.

16 Farrow and Mayer, "Senate Democrats Investigate New Allegation of Sexual Misconduct."

17 Jane Mayer and Ronan Farrow, "The F.B.I. Probe Ignored Testimonies from Former Classmates of Kavanaugh," *New Yorker*, October 3, 2018, https:// www.newyorker.com/news/news-desk/will-the-fbi-ignore-testimonies-from -kavanaughs-former-classmates.

18 Mike Davis to Stan Garnett, cc Heather Sawyer and Jennifer Duck, "Subject: SCOTUS—request for evidence," September 23, 2018, 9:43 p.m.

19 Heather Sawyer to Stan Garnett and Mike Davis, cc Jennifer Duck, "Subject: SCOTUS—request for evidence," September 23, 2018, 9:48 p.m.

20 Farrow and Mayer, "Senate Democrats Investigate New Allegation of Sexual Misconduct."

21 Avi Selk, "'Left-wing conspiracy': The White House abandons restraint after second Kavanaugh accusation," *Washington Post*, September 24, 2018, https://beta.washingtonpost.com/politics/2018/09/24/left-wing-conspiracy -white-house-abandons-restraint-after-second-kavanaugh-accusation/.

22 Ibid.

23 The White House, "Remarks by President Trump and President Duque of the Republic of Colombia before Bilateral Meetings," September 25, 2018, 11:32 a.m., United Nations Headquarters, New York, New York, https://www .whitehouse.gov/briefings-statements/remarks-president-trump-president -duque-republic-colombia-bilateral-meetings/.

24 Michael Avenatti, Twitter post, September 23, 2018, 7:33 p.m., https://twitter.com/michaelavenatti/status/1044006928416825344?lang=en.

25 Rachel Maddow, "Avenatti: Kavanaugh accuser client may pursue criminal case," *The Rachel Maddow Show*, MSNBC, September 24, 2018, https://www.msnbc.com/rachel-maddow/watch/avenatti-kavanaugh-accuser-client-may-pursue-criminal-case-1328359491812?v=raila&.

26 Declaration of Julie Swetnick, signed September 25, 2018, published on CNBC.com, September 26, 2018, http://fm.cnbc.com/applications/cnbc.com/resources/editorialfiles/2018/09/26/swetnickstatement.pdf.

27 Ibid.

28 According to the Montgomery County Police Department's Information Management and Technology division, Avenatti inquired about the cost of searching for any prior Montgomery County police interaction with Swetnick. He was informed that conducting such a search for a three-year period would cost $3,710, plus ten dollars for any report that was found, but never responded, according to a department official.

29 Steve Eder, Jim Rutenberg, and Rebecca R. Ruiz, "Julie Swetnick Is Third Woman to Accuse Brett Kavanaugh of Sexual Misconduct," *New York Times*, September 26, 2018, https://www.nytimes.com/2018/09/26/us/politics/julie-swetnick-avenatti-kavenaugh.html.

30 John Heilemann, Mark McKinnon, and Alex Wagner, *The Circus: Inside the Wildest Political Show on Earth*, season 3, episode 9: "Judgment Day," Showtime, aired September 30, 2018. Avenatti made that claim in an interview recorded on Tuesday, September 25.

31 Michael Kunzelman, Michael Biesecker, and Martha Mendoza, "3rd Kavanaugh accuser has a history of legal disputes," Associated Press, September 30, 2018, https://apnews.com/bccc4dd598df4e71bbf6c40ff4830373.

32 Michael E. Miller, Steve Hendrix, Jessica Contrera, and Ian Shapira, "Who is Julie Swetnick, the third Kavanaugh accuser?" *Washington Post*, October 1, 2018, https://beta.washingtonpost.com/local/who-is-julie-swetnick-the-third-kavanaugh-accuser/2018/09/26/91e16ed8-c1bc-11e8-97a5-ab1e46bb3bc7_story.html

33 Julie Swetnick to Lisa Banks, email, Subject: Regarding Kavanaugh Case, September 19, 2018.

34 Rachel Maddow, *The Rachel Maddow Show*, October 2, 2018, MSNBC, transcript. Maddow read from Rasor's affidavit, provided to the show by her attorney, Roberta Kaplan.

35 Cameron Joseph, "Collins Raised Renewed Concerns about Kavanaugh at Private GOP Meeting," *Talking Points Memo*, September 26, 2018, https://talkingpointsmemo.com/dc/collins-raised-renewed-concerns-about-kavanaugh-at-private-gop-meeting.

36 Senate Judiciary Committee Democrats to Chuck Grassley, public letter, "Postpone Hearing, Support FBI Investigation," September 26, 2018, https://www.judiciary.senate.gov/press/dem/releases/judiciary-committee -democrats-to-grassley-postpone-hearing-support-fbi-investigation.

37 Michael Avenatti, Twitter post, October 3, 2018, 4:26 a.m., https://twitter .com/MichaelAvenatti/status/1047226356831059970?ref_src=twsrc%5Etfw %7Ctwcamp%5Etweetembed%7Ctwterm%5E1047226356831059970&ref _url=https%3A%2F%2Fwww.dailykos.com%2Fstory%2F2018%2F10%2F 2%2F1800950%2F-Avenatti-puts-up-w-second-witness. Avenatti attached the declaration to the tweet.

38 Kate Snow and Anna Schecter, "New questions raised about Avenatti claims regarding Kavanaugh," NBC, October 25, 2018, https://www.nbcnews.com /politics/justice-department/new-questions-raised-about-avenatti-claims -regarding-kavanaugh-n924596.

39 Lindsey Graham, interview with author, August 24, 2019.

40 Mike Davis, interview with author, March 18, 2019.

CHAPTER FIFTEEN: ETERNITY

1 Martha MacCallum, interview with Brett and Ashley Kavanaugh, *The Story with Martha MacCallum*, Fox, September 24, 2018.

2 Sheldon Whitehouse to Charles Grassley and Dianne Feinstein, September 24, 2018.

3 Lara Quint email to Mike Davis, September 25, 2018, 2:49 p.m.

4 Mike Davis to Lara Quint, September 25, 2018, 2:55 p.m.

5 Mike Davis to John Clune and Heather Sawyer, cc Jennifer Duck and Stan Garnett, "Subject: SCOTUS—request for evidence," September 25, 2018, 10:05 a.m. These emails were later published by the *New Yorker*: Ronan Farrow and Jane Mayer, "E-mails Show That Republican Senate Staff Stymied a Kavanaugh Accuser's Effort to Give Testimony," *New Yorker*, September 28, 2018, https://www.newyorker.com/news/news-desk/e-mails -show-republican-senate-staff-stymied-a-kavanaugh-accusers-effort-to-give -testimony.

6 Heather Sawyer to John Clune, Stan Garnett, and Mike Davis, September 25, 2018, 8:45 a.m, link ibid.

7 Mike Davis to Stan Garnett and Heather Sawyer, cc John Clune, Jennifer Duck, and Bill Pittard, "Subject: SCOTUS—request for evidence," September 25, 2018, 7:45 p.m, link ibid.

8 Heather Sawyer to Mike Davis and Stan Garnett, cc et al., September 25, 2018, 7:54 p.m, link ibid.

9　Mike Davis to Heather Sawyer and Stan Garnett, cc et al., September 25, 2018, 8:05 p.m, link ibid.

10　Rachel Maddow, interview with John Clune, *The Rachel Maddow Show*, MSNBC, September 25, 2018.

11　United States Congress, Senate, Committee on the Judiciary, *Hearing on the Nomination of Brett Kavanaugh to be an Associate Justice on the Supreme Court, Day 5, Focusing on Allegations of Sexual Assault*, 115th Cong., 2nd sess., September 27, 2018.

12　Office of Chuck Grassley, Chairman of the Judiciary Committee, to Senate Republicans, Memorandum re: Senate Judiciary Committee Investigation of Numerous Allegations against Justice Brett Kavanaugh during the Senate Confirmation Proceedings, November 2, 2018, p. 8, https://www.judiciary .senate.gov/imo/media/doc/2018-11-02%20Kavanaugh%20Report.pdf.

13　Senate Judiciary Committee, "Summary of Actions by Chairman Grassley and the Senate Judiciary Committee Related to Allegations Made and Disputed Regarding Judge Brett Kavanaugh," September 26, 2018, https://www .judiciary.senate.gov/press/rep/releases/summary-of-actions-by-chairman -grassley-and-the-senate-judiciary-committee-related-to-allegations-made -and-disputed-regarding-judge-brett-kavanaugh.

14　Orrin Hatch, Twitter post, September 27, 2018, 12:05 a.m., https://twitter .com/senorrinhatch/status/1045162374645403648.

15　Brett Samuels, "Graham dismisses two men who claim Ford may have mistaken Kavanaugh for them," *The Hill*, September 27, 2018, https://thehill .com/homenews/senate/408736-graham-dismisses-two-men-who-claim -ford-may-have-mistaken-kavanaugh-for-them.

16　Mike Davis to Jennifer Duck and Heather Sawyer, "Subject: FW: Ramirez allegation against Kavanaugh," September 29, 2018.

17　Peter Baker, "Christine Blasey Ford's Credibility Under New Attack by Senate Republicans," *New York Times*, October 3, 2018, https://www.nytimes .com/2018/10/03/us/politics/blasey-ford-republicans-kavanaugh.html.

18　Michael Bromwich, interview with author, November 26, 2018.

19　Senate Judiciary Committee, interview with Brett Kavanaugh, September 26, 2018, https://www.judiciary.senate.gov/imo/media/doc/09.26.18%20BMK %20Interview%20Transcript%20(Redacted).pdf.

20　Ibid.

CHAPTER SIXTEEN: INDELIBLE IN THE HIPPOCAMPUS

1　Ford interview.

2　Michael Bromwich, interview with author, November 26, 2018.

3　Senate Judiciary Committee, *Hearing on the Nomination of Brett Kavanaugh to be Associate Justice of the Supreme Court, Day 5, Focusing on Allegations of Sexual Assault*, September 27, 2018.

4 Ibid.

5 Ibid.

6 Ibid.

7 Ibid.

8 Jeff Flake, interview with author, November 27, 2018.

9 Bob Corker, interview with author, May 15, 2019.

10 Aris Foley, "Chris Wallace: Ford's testimony is 'a disaster for the Republicans,'" *The Hill*, September 27, 2018, https://thehill.com/homenews/media/408747 -chris-wallace-christine-blasey-fords-testimony-is-a-disaster-for-the.

11 Annie Karni, "'This is march or die': Kavanaugh urged to hit back hard," *Politico*, September 30, 2018, https://www.politico.com/story/2018/09/30 /kavanaugh-response-senate-confirmation-854297.

12 Senate Judiciary Committee, Brett Kavanaugh nomination hearing, focusing on allegations of sexual assault.

13 Ibid.

14 Richard L. Berke, "The Thomas Nomination; Thomas Accuser Tells Hearing of Obscene Talk and Advances; Judge Complains of 'Lynching,'" *New York Times*, October 12, 1991, https://www.nytimes.com/1991/10/12/us/thomas -nomination-thomas-accuser-tells-hearing-obscene-talk-advances-judge.html.

15 Armstrong Williams, interview with author, January 24, 2019.

16 Senate Judiciary Committee, Brett Kavanaugh nomination hearing, focusing on allegations of sexual assault.

17 Ibid.

18 Graham interview.

19 Rudolph Bell, "Graham foes find fodder in his votes for Obama nominees," *Greenville News*, April 28, 2014, https://www.greenvilleonline.com/story /news/politics/2014/04/28/graham-foes-find-fodder-votes-obama-nominees /8350277/.

20 Senate Judiciary Committee, Brett Kavanaugh nomination hearing, focusing on allegations of sexual assault.

21 Kate Kelly and David Enrich, "Kavanaugh's Yearbook Page Is 'Horrible, Hurtful' to a Woman It Named," *New York Times*, September 24, 2018, https://www.nytimes.com/2018/09/24/business/brett-kavanaugh-yearbook -renate.html.

22 Senate Judiciary Committee, Brett Kavanaugh nomination hearing, focusing on allegations of sexual assault.

23 Ibid.

24 "Kavanaugh Hearing Cold Open," *Saturday Night Live*, NBC, September 29, 2018, https://www.youtube.com/watch?v=VRJecfRxbr8&app=desktop.

25 The Brennan Center found that groups supporting Kavanaugh's confirmation

spent $7.3 million on television ads, with the Judicial Crisis Network, the National Rifle Association, and the Trump-affiliated America First Policies making the biggest buys. Kavanaugh opponents spent just under $3 million dollars on TV ads, and only Demand Justice spent more than one million. See: Brennan Center for Justice, "Follow the Money: Tracking TV Spending on the Kavanaugh Nomination," BrennanCenter.org, page launched July 26, 2018, and last updated October 8, 2018, https://www.brennancenter.org/analysis /buying-time-supreme-court-advertisements?splash=.

26 Jon Kyl, interview with author, January 21, 2019.

27 Corker interview.

28 Elaina Plott, "Jeff Flake: 'We Can't Have That on the Court,'" *Atlantic*, October 2, 2018, https://www.theatlantic.com/politics/archive/2018/10/jeff -flake-criticizes-supreme-court-nominee-kavanaugh/571915/.

29 Flake interview.

30 Senate Judiciary Committee, Brett Kavanaugh nomination hearing, focusing on allegations of sexual assault.

31 Ford interview.

32 Jessica Contrera, Ian Shapira, Emma Brown, and Steve Hendrix, "Kava-naugh accuser Christine Blasey Ford moved 3,000 miles to reinvent her life. It wasn't far enough," *Washington Post*, September 27, 2018, https://beta .washingtonpost.com/local/christine-blasey-ford-wanted-to-flee-the-us-to -avoid-brett-kavanaugh-now-she-may-testify-against-him/2018/09/22/db 942340-bdb1-11e8-8792-78719177250f_story.html?noredirect=on.

33 Jessica Contrera and Ian Shapira, "Christine Blasey Ford's family has been nearly silent amid outpouring of support," *Washington Post*, September 27, 2018, https://beta.washingtonpost.com/local/christine-blasey-fords-own -family-has-been-nearly-silent-amid-outpouring-of-support/2018/09/26 /49a3f4a6-c0d6-11e8-be77-516336a26305_story.html.

34 Ford interview.

35 Flake interview.

36 Laura Ingraham and Newt Gingrich, "Kellyanne Conway on the Kavanaugh Hearing," *Ingraham Angle*, Fox News, September 27, 2018.

37 John Clune, interview with author, November 2, 2018.

38 Flake interview.

CHAPTER SEVENTEEN: BY THE BOOK

1 "Tearful woman confronts Senator Flake on elevator," CNN, September 28, 2018, https://www.youtube.com/watch?v=bshgOZ8QQxU.

2 Ibid.

3 Alex Isenstadt, "Coons took 'bearded Marxist' turn," *Politico*, May 4, 2010, https://www.politico.com/story/2010/05/coons-took-bearded-marxist-turn -036726.

4 Mary Clare Jalonick, "From Africa to the anteroom: Flake, Coons forge rare bond," Associated Press, October 2, 2018, https://www.apnews.com /31b4e77aa91549e9a1a34b39777ecb75.

5 Joe Scarborough, Mika Brzezinski, and Willie Geist, "Senator Jeff Flake on White House Behavior: We Can't Continue to Remain Silent," *Morning Joe*, MSNBC, October 25, 2017, https://www.youtube.com/watch?v=rou Ze4nErx0&app=desktop.

6 Jeff Flake, "Jeff Flake's full speech announcing he won't run for re-election," transcript published by CNN, October 24, 2017, https://www.cnn.com/2017 /10/24/politics/jeff-flake-retirement-speech-full-text/index.html.

7 Nash Jenkins, "Fighting Donald Trump Cost Jeff Flake His Job. But He's Not Going Quietly," *Time*, November 30, 2017, https://time.com/5042705/donald -trump-jeff-flake-not-going-quietly/.

8 Jordain Carney, "Flake to back tax bill, giving GOP 50 votes," *The Hill*, December 1, 2017, https://thehill.com/policy/finance/362784-flake-announces -support-of-tax-plan-giving-gop-votes-needed-to-pass-bill.

9 Sunlen Serfaty and Elizabeth Landers, "Jeff Flake's friend in the Senate got emotional when he heard he's voting yes," CNN, September 28, 2018, https://www.cnn.com/politics/live-news/kavanaugh-senate-committee-vote /h_c8ba66f1c35797187065b92786033782.

10 Senate Judiciary Committee Meeting on Brett Kavanaugh nomination, September 28, 2018, broadcast on and recorded by C-SPAN, https://www.c -span.org/video/?452084-1/senator-flake-calls-delaying-kavanaugh-vote-fbi -background-check-reopen.

11 Senate Judiciary Committee Meeting on Brett Kavanaugh nomination, September 28, 2018.

12 McKay Coppins, "Jeff Flake Explains Himself," *Atlantic*, September 29, 2018, https://www.theatlantic.com/politics/archive/2018/09/flake-Kavanaugh -interview/571735/.

13 Senate Judiciary Committee Meeting on Brett Kavanaugh nomination, September 28, 2018.

14 Ibid.

15 Flake interview.

16 Rachel Mitchell, Memorandum to All Republican Senators re: Analysis of Dr. Christine Blasey Ford's Allegations, September 30, 2018, published by the *Washington Post*, https://apps.washingtonpost.com/g/documents/politics /rachel-mitchells-analysis/3221/.

17 Ibid.

18 Office of Senator Dianne Feinstein, Ranking Member, Senate Judiciary Committee, "Response to Memo Prepared by Republican Attorney Rachel Mitchell," October 1, 2018, https://static.politico.com/fd/5f/8713aa9d40a5 a272b29b33a4250e/response-to-memo-prepared-by-republican-attorney -rachel-mitchell-october-1-2018.pdf.

19 Ford interview.

20 Michael Bromwich to Dana Boente, email, "Subject: Supplemental Background Investigation of Judge Brett Cavanaugh [*sic*]," September 29, 2018, 11:49 a.m.

21 Michael Bromwich to Dana Boente, email, "Subject: Letter to Director Wray re Supplemental Background Investigation," September 29, 2018, 2:05 p.m.

22 Dana Boente to Michael Bromwich, email, "Subject: Letter to Director Wray re Supplemental Background Investigation," September 29, 2018, 2:50 p.m.

23 Michael Bromwich to Dana Boente, email, "Subject: Letter to Director Wray re Supplemental Background Investigation," September 30, 2018, 1:07 p.m.

24 Dana Boente to Michael Bromwich, email, "Subject: Letter to Director Wray re Supplemental Background Investigation," September 30, 2018, 3:00 p.m.

25 Michael Bromwich and Debra Katz to Christopher Wray and Dana Boente, email and letter "Re: Supplemental Background Investigation of Judge Brett Kavanaugh," September 30, 2018.

26 Lauren Egan, "Trump asks if Feinstein leaked allegation against Kavanaugh, says FBI probe may be 'blessing in disguise,'" NBC News, September 29, 2018, https://www.nbcnews.com/politics/donald-trump/trump-kavanaugh -fbi-investigation-n915091.

27 Clune interview.

28 Jane Mayer and Ronan Farrow, "The F.B.I. Probe Ignored Testimonies from Former Classmates of Kavanaugh," *New Yorker*, October 3, 2018, https:// www.newyorker.com/news/news-desk/will-the-fbi-ignore-testimonies-from -kavanaughs-former-classmates.

29 Declaration of Dr. Richard Oh, included in letter from William Pittard to Christopher Wray, October 4, 2018, https://hutchinsonblackandcookitdepart ment.sharefile.com/share/view/s4065775f35b42069.

30 Leigh Ann Caldwell and Heidi Przybyla, "FBI has not contacted dozens of potential sources in Kavanaugh investigation," NBC News, October 3, 2018, https://www.nbcnews.com/politics/supreme-court/dozens-potential-sources -information-have-not-been-contacted-fbi-kavanaugh-n916146.

31 Statement to FBI of Kathleen Charlton, Yale Class of 1987, sent to Dianne Feinstein and Charles Grassley, October 3, 2018.

32 Donald Trump, Twitter post, September 28, 2018, 10:49 p.m., https:// twitter.com/realDonaldTrump. The tweet read in full: "NBC News incorrectly reported (as usual) that I was limiting the FBI investigation of Judge

Kavanaugh, and witnesses, only to certain people. Actually, I want them to interview whoever they deem appropriate, at their discretion. Please correct your reporting!"

33 Michael D. Shear, Michael S. Schmidt, and Adam Goldman, "F.B.I. Review of Kavanaugh Was Limited from the Start," *New York Times*, October 5, 2018, https://www.nytimes.com/2018/10/05/us/politics/trump-kavanaugh -fbi.html?smid=nytcore-ios-share.

34 Chris Coons, interview with author, October 24, 2018.

35 Michael Bromwich and Debra Katz to Christopher Wray, email and letter, September 29, 2018.

36 John Clune to Supervising Agent Todd Stanstedt, email and letter, September 30, 2018.

37 Michael Lewis, *The Fifth Risk* (New York: W. W. Norton, 2018) [e-book edition], "Prologue: Lost in Transition."

38 Chris Coons, interview with author, September 30, 2019.

39 Chris Coons to Chris Wray, cc Chuck Grassley and Dianne Feinstein, October 2, 2018.

40 Seung Min Kim, "Inaction on Kavanaugh allegations reignites political rancor," *Washington Post*, September 16, 2018, https://www.washingtonpost .com/politics/inaction-on-kavanaugh-allegations-reignites-political-rancor /2019/09/16/facf6518-d8ad-11e9-adff-79254db7f766_story.html.

41 Ibid.

42 Flake said he did not recall this conversation. Jeff Flake, interview with author, July 12, 2019.

43 Collins interview.

44 Josh Gerstein, "FBI's Wray confirms White House limited Kavanaugh probe," *Politico*, October 10, 2018, https://www.politico.com/story/2018/10 /10/kavanaugh-fbi-probe-limit-888667.

CHAPTER EIGHTEEN: THE VOTE

1 David Jackson, "Donald Trump has treated Kavanaugh accuser Christine Blasey Ford like a Faberge egg, Kellyanne Conway says," *USA Today*, October 3, 2018, https://www.usatoday.com/story/news/politics/2018/10/03 /kavanaugh-accuser-christine-ford-treated-like-faberge-egg-conway-says /1509135002/.

2 Donald Trump, remarks at Make America Great Again rally, Southaven, Mississippi, October 2, 2018.

3 Graham interview.

4 Susan Collins, "GOP senator Susan Collins: Why I cannot support Trump,"

Washington Post, August 8, 2016, https://www.washingtonpost.com/
opinions/gop-senator-why-i-cannot-support-trump/2016/08/08/821095be
-5d7e-11e6-9d2f-b1a3564181a1_story.html.

5 Francine Kiefer, "Can the center hold? Susan Collins and the high-wire act
of being a moderate," *Christian Science Monitor*, July 23, 2018, https://www
.csmonitor.com/USA/Politics/2018/0723/can-the-center-hold-susan-collins
-and-the-high-wire-act-of-being-a-moderate.

6 Susan Collins closed-door impeachment statement, February 12, 1999,
transcript published by CNN, https://www.cnn.com/ALLPOLITICS/stories
/1999/02/12/senate.statements/collins.html.

7 Stephen Diamond, interview with author, May 22, 2019.

8 Collins interview.

9 Elise Viebeck and Gabriel Pogrund, "Sen. Susan Collins says Kavanaugh
sees *Roe v. Wade* as 'settled law,'" *Washington Post*, August 21, 2018, https://
beta.washingtonpost.com/powerpost/sen-susan-collins-said-kavanaugh
-sees-roe-v-wade-as-settled-law/2018/08/21/214ae5dc-a54c-11e8-8fac
-12e98c13528d_story.html.

10 Emily Birnbaum, "Collins calls crowdfunding to get her to oppose Kavanaugh
a 'bribe,'" *The Hill*, September 11, 2018, https://thehill.com/homenews/senate
/406041-collins-calls-crowdfunding-to-get-her-to-oppose-kavanaugh-a
-bribe.

11 Ramsey Touchberry, "Republican Senator's staffers receive violent
threats, vulgar calls over Brett Kavanaugh nomination: report," *Newsweek*,
September 12, 2018, https://www.newsweek.com/brett-kavanaugh-susan
-collins-threats-1118121.

12 Patti Epler, "Alaska Senate race: The untold story of Lisa Murkowski's write
-in decision," *Anchorage Daily News*, November 11, 2010, https://www.adn
.com/politics/article/alaska-senate-race-untold-story-lisa-murkowski-s-write
-decision/2010/11/12/, 2010.

13 Shira Toeplitz, "Murkowski quits Senate GOP leadership," *Politico*,
September 18, 2010, https://www.politico.com/story/2010/09/murkowski
-quits-gop-leadership-042362.

14 Alex DeMarban, "Alaska Federation of Natives, a key supporter of Murkowski,
opposes Kavanaugh appointment," *Anchorage Daily News*, September 12,
2018, https://www.adn.com/politics/2018/09/12/alaska-federation-of-natives
-a-key-supporter-of-murkowski-opposes-kavanaugh-appointment/.

15 Phil Mattingly, "The single copy of the FBI's Kavanaugh report is behind
closed doors. Here's what senators have to do to see it," CNN, October 4,
2018, https://www.cnn.com/2018/10/04/politics/senator-fbi-report-review
/index.html.

16 Debra Katz, Lisa Banks, and Michael Bromwich to Christopher Wray,

October 4, 2018, published by CNN, http://cdn.cnn.com/cnn/2018/images /10/04/181004ltr.to.wray.pdf.

17 William Pittard to Christopher Wray, October 4, 2018, published on the website of his law firm, KaiserDillon PLLC, https://hutchinsonblackandcook itdepartment.sharefile.com/share/view/s4065775f35b42069.

18 Elana Schor, Burgess Everett, and Nancy Cook, "A GOP 'disaster' averted: The final harrowing hours of Kavanaugh's confirmation," *Politico*, October 6, 2018, https://www.politico.com/story/2018/10/06/how-republicans-got -Kavanaugh-confirmed-878748.

19 Alexander Bolton and Jordain Carney, "Kavanaugh's path to confirmation begins to solidify," *The Hill*, October 4, 2018, https://thehill.com/homenews /senate/409936-kavanaughs-path-to-confirmation-begins-to-solidify.

20 Dianne Feinstein, "Feinstein on FBI Investigation: Incomplete, Limited," press release and remarks, October 4, 2018, https://www.feinstein.senate.gov /public/index.cfm/press-releases?ID=BBF0B8EB-D2B5-4A34-A769-5A1 8839B9A6B.

21 Dick Durbin, interview with author, June 11, 2019.

22 Ibid.

23 Adam Liptak, "Retired Justice John Paul Stevens Says Kavanaugh Is Not Fit for Supreme Court," *New York Times*, October 4, 2018, https://www.nytimes .com/2018/10/04/us/politics/john-paul-stevens-brett-kavanaugh.html.

24 Kristine Phillips, "The ACLU typically stays neutral about Supreme Court nominees. It didn't with Kavanaugh," *Washington Post*, September 29, 2018, https://beta.washingtonpost.com/politics/2018/09/29/aclu-typically-stays -quiet-about-supreme-court-nominees-it-didnt-with-kavanaugh/.

25 Matt Buxton, "More than 100 women are flying from Alaska to D.C. to meet with Murkowski, Sullivan on Kavanaugh," *Midnight Sun*, October 3, 2018, http://midnightsunak.com/2018/10/03/more-than-100-women-are-flying -from-alaska-to-d-c-to-meet-with-murkowski-sullivan-on-kavanaugh/.

26 Liz Ruskin, "Murkowski: Kavanaugh debate now about 'victims and their ability to tell their story,'" *Alaska Public Media*, September 26, 2018, https:// www.alaskapublic.org/2018/09/26/murkowski-kavanaugh-debate-now -about-victims-and-their-ability-to-tell-their-story/.

27 Peter Baker and Nicholas Fandos, "Trump Unleashes on Kavanaugh Accuser as Key Republican Wavers," *New York Times*, September 25, 2018, https://www .nytimes.com/2018/09/25/us/politics/lisa-murkowski-brett-kavanaugh.html.

28 Marcia Coyle, "Young Scholar, Now Lawyer, Says Clarence Thomas Groped Her in 1999," *National Law Journal*, October 27, 2016, https://www.law .com/nationallawjournal/almID/1202770918142/Young-Scholar-Now -Lawyer-Says-Clarence-Thomas-Groped-Her-in-1999/.

29 Schor, Everett, and Cook, "A GOP 'disaster' averted."

30 Charles Grassley, remarks on the Senate Floor, recorded by C-SPAN, "Senate and Judiciary Committee Leaders Speak Ahead of Cloture Vote," October 5, 2018, https://www.c-span.org/video/?c4753664/senate-judiciary-committee -leaders-speak-ahead-cloture-vote.

31 Ibid.

32 Dianne Feinstein, remarks on the Senate floor, recorded by C-SPAN, "Senate and Judiciary Committee Leaders Speak ahead of Cloture Vote," October 5, 2018.

33 Chuck Schumer, remarks on the Senate floor, recorded by C-SPAN, "Senate and Judiciary Committee Leaders Speak ahead of Cloture Vote," October 5, 2018.

34 Collins interview.

35 Michael Kirk, interview with Susan Collins, conducted December 18, 2018, for film "Supreme Revenge," *Frontline*, broadcast on PBS, May 21, 2019, https://www.pbs.org/wgbh/frontline/interview/susan-collins/.

36 "Senator Collins Announces She Will Vote to Confirm Judge Kavanaugh," press release, Susan Collins website, October 5, 2018, https://www.collins .senate.gov/newsroom/senator-collins-announces-she-will-vote-confirm -judge-kavanaugh.

37 Ibid.

38 Joe Manchin, Twitter post, October 5, 2018, 3:54 p.m., https://twitter.com /sen_joemanchin/status/1048300503099170817?lang=en.

39 Office of Joe Manchin, press release, "Manchin to support Supreme Court nominee Brett Kavanaugh," October 5, 2018, https://www.manchin.senate .gov/newsroom/press-releases/manchin-to-support-supreme-court-nominee -brett-kavanaugh-.

40 Donald Trump,. Jr., Twitter post, October 5, 2018. 5:46 p.m., https://twitter .com/donaldjtrumpjr/status/1048328508831936517?lang=en.

41 George Herbert Walker Bush, Twitter post, October 5, 2018, 4:03 p.m., https://twitter.com/GeorgeHWBush/status/1048302670929436673.

42 Lisa Murkowski, "Senator Murkowski Speaks on Supreme Court Nomination," press release including transcript, October 5, 2018, https://www.murkowski .senate.gov/press/release/senator-murkowski-speaks-on-supreme-court -nomination_.

43 Ibid.

44 Jeff Merkley floor remarks on Brett Kavanaugh, *Congressional Record* 164, no. 166 (Friday, October 5, 2018): S6648-S6656, https://www.govinfo .gov/content/pkg/CREC-2018-10-05/html/CREC-2018-10-05-pt2-PgS6635 -2.htm.

45 "'This is how victims are isolated and silenced': Deborah Ramirez releases statement prior to Kavanaugh confirmation vote," *Denver Post*, October 6,

2018, https://www.denverpost.com/2018/10/06/deborah-ramirez-statement
-kavanaugh-confirmation/.

46 Jason Dick, "Final Kavanaugh Vote Comes with a Whimper, Not a Bang,"
Roll Call, October 6, 2018, https://www.rollcall.com/news/politics/kava
naugh-vote-whimper.

47 Ralph Blasey and Ed Kavanaugh declined to comment.

48 "Remarks by President Trump before Marine One Departure," White House
release, October 8, 2018, https://www.whitehouse.gov/briefings-statements
/remarks-president-trump-marine-one-departure-14/.

49 "Remarks by President Trump at Swearing-in Ceremony of the Honorable
Brett M. Kavanaugh as Associate Justice of the Supreme Court of the United
States," White House release, October 8, 2018, https://www.whitehouse.gov
/briefings-statements/remarks-president-trump-swearing-ceremony-honorable
-brett-m-kavanaugh-associate-justice-supreme-court-united-states/.

50 Brett Kavanaugh, remarks at White House swearing-in ceremony as associate
justice, White House release, October 8, 2018, https://www.whitehouse.gov
/briefings-statements/remarks-president-trump-swearing-ceremony-honorable
-brett-m-kavanaugh-associate-justice-supreme-court-united-states/.

EPILOGUE

1 Seung Min Kim, "McConnell calls opposition to Kavanaugh a 'great political
gift' to Republicans," *Washington Post*, October 6, 2018, https://www
.washingtonpost.com/politics/mcconnell-calls-opposition-to-kavanaugh-a
-great-political-gift-to-republicans/2018/10/06/761b8610-c988-11e8-9158
-09630a6d8725_story.html.

2 Heidi Heitkamp, interview with author, December 5, 2018.

3 Claire McCaskill, interview with author, March 14, 2019.

4 Rebecca Klar, "Susan Collins raises $2M in second quarter fundraising,
surpassing 2014 reelection bid," *The Hill*, July 15, 2019, https://thehill.com
/homenews/campaign/453094-susan-collins-raises-2m-earnings-in-second
-quarter.

5 Figures on proportion of Collins's out-of-state fund-raising from OpenSecrets
.org, run by the Center for Responsive Politics, accessed September 15, 2019;
"Maine Senate 2020 Race: In State Contributions vs. Out of State Contributions," https://www.opensecrets.org/races/geography?cycle=2020&id
=MES2&spec=N; "Maine Senate 2014 Race: In State Contributions vs. Out
of State Contributions," https://www.opensecrets.org/races/geography?cycle
=2014&id=MES2&spec=N.

6 Federal Election Commission, Collins for Senate individual contribu-

tions list, January 1 to June 30, 2019, https://www.fec.gov/data/receipts
/individual-contributions/?committee_id=C00314575&contributor_name
=adelson&two_year_transaction_period=2020&min_amount=2%2C000.00.

7 Steve Mistler, "Protesters met Susan Collins outside a fundraiser hosted by
   Trump's 'judge whisperer,'" *Bangor Daily News*, August 9, 2019, https://
   bangordailynews.com/2019/08/09/politics/protesters-met-susan-collins
   -outside-a-fundraiser-hosted-by-trumps-judge-whisperer/.

8 John Bowden, "Cook Political Report moves Susan Collins Senate race to
   'toss up,'" *The Hill*, August 16, 2019, https://thehill.com/homenews/campaign
   /457739-cook-political-report-moves-susan-collins-senate-race-to-toss-up.

9 Dartunorro Clark, "Christine Blasey Ford presents award to Nassar accuser
   Rachael Denhollander," NBC News, December 12, 2018, https://www
   .nbcnews.com/news/us-news/christine-blasey-ford-presents-award-nassar
   -accuser-rachael-denhollander-n946976.

10 Office of Chuck Grassley, "Senate Judiciary Committee Releases Summary
   of Investigation from Supreme Court Confirmation," November 3, 2018,
   https://www.grassley.senate.gov/news/news-releases/senate-judiciary
   -committee-releases-summary-investigation-supreme-court-0.

11 Mollie Hemingway and Carrie Severino, *Justice on Trial: The Kavanaugh
   Confirmation and the Future of the Supreme Court* (Washington, D.C.:
   Regnery Publishing, 2019), p. 215.

12 Ford interview.

13 Isaac Stanley-Becker, "'Kick Kavanaugh off campus': Students decry George
   Mason's decision to hire Supreme Court justice," *Washington Post*, April 9,
   2019, https://www.washingtonpost.com/nation/2019/04/09/kick-kavanaugh-off
   -campus-students-decry-george-masons-decision-hire-supreme-court-justice/.

14 Adam Liptak, "Three Supreme Court Justices Return to Yale," *New York
   Times*, October 25, 2014, https://www.nytimes.com/2014/10/26/us/three
   -supreme-court-justices-return-to-yale.html.

15 Nat Hentoff, "The Constitutionalist," *New Yorker*, March 12, 1990, https://
   www.newyorker.com/magazine/1990/03/12/the-constitutionalist.

16 Paul LeBlanc, "Sotomayor says Kavanaugh a part of the Supreme Court
   'family,'" CNN, November 17, 2018, https://www.cnn.com/2018/11
   /17/politics/sotomayor-kavanaugh-axe-files-axelrod/index.html?utm
   _medium=social&utm_content=2018-11-17T15%3A32%3A03&utm
   _source=twCNNp&utm_term=image.

17 Jess Bravin, "Sotomayor Works to Build Ties with Trump's Court
   Appointees," *Wall Street Journal*, September 10, 2019, https://www.wsj
   .com/articles/sotomayor-works-to-build-ties-with-trumps-court-appointees
   -11568157992.

18 John McCormack, "Ruth Bader Ginsburg Insists She's Not Going Anywhere,"

National Review, July 25, 2019, https://www.nationalreview.com/2019/07/ruth-bader-ginsburg-insists-shes-not-going-anywhere/.

19 Adam Liptak, "Chief Justice Defends Judicial Independence after Trump Attacks 'Obama Judge,'" *New York Times*, November 21, 2018, https://www.nytimes.com/2018/11/21/us/politics/trump-chief-justice-roberts-rebuke.html.

20 Sonia Sotomayor and Elena Kagan, remarks at "She Roars—A Conversation with the Justices," Princeton University, Princeton, N.J., October 5, 2018.

21 David Savage, "Justice Consistently Conservative; Kennedy's Record Sours Liberals' Victory on Bork," *Los Angeles Times*, June 11, 1989.

22 Ruth Marcus, "Energized Conservativism Rules High Court; Solid Majority Starting to Reverse Decades of Liberal Precedents," *Washington Post*, June 30, 1991.

23 Adam Feldman, "Final Stat Pack for October Term 2018," *SCOTUSblog*, June 28, 2019, https://www.scotusblog.com/2019/06/final-stat-pack-for-october-term-2018/.

24 *Gee v. Planned Parenthood of Gulf Coast*, 585 U.S. ___ (2018), Thomas, J., dissenting, https://www.supremecourt.gov/opinions/18pdf/17-1492_g3bi.pdf.

25 Adam Liptak, "Supreme Court Bars Challenges to Partisan Gerrymandering," *New York Times*, June 27, 2018, https://www.nytimes.com/2019/06/27/us/politics/supreme-court-gerrymandering.html.

26 Joan Biskupic, "Exclusive: How John Roberts killed the census citizenship question," CNN, September 12, 2019, https://www.cnn.com/2019/09/12/politics/john-roberts-census-citizenship-supreme-court/index.html.

27 *Kisor v. Wilkie*, 588 U.S. ___ (2019), Kavanaugh, J., concurring in judgment, https://www.supremecourt.gov/opinions/18pdf/18-15_9p6b.pdf.

28 *Kisor v. Wilkie*, Gorsuch, J., concurring in judgment.

29 *June Medical Services L.L.C v. Gee*, 586 U.S. ___ (2019), Kavanaugh, J., dissenting from grant of application for stay, https://www.supremecourt.gov/opinions/18pdf/18a774_3ebh.pdf.

30 *Flowers v. Mississippi*, 588 U.S. ___ (2019), June 21, 2019, Kavanaugh, J., 15–16, https://www.supremecourt.gov/opinions/18pdf/17-9572_k536.pdf.

31 Amelia Thomson-DeVeaux, "The Supreme Court Might Have Three Swing Justices Now," *FiveThirtyEight*, July 2, 2019, https://fivethirtyeight.com/features/the-supreme-court-might-have-three-swing-justices-now/.

32 Tucker Higgins, "Trump's two Supreme Court justices Kavanaugh and Gorsuch split in first term together," CNBC, June 29, 2019, https://www.cnbc.com/2019/06/28/trumps-two-supreme-court-justices-kavanaugh-and-gorsuch-diverge.html.

33 Kedar Bhatia, "Final October Term 2017 Stat Pack and key takeaways," *SCOTUSblog*, June 29, 2018, pp. 18–21, https://www.scotusblog.com/2018/06/final-october-term-2017-stat-pack-and-key-takeaways/.

34 Feldman, "Final Stat Pack for October Term 2018," p. 19.

35 *Franchise Board of California v. Gilbert P. Hyatt*, 587 U.S. ___ (2019), May 13, 2019, Breyer, J., dissenting, p. 13, https://www.supremecourt.gov /opinions/18pdf/17-1299_8njq.pdf.

36 *Knick v. Township of Scott, Pennsylvania*, 588 U.S. ___ (2019), June 21, 2018, Kagan, J., dissenting, p. 19, https://www.supremecourt.gov/opinions /18pdf/17-647_m648.pdf.

37 Nicholas Bagley, "'Most of Government Is Unconstitutional,'" *New York Times*, June 21, 2018, https://www.nytimes.com/2019/06/21/opinion/sunday /gundy-united-states.html.

38 *Gundy v. United States*, 588 U.S.___ (2019), June 20, 2019, Alito, J., concurring in judgment, p. 1, https://www.supremecourt.gov/opinions/18pdf /17-6086_2b8e.pdf.

39 *Gundy v. United States*, ibid, Kagan, J., dissenting, p. 17.

FINAL THOUGHTS: ZEAL TO WIN

1 Brett Kavanaugh to Alberto Gonzales and Timothy Flanigan cc Robert Cobb, "Subject: event policy question," March 5, 2001, WHCO emails from Brett Kavanaugh.

2 Stephen Carter, *The Confirmation Mess: Cleaning Up the Federal Appointments Process* (New York: Basic Books, 1994), 134.

3 Robin Pogrebin and Kate Kelly, *The Education of Brett Kavanaugh: An Investigation* (New York: Portfolio/Penguin, 2019), 284–86.

4 Davis interview.

5 Max Stier donor lookup, OpenSecrets.org, accessed September 25, 2019, https://www.opensecrets.org/donor-lookup/results?name=max+stier.

6 Office of the Press Secretary, "President Obama Nominates Eight to Serve on United States District Courts," Obama White House press release, April 28, 2016, https://obamawhitehouse.archives.gov/the-press-office/2016/04 /28/president-obama-nominates-eight-serve-united-states-district-courts.

7 Lisa Murkowski, remarks on the Senate floor on the Supreme Court nomination of Brett Kavanaugh, released by her office, October 5, 2018, https://www.murkowski.senate.gov/press/release/senator-murkowski-speaks -on-supreme-court-nomination_.

8 Robert Byrd, remarks on the Senate floor against the confirmation of Clarence Thomas to the Supreme Court, *Congressional Record*, Senate, October 15, 1991, 26278–82, https://www.govinfo.gov/content/pkg/GPO-CRECB-1991 -pt18/pdf/GPO-CRECB-1991-pt18-8-2.pdf.

INDEX